Along These Lines

Writing Sentences and Paragraphs

with Writing from Reading Strategies

Sixth Edition

John Sheridan Biays, professor emeritus of English
Broward College

Carol Wershoven, professor emerita of English
Palm Beach State College

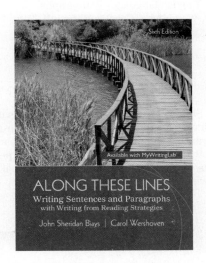

PEARSON

Boston   Columbus   Hoboken   Indianapolis   New York   San Francisco
Amsterdam   Cape Town   Dubai   London   Madrid   Milan   Munich   Paris   Montreal   Toronto
Delhi   Mexico City   São Paulo   Sydney   Hong Kong   Seoul   Singapore   Taipei   Tokyo

Executive Editor: Matthew Wright
Senior Development Editor: Anne Brunell Ehrenworth
Marketing Manager: Jennifer Edwards
Executive Digital Producer: Stefanie Snajder
Content Specialist: Erin E. Reilly
Program Manager: Eric Jorgensen
Project Manager: Denise Phillip Grant
**Project Coordination, Text Design, and Electronic
   Page Makeup:** Laserwords Private Ltd.
Design Lead: Barbara Atkinson
Cover Designer: Kristina Mose-Libon/Lumina Datamatics, Inc.
Cover Photo: monysasu/Shutterstock
Senior Manufacturing Buyer: Roy L. Pickering Jr.
Printer/Binder: Courier/Kendallville
Cover Printer: Phoenix Color/Hagerstown

Acknowledgments of third-party content appear on page 453, which constitutes an extension of this copyright page.

PEARSON, ALWAYS LEARNING, and MYWRITINGLAB are exclusive trademarks, in the United States and/or other countries, of Pearson Education, Inc., or its affiliates.

Library of Congress Cataloging-in-Publication Data

Biays, John Sheridan.
   Along these lines : writing sentences and paragraphs with, writing
      from reading strategies / John Sheridan Biays, Broward College;
      Carol Wershoven, Palm Beach State College.
      pages cm—(Sixth edition)
   Includes bibliographical references and index.
   ISBN 978-0-321-98401-2—ISBN 0-321-98401-3
      1. English language—Sentences.   2. English language—Paragraphs.
      3. English language—Rhetoric.   I. Wershoven, Carol, author.   II. Title.
PE1441.B53 2015
808'.042—dc23

2014037261

10 9 8 7 6 5 4 3 2 1—CRK—18 17 16 15

www.pearsonhighered.com

Student Edition
ISBN 10:   0-321-98401-3
ISBN 13: 978-0-321-98401-2

A la Carte
ISBN 10:   0-321-99123-0
ISBN 13: 978-0-321-99123-2

PEARSON

Contents

Preface for Instructors

As you know all too well, developmental education has been under intense scrutiny nationwide, and severe budget cuts have taken their toll on many college campuses. Whether your department has been actively involved in course redesign and/or your state legislature has mandated that developmental courses become strictly optional, one thing remains clear: *Students need more help than ever in becoming proficient writers and effective communicators.* We applaud your commitment to helping students become confident learners, and we remain extremely grateful for your trust in our work.

Along These Lines: Writing Sentences and Paragraphs with Writing from Reading Strategies, 6e, retains the intensive grammar coverage and writing-process instruction adopters have praised, and the self-contained chapters provide a flexible framework that can easily be adapted for myriad learning styles and instructional preferences. A host of caring reviewers offered insightful, practical, and creative revision suggestions; thanks to them, we feel that this edition is the most visually appealing and engaging text to date. We hope you'll agree.

NEW FEATURES AND ENHANCEMENTS IN THE SIXTH EDITION

- **New visuals, including charts and expanded checklists**, guide students through the writing process and help them grasp basic principles and patterns.

- **New critical-thinking references and tips** underscore critical thinking's connection to effective writing, focused reading, and logical sequencing of details.

- **New English language learner (ELL) teaching tips** are provided in the *Annotated Instructor's Edition*, including special emphasis on interactive class activities.

- **New exercises on fragments, run-ons, coordination and subordination, and verb tense consistency** provide ample reinforcement of basic rules.

- **New high-interest readings and related topics** are ideal for in-class reaction papers or point–counterpoint discussions; vocabulary lists and comprehension questions are also included.

- **New learning objectives in bulleted format** provide students with a quick preview of chapter content and enable instructors to plan assignments based on departmental objectives or core curricula.

A SAMPLING OF PRAISE FROM *ALONG THESE LINES* ADOPTERS:

"My students' experiences with Along These Lines *have been very good . . . The text aptly manages to provide instruction in some of the most fundamental writing skills; however, the subject matter used in examples and exercises is very appropriate for college developmental students."*

Elizabeth Andrews, South Florida State College

"The strengths of Along These Lines *include the teaching tips, the amount of practice exercises in each chapter, and the detailed writing process [instruction], which helps students see that there is more than one way to gather and arrange ideas."*

Cassi Lapp, Northwest Arkansas Community College

I think that Along These Lines *is a thoughtful book. . . . It's easy to use and easy to access. [Additionally,] the white space is used well and I like the tone of the instruction."*

Elizabeth Barnes, Daytona State College

POPULAR FEATURES RETAINED

Based on positive feedback from current adopters and new reviewers, the following popular and distinctive features have been retained:

The Grammar Chapters

- Grammar concepts taught step-by-step, as in "Two Steps to Check for Sentence Fragments"
- A Chapter Test at the end of chapters, ideal for class review or quick quizzes
- A "Quick Question" opener in each chapter that provides an incentive for students to preview a chapter's content
- Three types of grammar exercises: **Practice** (simple reinforcement), **Collaborate** (partner or group work), and **Connect** ("in context" application of a grammar principle to paragraphs requiring revision and/or editing)

The Writing Chapters

- Easy-to-follow checklists, charts, diagrams, and color "Info Boxes"
- Framed examples of an outline, draft, and final version of a formal assignment
- A "Walk-Through" writing assignment at the end of each chapter that guides students, step-by-step, through the stages of the writing process
- Numerous, timely writing topics that promote critical-thinking skills and spark collaborative or individual assignments

The Reading Sections

- A separate "Writing from Reading" chapter providing instruction on prereading strategies, marking a selection, taking notes, summarizing, and reacting to a writer's premise, and writing timed papers for in-class tests
- Carefully selected reading selections grouped in a separate appendix, *Readings for Writers*, for easy reference
- Writing options, including critical-thinking topics, sparked by a selection's content and designed to elicit informed, reasoned responses

WRITING RESOURCES AND SUPPLEMENTS

Annotated Instructor's Edition for *Along These Lines: Writing Sentences and Paragraphs with Writing from Reading Strategies*
ISBN 0321985974 / 9780321985972

Instructor's Resource Manual for *Along These Lines: Writing Sentences and Paragraphs with Writing from Reading Strategies*
ISBN 0321991052 / 9780321991058

Test Bank for Along These Lines: Writing Sentences and Paragraphs with Writing from Reading Strategies
ISBN 0133928748 / 9780133928747

PowerPoint Presentation for Along These Lines: Writing Sentences and Paragraphs with Writing from Reading Strategies
ISBN 0321991249 / 9780321991249

Answer Key for Along These Lines: Writing Sentences and Paragraphs with Writing from Reading Strategies
ISBN 0321985419 / 9780321985415

MyWritingLab™

Where Practice, Application, and Demonstration Meet to Improve Writing

MyWritingLab, a complete online learning program, provides additional resources and effective practice exercises for developing writers. *MyWritingLab* accelerates learning through layered assessment and a personalized learning path utilizing the Knewton Adaptive Learning Platform™ which customizes educational content to piece together the perfect personalized content for each student. With over eight thousand exercises and immediate feedback to answers, the integrated learning aids of *MyWritingLab* reinforce learning throughout the semester.

What Makes MyWritingLab More Effective?

Diagnostic Testing: *MyWritingLab's* diagnostic Path Builder test comprehensively assesses students' skills in grammar. Students are provided with an individualized learning path based on the diagnostic's results, identifying the areas where they most need help.

Progressive Learning: The heart of *MyWritingLab* is the progressive learning that students experience as they complete the Overview, Animation, Recall, Apply, and Write exercises along with the Post-test within each topic. Students move from preparation (Overview, Animation) to literal comprehension (Recall) to critical understanding (Apply) to the ability to demonstrate a skill in their own writing (Write) to total mastery (Post-test). This progression of critical thinking enables students to master the skills and concepts they need to become successful writers.

Online Gradebook: All student work in *MyWritingLab* is captured in the Online Gradebook. Instructors can see what and how many topics their students have mastered. They can also view students' individual scores on all assignments throughout *MyWritingLab* as well as class performance by module. Students can monitor their progress in new Completed Work pages, which show them their totals, scores, time on task, and the date and time of their work by module.

A Deeper Connection between Print and Media: The *MyWritingLab* logo MyWritingLab™ is used throughout the book to indicate exercises and writing activities that can be completed and submitted through *MyWritingLab* (appropriate results flow directly to the Instructor Gradebook).

ACKNOWLEDGMENTS

We are indebted to the following professionals for their comprehensive reviews, practical advice, and creative suggestions regarding the *Along These Lines* series:

Stephanie Alexander	Mountwest Community and Technical College
Elizabeth Andrews	South Florida State College
Elizabeth Barnes	Daytona State College
Iris Chao	Saddleback College
Patty Crockett	Bishop State Community College
Mellisa Dalton	Lanier Technical College
Linda Hasty	Motlow State Community College
Gregg Heitschmidt	Surry Community College
Johnnerlyn Johnson	Sandhills Community College
Therese Jones	Lewis University
Cassi Lapp	Northwest Arkansas Community College
Ann Moore	Florence Darlington Technical College
Deana Pendley	Copiah-Lincoln Community College
Sandra Valerio	Del Mar College

The success of any new edition relies on a wealth of expertise from talented individuals. We are very grateful to Matt Wright, senior acquisitions editor, for his ongoing support and enthusiasm for our series. Additionally, we are indebted to Anne Brunell Ehrenworth, senior development editor, for mapping out revision plans so expertly and efficiently. Anne suggested practical ways to streamline chapters, guided two new contributors, reviewed every page with us, and kept us current on the permissions status of proposed readings. With enviable tenacity and welcome humor, Anne made sure we made it to the finish line on time and in good spirits, a rare feat indeed!

We also extend our deepest gratitude to Christina Cavage and Paula Bonilla for taking on the lion's share of revisions. Christina updated many of our grammar exercises, devised creative ELL teaching tips, and provided crucial critical-thinking instruction. Paula updated many of our "Jumping In" chapter openers, contributed new writing topics and exercises, and even found time to write the *Instructor's Resource Manuals* (IRMs) for the *ATL* series. We can't thank Christina and Paula enough for their generous time and valuable contributions during the entire production period.

Rebecca Lazure, full-service production manager at SPi Global (Maine), once again worked her magic and calmly reassured everyone that all would be fine. We know our series couldn't have been in more caring hands. Additionally, we extend thanks and kudos to the charter members of "Team ATL," including Laura Marenghi, editorial assistant, for coordinating reviews and corresponding with us regularly; Laura Specht Patchkofsky, copy editor; the entire design team at SPi Global; Joe Croscup, permissions project manager; Jennifer Edwards, marketing manager; and Megan Zuccarini, marketing assistant extraordinaire, whose professionalism, good cheer, and attention to detail keep us sane even during the hectic selling season.

We also want to pay tribute to all of the unsung heroes in the classroom who help struggling students overcome adversity, find their voice, and reach their potential. We are humbled by your dedication and resilience, and you exemplify effective teaching at its best.

Finally, and most importantly, we send heartfelt thanks to the thousands of students who have intrigued, impressed, and inspired us through the years. You have taught us far more than you can ever imagine, and you have made our journey extraordinary along *all* lines.

John Sheridan Biays
Carol Wershoven

The Simple Sentence

CHAPTER 1

Quick Question MyWritingLab™

True or False: There is only one verb in this sentence: *Students should come to class on time.*

(After you study this chapter, you will be confident of your answer.)

Learning Objectives

In this chapter, you will learn to:

1. Identify subjects and verbs in sentences.
2. Identify action verbs and being verbs in sentences.
3. Identify helping verbs in sentences.
4. Identify prepositional phrases and correct word order.
5. Use verbs correctly in sentences.

Identifying the crucial parts of a sentence is the first step in many writing decisions: how to punctuate, how to avoid sentence fragments, and how to be sure that subjects and verbs *agree* (match). Moving forward to these decisions requires a few steps backward—to basics.

RECOGNIZING A SENTENCE

1 Identify subjects and verbs in sentences.

Let's start with a few definitions. A basic unit of language is a **word**.

> **examples:** tablet, desk, tree

A group of related words can be a **phrase**.

> **examples:** new smartphone, on the desk, tall palm tree

When a group of words contains a subject and a verb, it is called a **clause**. When the word group has a subject and a verb and makes sense by itself, it is called a **sentence** or an independent clause.

If you want to check whether you have written a sentence and not just a group of related words, you first have to check for a subject and a verb. Locating the verbs first can be easier.

2 Identify action verbs and being verbs in sentences.

RECOGNIZING VERBS

Verbs are words that express some kind of action or being. **Action verbs** tell what somebody or something does.

> **action verbs:**
> Computers *hold* an amazing amount of information.
> She *writes* a blog.
> They *post* on the discussion board every day.
> You *wrote* a paper for psychology class yesterday.
> Marco *completed* the job application.
> He *drives* like a maniac.
> They *study* together in the library.
> I *believe* her story.

Sometimes a verb tells what something or somebody is. Such verbs are called **being verbs**. Words like *feels, looks, seems, smells, sounds,* and *tastes* are part of the group called being verbs. Look at some examples of being verbs and their functions in the following sentences:

> **being verbs:**
> The computer *is* a great invention.
> The instructor *looks* tired today.
> You *sound* happy.
> David *is* a good candidate for traffic school.
> He *seems* unaware of traffic lights.
> They *are* the best students in my class.
> I *feel* confident about her story.
> His workplace *is* nearby.

Exercise 1   **Practice: Recognizing Action Verbs**

Underline the action verbs in the following sentences.

1. The grandmother hugged the child.

2. On Friday, traffic blocked the intersection.

3. The Web site loaded slowly.

4. Old clothes remind me of the past.

5. The bookstore opens at 9:00 a.m.

6. Mitchell goes to a gym on the weekends.

7. A city bus takes me to work in the morning.

8. Karen needs your help today.

Exercise 2   **Practice: Recognizing Being Verbs**

Underline the being verbs in the following sentences.

1. My study habits were not effective.

2. The homemade apple pie tastes delicious.

3. Your sister was a good and loyal friend.

4. Snapchatting seems fun.

5. Jade Beach is a popular gathering place for students.

6. Professor Duvall is a well-known jazz musician.

7. Yesterday your plan sounded clear and reasonable.

8. The fall foliage looks magnificent today.

Exercise 3   **Collaborate: Writing Sentences with Specific Verbs**

Collaborate

With a partner or group, write two sentences using each of the verbs listed below. Each sentence must have at least five words. When you have completed the exercise, share your answers with another group or with the class. The first one is done for you.

1. **verb:** dragged

   sentence 1: _I dragged the heavy bag across the floor._

   sentence 2: _Lori dragged herself to class on Friday morning._

2. **verb:** smells

   sentence 1: _____

   sentence 2: _____

3. **verb:** argues

   sentence 1: _____

   sentence 2: _____

4. **verb:** seem

   sentence 1: _____

   sentence 2: _____

5. **verb:** chatted

   sentence 1: _____

   sentence 2: _____

6. **verb:** wins

   sentence 1: _____

   sentence 2: _____

7. verb: was

sentence 1: _____

sentence 2: _____

8. verb: were

sentence 1: _____

sentence 2: _____

3 Identify helping verbs in sentences.

Helping Verbs

The verb in a sentence can be more than one word. There can be **helping verbs** in front of the main verb (the action verb or being verb) in statements. Questions often have a helping verb. *Do*, *does*, and *did* are used in questions without the verb *to be* or another helping verb. Here is a list of some frequently used helping verbs:

INFO BOX Common Helping Verbs			
am	had	might	were
can	has	must	will
could	have	shall	would
did	is	should	
do/does	may	was	

Here are some examples of sentences with main and helping verbs:

main and helping verbs:
You *should have answered* the question. (The helping verbs are *should* and *have*.)
Laurie *will notify* the lottery winner. (The helping verb is *will*.)
Babies *can recognize* their mothers' voices. (The helping verb is *can*.)
I *am thinking* about a career in medicine. (The helping verb is *am*.)

Exercise 4 **Practice: Recognizing the Complete Verb: Main and Helping Verbs**

Underline the complete verb (both main and helping verbs) in each of the following sentences.

1. Caroline has studied English since noon.
2. Did she build her Web site alone?
3. You will be taking your final exams next week.
4. Annette could have apologized for her rude remark to my uncle.
5. Gina and Larry are paying for their son's trip to Disney World.
6. My little nephew can sing several children's songs.
7. By Monday, you must make a decision about replacing the hot water heater.
8. Does this class end at 11:00 a.m.?

Collaborate

| **Exercise 5** | **Collaborate: Writing Sentences with Helping Verbs** |

Complete this exercise with a partner or group. First, ask one person to add at least one helping verb to the verb given. Then work together to write two sentences using the main verb and the helping verb(s). Appoint one spokesperson for your group to read all your sentences to the class. Notice how many combinations of main and helping verbs you hear. The first one is done for you.

1. **verb:** complained

    verb with helping verb(s): must have complained _____

    sentence 1: My supervisor must have complained about me. _____

    sentence 2: She must have complained twenty times yesterday. _____

2. **verb:** denying

    verb with helping verb(s): _____

    sentence 1: _____

    sentence 2: _____

3. **verb:** forgive

    verb with helping verb(s): _____

    sentence 1: _____

    sentence 2: _____

4. **verb:** said

    verb with helping verb(s): _____

    sentence 1: _____

    sentence 2: _____

5. **verb:** given

    verb with helping verb(s): _____

    sentence 1: _____

    sentence 2: _____

6. **verb:** expecting

    verb with helping verb(s): _____

    sentence 1: _____

    sentence 2: _____

7. **verb:** broken

    verb with helping verb(s): _____

    sentence 1: _____

    sentence 2: _____

8. **verb:** encourage

    verb with helping verb(s): _____

    sentence 1: _____

    sentence 2: _____

More Than One Main Verb

Helping verbs can make the verb in a sentence longer than one word, but there can also be more than one main verb.

> **more than one main verb:**
> Antonio *begged* and *pleaded* for mercy.
> I *ran* to the car, *tossed* my books on the back seat, and *jammed* the key in the ignition.
> The tutor *reviews* verbs and *explains* sentence structure.

Exercise 6   Practice: Recognizing Main Verbs

Some of the sentences below have one main verb; some have more than one main verb. Underline all the main verbs in each sentence.

1. Every night, my brother drives to his girlfriend's house, honks his car horn, and waits for her in his car.

2. Edward Kansky and Nick Stamos sell silver jewelry and leather belts at the flea market.

3. Alicia borrowed my clothes but rarely returned them.

4. My favorite place on campus has private study rooms.

5. Your mother called and invited us to dinner tomorrow night.

6. A drunk driver shattered one car's taillight, smashed another's front end, and skidded into a trash can.

7. Felice ordered a salad for lunch and cut the lettuce into tiny pieces.

8. Some of the animals in his paintings look like dragons or other fantastic creatures from an imaginary world.

Exercise 7   Practice: Recognizing Verbs in a Selection from "The Tell-Tale Heart"

This selection is from "The Tell-Tale Heart," a horror story by Edgar Allan Poe. In it, an insane murderer has killed an old man and buried him under the floor. When the police arrive, they find nothing, but the murderer is convinced that he—and the police—can hear the old man's heart beating under the floor. In this selection, the murderer describes what he feels as he hears the heart beat louder and louder.

Underline all of the verbs in the selection. Notice how a careful choice of verbs can make writing exciting and suspenseful.

The officers were satisfied. My manner had convinced them. I was singularly at ease. They sat, and while I answered cheerfully, they chatted of familiar things. But, ere* long, I felt myself getting pale and wished them gone. My head ached, and I fancied* a ringing in my ears: but still they sat and still chatted. The ringing became more distinct: —it continued and became more distinct: I talked more freely to get rid of the feeling: but it continued and gained definitiveness—until, at length,* I found that the noise was not within my ears.

No doubt I now grew very pale; —but I talked more fluently, and with a heightened voice. Yet the sound increased—and what could I do? . . . I gasped for breath—and yet the officers heard it not. I talked more quickly, more vehemently*; but the noise steadily increased. I arose and argued about trifles, in a high key and with violent gesticulations,* but the noise steadily increased. Why would they not be gone? I paced the floor to and fro with heavy strides, as if excited to fury by the observation of the men—but the noise steadily increased. Oh God! What could I do? I foamed—I raved—I swore! . . . It grew louder—louder—louder! And still the men chatted pleasantly, and smiled. Was it possible they heard not? Almighty God! —no, no! They heard! —they suspected! —they knew!

*__ere:__ before
*__fancied:__ imagined
*__at length:__ after a time
*__vehemently:__ furiously
*__gesticulations:__ gestures

RECOGNIZING SUBJECTS

After you learn to recognize verbs, you can easily find the subjects of sentences because subjects and verbs are linked. If the verb is an action verb, for example, the **subject** will be the word or words that answer the question "Who or what is doing that action?" Follow these steps to identify the subject:

> **sentence with an action verb:**
> The cat slept on my bed.
>
> **Step 1:** Identify the verb: *slept*
>
> **Step 2:** Ask, "Who or what slept?"
>
> **Step 3:** The answer is the subject: The *cat* slept on my bed. The *cat* is the subject.

If the verb is a being verb, the same steps apply to finding the subject.

> **sentence with a being verb:**
> Clarice is his girlfriend.
>
> **Step 1:** Identify the verb: *is*
>
> **Step 2:** Ask, "Who or what is his girlfriend?"
>
> **Step 3:** The answer is the subject: *Clarice* is his girlfriend. *Clarice* is the subject.

Just as there can be more than one verb, there can be more than one subject.

examples:
Coffee and a *doughnut* are a typical breakfast for me.
His *father* and *grandfather* own a landscaping service.

Exercise 8 Practice: Recognizing Subjects in Sentences

Underline the subjects in the following sentences.

1. The students like to share files.
2. Sylvia Jong might have left a message on my cell phone.
3. Psychology and algebra are difficult subjects for me.
4. Something woke me in the middle of the night.
5. Lorraine and Pierre have family members in Haiti.
6. Smoking is becoming an expensive and socially unacceptable habit.
7. Greed and arrogance led William to a series of bad decisions.
8. Peanuts can cause dangerous allergic reactions in some people.

Collaborate

Exercise 9 Collaborate: Adding Subjects to Sentences

Working with a partner or group, complete the paragraph below by adding subjects to the blank lines. Before you fill in the blanks, discuss your answers and try to come to an agreement about the worst movie, the worst music video, and so on. When you have completed the paragraph, share your answers with another group or with the class.

This year has seen many achievements in the arts and entertainment,

but it has also seen many creative disasters. On movie screens, there have

been some terrible movies. Without a doubt, _____

was the worst movie of the year. It should never have been made. On televi-

sion, _____ was the worst and also the most irritating

show. Every time I see it, I want to turn it off or kick in the television screen.

_____ and _____ take the prize

for the worst actor and actress of the year. They should consider other careers.

In the field of music, _____ ranks as the least successful

music video of the year. _____ is the most annoying song

because the radio played it far too often. Last, _____ is

the most annoying singer.

MORE ABOUT RECOGNIZING SUBJECTS AND VERBS

Recognizing the Core Subject

When you look for the subject of a sentence, look for the core word or words; do not include descriptive words around the subject. Look for the noun (people, places, or things), not for the words that describe it.

> **the core subject:**
> Interesting digital *texts* are needed to engage students.
>
> Cracked *sidewalks* and rusty *railings* made the old school dangerous for children.

Prepositions and Prepositional Phrases

Prepositions are usually short words that often signal a kind of position or possession, as shown in the following list.

④ Identify prepositional phrases and correct word order.

INFO BOX Some Common Prepositions

about	before	by	inside	on	under
above	below	down	into	onto	up
across	behind	during	like	over	upon
after	beneath	except	near	through	with
among	beside	for	of	to	within
around	between	from	off	toward	without
at	beyond	in			

A **prepositional phrase** is made up of a preposition and its object. Here are some prepositional phrases. In each one, the first word is the preposition; the other words are the object of the preposition.

> **prepositional phrases:**
> about the lecture   of mice and men
> around the corner   off the wall
> between two lanes   on the mark
> during class   up the big hill
> near my house   with my sister and brother

An old memory trick can help you remember prepositions. Think of a chair. Now, think of a series of words you can put in front of the chair:

> *around* the chair   *with* the chair
> *by* the chair   *to* the chair
> *behind* the chair   *near* the chair
> *between* the chairs   *under* the chair
> *of* the chair   *on* the chair
> *off* the chair   *from* the chair

These words are prepositions.

You need to know about prepositions because they can help you identify the subject of a sentence. Here is an important grammar rule about prepositions:

Nothing in a prepositional phrase can ever be the subject of a sentence.

Prepositional phrases describe people, places, or things. They may also describe the subject of a sentence, but they never *include* the subject. Whenever you are looking for the subject of a sentence, begin by putting parentheses around all the prepositional phrases:

parentheses and prepositional phrases:
The park (behind my apartment) has a playground (with swings and slides).

Nothing in the prepositional phrase can be the subject. Once you have eliminated these phrases, you can follow the steps to find the subject of the sentence.

Step 1: Identify the verb: *has*

Step 2: Ask, "Who or what has?"

Step 3: The answer is the subject: The *park.* The *park* is the subject.

By marking off the prepositional phrases, you are left with the core of the sentence. There is less to look at.

(Across the street) a *child* (with a teddy bear) sat (among the flowers).
subject: *child*

The *student* (from Jamaica) won the contest (with ease).
subject: *student*

Exercise 10 **Practice: Recognizing Prepositional Phrases, Subjects, and Verbs**

Put parentheses around the prepositional phrases in the following sentences. Then underline the subjects and verbs, putting *S* above the subject and *V* above the verb.

1. Two of my friends graduated from Western High School in 2004.

2. The athlete ran across the field and flew over the finish line.

3. A bunch of flowers and a card lay on the kitchen counter.

4. The girl with the long black hair was the most attractive stranger at my brother's party.

5. The mud on the side of my car came from a deep puddle at the end of the street.

6. Nothing except a sincere apology from that man can soothe the anger in my heart.

7. The employees worked over a long weekend to complete the project behind the new building.

8. At one point, the troops were driving through dangerous territory without clear directions.

Collaborate

Exercise 11 **Collaborate: Writing Sentences with Prepositional Phrases**

Do this exercise with a partner. First, add one prepositional phrase to the core sentence. Then ask your partner to add a second prepositional phrase to the same sentence. For the next sentence, switch places. Let your partner add the first phrase; you add the second. Keep switching places throughout the exercise. When you have completed the exercise, share your sentences (the ones with two prepositional phrases) with the class. The first one is done for you.

1. **core sentence:** Employees are concerned.

   Add one prepositional phrase: Employees are concerned about their paychecks.

   Add another prepositional phrase: Employees at the central plant are concerned about their paychecks.

2. **core sentence:** Eduardo studied.

   Add one prepositional phrase: _____

   _____

   Add another prepositional phrase: _____

   _____

3. **core sentence:** The lecture began.

   Add one prepositional phrase: _____

   _____

   Add another prepositional phrase: _____

   _____

4. **core sentence:** A man in black appeared.

   Add one prepositional phrase: _____

   _____

   Add another prepositional phrase: _____

   _____

Word Order

When we speak, we often use a very simple word order: first, the subject; then, the verb. For example, someone would say, "He lost the key." *He* is the subject that begins the sentence; *lost* is the verb that comes after the subject.

However, not all sentences use such a simple word order. Prepositional phrases, for example, can change the word order. To identify the subject and verb, follow these steps:

prepositional phrase and changed subject–verb order:
Behind the cabinet was a box of coins.

Step 1: Mark off the prepositional phrases with parentheses: (Behind the cabinet) was a box (of coins). Remember that nothing in a prepositional phrase can be the subject of a sentence.

Step 2: Find the verb: *was*

Step 3: Who or what was? A box was. The subject of the sentence is *box*.

After you change the word order of this sentence, you can see the subject (S) and the verb (V) more easily.

      S   V
A *box* of coins *was* behind the cabinet.

(Even though *coins* is a plural word, you must use the singular verb *was* because *box* is the singular subject.)

Exercise 12   **Practice: Finding Prepositional Phrases, Subjects, and Verbs in Complicated Word Order**

Put parentheses around the prepositional phrases in the following sentences. Then underline the subjects and verbs, putting an *S* above each subject and a *V* above each verb.

1. Across the street from my grandmother's apartment is an empty lot with cracked cement.

2. By a border of white roses stood a small dog without a collar.

3. Behind all Mario's bragging and bluster hid a shy man with a longing for approval.

4. Inside her desk is a new tablet in a leather case.

5. From the back of the auditorium came the loud sound of someone snoring happily.

6. Among the items in the old wooden chest is a faded photograph of my grandparents on their wedding day.

7. Through the halls echoed the sound of frustrated students on their

   way to an exam.

8. Down the snow-covered street raced two boys on shiny new sleds.

More on Word Order

The expected word order of a subject followed by a verb will change when a sentence starts with *There is/are, There was/were, Here is/are,* or *Here was/were.* In such cases, look for the subject after the verb:

> **S–V order with *There is/are, Here is/are*:**
>
>   V   S   S
> There *are* a *supermarket* and a *laundromat* near my apartment.
>
>   V   S
> Here *is* my best *friend.*

To understand this pattern, you can change the word order:

>   S   S   V
> A *supermarket* and a *laundromat are* there, near my apartment.
>
>   S   V
> My best *friend is* here.

You should also note that even when the subject comes after the verb, the verb has to *match* the subject. For instance, if the subject refers to more than one thing, the verb must refer to more than one thing:

> There are a *supermarket* and a *laundromat* near my apartment.
> (Two things, a supermarket and a laundromat, *are* near my
> apartment.)

Word Order in Questions

Questions have a different word order. The main verb and helping verb are not next to each other, except in short questions (often called *tag questions*).

> **Word order in questions:**
>
> **question:** Did you study for the test?
>   (tag question version: You studied for the test, didn't you?)
> **subject:** *you*
> **verbs:** *did, study*

To understand this concept, you can think about answering the question. If someone accused you of not studying for the test, you might say, "I *did study* for it." You would use two words as verbs.

> **question:** Will she take that history course next semester?
>   (tag question version: She'll take that history course next
>   semester, won't she?)
> **subject:** *she*
> **verbs:** *will, take*
>
> **question:** Is Charles making the coffee?
> **subject:** *Charles*
> **verbs:** *is, making*

> Exercise 13 Practice: Recognizing Subjects and Verbs in Questions
> and *Here is/are, There is/are* Word Order

Underline the subjects and verbs in the following sentences, putting an *S* above each subject and a *V* above each verb.

1. There is somebody with a package at the front door.

2. Have we driven off the main road and missed the right exit?

3. Do you expect an answer to your letter?

4. Here is our chance for a family vacation.

5. Would Mrs. Sung like a gift card for her birthday?

6. On the left side of the street there are a barber shop and an electronics store.

7. There was a long line at the college bookstore today.

8. Can I borrow your notes from Thursday's class?

5 Use verbs correctly in sentences.

Words That Cannot Be Verbs

Sometimes there are words that look like verbs in a sentence but are not verbs. Such words include *adverbs* (words like *always, often, nearly, never, ever*) that are placed close to the verb but are not verbs. Another word that is placed between a helping verb and a main verb is *not*. *Not* is not a verb. When you are looking for verbs in a sentence, be careful to eliminate words like *often* and *not*.

> They will not accept his apology. (The complete verb is *will accept*.)
> Matthew can often repair his truck by himself. (The complete verb is *can repair*.)

Be careful with *contractions*.

> He hasn't called me in a long time. (The complete verb is *has called*. *Not* is not a part of the verb, even in contractions.)
> Don't you speak Spanish? (The complete verb is *do speak*.)
> Won't you come inside? (The complete verb is *will come*. *Won't* is a contraction for *will not*.)

Recognizing Main Verbs

If you are checking to see if a word is a main verb, try the pronoun test. Combine your word with this simple list of pronouns: *I, you, he, she, it, we, they*. A main verb is a word such as *look* or *pulled* that can be combined with the words on this list. Now try the pronoun test.

> For the word *look:* I look, you look, he looks, she looks, it looks, we look, they look

For the word *pulled:* I pulled, you pulled, he pulled, she pulled, it
   pulled, we pulled, they pulled
But the word *never* can't be used alone with the pronouns:
~~I never, you never, he never, she never, it never, we never, they never~~
   (Never did what?)
Never is not a verb. *Not* is not a verb either, as the pronoun test indicates:
~~I not, you not, he not, she not, it not, we not, they not~~ (These combi-
   nations don't make sense because *not* is not a verb.)

Verb Forms That Cannot Be Main Verbs

There are two verb forms that are not main verbs. An *-ing* verb by itself cannot be the main verb, as the pronoun test shows.

> For the word *taking:* ~~I taking, you taking, he taking, she taking, it tak-
> ing, we taking, they taking~~

If you see an *-ing* verb by itself, correct the sentence by adding a helping verb.

> He ~~taking~~ his time. (*Taking*, by itself, cannot be a main verb.)
> **correction:** He *is taking* his time.

The other verb form is called an *infinitive*. An infinitive is the form of the
verb that has *to* placed in front of it.

INFO BOX   **Some Common Infinitives**

to call	to eat	to live	to smile
to care	to fall	to make	to talk
to drive	to give	to run	to work

Try the pronoun test and you'll see that infinitives can't be main verbs:

> For the infinitive *to live:* ~~I to live, you to live, he to live, she to live,
> we to live, they to live~~

So if you see an infinitive being used as a verb, correct the sentence by adding a main verb.

> He ~~to live~~ in a better house.
> **correction:** He *wants* to live in a better house.

The infinitives and the *-ing* verbs just don't work as main verbs. You must
put a verb with them to make a correct sentence.

Exercise 14   **Practice: Correcting Problems with Infinitive or *-ing* Verb
                  Forms**

Most—but not all—of the following sentences are faulty; an *-ing* verb or an
infinitive may be taking the place of a main verb. Correct the sentences that
have errors.

   1. Nobody in the store paying attention to the jumbled piles of mer-
      chandise on the sales tables.

   2. A lack of jobs in our state sending many people into debt, bank-
      ruptcy, and homelessness.

3. Mark's talent for putting people at ease was a real asset in his volunteer work at the free clinic near the edge of town.

4. In the middle of a cold winter, my father wondering about a move to a state with a warmer climate.

5. For me, the most challenging parts of the charity walkathon to be the hot weather and the hills along the route.

6. At the end of the weekend, I thinking about the responsibilities of the days ahead.

7. A tropical storm with strong winds and heavy rain is expected to move into our area in the next two or three days.

8. Joshua to graduate next June.

Exercise 15 **Practice: Finding Subjects and Verbs: A Comprehensive Exercise**

Underline the subjects and verbs in the following sentences, putting an *S* above each subject and a *V* above each verb.

1. My sisters don't like to study with me.

2. Behind all the bragging and the smart talk is an insecure young man with a need for acceptance.

3. Keith has always wanted a career in the U.S. Navy.

4. Matt hoped to send a message to his wife before her meeting with the cardiologist.

5. Didn't you ever think about the risks of traveling in a war-torn country?

6. There are a few problems with buying a used laptop from a pawn shop.

7. Deep love and constant patience helped my parents to survive the first years of a marriage between two people with opposing temperaments.

8. Where did you and Tina go after our geography class on Thursday afternoon?

Exercise 16   **Practice: Finding Subjects and Verbs: A Comprehensive Exercise**

Underline the subjects and verbs in the following sentences, putting an *S* above each subject and a *V* above each verb.

1. Beneath the pile of dirty clothes was a pair of old leather boots in terrible condition.

2. In the summer, Wallace drives to the mountains and hikes on trails at McLendon Park.

3. The Cuban coffee and pastries at Sylvia's restaurant attracted customers from miles away.

4. Without Peter's help, Jamie might never have gotten the chance to start a new career.

5. Below street level is an underground mall with fifty shops and restaurants.

6. Paul's dedication to his job has made him an honored employee.

7. There was a gold border around the rim of the blue vase.

8. Isaac's cat leaped onto my lap and became a blissful ball of orange fur.

Exercise 17   **Collaborate: Creating Your Own Text**

Collaborate

Do this exercise with a partner or a group. Following is a list of rules you have just studied. Write two examples for each rule. When your group has completed the examples for each rule, trade your group's completed exercise with another group's and check their examples while they check yours. The first rule has been done for you.

   Rule 1: The verb in a sentence can express some kind of action.

   example 1: My cousin studies biology in college.

   example 2: Yesterday the rain destroyed the rose bushes.

   Rule 2: The verb in a sentence can express some state of being.

   example 1: _____

   example 2: _____

Rule 3: The verb in a sentence can consist of more than one word.

example 1: _____

example 2: _____

Rule 4: There can be more than one subject in a sentence.

example 1: _____

example 2: _____

Rule 5: If you take out the prepositional phrases, it is easier to identify the subject of a sentence because nothing in a prepositional phrase can be the subject of a sentence. (Write sentences containing at least one prepositional phrase. Put parentheses around the prepositional phrases.)

example 1: _____

example 2: _____

Rule 6: Not all sentences have the simple word order of first subject, then verb. (Give examples of sentences with more complicated word order.)

example 1: _____

example 2: _____

Rule 7: Words like *not, never, often, always,* and *ever* are not verbs. (Write sentences using one of those words, but put a *V* above the correct verb.)

example 1: _____

example 2: _____

Rule 8: An *-ing* verb form by itself or an infinitive (*to* preceding the verb) cannot be a main verb. (Write sentences with *-ing* verb forms or infinitives, but put a *V* above the main verb.)

example 1: _____

example 2: _____

Connect

Exercise 18   Connect: Recognizing Subjects and Verbs in a Paragraph

Underline the subjects and verbs in the following paragraph, putting an *S* above each subject and a *V* above each verb.

A major event in our town is the annual weekend of hot rod racing. From every part of the state come thousands of people. Neighboring states also send their share of competitors and spectators. During this weekend there are huge economic benefits to our town. Many visitors arrive in their campers. Consequently, the local campgrounds fill with every kind of recreational vehicle. Other racing fans stay at nearby hotels and motels. Everyone in town for the races needs to eat, too. During this weekend, the restaurants and supermarkets in our town never complain about a lack of business. Other places sell souvenirs. There are shirts, caps, cups, stickers, bandanas, and flags for sale in every service station, drug store, and superstore. Visitors, merchants, and hotelkeepers love race weekend. In addition, many local residents love this time, too. Thousands of old timers in town have never missed a visit to the races. Without the fun and action of this event, our town would be a sad place.

Chapter Test **The Simple Sentence**   MyWritingLab™

Underline the subjects and verbs in the following sentences, putting an *S* above each subject and a *V* above each verb.

1. With a strong reliance on common sense, a person will nearly always find a way to handle tough decisions.

2. Shouldn't Maria take an early-morning flight to Atlanta and rent a car at the airport?

3. From the back of the audience at the comedy came the loudest laughter of anyone in the room.

4. Without a penny in his pocket, my grandfather arrived in a strange country and found work.

5. Mosquitoes have been making my life miserable during the endless hot and rainy days of a South Carolina summer.

6. Beyond the glamorous sights and sounds of the city center are abandoned apartment buildings and empty shops in a state of decay.

7. Do you think that computers will be obsolete one day?

8. After a few minutes of assessing the situation, the plumber went to his truck, grabbed his tools, and started the long process of fixing the leak.

CHAPTER 2 Beyond the Simple Sentence: Coordination

Quick Question MyWritingLab™

Which sentence(s) is/are correct?

A. Carla made coffee, and she offered us some cookies.

B. Carla made coffee and offered us some cookies.

(After you study this chapter, you will be confident of your answer.)

Learning Objectives

In this chapter, you will learn to:

1. Combine simple sentences using a comma and a coordinating conjunction.
2. Combine simple sentences using a semicolon.
3. Combine simple sentences using a semicolon and a conjunctive adverb.

A group of words containing a subject and a verb is called a **clause**. When that group makes sense by itself, it is called a sentence or an independent clause. A sentence that has one independent clause is called a **simple sentence**. If you rely too heavily on a sentence pattern of simple sentences, you risk writing paragraphs like this:

> My father never got a chance to go to college. He had to struggle all his life. He struggled to make a good living. He dreamed of sending his children to college. He saved his money for their education. Today, all three of his children are in college. Two of them are working toward degrees in business. My father is very proud of them. His third child has pleased my father the most. The third child, my brother, is majoring in

education. My father will be proud of his son the teacher. He thinks a teacher in the family is a great gift.

instead of

> My father never got a chance to go to college, and he had to struggle all his life to make a good living. He dreamed of sending his children to college, so he saved his money for their education. Today, all three of his children are in college. Two of them are working toward degrees in business. My father is very proud of them, yet his third child has pleased my father the most. The third child, my brother, is majoring in education. My father will be proud of his son the teacher, for he thinks a teacher in the family is a great gift.

If you read the two paragraphs aloud, you'll notice how choppy the first one sounds. The second one is smoother. The first one is made up of simple sentences, while the second one combines some simple sentences for a more flowing style.

OPTIONS FOR COMBINING SIMPLE SENTENCES

Good writing involves **sentence variety**. This means mixing a simple sentence with a more complicated one and using both short and long sentences. Sentence variety is easier to achieve if you can combine related, short sentences into one.

Punctuating is often the most difficult part of sentence combining. It's true that punctuating involves memorizing a few rules, but once you know them, you'll be able to use them automatically and write with more confidence. Here are three options for combining simple sentences followed by the punctuation rules you need to use in each case.

OPTION 1: USING A COMMA WITH A COORDINATING CONJUNCTION

1 Combine simple sentences using a comma and a coordinating conjunction.

You can combine two simple sentences with a comma and a coordinating conjunction. The coordinating conjunctions are *for, and, nor, but, or, yet,* and *so.*

To **coordinate** means to *join equals.* When you join two simple sentences with a comma and a coordinating conjunction, each half of the combination remains an **independent clause**, with its own subject (S) and verb (V).

Here are two simple sentences:

>   S   V   S   V
> *Joanne drove* the car. *Richard studied* the map.

Here are two simple sentences combined with a comma and with the word *and*, a coordinating conjunction (CC).

>   S   V   , CC S   V
> *Joanne drove* the car, *and Richard studied* the map.

The combined sentences keep the form they had as separate sentences; that is, they are still both independent clauses, with a subject and verb and with the ability to stand alone.

The word that joins them is the **coordinating conjunction**. It is used to join *equals.* Look at some more examples. These examples use a variety of coordinating conjunctions to join two simple sentences (also called independent clauses).

sentences combined with *for*:

```
       S     V            , CC      S     V
```
My *mother was* furious, *for* the *doctor was* two hours late. (Notice that *for* means *because.)*

sentences combined with *nor*:

```
     S     V      V          , CC   V    S    V
```
We *couldn't see* the stage, *nor could we hear* the music. (Notice what happens to the word order when you use *nor.)*

sentences combined with *but*:

```
   S    V                   , CC      S     V
```
She *parked* in the commuter lot, *but* her *car had* no parking decal.

sentences combined with *or*:

```
       S       V          , CC  S    V
```
Mr. *Chang can call* my office, *or he can write* me.

sentences combined with *and*:

```
   S       V                  S    V
```
She *downloaded* a new app, and *she used* it right away. *(And* means *in addition to.)*

sentences combined with *yet*:

```
 S   V              , CC  S        V
```
I *loved* earth science, *yet I* never *got* a good grade in it. (Notice that *yet* means *but* or *nevertheless.)*

sentences combined with *so*:

```
      S        V          , CC  S      V
```
Marshall *brought* her flowers, *so she forgave* him for his rudeness. (Notice that *so* means *therefore* or *as a result.*

> **Note:** One easy way to remember the coordinating conjunctions is to call them, as a group, **fanboys** (*for, and, nor, but, or, yet, so*).

Where Does the Comma Go?

The comma goes *before* the coordinating conjunction (*for, and, nor, but, or, yet, so*). It comes before the new idea—the second independent clause. It goes where the first independent clause ends. Try this punctuation check. After you've placed the comma, look at the combined sentences. For example,

John saved his money, and he bought a new car.

Now split it into two sentences at the comma:

John saved his money. And he bought a new car.

If you put the comma in the wrong place, after the coordinating conjunction, like this:

comma in wrong place:

~~John saved his money and, he bought a new car.~~

your split sentences would look like this:

> John saved his money and. He bought a new car. (The split doesn't make sense.)

This test helps you see whether the comma has been placed correctly—where the first independent clause ends. (Notice that, in addition to starting a sentence with *and,* you can also begin a sentence with *for, nor, but, or, yet,* or *so*—as long as you've written a complete sentence.)

Caution: Do *not* use a comma every time you use the words *for, and, nor, but, or, yet, so;* use one only when the coordinating conjunction joins independent clauses. Do not use a comma when the coordinating conjunction joins words:

> tea or coffee
> exhausted but relieved
> love and happiness

Do not use a comma when the coordinating conjunction joins phrases:

> on the patio or in the garden
> in the glove compartment and under the seats
> with harsh words but without anger

A comma is used when the coordinating conjunction joins two independent clauses. Another way to state this rule is to say that a comma is used when the coordinating conjunction joins two simple sentences.

Placing the Comma by Using S–V Patterns

An independent clause, or simple sentence, follows this basic pattern:

> S (subject) V (verb)

Here is an example:

> S V
> *He ran.*

You can add to the basic pattern in several ways:

> S S V
> *He* and *I ran.*
>
> S V V
> *He ran* and *swam.*
>
> S S V V
> *He* and *I ran* and *swam.*

Study all the examples above, and you'll notice that you can draw a line separating the subjects on one side and the verbs on the other:

S	V
SS	V
S	VV
SS	VV

So whether the simple sentence has one subject (or more than one), the pattern is subject(s) followed by verb(s).

Compound Sentences

When you combine two simple sentences, the pattern changes:

two simple sentences:

S V
He swam.

S V
I ran.

two simple sentences combined:

S V   S V
He swam, but *I ran.*

In the new pattern, SVSV, you can't draw a line separating all the subjects on one side and all the verbs on the other. The new pattern is called a **compound sentence**: two simple sentences, or independent clauses, combined into one.

Learning the Coordinating Conjunctions

You've just studied one way to combine simple sentences. If you are going to take advantage of this method, you need to memorize the coordinating conjunctions—*for, and, nor, but, or, yet, so*—so that your use of them, with the correct punctuation, will become automatic.

Exercise 1 Practice: Recognizing Compound Sentences and Adding Commas

Add commas only where they are needed in the following sentences.

1. Denise decorated her room in shades of green but I chose purple as the color for my room.

2. An acquaintance at the music store told me about a sale on guitars and advised me about the best deals.

3. At the end of the month, Robin pays all his bills for he fears getting into debt.

4. I have numerous files from high school that I probably don't need but I don't want to delete them.

5. The chef at the vegetarian restaurant creates meals with great flavor yet very little fat or salt.

6. My boyfriend spent Saturday afternoon at a soccer match so I went to the movies with my cousin.

7. Phil must not see his sister before Saturday or he will ruin the surprise about the farewell party.

8. The actor wasn't particularly handsome nor was he a typical action hero.

Exercise 2 Practice: More on Recognizing Compound Sentences and Adding Commas

Add commas only where they are needed in the following sentences.

1. We took the college van to the museum and our instructor drove.

2. My next door neighbor has neither a sense of humor nor a tolerance for young people's parties.

3. Coffee gets me started in the morning but too much caffeine leaves me with a bad headache.

4. Ricky's sister can take Ricky to work on Tuesday or he can get a ride with me.

5. The tea kettle was screeching so Miriam ran to turn off the heat on the stove.

6. My four-year-old dropped his bowl of oatmeal on the floor and I reached for the roll of paper towels.

7. I will never speak to Frank again for he betrayed my trust in him.

8. Patrick loves to watch NASCAR events on television so I got him tickets to a live race for his birthday.

Exercise 3 **Collaborate: Writing and Punctuating Compound Sentences**

Collaborate

Working with a partner or a group, write the compound sentences described below. Be sure to punctuate them correctly. When you have completed the exercise, share your answers with another group or with the class.

1. Write a compound sentence using the coordinating conjunction *for*.

_____

2. Write a compound sentence using the coordinating conjunction *and*.

_____

3. Write a compound sentence using the coordinating conjunction *nor*.

_____

4. Write a compound sentence using the coordinating conjunction *but*.

_____

5. Write a compound sentence using the coordinating conjunction *or*.

_____

6. Write a compound sentence using the coordinating conjunction *yet*.

_____

7. Write a compound sentence using the coordinating conjunction *so*.

_____

OPTION 2: USING A SEMICOLON BETWEEN TWO SIMPLE SENTENCES

2 Combine simple sentences using a semicolon.

Sometimes you want to combine two simple sentences (independent clauses) without using a coordinating conjunction. If you want to join two simple sentences that are related in their ideas and you do not want to use a coordinating conjunction, you can combine them with a semicolon.

two simple sentences:

S   V   S   V
I washed the floor. *He dusted* the furniture.

two simple sentences combined with a semicolon:

S   V   ; S   V
I washed the floor; *he dusted* the furniture.

Here are more examples of this option in use:

S   V ; S V
He swam; I ran.

S   V   V ; S   V   V
Jacy couldn't sleep; she was thinking about her job.

S   V   ; S   V
Skindiving is expensive; *you need* money for equipment.

Notice that when you join two simple sentences with a semicolon, the second sentence begins with a lowercase letter, not a capital letter.

Exercise 4 Practice: Recognizing Compound Sentences and Adding Semicolons

Add semicolons only where they are needed in the following sentences.

1. I went to the campus bookstore to get a book I studied it in the library.

2. David doesn't like Italian food he prefers Indian cooking.

3. Today has been horrible everything has gone wrong.

4. Anita's fear of driving on the freeway is hurting her chances for a position in sales many salespeople must travel frequently as part of their jobs.

5. The weekend at my brother's house was wonderful we had some good conversations and laughed at each other's stories.

6. You might need glasses you seem to be squinting often.

7. A doctor examined my ankle but seemed unconcerned about the possibility of broken bones.

8. My boyfriend is in jail last night he was arrested for driving with an expired license.

Exercise 5 Practice: More on Recognizing Compound Sentences and Adding Semicolons

Add semicolons only where they are needed in the following sentences.

1. Sammy gossips about all his friends I can never trust him with a secret.

2. Tamara sometimes changes the oil in the car Phil never does.

3. Jessica or her cousin could invite their aunt to dinner and pay a little attention to the elderly woman.

4. Everything in our bedroom is dusty or dirty we really need to clean.

5. My clothes don't fit me anymore and are not worth giving away to a charity.

6. Bill won't marry again he is afraid of getting hurt and wants to protect himself from rejection.

7. A kind little man with a huge heart and a tough-talking lady guided me through some terrible times and inspired me to change.

8. The test is tomorrow we need to study.

OPTION 3: USING A SEMICOLON AND A CONJUNCTIVE ADVERB

③ Combine simple sentences using a semicolon and a conjunctive adverb.

Sometimes you may want to join two simple sentences (independent clauses) with a connecting word or phrase called a **conjunctive adverb**. This word points out or clarifies a relationship between the sentences.

INFO BOX **Some Common Conjunctive Adverbs**			
also	furthermore	likewise	otherwise
anyway	however	meanwhile	similarly
as a result	in addition	moreover	still
besides	in fact	nevertheless	then
certainly	incidentally	next	therefore
consequently	indeed	now	thus
finally	instead	on the other hand	undoubtedly

You can put a conjunctive adverb (CA) between simple sentences, but when you do, you still need a semicolon in front of the adverb.

two simple sentences:

S V   S   V
I got a tutor for College Algebra. *I improved* my grade.

two simple sentences joined by a conjunctive adverb and a semicolon:

S V   ; CA S   V
I got a tutor for College Algebra; *then I improved* my grade.

S V   ;   CC   S   V
I got a tutor for College Algebra; *consequently, I improved* my grade.

Punctuating After a Conjunctive Adverb

Notice the comma after the conjunctive adverb in the sentence, *I got a tutor for college algebra; consequently, I improved my grade.* Here's the generally accepted rule:

Put a comma after the conjunctive adverb if the conjunctive adverb is more than one syllable long.

For example, if the conjunctive adverb is a word like *consequently, furthermore,* or *moreover,* you use a comma. If the conjunctive adverb is one syllable, you do not have to add a comma after it. One-syllable conjunctive adverbs are words like *then* or *thus*.

punctuating with conjunctive adverbs:

Every month, I paid my whole credit card debt; *thus* I avoided paying interest.

Every month, I paid my whole credit card debt; *consequently,* I avoided paying interest.

Exercise 6 **Practice: Recognizing and Punctuating Compound Sentences with Conjunctive Adverbs**

Add semicolons and commas only where they are needed in the following sentences.

1. We worked on our plans for a trip to the beach meanwhile the rain poured onto the roof and into the gutters.

2. We worked on our plans for a trip to the beach then the rain poured onto the roof and into the gutters.

3. I hate writing with ballpoint pens in fact I always carry a gel or felt-tip pen.

4. My commute to college is a long bus ride however it gives me time to study.

5. Lindsay used to read stacks of romance novels now she is involved in her own love story.

6. My car has been making a strange noise undoubtedly I should get the car checked by a mechanic.

7. Ren really wants to study drama however his father wants him to study computer science.

8. They could have their study group in the cafeteria on the other hand, they could meet in the library.

Exercise 7 **Practice: More on Recognizing and Punctuating Compound Sentences with Conjunctive Adverbs**

Add semicolons and commas only where they are needed in the following sentences.

1. Jim has always been a loyal friend to Adam certainly he will come to Adam's wedding.

2. Jonetta's love of animals certainly played a role in her choice of a college major.

3. Greg might work in his father's landscaping business and even study accounting at night.

4. I'll wash my clothes on Saturday morning next I'll treat myself to breakfast at the Pancake Palace.

5. Keira begged and pleaded with her father still he would not lend her the money for a tattoo.

6. Al never seems to have any money on him yet always wears expensive clothes.

7. I'll set up the file sharing then we can work on the project together.

8. Tina is not interested in me besides she already has a boyfriend.

Exercise 8   **Practice: Selecting the Correct Conjunctive Adverb**

In the sentences below, underline the conjunctive adverb that expresses the meaning given in the hint. The first one is done for you.

1. Hint: Select the word that means *yet.*

   The best vegetarian restaurant is Fresh and Fabulous Food; (moreover, <u>however</u>), it's too expensive for a person on a budget.

2. Hint: Select the word that means *as a substitute.*

   Nathan has stopped smoking cigarettes; (instead, incidentally), he chews nicotine gum to deal with his cravings.

3. Hint: Select the word that means *in the same way or manner.*

   San Diego has a nearly perfect climate; (undoubtedly, similarly), the weather in the Bahamas is mild and welcoming.

4. Hint: Select the word that means *at the same time.*

   I ran to turn off the water in the overflowing bathtub; (meanwhile, anyway), Denise gathered a pile of dry towels and began wiping up the mess.

5. Hint: Select the word that means *without question.*

   My daughter has more training in dance than the other contestants; (otherwise, undoubtedly), she will win the dance competition.

6. Hint: Select the word that means *in spite of that.*

   Mitchell doesn't have much money to buy clothes; (likewise, nevertheless), he always looks clean and neat.

7. Hint: Select the word that means *as a result.*

   I worked in the kitchen of a pizza restaurant all summer; (therefore, furthermore), I am ready for a job in a less stifling atmosphere.

8. Hint: Select the word that means *without a doubt.*

   My lab partner is the best choice for the job of team leader; (certainly, furthermore), he has more experience than any of the other students.

Exercise 9   **Collaborate: Writing Sentences with Conjunctive Adverbs**

Collaborate

Working with a partner or group, write one sentence for each of the conjunctive adverbs below. When you have completed this exercise, share your answers with another group or with the class. The first one is done for you.

1. Write a compound sentence using *instead.*

   She couldn't find her notes for her speech to the jury; instead, she relied on

   her memory.

  2. Write a compound sentence using *then*.

_____

_____

  3. Write a compound sentence using *furthermore*.

_____

_____

  4. Write a compound sentence using *on the other hand*.

_____

_____

  5. Write a compound sentence using *otherwise*.

_____

_____

  6. Write a compound sentence using *therefore*.

_____

_____

  7. Write a compound sentence using *thus*.

_____

_____

  8. Write a compound sentence using *in addition*.

_____

_____

Exercise 10   Practice: Combining Simple Sentences Three Ways

Add (1) a comma, (2) a semicolon, or (3) a semicolon and a comma to the following sentences. Do not add, change, or delete any words. Just add the correct punctuation.

  1. Send a sympathy card to Uncle Leo then call him in a few days.

  2. I admire my father very much but some of his ideas about raising a family seem old-fashioned.

  3. Melissa is out of town so I am taking care of her tropical fish and walking her terrier for a few days.

  4. Nothing is happening this weekend consequently I am bored and restless.

  5. Ryan used to be engaged to the star of a reality television show anyway he brags about this love affair all the time.

  6. We may not get to Spring Hills before dark still we can try.

  7. I have to use a special cream rinse on my hair otherwise the top of my head looks like a thatch of dead grass.

  8. Working the night shift is very hard it's even more difficult to be alert at school the next day.

Exercise 11   **Practice: More on Combining Simple Sentences Three Ways**

Add (1) a comma, (2) a semicolon, or (3) a semicolon and a comma to the following sentences. Do not add, change, or delete any words. Just add the correct punctuation.

1. Sandra might have run into bad weather on the highway or she might have gotten a late start.

2. Eli called every paint store in town finally he found a place with the right color of latex paint.

3. The instructor explained the new theory clearly therefore we scored very well on the exam.

4. I am tired of getting up early in the morning in fact I would like to sleep until noon every day for a year.

5. The new shoe store is in a great location yet it hasn't attracted many customers.

6. Yesterday, Shareena was flirting with me now she walks by without talking to me.

7. Lionel was hungry so he made some toast with strawberry jelly.

8. My husband and his brother cleaned out our garage on Saturday and I sorted through the boxes in the basement.

Exercise 12   **Collaborate: Combining Simple Sentences**

Collaborate

Following are pairs of simple sentences. Working with a partner or group, combine each pair into one sentence. Remember the three options for combining sentences: (1) a comma and a coordinating conjunction, (2) a semicolon, (3) a semicolon and a conjunctive adverb. When you have combined each pair into one sentence, exchange your exercise with another group. Write a new sentence below each sentence prepared by the other group. The first one is done for you.

1. Takeout pizza for a family of six is expensive.

   My children and I make our own pizza at home.

   combination 1: *Takeout pizza for a family of six is expensive, so my children and I make our own pizza at home.*

   combination 2: *Takeout pizza for a family of six is expensive; instead, my children and I make our own pizza at home.*

2. Alicia recently earned her G.E.D.

   She is thinking about taking some college courses.

   combination 1: _____

   _____

   combination 2: _____

   _____

3. You never kept your friends' secrets.

 Most people no longer trust you.

 combination 1: _____

 _____

 combination 2: _____

 _____

4. Mrs. Garcia's house was always a mess.

 Everyone loved the warmth and happiness in her home.

 combination 1: _____

 _____

 combination 2: _____

 _____

5. We moved to a new city.

 I began college there.

 combination 1: _____

 _____

 combination 2: _____

 _____

6. Andrea never complained about being poor.

 She did not want sympathy from others.

 combination 1: _____

 _____

 combination 2: _____

 _____

7. The community center has been closed for three years.

 Teens have nowhere to go after school.

 combination 1: _____

 _____

 combination 2: _____

 _____

8. We can go to a movie at the multiplex.

 We can play games at the arcade.

 combination 1: _____

 _____

 combination 2: _____

 _____

Exercise 13 **Connect: Punctuating Compound Sentences in a Paragraph** Connect

Add commas and semicolons only where they are needed in the paragraph below.

Losing a dog is a terrible experience finding one can be a stressful occasion, too. One morning, a woman from the neighborhood came to our door. She had a small, fluffy dog in her arms. She knew that we had a small poodle and she had found the fluffy dog wandering in the street. She asked us if the dog in her arms belonged to us. We said it wasn't ours but we offered to take the lost dog to our veterinarian's office. Our vet keeps part of her office for rescuing lost or abandoned pets however the rescue part accepts strays only in the late afternoon. In the meantime, we waited and worried. Our first worry concerned our dog she did not like the newcomer. The intruder dog sniffed our poodle consequently our dog growled. Soon the lost dog was exiled to our screened porch. We gave him water and food. He lapped the water enthusiastically then he peered through the sliding glass door of the porch and gazed lovingly at our dog. Our dog growled meanwhile we worried about the little stranger. We thought about dogs without homes and worried about a dog's life in a shelter. We went to the porch and petted the little dog immediately our dog growled. Soon the time came for taking the strange dog to our veterinarian's shelter. Fortunately, this story has a happy ending. The next day, the dog's owner checked the shelter. The lost dog became the found dog. All of the humans felt relieved and two dogs were safe in their own homes.

MyWritingLab™   **Chapter Test**   **Beyond the Simple Sentence: Coordination**

Add a comma, a semicolon, or a semicolon and a comma to the following sentences. Do not add, change, or delete any words; just add the correct punctuation.

1. On her birthday, Carlotta received a call from her father still she would have preferred a visit from him.

2. It rained for six hours on Saturday night finally the rain stopped on Sunday morning.

3. Ben wouldn't talk about his childhood in foster homes nor would he discuss his years as a runaway.

4. Your boyfriend is a kind and understanding person certainly he will support you in this sad time.

5. Many of the stores at Tower Mall are losing business for a new shopping center has opened nearby.

6. I will get better grades on my next two chemistry tests anyway I will study harder.

7. The newest tablet is so light it's hard to believe what it can do.

8. Carlton has a barbecue grill in his back yard thus he can invite his friends for cookouts during the summer.

Avoiding Run-on Sentences and Comma Splices

Learning Objectives

In this chapter, you will learn to:

1. Recognize and correct run-on sentences.
2. Recognize and correct comma splices.

RUN-ON SENTENCES

1. Recognize and correct run-on sentences.

If you run two independent clauses together without the necessary punctuation, you make an error called a **run-on sentence**. This error is also called a **fused sentence**.

run-on sentence error:
I worked hard in the class I earned a good grade.

run-on sentence error corrected:
I worked hard in the class, and I earned a good grade. (To correct this error, you need a comma before the coordinating conjunction *and*.)

run-on sentence error:
I worked hard in the class I earned a good grade.

run-on sentence error corrected:
I worked hard in the class; I earned a good grade. (To correct this error, you need a semicolon between the two independent clauses.)

run-on sentence error:
I worked hard in the class I earned a good grade.

run-on sentence error corrected:
I worked hard in the class. I earned a good grade. (To correct this error, you need to create two sentences with a period after "class" and a capital letter to begin the second sentence.)

Steps for Correcting Run-on Sentences

When you edit your writing, you can correct run-on sentences by following these steps:

Step 1: Check for two independent clauses.

Step 2: Check that the clauses are separated by either a coordinating conjunction (*for, and, nor, but, or, yet, so*) and a comma, or by a semicolon.

Follow the steps in checking this sentence:

Tablets are handy devices I use mine often.

Step 1: Check for two independent clauses. You can do this by checking for the subject–verb, subject–verb pattern that indicates two independent clauses.

    S   V   S V
Tablets are handy devices *I use* mine often.

The pattern indicates that you have two independent clauses.

Step 2: Check that the clauses are separated by either a coordinating conjunction (*for, and, nor, but, or, yet, so*) and a comma, or by a semicolon.

There is no punctuation between the independent clauses, and there is no coordinating conjunction. You therefore have a run-on sentence. You can correct it three ways:

run-on sentence corrected with a coordinating conjunction and a comma:
Tablets are handy devices, *so* I use mine often.

run-on sentence corrected with a semicolon:
Tablets are handy devices; I use mine often.

run-on sentence corrected with a period and a capital letter:
Tablets are handy devices. I use mine often.

Follow the steps once more, checking this sentence:

I bought a new computer it is too complicated for me.

Step 1: Check for two independent clauses. Do this by checking the subject–verb, subject–verb pattern.

S   V   S V
I bought a new computer *it is* too complicated for me.

Step 2: Check that the clauses are separated by either a coordinating conjunction (*for, and, nor, but, or, yet, so*) and a comma, or by a semicolon.

There is no punctuation between the independent clauses. There is no coordinating conjunction, either. Without the proper punctuation, this is a run-on sentence. Correct it three ways:

run-on sentence corrected with a coordinating conjunction and a comma:
I bought a new computer, *but* it is too complicated for me.

run-on sentence error corrected with a semicolon:
I bought a new computer; it is too complicated for me.

run-on sentence error corrected with a period and a capital letter:
I bought a new computer. It is too complicated for me.

Using the steps to check for run-on sentences can also help you avoid unnecessary punctuation. Consider this sentence:

Amelia worked at a day care Monday through Friday and took classes in the evening.

Step 1: Check for two independent clauses. Do this by checking the subject–verb, subject–verb pattern.

S   V   V
Amelia worked at a day care Monday through Friday and *took* classes in the evening.

The pattern is SVV, not SV, SV. You have one independent clause, not two. The sentence is not a run-on sentence.

Following the steps in correcting run-on sentences can help you avoid a major grammatical error.

Exercise 1 **Practice: Correcting Run-on Sentences**

Some of the sentences below are correctly punctuated. Some are run-on (fused) sentences—two simple sentences run together without any punctuation. If a sentence is correctly punctuated, write *OK* in the space provided. If it is a run-on sentence, put an *X* in the space provided and correct the sentence above the lines.

1. _____ My father never went to college yet knows a great deal about the history of World War II.

2. _____ The job applicant completed the application it was four pages long.

3. _____ Water was leaking from the bottom of the refrigerator and spreading across the kitchen floor.

4. _____ The high price of fuel makes long road trips more difficult for vacationers but hasn't resulted in more people traveling by air.

5. _____ Marcus could visit his family during the spring he could also wait until the summer months.

6. _____ I like writing with gel pens they write more smoothly than ballpoint pens and require less pressure than pencils.

7. _____ Nobody was home at my parents' house I opened the front door with my house key.

8. _____ The e-book is less expensive I wish all texts had e-books.

> **Exercise 2** Practice: More on Correcting Run-on Sentences

Some of the following sentences are correctly punctuated. Some are run-on (fused) sentences—two simple sentences run together without any punctuation. If the sentence is correctly punctuated, write *OK* in the space provided. If it is a run-on sentence, put an *X* in the space provided and correct the sentence above the lines.

1. _____ Selecting next semester's classes is difficult many classes conflict with my work schedule.

2. _____ I'm going to get my hair cut tomorrow I want to look good for Emily's party.

3. _____ The store detective looked at me with suspicion and asked to see the contents of my bag.

4. _____ My car radio is not working right I can get only two radio stations.

5. _____ Tom complained about his brother Rick's clothes Rick wears Tom's clothes now.

6. _____ Sabrina still thinks about her first love she sighs over old photographs of the two of them together and listens to their special songs.

7. _____ I studied my psychology notes for an hour then I fell asleep in my chair.

8. _____ The instructor quietly handed back papers thus students believed they didn't do well.

② Recognize and correct comma splices.

COMMA SPLICES

A **comma splice** is an error that occurs when you punctuate with a comma but should use a semicolon instead. If you are joining two independent clauses without a coordinating conjunction, you *must* use a semicolon. A comma isn't enough.

comma splice error:
The new office building has a cafeteria, the food choices are plentiful.

comma splice error corrected:
The new office building has a cafeteria; the food choices are plentiful.

comma splice error:
I lost my umbrella, now I have to buy a new one.

comma splice error corrected:
I lost my umbrella; now I have to buy a new one.

Correcting Comma Splices

When you edit your writing, you can correct comma splices by following these steps:

Step 1: Check for two independent clauses.

Step 2: Check that the clauses are separated by a coordinating conjunction (*for, and, nor, but, or, yet, so*). If they are, then a comma in front of the coordinating conjunction is sufficient. If they are not separated by a coordinating conjunction, you have a comma splice. Correct it by changing the comma to a semicolon.

Follow the steps to check for a comma splice in this sentence:

The college auditorium is huge, I have my history class there.

Step 1: Check for two independent clauses. You can do this by checking for the subject–verb, subject–verb pattern that indicates two independent clauses.

$$\text{S} \qquad \text{V} \qquad \text{S} \quad \text{V}$$
The college *auditorium is* huge, *I have* my history class there.

Step 2: Check that the clauses are separated by a coordinating conjunction.

There is no coordinating conjunction. To correct the comma splice error, you must use a semicolon instead of a comma:

comma splice error corrected:
The college auditorium is huge; I have my history class there.

Be careful not to mistake a short word like *then* or *thus* for a coordinating conjunction. Only the seven coordinating conjunctions (*for, and, nor, but, or, yet, so*) with a comma in front of them can join independent clauses.

comma splice error:
Suzanne opened the letter, then she screamed with joy.

comma splice error corrected:
Suzanne opened the letter; then she screamed with joy.

Then is not a coordinating conjunction; it is a conjunctive adverb. When it joins two independent clauses, it needs a semicolon in front of it.

Also remember that conjunctive adverbs that are two or more syllables long (such as *consequently, however, therefore*) need a comma after them *as well as* a semicolon in front of them when they join independent clauses.

Anthony passed the placement test; consequently, he can take Advanced Mathematics.

Note: For a list of some common conjunctive adverbs, see Chapter 2.

Sometimes writers use commas before and after a conjunctive adverb and think the commas are sufficient. Check this sentence for a comma splice by following the steps:

The van held all my tools, however, it used too much gas.

Step 1: Check for two independent clauses by checking for the subject–verb, subject–verb pattern.

             S   V   S   V
The van held all my tools, however, it used too much gas.

Step 2: Check for a coordinating conjunction.

There is no coordinating conjunction. *However* is a conjunctive adverb, not a coordinating conjunction. Without a coordinating conjunction, a semicolon is needed between the two independent clauses.

comma splice corrected:
The van held all my tools; however, it used too much gas.

Following the steps in correcting comma splices can help you avoid a major grammar error.

Exercise 3 Practice: Correcting Comma Splices

Some of the following sentences are correctly punctuated. Some contain comma splices. If the sentence is correctly punctuated, write *OK* in the space provided. If it contains a comma splice, put an *X* in the space provided and correct the sentence. To correct the sentence, you do not need to add words; just correct the punctuation.

1. _____ We don't need an expensive television, nor should we spend any money on a new and faster computer.

2. _____ I ran to algebra class, then I had to go to the lab for extra help.

3. _____ Sandra's little brother was reading all her email, also, he was telling his friends about some of the romantic messages.

4. _____ I lost my wallet, then I had to take quick action to protect my identity and savings.

5. _____ Eric spent most of his life in Norway, so he never complains about a few days of snow.

6. _____ You have to attend every one of your accounting classes, otherwise, you will miss too much explanation and be hopelessly lost.

7. _____ The food in the cafeteria is organic, so it is always fresh and tasty.

8. _____ The children's chorus worked on its spring concert for months, very few people came to hear the program.

Exercise 4   **Practice: More on Correcting Comma Splices**

Some of the following sentences are correctly punctuated. Some contain comma splices. If the sentence is correctly punctuated, write *OK* in the space provided. If it contains a comma splice, put an *X* in the space provided and correct the sentence. To correct the sentence, you do not need to add words; just correct the punctuation.

1. _____ My two-year-old has a cold, so I can't drop him off at his preschool today.

2. _____ Mr. Scheindlin enjoys Greek food, he comes to the annual Greek festival every year.

3. _____ Wen and Jack have English at noon, moreover, they go to sociology together afterwards.

4. _____ Jeans with status labels cost too much, I buy my jeans at a discount store.

5. _____ Someone broke into my parents' house, as a result, my parents have to get all their locks changed.

6. _____ I have been seeing Lisa for six months, yet I sometimes think about my former girlfriend.

7. _____ Pete wouldn't go to the fair with me, however, he promised he would meet me for breakfast next week.

8. _____ Andre always borrowed money from me and my sister, then he found a good job and paid us back.

Exercise 5   **Collaborate: Completing Sentences**

Collaborate

With a partner or group, write the first part of each of the following incomplete sentences. Make your addition an independent clause. Be sure to punctuate your completed sentences correctly. The first one is done for you.

1. <u>My candle suddenly blew out;</u>_____ then I saw the ghost.

2. _____ meanwhile, someone screamed.

3. _____ yet he kept smiling at me.

4. _____ next we'll pay our tuition bill.

5. _____ now I can't sleep.

6. _____ consequently, he won't speak to me.

7. _____ for I'm really hungry.

8. _____ and a swarm of bees appeared.

Connect

Exercise 6   **Connect: Editing a Paragraph for Run-on Sentences and Comma Splices**

Edit the following paragraph for run-on sentences and comma splices. There are eight errors.

Waiting in line at a crowded restaurant can provide a lesson in personality types and in keeping the peace. First of all, there are the calm people, they wait patiently and quietly. Unfortunately, the calm people are often outnumbered by the other types. Some people see the wait as a social opportunity they like to make new friends. Social types start conversations they will talk to anyone. Such people are generally kind and don't mean any harm. They have sweet dispositions, however, a few shy or very private people may feel uneasy around the social people. A more irritating type is the loud cell phone conversationalist. The conversationalist needs to be on the phone all the time. Unfortunately, the conversationalist loves an audience. With a captive audience of people in line, the conversationalist is elated. He or she will reveal family secrets and disturbing emotional problems and never blink, meanwhile, the listeners in line are horrified. No one knows whether to look at the speaker or to look away. The last kind of line personality is physically aggressive. Restless and impatient people in line may push others, they may even jump to the head of the line. Line jumpers often try to look confident they walk boldly to the front, ask a question of a staff member, and then stay at the front of the line. With cell phone dramatics and line jumping, even patient people can become distressed. A mix of impatience and irritation can be dangerous but everyone in line should remember the value of peaceful coexistence and think of the delicious food to come.

Chapter Test Avoiding Run-on Sentences and Comma Splices

Some of the sentences below are correctly punctuated. Some are run-on sentences, and some contain comma splices. If a sentence is correctly punctuated, write *OK* in the space provided. If it is a run-on sentence or contains a comma splice, put an *X* in the space provided and correct the sentence above the lines. To correct a sentence, add the necessary punctuation. Do not add any words.

1. _____ Someone at the back of the room sneezed loudly I began to worry about the recent flu epidemic.

2. _____ Ella met a kind, bright, and attractive man at college in Chicago and became engaged to him at the end of her sophomore year.

3. _____ This class is getting more difficult, consequently, I worry about my ability to pass it.

4. _____ You forgot our anniversary such thoughtlessness hurts me.

5. _____ It's too late for a big meal, so let's have soup and a salad.

6. _____ My bedroom is dark, in fact, it's the darkest room in the house.

7. _____ Calvin loves special effects thus he wants to be a visual effects artist.

8. _____ My mother is not fond of her older brother, nevertheless, she invites him to all the family gatherings.

CHAPTER 4

Beyond the Simple Sentence: Subordination

Quick Question MyWritingLab™

Which sentence(s) is/are correct?

A. Unless my test scores improve, I won't be able to pass this course.
B. I won't be able to pass this course unless my test scores improve.

(After you study this chapter, you will be confident of your answer.)

Learning Objectives

In this chapter, you will learn to:

1 Use a dependent clause to begin a sentence.
2 Use a dependent clause to end a sentence.
3 Generate and punctuate sentences correctly.

MORE ON COMBINING SIMPLE SENTENCES

You may remember these principles of grammar:

- A clause has a subject and a verb.
- An independent clause is a simple sentence; it is a group of words, with a subject and a verb, that makes sense by itself.

Chapter 2 described three options for combining simple sentences (independent clauses). There is another kind of clause called a **dependent clause**. It has a subject and a verb, but it does not make sense by itself. It cannot stand alone because it is not complete by itself. That is, it *depends* on the rest of the sentence to give it meaning. You can use a dependent clause in another option for combining simple sentences.

OPTION 4: USING A DEPENDENT CLAUSE TO BEGIN A SENTENCE

Often, you can combine simple sentences by changing an independent clause into a dependent clause and placing it at the beginning of the new sentence.

two simple sentences:

S   V   S V
I missed my bus. *I slept* through my alarm.

changing one simple sentence into a beginning dependent clause:

      S V   S   V
Because *I slept* through my alarm, *I missed* my bus.

OPTION 5: USING A DEPENDENT CLAUSE TO END A SENTENCE

You can also combine simple sentences by changing an independent clause into a dependent clause and placing it at the end of the new sentence:

S   V   S V
I missed my bus because *I slept* through my alarm.

Notice how one simple sentence can be changed into a dependent clause in two ways:

two simple sentences:

      S   V   S   V
Nicholas played his guitar. *Jared sang* an old song.

changing one simple sentence into a dependent clause:

      S   V   S   V
Nicholas played his guitar while *Jared sang* an old song.

or

        S   V   S   V
While *Jared sang* an old song, *Nicholas played* his guitar.

Using Subordinating Words: Subordinating Conjunctions

Changing an independent clause to a dependent one is called **subordinating**. How do you do it? You add a subordinating word, called a **subordinating conjunction**, to an independent clause, which makes it dependent—less "important"—or subordinate, in the new sentence.

Keep in mind that the subordinate clause is still a clause; it has a subject and a verb, but it doesn't make sense by itself. For example, here is an independent clause:

    S   V
David studies.

Somebody (David) does something (studies). The statement makes sense by itself. But if you add a subordinating conjunction to the independent clause, the clause becomes dependent—incomplete, unfinished—like this:

1. Use a dependent clause to begin a sentence.

2. Use a dependent clause to end a sentence.

3. Generate and punctuate sentences correctly.

When David studies (When he studies, what happens?)
Unless David studies (Unless he studies, what will happen?)
If David studies (If he studies, what will happen?)

Now, each dependent clause needs an independent clause to finish the idea:

dependent clause   independent clause
When David studies, he does well in his courses.

dependent clause   independent clause
Unless David studies, he will not do well in his courses.

dependent clause   independent clause
If David studies, his grades will be good.

There are many subordinating conjunctions. When you put any of these words in front of an independent clause, you make that clause dependent. Here is a list of some subordinating conjunctions:

INFO BOX   **Common Subordinating Conjunctions**

after	before	so that	whenever
although	even though	though	where
as	if	unless	whereas
as if	in order that	until	whether
because	since	when	while

If you pick the right subordinating conjunction, you can effectively combine simple sentences (independent clauses) into a more sophisticated sentence pattern. Such combining helps you add sentence variety to your writing and helps to explain relationships between ideas.

simple sentences:

S   V   V   S   V
Emily had never *studied* art. *She was* a gifted painter.

new combination:

dependent clause   independent clause
Although Emily had never studied art, she was a gifted painter.

simple sentences:

S   V   S   V
I have a dictionary app on my smartphone. *I can check* the meanings of new words easily.

new combination:

independent clause   dependent clause
I have a dictionary app on my smartphone so that I can check the meanings of new words.

Punctuating Complex Sentences

The new combination, which has one independent clause and one or more dependent clauses, is called a **complex sentence**. Complex sentences are very easy to punctuate. See if you can figure out the rule for punctuating by yourself. Look at the following examples. All are punctuated correctly:

dependent clause   independent clause
Whenever I visit my mother, I bring flowers.

independent clause   dependent clause
I bring flowers whenever I visit my mother.

dependent clause   independent clause
While he was talking, I was daydreaming.

independent clause   dependent clause
I was daydreaming while he was talking.

In the examples above, look at the sentences that have a comma. Now look at the ones that don't have a comma. Both kinds of sentences are punctuated correctly. Do you see the rule?

When a dependent clause comes at the beginning of a sentence, the clause is followed by a comma. When a dependent clause comes at the end of a sentence, the clause does not need a comma.

Here are some correctly punctuated complex sentences:

Although he studied hard, he failed the test.
He failed the test although he studied hard.
Until I started running, I was out of shape.
I was out of shape until I started running.

Exercise 1   Practice: Punctuating Complex Sentences

All of the following sentences are complex sentences—they have one independent and one or more dependent clauses. Add a comma to each sentence that needs one.

1. Unless I get a part-time job during the summer I won't have enough money for fall tuition and fees at college.

2. Bring me some fresh orange juice when you go to the supermarket.

3. After Victoria heard about the robbery on the other side of town she stopped jogging through the local park on her own.

4. When daylight savings time begins I feel disoriented for a few days.

5. Andrea struggled with finding a part-time job because she had to be on campus five days a week for classes.

6. Before Aunt Ella saw a physician my aunt had no idea of the dangers of diabetes.

7. Whenever the weather changes suddenly allergy sufferers are likely to experience symptoms.

8. Pedestrians huddled against the walls of the nearest buildings as a sudden storm blasted through the city.

Exercise 2 **Practice: More on Punctuating Complex Sentences**

All of the following sentences are complex sentences—they have one independent and one or more dependent clauses. Add a comma to each sentence that needs one.

1. Although the area once had a reputation for criminal activity and urban decay it is slowly renewing itself and emerging as an attractive neighborhood.

2. Lewis is taking care of his two nephews while his sister is in the hospital.

3. Toby smiled at me as if he had a wonderful secret.

4. Since there's nothing I want to watch on television I'm going to listen to some music.

5. Even if Laura can't find the perfect job she can earn money and learn about her field in a less attractive job.

6. When the instructor announced the final project the students let out a collective sigh of relief.

7. Tom will drive me to Tulsa next week unless he has to fill in for someone at the station.

8. Because my parents spoke Spanish at home I grew up knowing two languages.

Exercise 3 **Practice: Combining Sentences**

Combine each pair of sentences below into one smooth, clear sentence. The new combination should include one independent and one dependent clause and an appropriate subordinating word.

1. I am hoping for sunny weather on Saturday. I can spend the afternoon at the beach.

   combined: _____

   _____

2. Angela rehearsed her speech in front of family members and friends. She became more confident about giving the speech in front of her speech class.

   combined: _____

   _____

   _____

3. Charles has been working hard in his classes. He wants to get an internship this summer.

   combined: _____

   _____

4. Eric developed a sudden interest in the theater. He met a pretty and dynamic drama student.

   combined: _____

   _____

5. You never admit your mistakes. They always come to my attention in some way.

   combined: _____

   _____

6. We lose our electricity during the storm. We have plenty of battery-powered lights and lanterns.

   combined: _____

   _____

7. I plan on a quiet Saturday night. My sister asks me to babysit for her toddlers.

   combined: _____

   _____

8. I am engrossed in the second book. The third book comes out today.

   combined: _____

   _____

Exercise 4 **Collaborate: Creating Complex Sentences**

Collaborate

Do this exercise with a partner or group. Each item below lists a dependent clause. Write two different sentences that include the dependent clause. One sentence should begin with the dependent clause; the other sentence should end with the dependent clause. The first one is done for you.

1. **dependent clause:** whenever I visit my grandmother

   sentence 1: Whenever I visit my grandmother, she tells me stories about

   life in Havana.

   sentence 2: I bring a box of chocolates whenever I visit my grandmother.

   _____

2. **dependent clause:** even if Kevin texts me

   sentence 1: _____

   _____

   sentence 2: _____

   _____

3. **dependent clause:** as shots were fired at the soldiers

   sentence 1: _____

   _____

   sentence 2: _____

   _____

4. **dependent clause:** before our baby is born

   sentence 1: _____

   _____

   sentence 2: _____

   _____

5. **dependent clause:** since I have to work overtime this weekend

   sentence 1: _____

   _____

   sentence 2: _____

   _____

6. **dependent clause:** unless you can think of a better place

   sentence 1: _____

   _____

   sentence 2: _____

   _____

7. **dependent clause:** although my room is a mess

   sentence 1: _____

   _____

   sentence 2: _____

   _____

8. **dependent clause:** because my boss was a kind person

   sentence 1: _____

   _____

   sentence 2: _____

   _____

Connect

Exercise 5 **Connect: Editing a Paragraph with Complex Sentences**

Edit this paragraph by adding or deleting commas. There are eight places that contain errors.

For fifteen years, my family has moved often and has had to deal with mixed

effects of constant change. Because my parents and I have seen many parts of the country we have learned about different places. We know about the beauty

of Northern California and the friendliness of people in small Southern towns.

We have learned how to adjust quickly to a new house or a new town, so that

we can feel secure and stable. We have learned not to judge strangers, before we

get to know them. While some people have been known to judge us too quickly

we have tried to understand them. Although our many travels have widened our

perspective and brought us happiness we have missed a few important parts of a

stable life. My parents suffered, whenever they were forced to look for new jobs.

Since I changed schools six times I never enjoyed an enduring friendship. Loneli-

ness followed us from place to place even though we found good people in each

city or town. Fortunately, my family has now settled for good in a warm and safe

community, where we can develop permanent friendships and deep bonds.

Chapter Test Beyond the Simple Sentence: Subordination

MyWritingLab™

All of the following sentences are complex sentences, but some are not correctly punctuated. Write *OK* next to the ones that are correctly punctuated and *X* next to the ones that are not.

1. _____ My grandmother could barely walk, before she started physical therapy at the orthopedic center.

2. _____ Whenever the doorbell rings my dog hides.

3. _____ Because I did well on the essay, everyone comes to me for help.

4. _____ I can't wait until my husband gets back from active duty in Iraq and can see our new baby.

5. _____ Since her hair is thick and unmanageable, my cousin spends a great deal of money on hair products and visits to hair salons.

6. _____ The college president gave students an update on the campus construction project, while the bulldozers were running in the background.

7. _____ After you finish summer school, you can take a short break and relax.

8. _____ Let me know, if you need a ride to work.

CHAPTER 5

Combining Sentences: A Review of Your Options

Quick Question MyWritingLab™

Which sentence(s) is/are correct?

A. When March arrives, I am ready for a break from studying.
B. I am ready for a break from studying, when March arrives.

(After you study this chapter, you will be confident of your answer.)

Learning Objectives

In this chapter, you will learn to:

1. Combine sentences to achieve sentence variety in your writing.
2. Recognize and apply options for combining dependent clauses and independent clauses.

1 Combine sentences to achieve sentence variety in your writing.

Combining sentences helps you to avoid a choppy writing style in which all your sentences are short. The pattern of one short sentence after another makes your writing repetitive and boring. When you mix the length of sentences, using some long ones and some short ones, you use a strategy called **sentence variety**.

You can develop a style that includes sentence variety by combining short, related sentences clearly and smoothly. There are several ways to combine sentences. The following chart will help you see them all at a glance, and it includes the necessary punctuation for each combination:

INFO BOX **Options for Combining Sentences**

Coordination

| Option 1 Independent clause | { , for
, and
, nor
, but
, or
, yet
, so } | independent clause. |

| Option 2 Independent clause | { ; } | independent clause. |

| Option 3 Independent clause | { ; also,
; anyway,
; as a result,
; besides,
; certainly,
; consequently,
; finally,
; furthermore,
; however,
; in addition,
; in fact,
; incidentally,
; indeed,
; instead,
; likewise,
; meanwhile,
; moreover,
; nevertheless,
; next
; now
; on the other hand,
; otherwise,
; similarly,
; still
; then
; therefore,
; thus
; undoubtedly, } | independent clause. |

(Continued)

2 Recognize and apply options for combining dependent clauses and independent clauses.

Subordination

Option 4	After Although As As if Because Before Even though If In order that Since So that Though Unless Until When Whenever Where Whereas Whether While	dependent clause, independent clause. (When you begin with a dependent clause, put a comma at the end of the dependent clause.)
Option 5 Independent clause	after although as as if because before even though if in order that since so that though unless until when whenever where whereas whether while	dependent clause

Note: In Option 4, words are capitalized because the dependent clause will begin your complete sentence.

Exercise 1 **Practice: Combining Simple Sentences**

Following are pairs of simple sentences. Combine each pair of sentences into one clear, smooth sentence. Create two new combinations for each pairing. The first one is done for you.

1. The instructor was late for class yesterday.

   Some students left the classroom.

   combination 1: _Because the instructor was late for class yesterday, some_

   students left the classroom.

   combination 2: _The instructor was late for class yesterday; as a result,_

   some students left the classroom.

2. Allison was afraid to go back to school.

   She hadn't done well on the exam.

   combination 1: _____

   _____

   combination 2: _____

   _____

3. My brother has to get up early to go to work every day.

   He feels lucky to have a little job security.

   combination 1: _____

   _____

   combination 2: _____

   _____

4. Professor Montand is friendly and understanding.

   He demands his students' best work.

   combination 1: _____

   _____

   combination 2: _____

   _____

5. My brother and his friends get together on Sunday afternoons.

   They talk about sports for hours.

   combination 1: _____

   _____

   combination 2: _____

   _____

6. I cooked some fish last night.

My cat started circling the kitchen.

combination 1: _____

_____

combination 2: _____

_____

7. You can go to the new action film.

You won't like it much.

combination 1: _____

_____

combination 2: _____

_____

8. My four-year-old nephew found the salt shaker.

He sprinkled the entire living room carpet with salt.

combination 1: _____

_____

combination 2: _____

_____

Collaborate

Exercise 2 **Collaborate: Create Your Own Text**

Following is a list of rules for sentence combining through coordinating and subordinating sentences. Working with a group, create two examples of each rule and write those sentences on the lines provided. After your group has completed this exercise, share your examples with another group.

Option 1: You can join two simple sentences (two independent clauses) into a compound sentence with a coordinating conjunction and a comma in front of it. (The coordinating conjunctions are *for, and, nor, but, or, yet, so.*)

example 1: _____

_____

example 2: _____

_____

Option 2: You can combine two simple sentences (two independent clauses) into a compound sentence with a semicolon between independent clauses.

example 1: _____

_____

example 2: _____

_____

Option 3: You can combine two simple sentences (two independent clauses) into a compound sentence with a semicolon and a conjunctive adverb between independent clauses. (Some common conjunctive adverbs are *also, anyway, as a result, besides, certainly, consequently, finally, furthermore, however, in addition, in fact, incidentally, indeed, instead, likewise, meanwhile, moreover, nevertheless, next, now, on the other hand, otherwise, similarly, still, then, therefore, thus,* and *undoubtedly.*)

example 1: _____

_____

example 2: _____

_____

Option 4: You can combine two simple sentences (two independent clauses) into a complex sentence by making one clause dependent. The dependent clause starts with a subordinating conjunction. If the dependent clause begins the sentence, the clause ends with a comma. (Some common subordinating conjunctions are *after, although, as, because, before, even though, if, in order that, since, though, unless, until, when, whenever, where, whereas, whether, while.*)

example 1: _____

_____

example 2: _____

_____

Option 5: You can combine two simple sentences (two independent clauses) into a complex sentence by making one clause dependent. If the dependent clause comes after the independent clause, no comma is needed.

example 1: _____

_____

example 2: _____

_____

Exercise 3 **Connect: Combining Sentences in a Paragraph**

Connect

In the following paragraph, combine each pair of underlined sentences into one clear, smooth sentence. Write your combination in the space above the old sentences.

I made my choice of careers years ago. I was a child. My parents gave me a

puppy for my seventh birthday, and I fell in love. Most children love puppies instantly.

Most children lose interest in the dogs or take them for granted. I was not like

most children. My dog became my best friend. I took responsibility for his care.

I loved to walk him, feed him, and brush him. <u>Soon I wanted my dog to have a little brother or sister. I brought home a stray dog</u>. At age ten, I had three dogs, two cats, and three hamsters. <u>My parents accepted all these new members of the family. They could see my love for animals</u>. At fourteen, I volunteered to walk the dogs at the animal shelter. <u>I saw the kindness of the staff. I recognized the needs of the helpless animals</u>. I wanted to do more than walk the dogs. From my first puppy to my teen work at the shelter, I had been moving toward one goal. <u>Today, I am closer to that goal. I am studying veterinary science</u>.

Connect

Exercise 4   Connect: Editing a Paragraph with Compound and Complex Sentences

Edit the following paragraph, adding commas and semicolons where they are necessary and deleting unnecessary commas. There are nine errors.

My situation makes it difficult for me to meet people. I am a commuter student at a nearby college. In addition, I am the single parent of two children, and have a job. Because I am juggling so many responsibilities I have very little social life. I don't meet anyone at work, where I sit in front of a computer screen all day. I attend classes at night and on weekends. I rush to classes then, I rush home to my children. Most of my relatives are married and middle-aged. They don't know many young people so I meet few people of my age through my family. My friends have good intentions but I hate "fixed-up" dates. At this time in my life, I must focus on raising my children, finishing my education, and getting a better job. Now there is no time or opportunity for romance on the other hand I may find it later.

Chapter Test **Combining Sentences: A Review of Your Options**   MyWritingLab™

All of the following sentences are compound or complex sentences, but some are not correctly punctuated. Write *OK* next to the ones that are correctly punctuated and *X* next to the ones that are not.

1. _____ The new social networking site is fun to use, although few people are on it.

2. _____ Rafael told me a lie, then he covered it up with another lie.

3. _____ The singer was a role model for many young Latinas, for she had great talent, a strong spirit, and a big heart.

4. _____ Unless we get stuck in heavy traffic, we should make it to the stadium on time.

5. _____ My girlfriend can be stubborn and demanding; on the other hand, she is loyal and loving.

6. _____ Charlie doesn't know much about living on his own because, his mother cooked his meals, cleaned his room, and did all his laundry.

7. _____ While Danny stared at the phone bill in horror; I pretended not to notice his reaction.

8. _____ The student plagiarized a paper although he denied doing so when asked.

9. _____ My grandfather just completed a yoga class; now he is taking a course in creative writing.

10. _____ Clarissa rarely changes the style of her beautiful, curly hair, nor does she wear a great deal of makeup.

CHAPTER 6

Avoiding Sentence Fragments

Quick Question MyWritingLab™

True or False: If a group of words has a subject and a verb, it cannot be a sentence fragment.
  (After you study this chapter, you will be confident of your answer.)

Learning Objectives

In this chapter, you will learn to:

1. Recognize and correct sentence fragments by checking for subject and verb.
2. Recognize and correct sentence fragments by making sure the group of words makes a complete statement.

A **sentence fragment** is a group of words that looks like a sentence, is punctuated like a sentence, but is not a sentence. Writing a sentence fragment is a major error in grammar because it reveals that the writer is not sure what a sentence is. The following groups of words are all fragments:

fragments:
Because the cafeteria serves gluten-free breads, rice, and pasta.
Her father being an open-minded individual.
For example, the controversy over the safety of air bags.

There are two simple steps that can help you check your writing for sentence fragments.

INFO BOX **Two Steps in Recognizing Sentence Fragments**

Step 1: Check each group of words punctuated like a sentence; look for a subject and a verb.

Step 2: If you find a subject and a verb, check that the group of words makes a complete statement.

RECOGNIZING FRAGMENTS: STEP 1

Check for a subject and a verb. Some groups of words that look like sentences may actually have a subject but no verb, or they may have a verb but no subject, or they may have no subject *or* verb.

fragments:
The bowl with the bright gold rim. (*Bowl* could be the subject of the sentence, but there is no verb.)
Can't be a friend of mine from college. (There is a verb, *Can be*, but there is no subject.)
On the tip of my tongue. (There are two prepositional phrases, *On the tip* and *of my tongue*, but there is no subject or verb.)

Remember that an *-ing* verb by itself cannot be the main verb in a sentence. Therefore, groups of words like the following ones may look like sentences but are missing a verb and are really fragments.

fragments:
The woman working in the college's Learning Enrichment Center.
A few brave souls taking the plunge into the icy lake in mid-March.
My friend Cynthia being loyal to her selfish and manipulative sister.

An infinitive (*to* plus a verb) cannot be a main verb in a sentence, either. The following groups of words, which contain infinitives, are also fragments.

fragments:
Next week a representative of the airlines to meet with travel agents from across the country.
My hope to help the children of the war-torn nation.
Something interesting to write about.

Groups of words beginning with words such as *also, especially, except, for example, for instance, in addition,* and *such as* need subjects and verbs. Without subjects and verbs, these groups can be fragments, like the ones below:

fragments:
Also a dangerous neighborhood in the late hours of the evening.
Especially a new roommate.
For example, a box of high-priced chocolates.

Checking for subjects and verbs is the first step in recognizing major sentence errors called fragments.

1 Recognize and correct sentence fragments by checking for subject and verb.

Exercise 1 Practice: Checking Groups of Words for Subjects and Verbs

Some of the following groups of words have subjects and verbs; these are sentences. Some groups are missing subjects, verbs, or both; these are fragments. Put an *S* next to each sentence; put an *F* next to each fragment.

1. _____ Especially someone with an extreme fear of heights.

2. _____ For example, sociology is a social science while physics is a lab science.

3. _____ Certainly shouldn't think about a trip to a country with an unstable government and armed rebels in the countryside.

4. _____ The thin walls between the apartments allowing the noise of each apartment to travel into the adjoining ones and preventing residents from getting to sleep at night.

5. _____ The new exit on the highway reduces the typical rush hour congestion.

6. _____ From the shimmering costumes of the dance team to the precision of the marching band.

7. _____ Except for the support of my loving family and the encouragement of the staff at the physical therapy center in Monroe.

8. _____ In the college bookstore near the lounge and cafeteria.

Exercise 2 Practice: More on Checking Groups of Words for Subjects and Verbs

Some of the following groups of words have subjects and verbs; these are sentences. Some groups are missing subjects, verbs, or both; these are fragments. Put an *S* next to each sentence; put an *F* next to each fragment.

1. _____ Learning a language takes practice.

2. _____ A hint of sadness appeared in his paintings.

3. _____ Needs a used car with low mileage and a good safety record.

4. _____ Because the architect spoke to the class.

5. _____ Especially a woman with a good education and excellent references from previous employers.

6. _____ From the end of the line came a loud voice.

7. _____ Might have chosen a partner with more common sense.

8. _____ Richard is working on the final version of his essay.

❷ Recognize and correct sentence fragments by making sure the group of words makes a complete statement.

RECOGNIZING FRAGMENTS: STEP 2

If you are checking a group of words to see if it is a sentence, the first step is to look for a subject and a verb. If you find a subject and a verb, Step 2 is to check that the group of words makes a complete statement. Many groups of words have both a subject and a verb but don't make sense by themselves. They are **dependent clauses**.

How can you tell if a clause is dependent? After you've checked each group of words for a subject and a verb, check to see if it begins with one of the subordinating conjunctions that start dependent clauses.

INFO BOX Subordinating Conjunctions			
after	before	so that	whenever
although	even though	though	where
as	if	unless	whereas
as if	in order that	until	whether
because	since	when	while

A clause that begins with a subordinating conjunction is a dependent clause. When you punctuate a dependent clause as if it were a sentence, you have a kind of fragment called a **dependent-clause fragment**. These fragments do not make a complete statement.

dependent-clause fragments:
After she registered for classes. (What happened after she registered for classes?)
Because lemonade tastes better than limeade. (What will happen because lemonade tastes better than limeade?)
Unless you leave for the movie right now. (What will happen unless you leave for the movie right now?)

It is important to remember both steps in checking for fragments:

Step 1: Check for a subject and a verb.

Step 2: If you find a subject and a verb, check that the group of words makes a complete statement.

Exercise 3 **Practice: Checking for Dependent-Clause Fragments**

Some of the following groups of words are sentences. Some are dependent clauses punctuated like sentences; these are sentence fragments. Put an *S* next to each sentence and an *F* by each fragment.

1. _____ Whenever I hear an old song from my senior year at Washington High School.

2. _____ At the orientation training for my new job was a woman in my chemistry lab.

3. _____ Whether I can get more child support from the father of my twins.

4. _____ Making a fuss is my sister's way of coping with anxiety.

5. _____ On Saturdays I always have good intentions about catching up on household chores.

6. _____ If you can pick Denise up at the airport next Sunday at 9:30 p.m.

7. _____ While I was composing my essay on my computer, the power went out.

8. _____ Because she's studying in the library now.

Exercise 4 **Practice: More on Checking for Dependent-Clause Fragments**

Some of the following groups of words are sentences. Some are dependent clauses punctuated like sentences; these are sentence fragments. Put an *S* next to each sentence and an *F* by each fragment.

1. _____ Then we waited in line at the bookstore.

2. _____ Unless Claudia asks for a transfer to another department.

3. _____ From my grandfather I inherited a love of fishing.

4. _____ Even though the prices at Classic Style can be high.

5. _____ Until we received our first draft on comparing and contrasting high school and college.

6. _____ Without my smartphone, I wouldn't contact anyone.

7. _____ Since Pete signed up for a class in electrical engineering.

8. _____ After Tower College opened a branch campus near Westburg and started offering weekend classes.

Exercise 5 **Practice: Using Two Steps to Recognize Sentence Fragments**

Some of the following are complete sentences; some are sentence fragments. To recognize the fragments, check each group of words by using the two-step process:

Step 1: Check for a subject and a verb.

Step 2: If you find a subject and a verb, check that the group of words makes a complete statement.

Then put an *S* next to each sentence and an *F* next to each fragment.

1. _____ One of the great features in the nature preserve being a wooden boardwalk across an area of wetlands.

2. _____ Doing the dishes is not a job for careless or sloppy people.

3. _____ When the instructor begins the lectures and starts the projector.

4. _____ On the top of the wedding cake were real roses in shades of yellow and peach.

5. _____ Without any hesitation or fear of the consequences of his difficult decision.

6. _____ A small group of people sacrificing their safety for the well-being of millions of citizens.

7. _____ As if Dina knew a secret about her former boss and was ready to tell it.

8. _____ For instance, someone who decided to go out rather than study.

Exercise 6 **Practice: More on Using Two Steps to Recognize Sentence Fragments**

Some of the following are complete sentences; some are sentence fragments. To recognize the fragments, check each group of words by using the two-step process:

Step 1: Check for a subject and a verb.

Step 2: If you find a subject and a verb, check that the group of words makes a complete statement.

Then put an *S* next to each sentence and an *F* next to each fragment.

1. _____ Some of the most distinguished heart surgeons in the country to meet in San Francisco next month and study new ways to prevent heart disease.

2. _____ In the middle of the crowd stood a man in a bumblebee costume and another man dressed as the team mascot.

3. _____ The reason being a lack of interest in participating in a talent show.

4. _____ Deciding on your major can be stressful.

5. _____ At times Christopher can be annoying or rude.

6. _____ Whenever my grandparents bring out the old photographs of the Jamaican branch of the family.

7. _____ From the drawer an alarm sounded.

8. _____ Because half the clothes in my closet are hand-me-downs from my two sisters.

CORRECTING FRAGMENTS

You can correct fragments easily if you follow the two steps for identifying them.

Step 1: Check for a subject and a verb. If a group of words is a fragment because it lacks a subject or a verb, or both, *add what is missing.*

fragment: Jonette giving ten percent of her salary. (This fragment lacks a main verb.)
corrected: Jonette gave ten percent of her salary. (The verb *gave* replaces *giving*, which is not a main verb.)

fragment: Can't study with the television on. (This fragment lacks a subject.)
corrected: Salvatore can't study with the television on. (A subject, *Salvatore*, is added.)

fragment: Especially at the end of the day. (This fragment has neither a subject nor a verb.)
corrected: I often feel stressed, especially at the end of the day. (A subject, *I*, and a verb, *feel*, are added.)

Step 2: If you find a subject and a verb, check that the group of words makes a complete statement. To correct the fragment, you can turn a dependent clause into an independent one by removing the subordinating conjunction, *or* you can add an independent clause to the dependent one to create a statement that makes sense by itself.

fragment: When Mrs. Diaz offered him a job. (This statement does not make sense by itself. The subordinating conjunction *when* leads the reader to ask, "What happened when Mrs. Diaz offered him a job?" The subordinating conjunction makes this a dependent clause, not a sentence.)

corrected: Mrs. Diaz offered him a job. (Removing the subordinating conjunction makes this an independent clause—a sentence.)

corrected: When Mrs. Diaz offered him a job, he was very happy. (Adding an independent clause to the end of the sentence turns this into a statement that makes sense by itself.)

corrected: He was very happy when Mrs. Diaz offered him a job. (Adding an independent clause to the beginning of the sentence turns this into a statement that makes sense by itself.)

Note: Sometimes you can correct a fragment by adding it to the sentence before or after it.

---

fragment (in italics): *Even if I get an A on the final.* I won't pass the class.

corrected: Even if I a get an A on the final, I won't pass the class.

fragment (in italics): Yvonne hates large parties. *Like the one at Matthew's house.*

corrected: Yvonne hates large parties like the one at Matthew's house.

You have several choices for correcting fragments. You can add words, phrases, or clauses; you can take words out or combine independent and dependent clauses. You can change fragments into simple sentences or create compound or complex sentences. If you create compound or complex sentences, be sure to use correct punctuation.

Exercise 7   Practice: Correcting Fragments

Correct each sentence fragment below in the most appropriate way.

1. Ms. Salvo has explained sentence types. Including simple, compound, and complex.

   corrected: _____

   _____

2. If you can lend me twenty dollars. I will pay you back on Saturday.

   corrected: _____

   _____

3. Seeing my brother and sister-in-law celebrating their tenth wedding anniversary. I hoped for a lasting relationship of my own.

   corrected: _____

   _____

4. Brian will eat any kind of chicken. Except chicken livers.

corrected: _____

_____

5. If she reads that post.

corrected: _____

_____

6. My obnoxious little brother scraping all the icing off the beautifully decorated birthday cake.

corrected: _____

_____

7. I need to see a tax adviser. To get some help in completing my income tax form.

corrected: _____

_____

Exercise 8 **Collaborate: Correcting Fragments Two Ways**

Collaborate

The following groups of words all contain fragments. With a partner or group, construct two ways to eliminate the fragment. You can add words, phrases, or clauses; take out words; combine independent and dependent clauses; or attach a fragment to the sentence before or after it. When you have completed the exercise, be ready to share your answers with another group or with the class. The first one is done for you.

1. While my children sat in the back of the car and tried to slap each other.

corrected: *While my children sat in the back of the car and tried to slap*

each other, I tried to keep my eyes on the road.

corrected: *I tried to keep my eyes on the road while my children sat in the*

back of the car and tried to slap each other.

2. After a group of firefighters had extinguished the fire. The family members surveyed the damage to their home.

corrected: _____

_____

corrected: _____

_____

3. If anyone asks about my grades.

corrected: _____

_____

corrected: _____

_____

4. Jay considering a job offer in Austin, Texas.

   corrected: _____

   _____

   corrected: _____

   _____

5. Whenever my partner talks about a trip to the rainforest. I think about exotic animals.

   corrected: _____

   _____

   corrected: _____

   _____

6. Carmen launched the new Web site. As her coworkers removed the old one.

   corrected: _____

   _____

   corrected: _____

   _____

7. Unless it rains within the next week. Our plants will die.

   corrected: _____

   _____

   corrected: _____

   _____

8. When my laptop started making strange noises.

   corrected: _____

   _____

   corrected: _____

   _____

Connect

Exercise 9 Connect: Editing a Paragraph to Eliminate Fragments

Edit the paragraph below, correcting the sentence fragments by writing in the space above each fragment. There are six fragments.

All my closest friends are optimists. Such as my cousin Jared. Jared is

always willing to expect the best outcome in a school, family, or work crisis. As a

child, Jared had cancer, yet he seemed to be the strongest member of the family.

Even though he suffered terrible pain and endured surgery, chemotherapy, and radiation treatments. Jared stayed calm and tough. He was an inspiration to me. Recently, Jared giving me strength and a positive attitude. I lost my job at the movie theater and was depressed about finding work. However, Jared encouraged me to transform my loss. Into an opportunity to find a job better suited to my personality. His support led me to make an active and thorough job search. After a few months, I got a position at a computer store. Where I enjoy helping the customers choose the best technology. I like the work; in addition, I appreciate the rise in salary. My loss turned into a gain. Because I took the advice of a close friend and acted on it.

Chapter Test Avoiding Sentence Fragments

MyWritingLab™

Some of the following are complete sentences; some are sentence fragments. Put an *S* by each sentence and an *F* by each fragment.

1. _____ Next to an attractive little house on Whittier Drive, an empty lot full of weeds, concrete blocks, and old tires.

2. _____ About four rows over from me sat my best friend.

3. _____ In order that the local police can reach people in trouble and get to the scene of an accident or crime as quickly as possible.

4. _____ When new students aimlessly wandered across the large campus.

5. _____ Then an angry man complained loudly about the long lines at the cash register.

6. _____ The rising price of cigarettes prompting many smokers to sign up for smoking cessation programs or to try to quit on their own.

7. _____ Except for an overcooked selection of vegetables, the meal at Maureen's house was tasty.

8. _____ Until Eliot finds a way to cover the cost of his textbooks, he is borrowing them from the library.

MyWritingLab™ Visit Chapter 6, "Avoiding Sentence Fragments," in *MyWritingLab* to test your understanding of the chapter objectives.

Using Parallelism in Sentences

Learning Objectives

In this chapter, you will learn to:

1. Recognize parallel structure in a sentence.
2. Use parallel structure to revise awkwardly worded sentences.

Parallelism means balance in sentences. To create sentences with parallelism, remember this rule:

Similar points should get similar structures.

Often, you will include two or more points—related ideas, examples, or details—in one sentence. If you express these ideas in a parallel structure, they will be clearer, smoother, and more convincing.

Here are some pairs of sentences with and without parallelism:

1. Recognize parallel structure in a sentence.

not parallel: Of all the assignments I have to do, the ones I dislike the most are writing essays and to give presentations.

parallel: Of all the assignments I have to do, the ones I dislike the most are *writing* essays and *giving* presentations. (Two words are parallel.)

not parallel: When I need a pencil, I look in my purse, the table, and beside the telephone.

parallel: When I need a pencil, I look *in my purse, on the table,* and *beside the telephone.* (Three prepositional phrases are parallel.)

> **not parallel:** Inez should get the promotion because she gets along with her coworkers, she works hard, and a knowledge of the business.
>
> **parallel:** Inez should get the promotion because *she gets along with her coworkers*, *she works hard*, and *she knows the business*. (Three clauses are parallel.)

From these examples, you can see that parallelism involves matching the structures of parts of your sentence. There are two steps that can help you check your writing for parallelism:

INFO BOX Two Steps in Checking a Sentence for Parallel Structure

Step 1: Look for the list in the sentence.

Step 2: Put the parts of the list into a similar structure.

You may have to change or add something to get a parallel structure.

ACHIEVING PARALLELISM

2 Use parallel structure to revise awkwardly worded sentences.

Let's correct the parallelism of the following sentence:

> **not parallel:** If you want to pass the course, you have to study hard, taking good notes, and attendance at every class.

To correct this sentence, we'll follow the steps.

> **Step 1:** Look for the list. If you want to pass the course, you have to do three things. Here's the list:
>
> **1.** study hard
> **2.** taking good notes
> **3.** attendance at every class

> **Step 2:** Put the parts of the list into a similar structure.
>
> **1.** *to study* hard
> **2.** *to take* good notes
> **3.** *to attend* every class

Now revise to get a parallel sentence.

> **parallel:** If you want to pass the course, you have *to study* hard, *to take* good notes, and *to attend* every class.

If you follow Steps 1 and 2, you can also write the sentence like this:

> **parallel:** If you want to pass the course, you have to *study* hard, *take* good notes, and *attend* every class.

But you can't write the sentence like this:

> **not parallel:** If you want to pass the course, you have to study hard, take good notes, and to attend every class.

Think of the list again. You can write:
If you want to pass the course, you have

1. to study ⎫
2. to take ⎬ parallel
3. to attend ⎭

Or you can write:
> If you want to pass the course, you have to

> 1. study
> 2. take   } parallel
> 3. attend

But your list can't be:
> If you want to pass the course, you have to

> 1. study
> 2. take   } not parallel
> 3. to attend

In other words, use *to* once (if it fits every part of the list), or use it with *every* part of the list.

> **Note:** Sometimes making ideas parallel means adding something to the sentence because all the parts of the list cannot match exactly.

> **not parallel:** While we were taking the midterm exam, a student tore up his paper, making it fly across the room, the floor, and my desk.

> **Step 1:** Look for the list. While we were taking the midterm exam, a student tore up his paper, making it fly

> > 1. across the room
> > 2. the floor
> > 3. my desk

As this sentence is written, *across* goes with *room*, but it doesn't go with *floor* or *my desk*. Check the sense of this sentence by looking at each part of the list and how it is working in the sentence: "While we were taking the midterm exam, a student tore up his paper, making it fly *across the room*" is clear. But "paper flew *across the floor*"? Or "paper flew *down my desk*"? These parts of the list are not right.

> **Step 2:** The sentence needs some words added to make the structure parallel.

> **parallel:** While we were taking the midterm exam, a student tore up his paper, making it fly *across* the room, *on* the floor, and *on* my desk.

When you follow the two steps to check for parallelism, you can write clear sentences and improve your style.

Exercise 1   Practice: Revising Sentences for Parallelism

Some of the following sentences need to be revised so they have parallel structures. Revise the ones that need parallelism. Write *OK* for sentences that already have parallel structures.

> 1. Getting up early in the morning is not as bad as when you get up in the middle of the night.

> **revised:** _____

> _____

2. Colin can be immature and irritating at times, yet he can also be sympathetic and generous.

   revised: _____

   _____

3. My roommate warned me about taking physics and to work at the same time but I didn't listen.

   revised: _____

   _____

4. Shane's outgoing personality, being naturally confident, and athletic ability made him popular in high school.

   revised: _____

   _____

5. In my family, children were taught to say "please" and "thank you," be kind to animals, and always telling the truth.

   revised: _____

   _____

6. André could grow up to be a man with strong principles and a heart that is filled with generosity.

   revised: _____

   _____

7. I keep running into Mrs. Kelly on the bus, the movies, and in the hall.

   revised: _____

   _____

8. If I go to the tutoring center, I will get help with my English essay or with my algebra homework.

   revised: _____

   _____

| Exercise 2 | **Collaborate: Writing Sentences with Parallelism** |

Collaborate

With a partner or group, complete each sentence. Begin by brainstorming a draft list; then revise the list for parallelism. Finally, complete the sentence in a parallel structure. You may want to assign one task (brainstorming a draft list, revising it, etc.) to each group member, then switch tasks on the next sentence. Following is a sample of how to work through each question, from list to sentence.

sample incomplete sentence: The three parts of college I like best are

Draft List	Revised List
1. new friends	1. making new friends
2. doing well in English	2. doing well in English
3. Fridays off	3. having Fridays off

sentence: The three parts of college I like best are making new friends, doing well in English, and having Fridays off.

1. Three reasons for getting regular exercise are

   Draft List   Revised List

   1. _____   1. _____
   2. _____   2. _____
   3. _____   3. _____

   sentence: _____

   _____

2. Two suggestions for fighting a cold are

   Draft List   Revised List

   1. _____   1. _____
   2. _____   2. _____

   sentence: _____

   _____

3. Three signs that a person is lying are

   Draft List   Revised List

   1. _____   1. _____
   2. _____   2. _____
   3. _____   3. _____

   sentence: _____

   _____

4. When choosing a major, you need to consider

   Draft List   Revised List

   1. _____   1. _____
   2. _____   2. _____

   3. _____   3. _____

   sentence: _____

   _____

Exercise 3 Collaborate: Recognizing Parallelism in Famous Speeches

Some of the most famous speeches in history contain parallel structures. This parallelism adds emphasis and dignity to the points expressed. Working in a group, have one member read each segment of a speech aloud while the others listen carefully. Then underline all the words, phrases, clauses, or sentences that are in parallel form. When you have completed the exercise, share your answers with another group.

1. Inaugural Address

John F. Kennedy

President John F. Kennedy delivered this speech when he was inaugurated on January 20, 1961. His theme was the renewal of American values and the changes and challenges we must face.

Let the word go forth from this time and place, to friend and foe alike, that the torch has been passed to a new generation of Americans— born in this century, tempered* by war, disciplined by a hard and bitter peace, proud of our ancient heritage—and unwilling to witness or permit the slow undoing of those human rights to which this nation has always been committed, and to which we are committed today at home and around the world.

*__tempered__ means hardened, toughened

2. The Gettysburg Address

Abraham Lincoln

Abraham Lincoln was the 16th President of the United States. He served during the Civil War, which was fought in the United States from 1861 until 1865 over the issue of slavery. In 1863, Lincoln, who was against slavery, delivered his famous Gettysburg Address at the site of one of the bloodiest battles in the Civil War.

Four score and seven years ago* our fathers brought forth on this continent a new nation, conceived in liberty and dedicated to the proposition that all men are created equal.

Now we are engaged in a great civil war, testing whether that nation, or any nation so conceived and so dedicated, can long endure. We are met on a great battlefield of that war. We have come to dedicate a portion of that field as a final resting place for those who here gave their lives that that nation might live. It is altogether fitting and proper that we should do this.

*__Four score and seven years ago__ equals eighty-seven years. Eighty-seven years prior to this speech, the Declaration of Independence was signed and the United States became a free country (no longer ruled by England).

Connect

Exercise 4   **Connect: Combining Sentences and Creating a Parallel Structure**

In the paragraph below, some sentences should be combined in a parallel structure. Combine each cluster of underlined sentences into one sentence with a parallel structure. Write your sentences in the lines above the old ones.

At my college, footwear suits the role of each group of people. For example, students have to come to class. They sit in a classroom. Listening to lectures is a major duty of being a student. Students are an important part of campus, and there are hundreds of them everywhere. Most of them dress in a similar style. <u>Their footwear tends to be flip flops in warm weather. Students wear sneakers when it gets cold outside.</u> Like students, most teachers wear a specific type of footwear. Their shoes have to be comfortable. <u>Teachers stand in front of the classroom. Sometimes they walk around the room. Heavy books and papers are often in their arms as they go from one classroom to another.</u> They need shoes that are stronger than flip flops and a little more formal than scuffed athletic shoes. These shoes tend to be loafers or another comfortable but professional-looking shoe. <u>Administrators deal with students and faculty. They interact with other administrators. Also, they are representatives of the college in the community.</u> They wear more traditional, businesslike footwear. <u>For example, male administrators tend to wear stiff black shoes. Black shoes also appear on female administrators. They wear black high heels.</u> Of course, not all college students, teachers, or administrators wear the same types of footwear. There are some professors in ratty-looking athletic shoes. In addition, some students come to class directly from their jobs and may appear in dressier shoes. However, most of the time, shoes tell the place of each person in the college community.

Connect

Exercise 5   **Connect: Revising a Paragraph for Parallelism**

The following paragraph contains sentences with errors in parallelism. In the space above the lines, correct the sentences that contain errors in parallelism. You can cross out any word(s) that should be deleted. There are five sentences with errors.

My favorite restaurant is hard to classify. It is not a part of a restaurant chain like Burger King or a fancy restaurant like the expensive steakhouse outside of town. It has roomy booths, tables made of wood, and colorful curtains. In good weather, a patio offers outdoor seating. The outdoor spots fill up quickly because a cluster of oak trees offer shade, and a soft breeze comes with the trees. This restaurant is in an old section of town. The place is famous for barbecue. Customers stand in line for seats or take out the homemade dinners. I love all the choices: barbecued pork, beef, chicken, or barbecued shrimp. A customer can eat one kind of barbecue or enjoy a mixed platter. The smoky smell of barbecue fills the air for miles, and people are called to the restaurant. This barbecue place regularly calls me back for more because of its relaxed atmosphere, reasonable prices, and the food that is irresistible.

Chapter Test Using Parallelism in Sentences

MyWritingLab™

Some of the following sentences have errors in parallelism; some are correct. Put *OK* next to the correct sentences and *X* by the sentences with errors in parallelism.

1. _____ After a long day of arguing with his parents, trying to sell shoes at a nearly empty store, and losing his car keys, Eric was exhausted.

2. _____ Horror movies can be ridiculous, love stories are often phony, and to sit through a long war movie bores me, so I rarely go to the movies.

3. _____ Every month, my supervisor observes my work style, makes me write a report, meets with me, and determines if I am eligible for a raise.

4. _____ A huge insect darted across the kitchen floor and hid under the stove.

5. _____ A dried-up tube of lip gloss, a collection of ratty cotton balls in a yellowed plastic bag, an ancient hairbrush, and half-empty bottle of cough medicine fell out of the rusty medicine cabinet.

6. _____ After my chemistry class, I always notice some of the students gathering in the hall, whispering complaints about the grading policy, and I hear them worrying about the next test.

7. _____ Somehow I was able to complete the college application, take the placement exam, get my results, and register for classes all in the same day.

8. _____ Ben goes to Miranda's Palace every weekend because the place offers live music, the low price of the tasty food, and the atmosphere is friendly.

CHAPTER 8

Using Adjectives and Adverbs

Quick Question MyWritingLab™

Which sentence(s) is/are correct?

A. Alexia is the most talkative in the class.
B. After Naomi argued with her instructor, she felt badly.

(After you study this chapter, you will be confident of your answer.)

Learning Objectives

In this chapter, you will learn to:
1. Identify adjectives.
2. Identify adverbs.
3. Use adjectives and adverbs correctly in your writing.

1. Identify adjectives.

WHAT ARE ADJECTIVES?

Adjectives describe nouns (words that name persons, places, or things) or pronouns (words that substitute for a noun).

adjectives:
She is a *talented* writer. (*Talented* describes the noun *writer*.)
I need a *little* help. (*Little* describes the noun *help*.)
She looked *happy*. (*Happy* describes the pronoun *she*.)

An adjective usually comes before the word it describes.

He gave me a *beautiful* ring. (*Beautiful* describes *ring*.)

Sometimes an adjective comes after a *being* verb, a verb that tells what something is. Being verbs are words like *is, are, was, am, has been*. Words like *feels, looks, seems, smells, sounds*, and *tastes* are part of the group called being verbs.

He seems *unhappy*. (*Unhappy* describes *he* and follows the being
   verb *seems*.)
Alan was *confident*. (*Confident* describes *Alan* and follows the being
   verb *was*.)
Your screen is *cracked*. (*Cracked* describes *screen* and follows the
   being verb *is*.)

Exercise 1 **Practice: Recognizing Adjectives**

Circle the adjective in each of the following sentences.

   1. The textbook I bought was used.

   2. Rick walked across the hot sand.

   3. My mother bought me an expensive bracelet for my birthday.

   4. His old phone needs to be replaced.

   5. Uncle Frank feels tired in the afternoon.

   6. The lavish praise embarrassed Cynthia.

   7. The tiny flash drive holds all of my files.

   8. Something in the sauce tastes bitter.

ADJECTIVES: COMPARATIVE AND SUPERLATIVE FORMS

The **comparative** form of an adjective compares two persons or things. The **superlative** form compares three or more persons or things.

comparative: Your car is *cleaner* than mine.
superlative: Your car is the *cleanest* one in the parking lot.

comparative: An e-book is *cheaper* than a used book.
superlative: An e-book is the *cheapest* way to buy a textbook at the
   bookstore.

comparative: Lisa is *friendlier* than her sister.
superlative: Lisa is the *friendliest* of the three sisters.

For one-syllable adjectives, add *-er* to form the comparative and add *-est* to form the superlative.

The weather is *colder* today than it was yesterday, but Friday was the
   coldest day of the year.
Orange juice is *sweeter* than grapefruit juice, but the *sweetest* juice is
   grape juice.

For two-syllable adjectives that end in *-y*, drop the *y* and add *-ier* to form the comparative and add *-iest* to form the superlative. For adjectives with two or more syllables, use *more* to form the comparative and *most* to form the superlative.

> I thought College Algebra was *more difficult* than English; however, Beginning Physics was the *most difficult* course I ever took.
>
> My brother is *more outgoing* than my sister, but my father is the *most outgoing* member of the family.

The three forms of adjectives usually look like this:

Adjective	Comparative	Superlative
sweet	sweeter	sweetest
fast	faster	fastest
short	shorter	shortest
quick	quicker	quickest
old	older	oldest

For adjectives that end in *y*, the three forms may look like this:

Adjective	Comparative	Superlative
happy	happier	happiest
easy	easier	easiest
busy	busier	busiest
friendly	friendlier	friendliest
lucky	luckier	luckiest

The three forms may even look like this:

Adjective	Comparative	Superlative
confused	more confused	most confused
specific	more specific	most specific
dangerous	more dangerous	most dangerous
confident	more confident	most confident
beautiful	more beautiful	most beautiful

However, there are some *irregular forms* of adjectives:

Adjective	Comparative	Superlative
good	better	best
bad	worse	worst
little	less	least
many, much	more	most

Exercise 2 **Practice: Selecting the Correct Adjective Forms**

Write the correct form of the adjective in each of the following sentences.

1. When money is involved, my sister has always been _____ (smart) about spending than my brother is.

2. The red-haired boy in the back row of the classroom was the _____ (funny) of all the students.

3. My truck gets _____ (good) gas mileage than my husband's van.

4. Which of your textbooks was the _____ (little) expensive?

5. Ignoring a nagging toothache can lead to _____ (bad) trouble than going to a dentist would.

6. Although my first apartment had many attractive features, my second one had even _____ (many) stylish and modern features.

7. Andrew's performance at the talent show was _____ (confident) than his first try at singing in public.

8. In the Jackson family, Jill is _____ (good) at playing video games than Ben, but their father is the _____ player in the family.

Exercise 3 **Collaborate: Writing Sentences with Adjectives**

Collaborate

Working with a partner or group, write a sentence that correctly uses each of the following adjectives. Be prepared to share your answers with another group or with the class.

1. more dangerous _____

_____

2. best _____

_____

3. sillier _____

_____

4. most talented _____

_____

5. brightest _____

_____

6. more stubborn _____

_____

7. cleaner _____

_____

8. worst _____

_____

WHAT ARE ADVERBS?

2 Identify adverbs.

Adverbs describe verbs, adjectives, or other adverbs.

adverbs:
As she spoke, Steve listened *thoughtfully*. (*Thoughtfully* describes the verb *listened*.)
I said I was *really* sorry for my error. (*Really* describes the adjective *sorry*.)
The clerk worked *very* quickly. (*Very* describes the adverb *quickly*.)

Adverbs answer questions like "How?" "How much?" "How often?" "When?" "Why?" and "Where?"

Exercise 4 **Practice: Recognizing Adverbs**

Circle the adverbs in the following sentences and underline the word they modify.

1. At a children's concert, I heard a naturally talented, seven-year-old pianist.

2. Offered a free ticket to a hockey game, Mitchell was not very enthusiastic.

3. We'll review those notes tomorrow.

4. The women looked suspiciously at the man with a briefcase full of cheap designer watches.

5. Pamela smiled shyly as the new boy looked at her.

6. If the traffic is heavy, the drive home can be really frustrating.

7. My boss is usually tolerant about sick days and other emergencies.

8. The instructor was very impressed with the students' discussion.

Collaborate

Exercise 5 **Collaborate: Writing Sentences with Adverbs**

Working with a partner or group, write a sentence that correctly uses each of the following adverbs. Be prepared to share your answers with another group or with the class.

1. usually _____

_____

2. exceptionally _____

_____

3. never _____

_____

4. magically _____

_____

5. mostly _____

_____

6. intentionally _____

_____

7. badly _____

_____

8. barely _____

_____

Hints About Adjectives and Adverbs

Do not use an adjective when you need an adverb. Some writers make the mistake of using an adjective when they need an adverb.

> **3** Use adjectives and adverbs correctly in your writing.

> **not this:** Talk to me ~~honest~~.
> **but this:** Talk to me honestly.
>
> **not this:** You can say it ~~simple~~.
> **but this:** You can say it simply.
>
> **not this:** He was breathing ~~deep~~.
> **but this:** He was breathing deeply.

Exercise 6 **Practice: Changing Adjectives to Adverbs**

In each pair of sentences, change the underlined adjective in the first sentence to an adverb in the second sentence. The first one is done for you.

1. a. That light is <u>bright</u>.

    b. That light gleams _brightly_.

2. a. The traffic officer made a <u>tactful</u> reply.

    b. The traffic officer replied _____.

3. a. The clerk did a <u>thorough</u> search for my transcript.

    b. The clerk searched _____ for my transcript.

4. a. The senator has a <u>decisive</u> way of speaking.

    b. The senator speaks _____.

5. a. Miguel has a <u>beautiful</u> voice.

    b. Miguel sings _____.

6. a. Taylor makes <u>constant</u> references to his luck with women.

    b. Taylor _____ refers to his luck with women.

7. a. Amy has a <u>simple</u> style of dressing.

    b. Amy dresses _____.

8. a. The tutor can be <u>impatient</u> at times.

    b. At times, the tutor acts _____.

Do Not Confuse *Good* and *Well*, *Bad* and *Badly*

Remember that *good* is an adjective; it describes nouns. It also follows being verbs like *is*, *are*, *was*, *am*, and *has been*. Words like *looks*, *seems*, *smells*, *sounds*, and *tastes* are part of the group called being verbs. *Well* is an adverb; it describes verbs. (The only time *well* can be used as an adjective is when it means *healthy*, as in *I feel well today*.)

> **not this:** You completed the assignment ~~good~~.
> **but this:** You completed the assignment well.

not this: I cook eggs ~~good~~.
but this: I cook eggs well.

not this: How ~~good~~ do you understand grammar?
but this: How well do you understand grammar?

Bad is an adjective; it describes nouns. It also follows being verbs like *is*, *are*, *was*, *am*, and *has been*. Words like *feels*, *looks*, *seems*, *smells*, *sounds*, and *tastes* are part of the group called being verbs. *Badly* is an adverb; it describes verbs.

not this: He feels ~~badly~~ about his mistake.
but this: He feels bad about his mistake. (*Feels* is a being verb; it is followed by the adjective *bad*.)

not this: That soup smells ~~badly~~.
but this: That soup smells bad. (*Smells* is a being verb; it is followed by the adjective *bad*.)

not this: He dances ~~bad~~.
but this: He dances badly.

Exercise 7 **Practice: Using *Good* and *Well*, *Bad* and *Badly***

Write the appropriate word in the following sentences.

1. Jonelle has been sick with the flu; she seemed really _____ (bad, badly) yesterday.

2. That room _____ (bad, badly) needs a new coat of paint.

3. André is behaving _____ (good, well) in his kindergarten class.

4. My chances of getting more financial aid look _____ (bad, badly).

5. Something in the cafeteria smells _____ (good, well).

6. When Terrance asked you an embarrassing question, you answered it _____ (good, well).

7. After the team performed _____ (bad, badly) in the first half, the fans began to lose hope.

8. That new jacket looks _____ (good, well) on you.

Do Not Use *More* + *-er*, or *Most* + *-est*

Be careful. Never write both an *-er* ending and *more*, or an *-est* ending and *most*.

not this: I want to work with someone ~~more smarter~~.
but this: I want to work with someone smarter.

not this: Alan is the ~~most richest~~ man in town.
but this: Alan is the richest man in town.

Use *Than*, Not *Then*, in Comparisons

When you compare things, use *than*. *Then* means *at a later time*.

not this: You are taller ~~then~~ I am.
but this: You are taller than I am.

not this: I'd like a car that is faster ~~then~~ my old one.
but this: I'd like a car that is faster than my old one.

Adjectives: Multiple Adjective Word Order

We often use more than one adjective to describe someone or something.

> **examples:**
> This is a **classic old American** classroom
> Where are my **black Italian leather** shoes?
> **Large modern glass** buildings are common in this city.

When we use more than one adjective, the correct order of adjectives is based on categories. Review the categories below and the examples of correct and incorrect adjective word order:

1. Opinion or evaluation (*beautiful, horrible, classic*)
2. Size/shape/condition (*small, triangular, broken*)
3. Age (*new, old*)
4. Color (*red, multicolored*)
5. Origin (*Italian, American*)
6. Material (*glass, leather*)

Note: Commas are only placed between adjectives that come from the same category.

> **example:** I live in a beautiful, friendly neighborhood. (Both *beautiful* and *friendly* are opinions or evaluations.)
> **incorrect:** I have a large, black, flat-screen TV. (These are all from *different* categories, so no commas are needed.)
> **correct:** I have a large black flat-screen TV.

Exercise 8   **Practice: A Comprehensive Exercise on Using Adjectives and Adverbs**

Correct any errors in the use of adjectives and adverbs (including punctuation errors) in the following sentences. Write your corrections in the space above the errors, and cross out any word(s) that should be deleted. Some sentences do not need correcting.

1. Both Alan and Meghan are excellent swimmers, but Meghan is the best one.

2. Katrina feels badly about her last conversation with her boyfriend.

3. It's hard to believe there's another class more livelier than this class.

4. Cocoa tastes good on a cold night in December.

5. I found a cheap kitchen table at a neighborhood garage sale.

6. Charlie was the least trustworthy of my two former boyfriends.

7. I will eat any kind of chocolate, but I like milk chocolate better then dark chocolate.

8. Emily wrote a personal insightful essay.

Connect

Exercise 9   **Connect: Editing a Paragraph for Errors in Adjectives and Adverbs**

Edit the following paragraph, correcting all the errors in the use of adjectives and adverbs. Write your corrections in the space above the errors. There are eight errors.

   Sometimes loneliness hurts me bad. I am a general outgoing person and

choose to spend my time with friends. However, sometimes everyone is busy.

I tend to feel nervously when I have to face an afternoon alone at home. Saturday

evenings by myself are even worst. Of course, I can send e-mails or text messages,

but those connections don't satisfy me. At such times, I don't know what I want.

I start feeling bored. Soon I wonder why everyone is having a best time then I am.

Sitting alone, I feel jealous and sorry for myself. Then loneliness creeps into my

brain. Being alone creates a terrible emptiness for me. My idea of happiness is

being with others and sharing extremely, wild adventures. To me, a day alone is

never a well day.

Chapter Test **Using Adjectives and Adverbs**   MyWritingLab™

Some of the following sentences have errors in the use of adjectives and adverbs. Some are correct. Put *OK* by the correct sentences and *X* by the sentences with an error.

1. _____ I have eaten all kinds of cakes, but the most delicious cake of all was one called Raspberry Surprise, a mix of white cake, butter cream icing, and raspberry filling.

2. _____ The students were proud of their careful review for the exam.

3. _____ One candidate for governor gave an explanation of her position on offshore oil drilling.

4. _____ Lamar was confident about his performance on the multiple-choice test, but he wasn't sure how good he did on the essay test.

5. _____ My four cousins are all excellent musicians, but the youngest is the more talented of the group.

6. _____ I'm considering a class in graphic design or one in advertising, but I'm not sure which one is a better choice for me.

7. _____ Mason has a boring, American history class and an engaging English class today.

8. _____ When my brother explained the math problem to me, he spoke very sarcastic.

Correcting Problems with Modifiers

Learning Objectives

In this chapter, you will learn to:

1. Identify modifiers within sentences.
2. Correct misplaced or dangling modifiers.

Modifiers are words, phrases, or clauses that describe (modify) something in a sentence. All of the following italicized words, phrases, and clauses are modifiers:

modifiers:
the *new* smartphone (word)
the smartphone *on the table* (phrase)
the smartphone *that he bought* (clause)

Sometimes modifiers limit another word. They make another word (or words) more specific.

Identify modifiers within sentences.

the basket *in the boy's bedroom* (tells which basket)
twenty cookies (tells how many cookies)
the card *that she gave me* (tells which card)
They *seldom* visit. (tells how often)

Exercise 1   **Practice: Recognizing Modifiers**

In each of the following sentences, underline the modifiers (words, phrases, or clauses) that describe the italicized word.

1. David's heavy old backpack, with its bright orange sticker, fell on the floor.

2. Peering into the window, *Ethan* saw someone asleep in a rocking chair.

3. A thin *man* in an overcoat waited at the end of a long line.

4. Yesterday a kind *stranger* returned my lost wallet.

5. Swept away by the flood, the *house* fell into pieces.

6. Ryan spent years in the jungles of South America, so he can tell amazing *stories*.

7. I want to read a book filled with exciting drama.

8. The *passengers* stuck at the airport waited for the storm to pass.

Exercise 2   **Practice: Finding Modifiers in Professional Writing**

Following is an excerpt from an essay by Pat Mora, an educator and writer. It is a remembrance of her favorite aunt, Lobo. The writing makes effective use of specific details, particularly through the use of modifiers. After you read the selection, underline the modifiers that describe each italicized word or phrase.

    We called her "Lobo." The word means "wolf" in Spanish, an odd name for a generous and loving *aunt*. Like all names it became synonymous* with her, and to this day returns me to my child self. Although the name seemed perfectly *natural* to us and to our friends, it did cause *frowns* from strangers throughout the years. I particularly remember one hot *afternoon* when on a crowded *streetcar* between the border cities of El Paso and Juarez, I momentarily *lost* sight of her. "Lobo! Lobo!" I cried in panic. Annoyed faces peered at me, disappointed at such disrespect to a white-haired woman.

    Actually the fault was hers. She lived with us for years, and when she arrived home from work in the evening, she'd knock on the front *door* and ask, "Donde estan mis lobitos?" "Where are my little *wolves*?" Gradually she became our lobo, a spinster* aunt who gathered the four of us around her, tying us to her life by giving us all she had.

*synonymous means having the same or a similar meaning

*spinster is an outdated term for an unmarried woman

② Correct misplaced or dangling modifiers.

CORRECTING MISPLACED MODIFIER PROBLEMS

Modifiers can make your writing more specific and more vivid. Used effectively and correctly, modifiers give the reader a clear picture of what you want to say, and they help you to say it precisely. But modifiers have to be used correctly. You can check for errors with modifiers, often called **misplaced modifiers**, as you revise your sentences.

INFO BOX **Three Steps to Check for Misplaced Modifiers**

Step 1: Find the modifier.

Step 2: Ask, "Does the modifier have something to modify?"

Step 3: Ask, "Is the modifier in the right place, as close as possible to the word, phrase, or clause it modifies?"

If you answer no to either Step 2 or Step 3, you need to revise your sentence.

Review the three steps in the following example:

sample sentence: They were looking for a man walking a dog smoking a cigar.

Step 1: Find the modifier. The modifiers are *walking a dog* and *smoking a cigar*.

Step 2: Ask, "Does the modifier have something to modify?" The answer is yes. The man is walking a dog. The man is smoking a cigar. Both modifiers go with *man*.

Step 3: Ask, "Is the modifier in the right place?" The answer is yes and no. One modifier is in the right place:

a man *walking a dog*

The other modifier is not in the right place:

a dog *smoking a cigar*

The dog is not smoking a cigar. The sentence needs to be revised.

revised sentence: They were looking for a man *smoking a cigar and walking a dog*.

Here is another example of how to apply the three steps:

sample sentence: Filled with new vocabulary, she attempted to understand the lengthy assigned reading.

Step 1: Find the modifiers. The modifiers are *Filled with new vocabulary* and *lengthy*

Step 2: Ask, "Does the modifier have something to modify?" The answer is yes. The assigned reading is *filled with new vocabulary* and it is *lengthy*.

Step 3: Ask, "Is the modifier in the right place?" The answer is yes and no. The phrase *lengthy assigned* is in the right place:

> *lengthy assigned* reading

But *Filled with new vocabulary* is in the wrong place:

> *Filled with new vocabulary*, she

She is not filled with new vocabulary. The assigned reading is. The sentence needs to be revised.

revised sentence: She attempted to understand the *lengthy assigned* reading *filled with new vocabulary.*

Caution: Be sure to put words like *almost, even, exactly, hardly, just, merely, nearly, only, scarcely,* and *simply* as near as possible to what they modify. If you put them in the wrong place, you may write a confusing sentence.

---

confusing sentence: Brian only wants to buy toothpaste and shampoo. (The modifier that creates confusion here is *only.* Does Brian have only one goal in life—to be a toothpaste and shampoo buyer? Or are these the only items he wants to buy? To create a clearer sentence, move the modifier.)

revised sentence: Brian wants to buy *only* toothpaste and shampoo.

As you can see, misplaced modifiers can easily be corrected if you test the modifier for proper placement in the sentence. Here is the rule to remember:

> **Put the modifier as close as possible to the word, phrase, or clause it modifies.**

Exercise 3 Practice: Correcting Sentences with Misplaced Modifiers

Some of the following sentences contain misplaced modifiers. Revise any sentences that have a misplaced modifier by putting the modifier as close as possible to whatever it modifies.

1. Fresh from the printer, I read my essay.

   revised: _____

   _____

2. On my first day of college, I nearly sat in the wrong classroom for an hour.

   revised: _____

   _____

3. Lewis used to know a beautiful woman with a rare disease named Lucinda.

   revised: _____

   _____

4. Cooking in a tiny kitchen all day, the chef became dizzy and dehydrated.

   revised: _____

   _____

5. My cousins like to study dinosaurs on their visits to the natural history museum.

   revised: _____

   _____

6. With a can of paint, all of the bathroom walls were brightened by a smart decorator.

   revised: _____

   _____

7. Leticia will regret today's foolish decision in later years.

   revised: _____

   _____

8. I learned about the oil spill on my cell phone.

   revised: _____

   _____

Correcting Dangling Modifiers

The three steps for correcting misplaced modifier problems can help you recognize another kind of error. For example, let's use the steps to check the following sentence.

> **sample sentence:** Cruising slowly through the Everglades, two alligators could be seen.

> **Step 1:** Find the modifier. The modifiers are *Cruising slowly through the Everglades* and *two.*

> **Step 2:** Ask, "Does the modifier have something to modify?" The answer is yes and no. The word *two* modifies *alligators.* But who or what is *cruising slowly through the Everglades*? There is no person mentioned in the sentence. The alligators are not cruising.

This kind of error is called a **dangling modifier**. It means that the modifier does not have anything to modify; it just dangles in the sentence. If you want to correct this kind of error, just moving the modifier will not work.

> **still incorrect:** Two alligators could be seen cruising slowly through the Everglades. (There is still no person cruising, and the alligators are not cruising.)

The way to correct this kind of error is to add something to the sentence. If you gave the modifier something to modify, you might come up with several correct sentences.

revised sentences: *As we cruised slowly through the Everglades,* two alligators could be seen.

Two alligators could be seen *when the visitors were cruising slowly through the Everglades.*

Cruising slowly through the Everglades, the people on the boat saw two alligators.

Try the process for correcting dangling modifiers once more:

sample sentence: Having struggled in the snow all day, hot coffee was welcome.

Step 1: Find the modifier. The modifiers are *Having struggled in the snow all day* and *hot.*

Step 2: Ask, "Does the modifier have anything to modify?" The answer is yes and no. *Hot* modifies *coffee,* but *Having struggled in the snow all day* doesn't modify anything. Who struggled? There is nobody mentioned in the sentence. To revise, put somebody in the sentence.

revised sentences: Having struggled in the snow all day, Dan welcomed hot coffee.

After struggling in the snow all day, we welcomed hot coffee.

Remember that you cannot correct a dangling modifier just by moving the modifiers. You have to give the modifier something to modify, so you must add something to the sentence.

Exercise 4   Practice: Correcting Sentences with Dangling Modifiers

Some of the following sentences use modifiers correctly, but some have dangling modifiers. Revise the sentences that have dangling modifiers. To revise, you will have to add words and change words.

1. When meeting people for the first time, highly personal questions are out of place.

   revised: _____

   _____

2. To finish a complicated task, small steps are useful.

   revised: _____

   _____

3. Motivated by fear and the pressure of my family's expectations, there was nothing but misery ahead.

   revised: _____

   _____

4. Lost in a forest and without warm clothes, the chances of surviving the night were slim.

   revised: _____

   _____

5. Preparing for a career in the military, good health is essential.

   revised: _____

   _____

6. Wrapped in an old blanket, the cat slept peacefully on the car's back seat.

   revised: _____

   _____

7. Without advanced training in electronics, a job at the new plant will be difficult to get.

   revised: _____

   _____

8. Surprised by the change in his schedule, Aidan was relieved he didn't have a math class at 8:00 a.m.

   revised: _____

   _____

REVIEWING THE STEPS AND THE SOLUTIONS

It is important to recognize modifier problems and correct them. Such problems can result in confusing or even silly sentences, and when you confuse or unintentionally amuse your reader, the reader misses your point.

Remember to check for modifier problems by using the three steps and to correct each kind of problem appropriately.

INFO BOX **A Summary of Modifier Problems**

Checking for Modifier Problems

Step 1: Find the modifier.

Step 2: Ask, "Does the modifier have something to modify?"

Step 3: Ask, "Is the modifier in the right place?"

Correcting Modifier Problems

- If a modifier is in the wrong place (a **misplaced modifier**), put it as close as possible to the word, phrase, or clause it modifies.

- If a modifier has nothing to modify (a **dangling modifier**), add or change words so that it has something to modify.

Exercise 5 **Practice: Revising Sentences with Misplaced or Dangling Modifiers**

All of the sentences below have some kind of modifier problem. Write a new, correct sentence for each one. You can move, remove, add, or change words. The first one is done for you.

1. Chewing on an old shoe, Lincoln discovered his puppy.

   revised: <u>Lincoln discovered his puppy chewing on an old shoe.</u>

   _____

2. Climbing several flights of old, steep stairs, aches and pains began to afflict the tourists.

   revised: _____

   _____

3. Worried by endless rain, flooding was constantly in the residents' thoughts.

   revised: _____

   _____

4. Dancing through the aisles of the theater, the audience applauded the performers.

   revised: _____

   _____

5. Covered in pollen, the class sat in the garden and sketched.

   revised: _____

   _____

6. Completing the calculus test nearly took me an hour.

   revised: _____

   _____

7. Wrapped in plastic, Lisa saw a huge stuffed teddy bear.

   revised: _____

   _____

8. To make friends, money or good looks are not required.

   revised: _____

   _____

| **Exercise 6** | **Collaborate: Completing Sentences with Modifiers** |

Collaborate

Do this exercise with a partner or group. Below are the beginnings of sentences. Complete each sentence by adding your own words. Be sure that each new sentence is free of modifier problems. When you have completed the exercise, share your sentences with another group or with the class. The first one is done for you.

1. Scorched and dry, <u>the toasted English muffin tasted like a chunk of</u>

   <u>charcoal.</u> _____

2. Furious about his friend's betrayal, _____

   _____

3. Sitting in our writing groups, _____

_____

4. When making an excuse, _____

5. Stuck at work until 9:00 p.m., _____

_____

6. To make friends in a new town, _____

_____

7. Suddenly realizing she forgot her homework, _____

_____

8. Loved by millions, _____

_____

Connect

Exercise 7   Connect: Revising for Modifier Problems

The following paragraph has some modifier problems. Correct the errors by writing above the lines. There are five errors.

Going online, the time speeds by. I am capable of sitting at my computer for five hours and losing all sense of the passing of time. After checking my messages, replies must be sent to all my friends. Involved in the resulting conversations, a new world is entered, one without clocks. I can spend hours on my favorite sites and blogs. I can play games, chat, watch videos, listen to music, and shop. My computer offers a new world for me. In this world, I can choose what I want to see and hear. First becoming popular years ago, some people worried about the power of television. They worried about television's ability to fascinate huge audiences. However, spending hours in front of a television does not erase a person's sense of time. An online experience can only do that.

Chapter Test Correcting Problems with Modifiers

MyWritingLab™

Some of the sentences below have problems with modifiers; some are correct. Put *OK* by each correct sentence and *X* by each sentence with a modifier problem.

1. _____ When I was short of cash, I took almost all the coins out of the cookie jar in the kitchen.

2. _____ With no sense of direction, getting lost on a huge campus was typical behavior for Sam.

3. _____ While taking a shower, a lizard crawled out of the drain.

4. _____ Broken-hearted, Lisa had difficulty learning to trust others again.

5. _____ Clutching his identification papers, the visitor to the United States waited at the end of a long line.

6. _____ Blended with strawberries and bananas, Sarah sipped the tropical drink.

7. _____ Constantly looking behind him, fear drove the escaped prisoner into a panic.

8. _____ At four years old, Callie's mother introduced her to the pleasures of reading.

MyWritingLab™ Visit Chapter 9, "Correcting Problems with Modifiers," in *MyWritingLab* to test your understanding of the chapter objectives.

CHAPTER 10

Verbs: The Present Tense

Quick Question MyWritingLab™

Which sentence(s) is/are correct?

A. Amanda has worked in the computer lab since she started college.

B. Most of the time, Trevor do not speak to his father.

(After you study this chapter, you will be confident of your answer.)

Learning Objectives

In this chapter, you will learn to:

1. Identify the simple present tense of verbs.
2. Identify irregular verbs in the simple present tense.
3. Identify the present progressive tense of verbs.
4. Identify the present perfect tense of verbs.

Verbs are words that show some kind of action or being:

> **verb**
> My brother *washes* my car.

> **verb**
> The teddy bear *is* his oldest toy.

> **verb**
> Your cinnamon cake *smells* wonderful.

Verbs also tell about time:

> **verb**
> My brother *will wash* my car. (The time is future.)

> **verb**
> The teddy bear *was* his oldest toy. (The time is past.)

> **verb**
> Your cinnamon cake *smells* wonderful. (The time is present.)

Verbs have time frames. Time frames tell us when the action happens: **present**, **past** or **future**. Verbs also have aspects. Aspects tell us how the action happens: **simple**, **progressive**, **perfect**, **perfect progressive**. (A time frame + an aspect = a verb tense)

THE SIMPLE PRESENT TENSE

Following are the verb forms of the verb *walk*:

1 Identify the simple present tense of verbs.

> **INFO BOX** Verb Forms in the Simple Present Tense
>
> | | |
> |---|---|
> | I walk | we walk |
> | you walk | you walk |
> | he, she, it walks | they walk |

Take a closer look at the simple present tense forms. Only one form is different:

> he, she, it *walks*

This is the only form that ends in *-s* in the simple present tense.

In the simple present tense, use an *-s* or *-es* ending on the verb only when the subject is *he*, *she*, or *it* or the equivalent of *he*, *she*, or *it*.

examples:
He *drives* to campus on Tuesdays and Thursdays.
Larry *walks* his dog on Saturdays. (*Larry* is the equivalent of *he*.)
The Web site *receives* a lot of hits. (The *Web site* is the equivalent of *it*.)
She *reminds* me of my sister.
It *looks* like a new car.
Your engine *sounds* funny. (The word *engine* is the equivalent of *it*.)
My daughter *watches* the news on television. (The word *daughter* is the equivalent of *she*.)

> **INFO BOX** Functions of Simple Present Tense
>
> The simple present tense is used to:
>
> > Describe regular or habitual (ongoing) activities
> > State a fact
> > Express thoughts or emotions

Exercise 1 Practice: Picking the Right Verb in the Simple Present Tense

To familiarize yourself with verb forms in the present tense, underline the subject and circle the correct verb form in each of the following sentences.

1. The sound of a car horn (wake / wakes) me up every morning.

2. Andrea is always thinking of her future; each week she (put / puts) a few dollars into a savings account.

3. Every semester my advisor (help / helps) me plan my schedule for next semester.

4. My job responsibilities (seem / seems) to grow every week.

5. Meeting at my house for dinner (give / gives) us a chance to catch up on the latest local gossip.

6. Cynthia and her sister (look / looks) like twins.

7. I have one instructor who always (wear / wears) a hat in the classroom.

8. Ricardo and his uncle (own / owns) a towing company.

Exercise 2   **Practice: Determining the Function of the Simple Present Tense**

To familiarize yourself with the use of the simple present tense, circle the correct function.

1. Every Monday, I work at 5:00 p.m.	Habitual	Fact	Thoughts/emotions
2. The earth revolves around the sun.	Habitual	Fact	Thoughts/emotions
3. James wakes up, takes a shower, and gets dressed.	Habitual	Fact	Thoughts/emotions
4. She loves literature.	Habitual	Fact	Thoughts/emotions
5. We always freewrite at the beginning of class.	Habitual	Fact	Thoughts/emotions
6. Constant jealousy damages a relationship.	Habitual	Fact	Thoughts/emotions

Collaborate

Exercise 3   **Collaborate: Writing Sentences with Verbs in the Simple Present Tense**

Below are pairs of verbs. Working with a partner or group, write a sentence using each verb. Be sure your verbs are in the simple present tense, and make your sentences at least five words long. When you have completed the exercise, share your sentences with another group. The first one is done for you.

1. **verbs:** ignore, ignores

    sentence 1: _Sometimes I ignore Jay's constant complaining._

    _____

    sentence 2: _Alan regularly ignores his mother's warnings about eating too much fatty food._

2. **verbs:** forget, forgets

    sentence 1: _____

    _____

    sentence 2: _____

    _____

3. **verbs:** demand, demands

   sentence 1: _____

   _____

   sentence 2: _____

   _____

4. **verbs:** reveal, reveals

   sentence 1: _____

   _____

   sentence 2: _____

   _____

5. **verbs:** evaluate, evaluates

   sentence 1: _____

   _____

   sentence 2: _____

   _____

6. **verbs:** remain, remains

   sentence 1: _____

   _____

   sentence 2: _____

   _____

7. **verbs:** lose, loses

   sentence 1: _____

   _____

   sentence 2: _____

   _____

8. **verbs:** prepare, prepares

   sentence 1: _____

   _____

   sentence 2: _____

   _____

Connect

Exercise 4	**Connect: Revising a Paragraph for Errors in the Simple Present Tense**

The following paragraph contains nine errors in the present tense verb forms. Correct the errors in the spaces above the lines.

   A sick person often take medicine to get well, but sometimes liquids

tastes disgusting and pills gets stuck in a person's throat. When I feel nauseous,

I take a pink liquid. Swallowing this liquid cause me to consider spitting it out.

Surely, other people with indigestion wonders about taking a nasty cure.

In addition, my doctor sometimes prescribes pills when I suffers from the flu

or a migraine headache. These medications seems much bigger than a tiny

aspirin or a cold pill. Most adults fear choking on such enormous pills. After

symptoms appears, I and other people wants a quick end to colds, infections,

allergies, and pain. However, the remedies often seem almost as unpleasant as

the ailment.

② Identify irregular verbs in the simple present tense.

IRREGULAR VERBS IN THE SIMPLE PRESENT TENSE

The Simple Present Tense of *Be, Have, Do*

Irregular verbs do not follow the same rules for creating verb forms that regular verbs do. Three verbs that we use all the time—*be, have,* and *do*—are irregular verbs. You need to study them closely. Look at the following simple present tense forms for all three.

simple present tense of *be*:

I am	we are
you are	you are
he, she, it is	they are

simple present tense of *have*:

I have	we have
you have	you have
he, she, it has	they have

simple present tense of *do*:

I do	we do
you do	you do
he, she, it does	they do

Spelling Note: Other verbs have spelling changes for third person singular. For example, verbs that end in a consonant + *y* drop the *y* and add *-ies*. Example: *try* becomes *tries*. Verbs that end in *-s, -sh, -ch,* or *-x* need *-es* for third-person singular. Example: *pass* becomes *passes*.

Caution: Be careful when you add *not* to *does*. If you're using the contraction of *does not*, be sure you write *doesn't* instead of *don't*. Contractions should be avoided in most formal reports and business writing courses. Always check with your instructor about the appropriate use of contractions in your assignments.

not this: ~~He don't call me very often.~~
but this: He doesn't call me very often.

Exercise 5 **Practice: Choosing the Correct Form of *Be, Have,* and *Do* in the Simple Present Tense**

Circle the correct form of the verb in each sentence.

1. After my boyfriend and I argue, we (are / be) ashamed of our bad tempers.

2. Leon, my friend from high school, (has / have) a job at the airport.

3. My new cell phone (do / does) everything but cook.

4. Stacks of books (be / are) extremely heavy items for carrying to class.

5. As we enter North Ridge, we (has / have) a beautiful view of hills and trees.

6. When I see my husband come home from his night class, I (am / be) proud of his determination.

7. At the club house, two or three members (does / do) a little cleaning once a month.

8. Once a year, the local library (has / have) a giant used book sale.

Exercise 6 **Connect: Revising a Paragraph with Errors in the Present Tense of *Be, Have,* and *Do***

Connect

The following paragraph contains nine errors in the use of the present tense forms of *be, have,* and *do.* Correct the errors above the lines.

A small park at the back of my apartment complex be causing some problems in our neighborhood. The park have swing sets, a slide, and a jungle gym designed for children in kindergarten or elementary school, but neighborhood teens has an interest in the park. The teens does not have a gathering place of their own, so they be regular visitors to the children's park. Sometimes the teens frighten the small children. In addition, the playground equipment be not designed to hold the weight of older children, so the swing sets, slide, and even the jungle gym has dents and cracks. The parents of the young children do not like this invasion of the park, but the teens are now in control of the property. It do not seem fair that small children are now the outsiders at a park for small children. On the other hand, local teens does not want to be stuck with no gathering place except the streets.

③ Identify the present progressive tense of verbs.

THE PRESENT PROGRESSIVE TENSE

The **present progressive tense** is used to describe actions in progress. Words indicating time such as *now* and *at this moment* are found in sentences in the present progressive tense. The present progressive occurs more in spoken English than in formal, academic written English.

Some verbs do not occur in the present progressive form. These verbs are **nonaction verbs**. Nonaction verbs include verbs that describe possession (*belong, have, own, possess*), verbs that describe senses (*feel, hear, see, smell, taste, touch*), verbs that describe emotions (*desire, like, love, hate*), verbs that describe mental activities (*believe, realize, remember, understand*), and verbs that describe states of being (*appear, be, consist, seem*).

Take a closer look at the present progressive tense forms. It is formed with the verb **to be + verb + ing**. The verb + *ing* is called a **present participle**. As an example, look at the forms for the present progressive tense of the verb *study*:

INFO BOX **Verb Forms in the Present Progressive Tense**

I am studying	we are studying
you are studying	you are studying
he, she, it is studying	they are studying

---

examples:
The professor *is explaining* the lesson.
Mario *is preparing* for a test.
The smartphone *is vibrating*.
We *are reviewing* the exam.
They *are planning* a vacation.

Collaborate

Exercise 7 **Collaborate: Writing Sentences with Verbs in the Present Progressive Tense**

Following is a verb with a time word. Working with a partner or group, write a sentence using the verb and time word. Be sure your verbs are in the present progressive tense, and make your sentences at least five words long. When you have completed the exercise, share your sentences with another group. The first one is done for you.

    1. **verb:** leave/now

        The bus is leaving now. _____

        _____

    2. **verb:** work/at this moment

        _____

        _____

    3. **verb:** rain/right now

        _____

        _____

   4. verb: assist/at this moment

   _____

   _____

   5. verb: write/now

   _____

   _____

   6. verb: walk/right now

   _____

   _____

Exercise 8   Practice: Choosing the Simple Present Tense or the Present
Progressive Tense

Circle the correct form of the verb in each sentence.

1. I can't believe the time! We (are having / have) to go to class.

2. Emma (is taking / takes) her exam now.

3. I (am loving / love) my history class; it's really interesting.

4. My college (is offering / offers) English I on Saturday mornings.

5. Please be quiet. I (am trying / try) to study at this moment.

6. Sondra (is doing / does) her homework every evening.

7. Jason (is owning / owns) two brand new cars.

8. The movie (is opening / opens) on Friday.

Exercise 9   Practice: Choosing the Correct Form of the Present
Progressive Tense

Write the correct form of the verb in parentheses in the following sentences.
Review the instruction on irregular verb forms.

1. The environmental scientist has _____ (draw) a clear picture of
   the danger to our lakes and rivers.

2. My grandfather has _____ (build) two houses in South Dakota.

3. It is my second time taking College Algebra. I have _____ (study)
   all this before!

4. We have _____ (bring) every book she has ever _____ (wrote).

5. Colin has _____ (give) his notice at work; he has a new job.

6. I'm not sure that I have _____ (find) a subject I really love.

7. Sarah has _____ (tell) me three different stories about her family
   background.

8. Jesse has _____ (stand) in line at the registrar's office for
   an hour.

| Exercise 10 | Practice: Choose the Simple Present Tense or the Present Progressive Tense |

Write the correct form of the verb in parentheses in the following sentences. Review the instruction on irregular verb forms.

1. When the spotlight turns to me, I _____ (shake) with nervousness.

2. Be careful; that little puppy _____ (bite) me with his sharp little teeth.

3. Every summer, I _____ (work) at a candy store on the boardwalk.

4. Since I _____ (be) a student here, I have worked in the tutoring center.

5. In class, Alicia _____ (participate) often.

6. My mother _____ (saved) every picture I have ever drawn for her.

7. I never _____ (sleep) on the top bunk of a bunk bed.

8. Every day, my father _____ (rise) at 5:30 a.m. and cooks himself a large breakfast.

4 Identify the present perfect tense of verbs.

THE PRESENT PERFECT TENSE

The **present perfect tense** is used for actions that began in the past and are still ongoing, or for actions that happened at an unspecified time in the past (we don't know the precise time that the action occurred).

Time words such as *for* and *since* are often used with sentences in the present perfect. The present perfect is often seen in academic writing.

Take a closer look at the present perfect tense. It is formed with the verb **to have + past participle**.

INFO BOX Verb Forms in the Present Perfect Tense

I have lived	we have lived
you have lived	you have lived
he, she, it has lived	they have lived

examples:
The instructor *has taught* here for twelve years.
We *have studied* this since September.
Smartphones *have changed* considerably.
We *have been* to Florida.
They *have worked* in the library all day.

It is important to familiarize yourself with past participles to form the present perfect tense correctly.

Base Form	**Past Participle**
(Today I arise.)	(I have/had arisen.)
arise	arisen
awake	awaked, awoken
bear	born, borne
beat	beaten
become	become
begin	begun
bend	bent
bite	bitten
bleed	bled
blow	blown
break	broken
bring	brought
build	built
burst	burst
buy	bought
catch	caught
choose	chosen
come	come
cling	clung
cost	cost
creep	crept
cut	cut
deal	dealt
draw	drawn
dream	dreamed, dreamt
drink	drunk
drive	driven
eat	eaten
fall	fallen
feed	fed
feel	felt
fight	fought
find	found
fling	flung
fly	flown
freeze	frozen
get	got, gotten
give	given
go	gone
grow	grown
hear	heard
hide	hidden
hit	hit
hold	held
hurt	hurt
keep	kept

(Continued)

Base Form	Past Participle
know	known
lay (to put)	laid
lead	led
leave	left
lend	lent
let	let
lie (to recline)	lain
light	lit, lighted
lost	lost
make	made
mean	meant
meet	met
pay	paid
ride	ridden
ring	rung
rise	risen
run	run
say	said
see	seen
sell	sold
send	sent
sew	sewn, sewed
shake	shaken
shine	shone, shined
shrink	shrunk
shut	shut
sing	sung
sit	sat
sleep	slept
slide	slid
sling	slung
speak	spoken
spend	spent
stand	stood
steal	stolen
stick	stuck
sting	stung
stink	stunk
string	strung
swear	sworn
swim	swum
teach	taught
tear	torn
tell	told
think	thought
throw	thrown
wake	waked, woken
wear	wore
win	won
write	written

Exercise 11   **Collaborate: Writing Sentences Using the Simple Present, Present Progressive, and Present Perfect**

Collaborate

Do this exercise with a partner or group. Below are pairs of verbs. Write a sentence for each verb. Your sentences should be at least five words long. When you have completed this exercise, share your answers with another group or with the class. The first one is done for you.

1. **verbs:** worry, worrying, worried

   sentence 1: _I rarely worry about my health or fitness._ _____

   _____

   sentence 2: _Colleen's parents are worrying about her reckless behavior._ ___

   _____

   sentence 3: _Colleen's parents have worried about her since she was a child._

   _____

2. **verbs:** study, studying, studied

   sentence 1: _____

   _____

   sentence 2: _____

   _____

   sentence 3: _____

   _____

3. **verbs:** scatters, scattering, scattered

   sentence 1: _____

   _____

   sentence 2: _____

   _____

   sentence 3: _____

   _____

4. **verbs:** praise, praising, praised

   sentence 1: _____

   _____

   sentence 2: _____

   _____

   sentence 3: _____

   _____

5. **verbs:** restore, restoring, restored

   sentence 1: _____

   _____

sentence 2: _____

_____

sentence 3: _____

_____

6. **verbs:** implies, implying, implied

sentence 1: _____

_____

sentence 2: _____

_____

sentence 3: _____

_____

MyWritingLab™ **Chapter Test** **Verbs: The Present Verb Forms**

Some of the sentences use verbs correctly; others do not. Put *OK* by each correct sentence and *X* by each sentence with an error in using verbs.

1. _____ After the argument at my house, my sister and her boyfriend done nothing to improve family relations.

2. _____ The comedian has hid his intelligence behind a mask of foolishness.

3. _____ Matthew and Lisa are going to a discount store to buy a window air conditioner.

4. _____ Even though Michael is a strict parent, he do have a warm heart and great love for his children.

5. _____ If you are ready to leave at 6:30 a.m., we are avoiding the morning rush hour on Cade Boulevard.

6. _____ The horror movie has had a lingering effect on me; it gave me nightmares for a week.

7. _____ Serena swims in the city pool whenever she has some free time.

8. _____ We are preparing for the exam by reviewing all of the class notes.

Quick Question MyWritingLab™

Which sentence(s) is/are correct?

A. *Maria had studied the entire chapter yesterday.*

B. *Before Tony moved to New Jersey, he had lived in Nebraska.*

(After you study this chapter, you will be confident of your answer.)

Learning Objectives

In this chapter, you will learn to:

1. Identify the simple past tense of verbs.
2. Identify irregular verbs in the simple past tense.
3. Identify the past progressive tense of verbs.
4. Identify the past perfect tense of verbs.

PAST VERB FORMS

A verb form tells us two things: *when* the action happened and *how* the action happened. The *when* is the time frame. The *how* is the aspect. As you already know, there are three basic time frames: *present, past,* and *future.*

In this chapter, you will learn about the **past time frame**. The past time frame is used for actions that occurred in the past and have been completed.

① Identify the simple past tense of verbs.

The Simple Past Tense

The **simple past tense** expresses actions that happened once and are completed. To form the simple past tense add -*ed* to the base form for regular verbs.

For verbs that end in -*e*, add -*d*.
For verbs that end in a consonant +*y*, drop the *y* and add -*ied*.

INFO BOX Simple Past Tense

I walked	We walked
I lived	We lived
I studied	We studied
You walked	You walked
You lived	You lived
You studied	You studied
He walked	They walked
It lived	They lived
She studied	They studied

Notice that the simple past tense verb forms for the third person (*he, she, it*) is the same as the verb forms for third person plural (*they*). All simple past forms are the same.

Exercise 1   Practice: Writing the Correct Form of the Simple Past Tense

To familiarize yourself with the simple past tense, write the correct simple past tense form of each verb in the blank space.

1. After planning a visit to a national park, my parents _____ (count) on good weather.

2. Before our wedding, my fiancé and I _____ (receive) many beautiful gifts.

3. When she was a child, my mother _____ (suffer) from a problem with her spine.

4. Last weekend, my car _____ (stall) in heavy traffic.

5. During my first semester of college, I _____ (learn) about the differences between high school and higher education.

6. Once in summer school, someone _____ (pull) the fire alarm in a classroom building.

7. At the end of the party, a friend _____ (offer) me a ride home.

8. In kindergarten, my older sister _____ (love) her teacher and the entire experience of school.

② Identify irregular verbs in the simple past tense.

IRREGULAR VERBS IN THE SIMPLE PAST TENSE

As you learned in Chapter 10, irregular verbs do not follow the same rules for creating verb forms that regular verbs do. While there are many irregular verbs in the simple past tense, there are three verbs that we use all the time: *be, have,* and *do.* Here are some simple past tense forms of **to be** we use frequently:

> I **was** late for class this morning.
> You **were** late, too.
> Ms. Taylor **was** pleased with the essays.
> We **were** all thankful spring break was coming.
> They **were** relieved to get passing grades.

Unlike other simple past tense verbs, the past tense verb forms of *to be* change according to the subject. However, that does not apply to other irregular verb forms:

> I **had** a terrible headache last night.
> She **had** four exams yesterday! She is exhausted.
>
> **Did** Professor Smith return our papers?
> They **did not** get the classes they wanted.

Exercise 2   Practice: Choosing the Correct Form of *Be, Have,* and *Do* in the Simple Past Tense

Circle the correct verb form in each sentence.

1. Lisa and Danny (done / did) most of the work in the office; the other members of the staff were on the road most of the time.

2. After my grandmother retired, she finally (have / had) the time to enjoy her favorite hobbies: photography and ballroom dancing.

3. For two years, I (was / were) the proud owner of a large snake.

4. When I first saw my sister's cats, they (was / were) tiny kittens curled up in an old baseball cap.

5. My brothers never helped with chores around the house; they always (have / had) a million excuses for getting out of housework.

6. The cake at Kelly's birthday party (was / were) so large that we all took leftover pieces home.

7. For months, Saul and his friends (done / did) nothing but complain about their bad luck.

8. Because our parents died young, my sister and I (has / had) very little guidance in our teen years.

Exercise 3   Connect: Revising a Paragraph with Errors in the Past Tense of *Be, Have,* and *Do*

Connect

The following paragraph contains twelve errors in the use of the past tense of *be, have,* and *do.* Correct the errors above the lines.

Yesterday I stood up to Jamie, my older brother, and I done it for some good

reasons. First, Jamie were an obnoxious person all afternoon. He ridiculed me,

and he done it for hours. He were especially cruel because he done the verbal bullying when my fiancée were present. I were convinced that he meant to shame me in front of her, and I were full of rage. In addition, the hurt of many years of Jamie's abuse seemed to collect in my heart. These two factors was enough to provoke me to fight back. I done nothing physical, but I stood my ground. "Watch it, Jamie," I said. "You has gone too far with your meanness." He glared at me in silence, but I did not back off. "Watch your words," I said, and my brother have nothing else to say. I felt free and strong for the first time in years, and I plan to keep challenging my brother's cruelty.

More Irregular Verb Forms

Be, have, and *do* are not the only verbs with irregular forms in the simple past tense. There are many such verbs, and everybody who writes uses some form of an irregular verb. When you write and you are not certain you are using the correct form of a verb, check the following list of irregular simple past tense verbs.

For each verb listed, the base form and the simple past tense are given.

Present (Today I arise.)	**Past** (Yesterday I arose.)
arise	arose
awake	awaked, awoke
bear	bore
beat	beat
become	became
begin	began
bend	bent
bite	bit
bleed	bled
blow	blew
break	broke
bring	brought
build	built
burst	burst
buy	bought
catch	caught
choose	chose
come	came
cling	clung
cost	cost
creep	crept
cut	cut
deal	dealt

Present	**Past**
draw	drew
dream	dreamed, dreamt
drink	drank
drive	drove
eat	ate
fall	fell
feed	fed
feel	felt
fight	fought
find	found
fling	flung
fly	flew
freeze	froze
get	got
give	gave
go	went
grow	grew
hear	heard
hide	hid
hit	hit
hold	held
hurt	hurt
keep	kept
know	knew
lay (to put)	laid
lead	led
leave	left
lend	lent
let	let
lie (to recline)	lay
light	lit, lighted
lost	lost
make	made
mean	meant
meet	met
pay	paid
ride	rode
ring	rang
rise	rose
run	ran
say	said
see	saw
sell	sold
send	sent
sew	sewed
shake	shook
shine	shone, shined
shrink	shrank
shut	shut

(Continued)

Present	Past
sing	sang
sit	sat
sleep	slept
slide	slid
sling	slung
speak	spoke
spend	spent
stand	stood
steal	stole
stick	stuck
sting	stung
stink	stank, stunk
string	strung
swear	swore
swim	swam
teach	taught
tear	tore
tell	told
think	thought
throw	threw
wake	waked, woke
wear	wore
win	won
write	wrote

Exercise 4   **Practice: Choosing the Correct Form of Irregular Past Tense Verbs**

Write the correct form of the verb in parentheses in the following sentences. Be sure to check the list of irregular verbs.

1. When the spotlight turned to me, I _____ (shake) with nervousness.

2. Be careful; that little puppy _____ (bite) me with his sharp little teeth.

3. In the summer, I _____ (sling) an old sheet over the curtain rod on my bedroom window to keep out the early morning sun.

4. When the storm hit, the wind _____ (blow) through the smallest cracks in the log cabin's walls.

5. After class, Alicia _____ (go) to the computer lab to work on her political science assignment.

6. My mother saved old buttons and _____ (string) them together to make a necklace for her little granddaughter.

7. I _____ (sleep) under the stars last night.

8. My father _____ (rise) at 5:30 a.m. and cooked himself a large breakfast.

| Exercise 5 | **Connect: Revising a Paragraph That Contains Errors in Irregular Past Tense Verb Forms** |

Connect

Twelve of the irregular verb forms in the following paragraph are incorrect. Write the correct verb forms in the space above the lines.

When the pipes bursted in our house, panic breaked loose among the family members. The disaster occurred on a Saturday evening while we were in the kitchen. As we sitted at the kitchen table, our supper was interrupted by a sudden flow of water. Within minutes, the water had covered the floor. Because it surprised us, no one knowed what to do. My mother was the first to act. She flinged kitchen mats, chairs, pet bowls, and other objects onto higher spaces such as the table and kitchen counters. The rest of us kept trying to figure out the cause of the damage. Meanwhile, the amount of water just growed. Of course, because this mess hit us on a Saturday night, we had a hard time finding a plumber. Finally, we finded a person who came to our rescue. The damage was extensive, and repairing it costed a great deal of money. Once the kitchen was repaired and restored, my sister and I still shrinked from sitting at the kitchen table. We remembered the awful time when the water stinked and the contractors teared our kitchen apart. Today, three years after the flood, I still spend very little time in the kitchen.

PAST PROGRESSIVE TENSE

Much like the simple past tense, the **past progressive tense** expresses actions that occurred in the past. It is used for actions that happened repeatedly, or continuously, in the past. The past progressive tense uses the present participle (the *-ing* form of the verb) plus some form of *to be*. Keep in mind that the present participle does not mean present time. It is the helping verb **to be** that determines the time frame.

> I **was working** on my paper all day yesterday.
> John and Madison **were studying** when the lights went out.

3 Identify the past progressive tense of verbs.

INFO BOX Past Progressive Tense

Singular	**Plural**
I was walking	we were walking
you were walking	you were walking
he, she, it was walking	they were walking

Be careful not to confuse the past progressive tense with the past tense:

past tense: George *took* the final exam. (This sentence implies that George is done with the final exam.)

past progressive tense: George *was taking* the final exam when the fire alarm sounded. (This sentence says that George was in the process of taking his exam when something else happened: the alarm sounded.)

Use the simple past tense to express completed or finished actions. Use the past progressive tense when you want to show that something was or is in progress.

Exercise 6   **Practice: Distinguishing Between the Simple Past Tense and the Past Progressive Tense**

Circle the correct verb tense in each of the following sentences. Be sure to look carefully at the meaning of each sentence.

1. Last week, the trip to Houston (was taking / took) more time than usual.

2. Eric (was packing / packed) his duffle bag last night.

3. After Kelly's trip to North Carolina, she (was talking / talked) about nothing but the beautiful mountains.

4. The hurricane (was devastating / devastated) parts of coastal Texas before it moved to the Florida Panhandle.

5. You (wore / were wearing) a hideous yellow sweater when we first met.

6. When I was a child, I (was loving / loved) cartoons with animal characters.

7. More than a month ago, Bill (was promising / promised) to pay his debt to me within twenty-four hours.

8. I (was typing / typed) my essay when the power went out.

PAST PERFECT TENSE

4 Identify the past perfect tense of verbs.

As you learned in Chapter 10, the *present perfect tense* can be used to express actions in the past if they happened at an unspecified time. That is, we don't know when the action occurred.

I have been to Florida. (Do you know when I was in Florida? Am I still in Florida? No. This is an unspecified time.)

The **past perfect tense** is made up of the past participle form + *had*. You can use the past perfect tense to show more than one event in the past; you can use it to show when two or more events happened in the past but at different times.

past tense: Alan *cut* the grass.

past perfect tense: Alan *had cut* the grass by the time David arrived. (Alan cut the grass *before* David arrived. Both events happened in the past, but one happened earlier than the other.)

past tense: The professor *lectured* for an hour.

past perfect tense: The professor *had lectured* for an hour when he pulled out a surprise quiz. (Lecturing came first; pulling out a surprise quiz came second. Both actions are in the past.)

The most challenging part of using the past perfect is choosing the correct form of the past participle. While many past participles look like simple past tense verbs, many do not. It is important that you familiarize yourself with past participles. Here is a list of irregular verb forms:

Base	Past	Past Participle
(Today I arise.)	(Yesterday I arose.)	(I had arisen.)
arise	arose	arisen
awake	awaked, awoke	awaked, awoken
bear	bore	born, borne
beat	beat	beaten
become	became	become
begin	began	begun
bend	bent	bent
bite	bit	bitten
bleed	bled	bled
blow	blew	blown
break	broke	broken
bring	brought	brought
build	built	built
burst	burst	burst
buy	bought	bought
catch	caught	caught
choose	chose	chosen
come	came	come
cling	clung	clung
cost	cost	cost
creep	crept	crept
cut	cut	cut
deal	dealt	dealt
draw	drew	drawn
dream	dreamed, dreamt	dreamed, dreamt
drink	drank	drunk
drive	drove	driven
eat	ate	eaten
fall	fell	fallen
feed	fed	fed
feel	felt	felt
fight	fought	fought
find	found	found
fling	flung	flung
fly	flew	flown
freeze	froze	frozen
get	got	got, gotten
give	gave	given
go	went	gone

(Continued)

Base	Past	Past Participle
grow	grew	grown
hear	heard	heard
hide	hid	hidden
hit	hit	hit
hold	held	held
hurt	hurt	hurt
keep	kept	kept
know	knew	known
lay (to put)	laid	laid
lead	led	led
leave	left	left
lend	lent	lent
let	let	let
lie (to recline)	lay	lain
light	lit, lighted	lit, lighted
lost	lost	lost
make	made	made
mean	meant	meant
meet	met	met
pay	paid	paid
ride	rode	ridden
ring	rang	rung
rise	rose	risen
run	ran	run
say	said	said
see	saw	seen
sell	sold	sold
send	sent	sent
sew	sewed	sewn, sewed
shake	shook	shaken
shine	shone, shined	shone, shined
shrink	shrank	shrunk
shut	shut	shut
sing	sang	sung
sit	sat	sat
sleep	slept	slept
slide	slid	slid
sling	slung	slung
speak	spoke	spoken
spend	spent	spent
stand	stood	stood
steal	stole	stolen
stick	stuck	stuck
sting	stung	stung
stink	stank, stunk	stunk
string	strung	strung
swear	swore	sworn
swim	swam	swum
teach	taught	taught
tear	tore	torn

Base	Past	Past Participle
tell	told	told
think	thought	thought
throw	threw	thrown
wake	waked, woke	waked, woken
wear	wore	wore
win	won	won
write	wrote	written

Exercise 7   **Practice: Distinguishing Between the Past and the Past Perfect Tense**

Circle the correct verb tense in the following sentences. Be sure to look carefully at the meaning of each sentence.

1. I was surprised when Lisa offered me another slice of her birthday cake before I (finished / had finished) eating my first slice.

2. Carlos suspected that his girlfriend (went / had gone) though his bureau drawers before he came home.

3. By the time I finished washing my car, the sky (turned / had turned) dark and cloudy.

4. At the movie, my brother (talked / had talked) on his cell phone while I tried to concentrate on the film.

5. Every Friday, my friends at work (met / had met) for a meal at a local Asian restaurant.

6. My father wondered if I (met / had met) any soccer players at school.

7. As Alan (wailed / had wailed) about the dismal performance of his favorite team, he clenched his fists in rage.

8. By the time we got to the airport, our flight (left / had left) the runway.

Some Tips About Verbs

There are a few errors that people tend to make with verbs. If you are aware of these errors, you will be on the lookout for them as you edit your writing.

Used to: Be careful when you write that someone *used to* do, say, or feel something. It is incorrect to write *use to*.

> **not this:** Wendy ~~use to~~ make pancakes for breakfast.
> **but this:** Wendy *used to* make pancakes for breakfast.

> **not this:** They ~~use to~~ live on my street.
> **but this:** They *used to* live on my street.

Supposed to: Be careful when you write that someone is *supposed to* do, say, or feel something. It is incorrect to write *suppose to*.

> **not this:** He was ~~suppose to~~ repair my watch yesterday.
> **but this:** He was *supposed to* repair my watch yesterday.

not this: I am ~~suppose to~~ make dinner tomorrow.
but this: I am *supposed to* make dinner tomorrow.

Could have, should have, would have: Using *of* instead of *have* is another error with verbs.

not this: He ~~could of~~ sent me a card.
but this: He *could have* sent me a card.

not this: You ~~should of~~ been more careful.
but this: You *should have* been more careful.

not this: Norman ~~would of~~ enjoyed the music.
but this: Norman *would have* enjoyed the music.

Would have/had: If you are writing about something that might have been possible but that did not happen, use *had* as the helping verb.

not this: If he ~~would have~~ been friendlier, he would not be alone now.
but this: If he *had* been friendlier, he would not be alone now.

not this: I wish the plane fare ~~would have~~ cost less.
but this: I wish the plane fare *had* cost less.

not this: If David ~~would have~~ controlled his temper, he would be a free man today.
but this: If David *had* controlled his temper, he would be a free man today.

Connect

Exercise 8   Connect: Editing a Paragraph for Common Errors in Verbs

Correct the six errors in *used to, supposed to, could have, should have, would have,* and *would have/had* in the following paragraph. Write your corrections above the lines.

When I fell in love for the first time, I was so overcome with emotion

that I made a fool of myself. Of course, I was twelve years old at the time, and

I had never spoken to the boy. He was in my class at middle school. I use to

stare at him while our teacher was talking, and I could of sworn that the boy

saw my adoring gaze. Now I know that a girl in love is suppose to be aloof and

cold. Then the man of her dreams is expected to notice her. Unfortunately, this

twelve-year-old boy of my dreams never noticed me at all. All my gazing and fan-

tasizing had no effect on him. I could of worn face paint to class and he wouldn't of

noticed. Of course, if I would have just waited a few years, that boy might have

noticed me at last.

Exercise 9   **Collaborate: Writing Sentences with the Correct Verb Forms**

Collaborate

Do this exercise with a partner or with a group. Write or complete each of the following sentences. When you have finished the exercise, be ready to share your answers with another group or with the class.

1. Complete this sentence and add a verb in the correct tense: Ethan had never seen the ocean until he _____

_____

2. Write a sentence that uses the words *gave me the same birthday gift.* _____

_____

3. Complete this sentence and add a verb in the correct tense: I was falling asleep at my desk when _____

_____

4. Write a sentence that includes the phrases *was studying.* _____

_____

_____

5. Complete this sentence: If only you had asked me, _____

_____

_____

6. Write a sentence that contains the words *should have.* _____

_____

_____

_____

7. Write a sentence that includes two actions in the past. _____

_____

_____

8. Complete this sentence: By the time the battle ended, six soldiers

_____

_____

MyWritingLab™   **Chapter Test**   **Verbs: Past Tense**

Some of the sentences below are correct; some have errors in verb tenses or other common errors. Put *OK* next to the correct sentences and *X* next to the sentences with errors.

1. _____ After a bumpy ride on a cramped, stuffy airplane, I were happy to be off that plane.

2. _____ Every weekend last year, Carter was taking his mother to visit his father's grave.

3. _____ My cousin was helping me paint my basement when we heard the news.

4. _____ My math professor wondered if I had forgotten last week's assignment.

5. _____ Allison tooked her books back to the bookstore.

6. _____ Henry have convinced Monica to go to the movies with him.

7. _____ Shane spent thirty minutes in front of the mirror, tried to style his hair, and then gave up.

8. _____ Jeffrey and Ron were in a good mood when I saw them at the game.

Verbs: Consistency and Voice

Learning Objectives

In this chapter, you will learn to:

1 Use consistent verb tense.

2 Identify the difference between active and passive voice.

3 Avoid unnecessary shifts in voice.

Remember that your choice of verb form indicates the time (tense) of your statements. Be careful not to shift from one time frame to another unless you have a reason to change the time.

CONSISTENT VERB TENSES

1 Use consistent verb tense.

Staying in one time frame (unless you have a reason to change that time frame) is called **consistency of verb tense**.

incorrect shifts in tense:
He *raced* through the yellow light, *stepped* on the gas, and *cuts* off a driver in the left lane.
A woman in a black dress *holds* a handkerchief to her face and *moaned* softly.

You can correct these errors by putting all the verbs in the same tense.

consistent present tense:

He *races* through the yellow light, *steps* on the gas, and *cuts* off a
   driver in the left lane.
A woman in a black dress *holds* a handkerchief to her face and *moans*
   softly.

consistent past tense:

He *raced* through the yellow light, *stepped* on the gas, and *cut* off a
   driver in the left lane.
A woman in a black dress *held* a handkerchief to her face and *moaned*
   softly.

Whether you correct the errors by changing all the verbs to the present time
frame or by changing them all to the past time frame, you are making the tense
consistent. Consistency of verb tenses is important when you describe events
because it helps the reader understand what happened and when it happened.

Exercise 1   **Practice: Correcting Sentences That Are Inconsistent in Tense**

In each sentence that follows, one verb is inconsistent in tense. Cross it out
and write the correct tense above. The first one is done for you.

1. Even though food ~~tasted~~ *tastes* better when I am hungry, food still tastes

   good whenever I eat it.

2. This class was useful because we study verbs, practiced sentence

   combining, and learned to use specific detail.

3. When autumn arrives, I brought out my sweaters and flannel shirts

   and prepare to enjoy the changing colors of the leaves, the brisk

   morning temperatures, and the deep blue skies.

4. For five days, I woke up at 3:00 a.m., struggled to get back to sleep,

   and wind up awake and exhausted.

5. My brother and I share a bedroom, so he usually knew when

   I wake up.

6. Andy missed most of the gossip at school because he paid no

   attention to rumors and never enjoys a nasty story about a rival.

7. For many years, Mike sent his niece a gift on her birthday and tol-

   erated her lack of gratitude, but when she does not invite him to

   her wedding, he lost his patience.

8. Yesterday evening, my husband cooked spaghetti and meatballs for our two children, gave them baths, but foolishly allows them to stay up long past their bedtime.

Exercise 2 **Connect: Editing a Paragraph for Consistency of Tense**

Read the following paragraph. Then cross out any verbs that are inconsistent in tense and write the corrections above them. The paragraph has five errors.

Every Friday evening, Sam calls me to ask about my plans for Saturday night. Almost always, I told him the same thing: I have no plans. After a brief sigh of disappointment, Sam bombards me with a list of suggestions for filling the Saturday evening hours. He mentioned the same old activities every week. They included going to a game, playing cards, meeting women at a club, or driving around aimlessly. When I tell him about my lack of money for socializing or filling the gas tank of my car, Sam admits his own lack of funds. At that point, we come to a realistic decision. We planned to meet at my house and watch an old movie. This dialogue and its outcome occur each week, and I thought they always happen for the same reason. Each time, Sam and I are hoping for a better outcome.

Exercise 3 **Collaborate: Rewriting a Paragraph for Consistent Verb Tenses**

The following paragraph has some inconsistencies in verb tenses; it shifts between past and present tenses. With a partner or a group, correct the errors in consistency by writing all the verbs in the past tense. You can write your corrections in the space above the errors. When you have completed the corrections, have one member of the group read the paragraph aloud as a final check.

When my parents bought an old house in a decrepit neighborhood, I had my doubts about their decision. I think the house was a hopeless wreck and I imagine my parents struggling to fix it up. Nothing about their plan seemed practical. I imagined a terrible struggle to deal with rotted wood, broken tiles, a leaky roof, bad plumbing, and an overgrown yard. I also believe that the other houses in the area are not worth repairing or restoring. I was wrong. Almost immediately after they bought the house, my parents started serious work on the property, and the changes are remarkable. Eventually, I was impressed and joined the group of family members who transformed the house and yard. My surprise grew when the changes spread to neighboring properties. Several people in the community watch my parents work and begin improving their homes. All my doubts about the power of hope, work, and determination are foolish, as my parents' efforts showed.

2 Identify the difference between active and passive voice.

ACTIVE AND PASSIVE VOICE

Verbs not only have tenses; they have voices. When the subject in the sentence is doing something, the verb is in the **active voice**. **Passive voice** is used when the subject of the sentence is unimportant or unknown.

active voice:
I designed the album cover. (*I*, the subject, did it.)
My friends from college raised money for the homeless shelter.
    (*Friends*, the subject, did it.)

passive voice:
The album cover was designed by me. (The *cover*, the subject, is what is important. It is not important that it was designed by me.)
The great work of art was stolen from the museum. (*The great work of art* the subject, was stolen. However, we don't know who stole it.)

Notice what happens when you use the passive voice instead of the active voice:

active voice: I designed the album cover.
passive voice: The album cover was designed by me.

The sentence in the passive voice is two words longer than the one in the active voice. Yet the sentence that used the passive voice doesn't say anything different, and it doesn't say it more clearly than the one in the active voice.

Using the passive voice can make your sentences wordy, it can slow them down, and it can make them boring. The passive voice can also confuse readers. When the subject isn't doing anything, readers may have to look carefully to see who or what *is doing* something. For example, look at this sentence:

A famous city landmark is being torn down.

Who is tearing down the landmark? In this sentence, it's impossible to find the answer to that question.

In general, you should avoid using the passive voice; instead, rewrite sentences so they are in the active voice.

Collaborate

| Exercise 4 | **Collaborate: Rewriting Sentences, Changing the Passive Voice to the Active Voice** |

Do this exercise with a partner or group. In the following sentences, change the passive voice to the active voice. If the original sentence doesn't tell you who or what performed the action, add words that tell you who or what did it. The first one is done for you.

1. One of Shakespeare's plays was performed at Peace River High School last night.

    rewritten: Students at Peace River High School performed one of

    Shakespeare's plays last night.

2. A series of safety measures was recommended by the superintendent of the Water Management District.

   rewritten: _____

   _____

3. Tremendous effort went into restoring the historic house.

   rewritten: _____

   _____

4. A new contract for workers at the plant has been proposed.

   rewritten: _____

   _____

5. A decision was made not to hire more security guards for the shopping center.

   rewritten: _____

   _____

6. A famous musician has been invited to speak at the college graduation ceremony.

   rewritten: _____

   _____

7. On most days, my mail is delivered after 5:00 p.m.

   rewritten: _____

   _____

8. Cigarette butts, plastic bottles, and soda cans had been tossed on the sand.

   rewritten: _____

   _____

Collaborate

Exercise 5   **Collaborate: Rewriting a Paragraph, Changing It to the Active Voice**

Do this exercise with a partner or group. Rewrite the paragraph below, changing all the verbs that are in the passive voice to the active voice. To make these changes, you may have to add words, omit words, and change the structure of sentences. Write your changes in the space above the lines. Be ready to read your new version of the paragraph to another group or to the class.

A better system for ensuring residents' safety has been initiated at Cedar

Forest Apartments. The change was designed by the Responsible Management

Company (RMC) as a quick response to residents' concerns about recent burglar-

ies and damages to vehicles at the Cedar Forest site. Beginning next month, all

residents will receive an electronic card that will enable them to pass through a new gated entrance to the community. A small electronic gatehouse will be installed by RMC next week. An introductory period of transition from an open community to a gated one has been planned for the following week. During this period, the gated entrance will be made accessible to all residents and visitors. This period was planned by RMC to familiarize residents with the new structure. A telephone line to the resident apartment manager will also be installed by management so that any discomfort with the new process can be minimized. When the gated entrance system is initiated by RMC next month, the structure will include a phone. Using this phone, a visitor to the apartments may call a resident and gain entry. Any further questions about the new system can be answered by your resident manager.

③ Avoid unnecessary shifts in voice.

Avoiding Unnecessary Shifts in Voice

Just as you should be consistent in the tense of verbs, you should be consistent in the voice of verbs. Do not shift from active to passive, or vice versa, without a good reason to do so.

> active   passive
> **shift:** *Carl wrote* the song, but the *credit was taken* by Tom.

> active   active
> **rewritten:** *Carl wrote* the song, but *Tom took* the credit.

> passive
> **shift:** Several *suggestions were made* by the vice president, yet the
> active
> *president rejected* all of them.

> active
> **rewritten:** The *vice president made* several suggestions, yet the
> active
> *president rejected* all of them.

Being consistent can help you write clearly and smoothly.

Exercise 6   **Practice: Rewriting Sentences to Correct Shifts in Voice**

Rewrite the following sentences so that all the verbs are in the active voice. You may change the wording to make the sentences clear, smooth, and consistent in voice.

1. André Hall was awarded a scholarship by the New Vistas Organization; André is a remarkable young man.

   rewritten: _____

   _____

2. My mother and her friends are obsessed with one television show; its stars and plots are constantly analyzed by the women.

    rewritten: _____

    _____

3. The drill sergeant bullied the new recruits, and the last drop of energy was squeezed from them.

    rewritten: _____

    _____

4. If plans for a holiday party were made by my parents, they didn't include me in their arrangements.

    rewritten: _____

    _____

5. Palmer Heights was a desirable place to live until the area was struck by a series of violent robberies.

    rewritten: _____

    _____

6. The spectators roared with approval as sports history was made by the pitcher.

    rewritten: _____

    _____

7. It has been arranged by volunteer firefighters to sponsor a food drive next week; they will collect canned goods.

    rewritten: _____

    _____

8. Because Kelly is so eager to please her boyfriend, her ambitions can easily be stifled by him.

    rewritten: _____

    _____

| Exercise 7 | Connect: A Comprehensive Exercise: Editing a Paragraph for Errors in Consistent Verb Tense and Voice |

Connect

The following paragraph has seven errors related to verb tense and voice. Correct the errors in the space above the lines.

I live in a town where college football dominates the autumn weekends.

Our local college's team is valued by the students and the community partly

because the team has a decent record of success. Whether the team was playing

at home or away, the team colors dominate the landscape before each game.

Flags with the colors are flown on cars, trucks, and even motorcycles, and

of course, these colors appear in clothing. Babies are dressed in the colors by
enthusiastic parents, and the babies' strollers carry team-colored streamers. Even
dogs wore collars or coats with pictures of the team mascot. On game days, floral
arrangements in the team colors are sold at local supermarkets. Football fever is
always fun because it linked thousands of people of all ages and backgrounds.

MyWritingLab™   **Chapter Test**   Verbs: Consistency and Voice

Some of the sentences below are correct; others have errors related to consistency in verb tense or voice. Put *OK* next to the correct sentences and *X* next to the incorrect ones.

1. _____ When Martin called me, he sounded tired and avoided the topic of his divorce.

2. _____ Sarah smiles at me and asks me about my family every time I see her at the supermarket.

3. _____ Although the heavy rain was good for my lawn, I want it to end because my basement is filling with water.

4. _____ When we have a family dinner at my sister's house, I bring the lemonade and soda, my mother cooked the main course, my sister prepares dessert, and my father supplies cheese and crackers.

5. _____ Sushi is considered delicious and healthy by millions of people in many parts of the world; however, I hate the thought of eating it.

6. _____ When I have a writing assignment, I like to complete it as quickly as possible; however, my rush to finish is criticized by my roommate, an English major.

7. _____ When I was home sick, a classmate lent me her dictionary, took class notes for me, and sent me the assignment online.

8. _____ After class last night, I took a chance and asked the woman sitting next to me if she wanted to go out, but she stares at me without saying a word.

MyWritingLab™ Visit Chapter 12, "Verbs: Consistency and Voice," in *MyWritingLab* to test your understanding of the chapter objectives.

Making Subjects and Verbs Agree

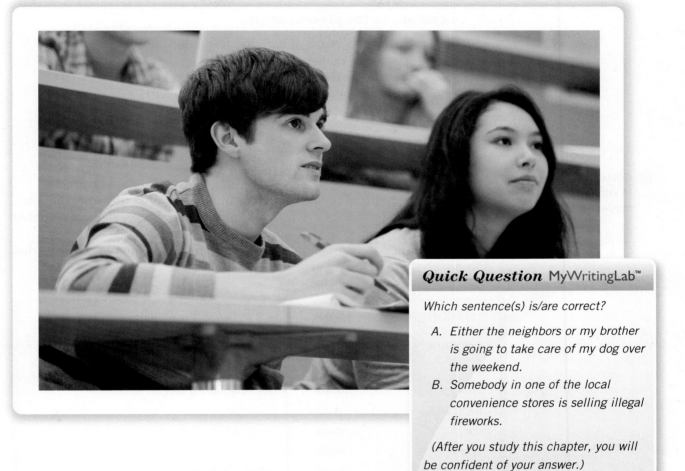

Learning Objectives

In this chapter, you will learn to:

1 Correct simple errors in subject–verb agreement.

2 Use a variety of methods to check for subject–verb agreement.

Subjects and verbs have to agree in number. That means a singular subject must be matched with a singular verb form; a plural subject must be matched with a plural verb form.

singular subject, singular verb
Nicole races out of the house in the morning.

plural subject, plural verb
Christine, Michael, and Marie take the train to work.

singular subject, singular verb
The old *song reminds* me of Mexico.

plural subject, plural verb
Greasy *hamburgers upset* my stomach.

133

> **Caution:** Remember that a regular verb has an -*s* ending in one singular form in the present tense—the form that goes with *he, she, it,* or their equivalents.

s endings in the present tense:

Marsha *takes* good care of her grandmother.
She *concentrates* on her assignments.
It *looks* like a nice day.
Eddie *buys* high-octane gasoline.
Nancy *seems* pleased.
The apartment *comes* with cable television.

① Correct simple errors in subject–verb agreement.

PRONOUNS USED AS SUBJECTS

Pronouns can be used as subjects. **Pronouns** are words that take the place of nouns. When pronouns are used as subjects, they must agree in number with verbs.

Following is a list of subject pronouns and the regular verb forms that agree with them in the present tense.

INFO BOX   **Subject Pronouns and Present Tense Verb Forms**

pronoun	verb	
I	walk	⎫
you	walk	⎬ (all singular forms)
he, she, it	walks	⎭
we	walk	⎫
you	walk	⎬
they	walk	⎭ all plural forms

In the following sentences, the pronoun used as the subject of the sentence agrees in number with the verb:

singular pronoun, singular verb
I take good care of my daughter.

singular pronoun, singular verb
You sing like a professional entertainer.

singular pronoun, singular verb
She argues with conviction and courage.

plural pronoun, plural verb
We want a better deal on the apartment.

plural pronoun, plural verb
They accept my decision about moving.

| **Exercise 1** | Connect: Editing a Paragraph for Simple Errors in Subject–Verb Agreement |

Connect

There are seven errors in subject–verb agreement in the following paragraph. If the verb does not agree with the subject, cross out the incorrect verb form and write the correct one above it.

A few children likes to get up when their parents wake them, but most

children, including mine, resist and stalls as long as they can. My older son, for

example, believe that my words about waking up signals a warning, but not a final

statement. He requires two or three more "warnings" before he slides out of bed.

My younger boy simply ignores my wake-up calls. He seem to have the power to

incorporate my words into a dream and to keep on dozing. Naturally, school days

at my house often deteriorates into a series of frustrations and confrontations. Of

course, I keeps my own secret from my boys: I love to sleep late, and I want their

few extra minutes in bed.

SPECIAL PROBLEMS WITH AGREEMENT

Agreement seems fairly simple, doesn't it? If a subject is singular, use a singular verb form; if a subject is plural, use a plural verb form. However, certain problems with agreement will come up in your writing. Sometimes it is difficult to find the subject of a sentence; at other times, it can be difficult to determine if a subject is singular or plural.

2 Use a variety of methods to check for subject–verb agreement.

Identifying Count and Noncount Nouns

When you are identifying the subject, you must first determine if it is a singular or plural subject. Nouns are either **count** or **noncount**. Count nouns can be singular or plural. Noncount nouns in English are always singular; they are not countable. Here are examples of count and noncount nouns:

count	**noncount**
joke	humor
movie	entertainment
dress	inspiration
automobile	transportation

One way to remember the difference between count and noncount nouns is to put the word *much* in front of the noun. For example, if you can say *much entertainment*, then *entertainment* is a noncount noun.

Exercise 2   **Practice: Identifying Count and Noncount Nouns**

Put **count** or **noncount** next to each word below.

1. _____ grandchild   5. _____ money

2. _____ gas   6. _____ sympathy

3. _____ support   7. _____ electricity

4. _____ coin   8. _____ animal

Using Articles with Nouns

Articles point out nouns. Articles are either **indefinite** (*a, an*) or **definite** (*the*). There are several rules for using these articles.

   a. Use *a* in front of consonant sounds; use *an* before vowel sounds.

a filter	an orphan
a room	an apple
a bench	an event
a thought	an issue
a necklace	an umbrella

   b. Use *a* or *an* in front of singular count nouns. *A* or *an* means *any one.*

     I saw *an* owl.

     She rode *a* horse.

   c. Do not use *a* or *an* with noncount nouns.
     not this: I need a~~a~~ money.
     but this: I need money.

     not this: Selena is passing ~~an~~ arithmetic.
     but this: Selena is passing arithmetic.

   d. Use *the* before both singular and plural count nouns whose specific identity is known to the reader.

     The dress with the sequins on it is my party dress.

     Most of *the* movies I rent are science fiction films.

   e. Use *the* before noncount nouns only when they are specifically identified.

     not this: He wants ~~the~~ sympathy. (Whose sympathy? What sympathy? The noncount noun *sympathy* is not specifically identified.)
     but this: I need *the sympathy* of a good friend. (Now *sympathy* is specifically identified.)

     not this: ~~Generosity~~ of the family who paid for my education was remarkable. (The noncount noun *generosity* is specifically identified, so you need *the*.)
     but this: *The generosity* of the family who paid for my education was remarkable.

| Exercise 3 | **Practice: Using _a_ or _an_**

Put _a_ or _an_ in the spaces where it is needed. Some sentences are correct as they are.

1. Once she started her new job, Elisa was filled with _____ enthusiasm.

2. Tommy offered me _____ cup of green tea.

3. On summer nights, _____ soft breeze cooled the back yard.

4. The neglected child was desperate for _____ affection.

5. There was nothing in the refrigerator except _____ apple and _____ box of stale crackers.

6. After listening to my girlfriend's obvious lies, I lost _____ control.

7. Mr. Stein has _____ allergy to _____ dust, so he avoids dusty rooms and objects.

8. _____ sense of _____ humor can break the tension at _____ interview.

| Exercise 4 | **Practice: Using _the_**

Put _the_ in the spaces where it is needed. Some sentences are correct as they are.

1. When Kevin gets a little older, he will have _____ physical strength of his father.

2. My mother never let me play near _____ canal behind my house.

3. Hank has _____ ability to meet a customer once and remember _____ person's name forever.

4. _____ city commission of _____ Forest Park met to discuss _____ possibility of building more low-cost housing.

5. _____ movies I prefer focus on _____ action rather than on _____ romance.

6. My father was _____ first person in his family to make _____ money in _____ real estate business.

7. With _____ help from his father, Matthew converted an old barn into an attractive house.

8. Sometimes Callie behaves foolishly because she wants _____ attention.

| Exercise 5 | **Connect: Correcting a Paragraph with Errors in Articles**

Connect

Correct the eleven errors with _a_, _an_, or _the_ in the following paragraph. You may need to add, change, or eliminate articles. Write the corrections in the space above the errors.

The traveling can be a frustrating experience. Last week, I spent four

hours at airport, waiting for plane that would take me to Atlanta. The person at

the check-in counter did not announce an delay until one hour after the plane was supposed to take off. One hour later, we finally boarded the plane, only

to sit for another two hours. During those two hours, the air conditioning was

turned off, and no one offered me the drink or the snack. Pilot kept coming on

the loudspeaker to say he had a news of bad weather ahead and had to wait.

Sitting in the tiny seat, sweltering in the heat, I felt the anger and an impatience.

I experienced bad side of travel.

Finding the Subject

When you are checking for subject–verb agreement, you can find the true
subject of the sentence by first eliminating the prepositional phrases. To find
the subject, put parentheses around the prepositional phrases. Then it will
be easy to determine the subject because nothing in a prepositional phrase
can be the subject of a sentence.

prepositional phrases in parentheses:

    S   V
A *person* (with good math skills) *is* a good candidate (for the job).

  S   V
One (of the children) (from the village) (in the hills) *is* my cousin.

      S   V
The *restaurant* (down the road) (from Cindy's house) *is* open all
night.

  S   V
Roy, (with his charm and style), *is* popular (with the ladies).

Exercise 6   **Practice: Finding the Subject and Verb by Recognizing Prepositional Phrases**

Put parentheses around all the prepositional phrases in the following sentences, and identify the subject and verb by writing an *S* or a *V* above them.

1. During my drive to North Dakota, I saw very little sunshine between the ominous gray clouds.

2. Cathy strolled through the garden with a watering can in her hand.

3. Before the end of winter, I sometimes wore a bright t-shirt under my heavy sweater and coat in an attempt at bringing some brightness into the day.

4. The happiest day of my life came at the end of my father's military duty in a dangerous part of the Middle East.

5. A box of castoff clothes and shoes turned into fabulous costumes for two little girls with lively imaginations and a love of playing roles.

6. The most interesting classes at college are ones that require participation from all the students.

7. Someone with an extensive knowledge of genealogy spoke at the local library last week.

8. From her first appearance in our tenth-grade classroom to her warm good-bye at graduation, Mrs. Klein was the most generous and caring mentor among many caring coaches and teachers.

Exercise 7   **Practice: Selecting the Correct Verb Form by Identifying Prepositional Phrases**

In the following sentences, put parentheses around all of the prepositional phrases; then circle the verb that agrees with the subject.

1. A representative of the insurance company (was / were) explaining the change in benefits to a group of employees during a staff meeting.

2. The miners' survival at the bottom of a deep, dark pit (is / are) almost unbelievable in a time of natural and man-made disasters, from earthquakes to oil spills.

3. Frowning at me from the other side of the room (was / were) my mother, with the look of someone in an extremely bad mood.

4. In the early morning hours, Bill's good intentions about cramming for his exams (do / does) not keep him alert or even awake.

5. The sight of red ants on the picnic table and in the cake and salads (was / were), without a doubt, a horror beyond my worst fears.

6. A cup of coffee from the vending machine at the site of our evening classes (make / makes) a person think about dish water.

7. Between the closing of the tile factory on Saturday afternoon and its opening on Monday morning, one of the back doors (was / were) pried open.

8. One of the most irritating sounds (is / are) the tapping on a desk when I am taking a test.

Changed Word Order

You are probably used to looking for the subject of a sentence in front of the verb, but not all sentences follow this pattern. Questions, sentences beginning with words like *here* or *there*, and other sentences change the word order. Therefore, you have to look carefully to check for subject–verb agreement.

sentences with changed word order:

      V   S
Where *are* the *packages*?

      V   S   V
When *is Mr. Hernandez giving* the exam?

              V   S
Behind the trees *is* a picnic *table*.

      V   S
There *are crumbs* on the floor.

      V   S
There *is* an *answer* to your question.

Exercise 8 Practice: Making Subjects and Verbs Agree in Sentences with Changed Word Order

In each of the following sentences, underline the subject; then circle the correct verb form.

1. Here (comes / come) my favorite niece and nephew in their new car.

2. There (is / are) freedom and optimism in my soul when I begin my summer vacation.

3. When (do / does) the new student center open?

4. Among the most cherished items in my closet (was / were) my first baseball glove.

5. Here (was / were) an unopened pack of playing cards from my grandfather's gambling days.

6. There (is / are) several reasons for Emilio's loss of interest in joining the U.S. Air Force.

7. At the top of my list of favorite items (is / are) my mountain bike.

8. Below Tyler Hill (stands / stand) a small monument with the names of local heroes of World War I.

Exercise 9   **Collaborate: Writing Sentences with Subject–Verb Agreement in Changed Word Order**

Collaborate

Do this exercise with a partner or group. Complete the following, making each into a sentence. Be sure the subject and verb agree. The first one is done for you.

   1. From the back of the room came _three loud cheers._____

   2. Behind the castle wall lurks _____

   3. Here are _____

   4. Under the pile of old newspapers was _____

   5. With a popular social network comes _____

   6. After the scream, there was _____

   7. Into the glass skylight crashes _____

   8. At the top of the mountain are _____

Compound Subjects

A **compound subject** is two or more subjects joined by *and, or,* or *nor.*
When subjects are joined by *and,* they are usually plural.

compound subjects joined by *and*:

  S   S   V
Bill and *Chris are* good tennis players.

        S   S   V
The *classroom* and the *hallway* are flooded.

      S   S   V
A *restaurant* and a *motel are* across the road.

Caution: Be sure to check for a compound subject when the word order changes.

---

compound subjects in changed word order:

      V   S   S
There *are* a *restaurant* and a *motel* across the road. (Two things, a restaurant and a motel, are across the road.)

     V   S   S
Here *are* your *notebook* and *pencil.* (Your notebook and pencil, two things, are here.)

When subjects are joined by *or, either . . . or, neither . . . nor, not only . . . but also,* the verb form agrees with the subject closest to the verb.

compound subjects with *or, either . . . or, neither . . . nor, not only . . . but also:*

singular S   plural S,   plural V
Christine or the *neighbors are* making dinner.

      plural S   singular S,   singular V
The *neighbors* or *Christine is* making dinner.

          singular S   plural S,   plural V
Not only my *mother* but also my *brothers were* delighted with the gift.

plural S   **singular S, singular V**

Not only my *brothers* but also my *mother was* delighted with the gift.

plural S   **singular S, singular V**

Either the *tenants* or the *landlord has* to back down.

singular S   **plural S, plural V**

Either the *landlord* or the *tenants have* to back down.

plural S   **singular S, singular V**

Neither the rose *bushes* nor the lemon *tree fits* in that corner of the yard.

singular S   **plural S, plural V**

Neither the lemon *tree* nor the rose *bushes fit* in that corner of the yard.

Exercise 10   **Practice: Making Subjects and Verbs Agree: Compound Subjects**

Circle the correct form of the verb in each of the following sentences.

1. While the physician examined the accident victim, his mother and sister (was / were) panicking in the emergency waiting room.

2. Either anger at losing my job or money problems (has / have) caused me to clench my jaw until it hurts.

3. There (is / are) a quick, risky way and a longer, safer way to fix a broken windshield.

4. Neither my sisters nor my mother (is / are) interested in cosmetic surgery.

5. In the kitchen drawer (is / are) an extra set of house keys and a small flashlight.

6. The tutor or teaching assistant usually (help / helps) me with my assignments.

7. Not only your shoes but also your coat (is / are) splashed with mud.

8. Here (is / are) a warm wool hat and a thick scarf for your long walk in the snow.

Exercise 11   **Practice: Recognizing Subjects and Verbs: A Review**

Being sure that subjects and verbs agree often depends on recognizing subjects and verbs in sentences with changed word order, prepositional phrases, and compound subjects. To review the subject–verb patterns of sentences, underline all the subjects and verbs in the following selection. Put an *S* above the subjects and a *V* above the verbs.

The following excerpt is from "Miami's Most Dangerous Profession" by Edna Buchanan, a former prize-winning journalist for the *Miami Herald* and now a famous crime novelist.

Miami's most dangerous profession is not police work or fire fighting; it

is driving a cab. For taxi drivers, many of them poor immigrants, murder is an

occupational hazard. All-night gas station attendants and convenience store clerks used to be at high risk, but steps were taken to protect them. All gas pumps now

switch to self-serve after dark, with exact change only, and the attendants

are locked in bullet-proof booths. Convenience stores were redesigned, and

drop safes were installed, leaving little cash available.

But the life of a taxi driver is just as risky as it was twenty years ago when I

covered my first killing of a cabbie.

Bullet-proof glass could be placed between the driver and passengers, but

most owners say it <u>is</u> too expensive, and besides, there is no foolproof way to pro-

tect oneself totally from somebody riding in the same car.

Indefinite Pronouns

Certain **indefinite pronouns**, such as *someone* and *anyone*, always take a
singular verb. Study the following list of common singular indefinite pronouns:

<table>
<tr><td colspan="5">**INFO BOX** Common Indefinite Pronouns: Singular</td></tr>
<tr><td>one</td><td>everyone</td><td>somebody</td><td>anything</td><td>each</td></tr>
<tr><td>anyone</td><td>nobody</td><td>everybody</td><td>something</td><td>either</td></tr>
<tr><td>someone</td><td>anybody</td><td>nothing</td><td>everything</td><td>neither</td></tr>
</table>

If you want to write clearly and correctly, you must memorize these words
and remember that they always use singular verbs. Using common sense isn't
enough because some of these words seem plural; for example, *everybody*
seems to mean more than one person, but in grammatically correct English,
it takes a singular verb. Here are some examples of the pronouns used with
singular verbs:

indefinite pronouns and singular verbs:

singular S   singular V
Each of my friends *is* athletic.

singular S   singular V
Everyone in the supermarket *is looking* for a bargain.

singular S   singular V
Anybody from our Spanish class *is* capable of translating the letter.

singular S   singular V
Someone from the maintenance department *is working* on the heater.

singular S   singular V
One of Roberta's nieces *is* in my sister's ballet class.

singular S   singular V
Neither of the cakes *is* expensive.

You can memorize the indefinite pronouns as the *-one*, *-thing*, and *-body*
words—*everyone, everything, everybody,* and so on—plus *each, either,*
and *neither.*

Exercise 12   **Practice: Making Subjects and Verbs Agree: Using Indefinite Pronouns**

Circle the correct verb in the following sentences.

1. Here (is / are) everyone in our study group.

2. Nobody in high heels (enjoys / enjoy) standing in line for thirty-five minutes.

3. Everybody from the two neighboring towns (knows / know) about the old rivalry between the two high schools.

4. (Has / Have) anyone from my study group called?

5. Last night at the movies, somebody in one of the back rows (was / were) throwing popcorn at me.

6. Take some time to see the Lincoln Memorial; nothing in the thousands of photographs and film clips (do / does) justice to its magnificence.

7. Unfortunately, neither of my sons (has / have) an interest in joining the family business.

8. Each of my electronic devices (needs / need) a software update.

Exercise 13   **Practice: Another Exercise on Making Subjects and Verbs Agree: Using Indefinite Pronouns**

Circle the correct verb in the following sentences.

1. Sal and Todd are both trustworthy and discreet; either (makes / make) a good listener when you are in trouble.

2. Anyone from our old graduating class still (remembers / remember) Mrs. Marciano, the sweetest lady in the cafeteria.

3. Each of the sequined t-shirts (costs / cost) more than my weekly paycheck.

4. Fortunately, neither of my sisters (has / have) inherited my mother's restless spirit.

5. Be sure to read the entire contract; nothing in all those pages (covers / cover) electrical problems.

6. Somebody from the airlines (was / were) explaining the flight delays.

7. (Has / Have) anyone in the office made coffee yet?

8. Everyone from my study group (has / have) problems with algebra.

Connect

Exercise 14   **Connect: Editing for Subject–Verb Agreement in a Paragraph with Indefinite Pronouns**

The following paragraph has six errors in the agreement of indefinite pronouns and verbs. Correct the errors in the spaces above the lines.

Many people would suspect that something are wrong with a small house

containing one woman and five cats. However, the stereotype of a weird, witchlike old lady and her mysterious animals does not fit this situation. The woman is Tamika, my sister, and she is a veterinarian with a big heart. Because she is a veterinarian, everybody in her neighborhood are eager to get her advice on animals. In addition, someone are always likely to bring her a stray kitten or a pregnant mother cat. Nothing touch my sister's emotions like a cat in trouble. Most of the time, she brings these homeless pets to her workplace: a no-kill animal shelter. There they receive care and a good chance at adoption. At times she is so touched by a kitten's helplessness or a mother cat's bravery that everything in her heart tell her to invite the newcomer into her home. Neither my parents' advice nor her own common sense keep her from nurturing her five cats. They are the most damaged or the least likely to be adopted, but in my sister's house, they are loved.

Collective Nouns

Collective nouns refer to more than one person or thing.

INFO BOX **Common Collective Nouns**

team	audience	family	government
class	company	jury	group
committee	corporation	council	crowd

Collective nouns usually take a singular verb.

collective nouns and singular verbs:

singular S, singular V
The *class is meeting* in the library today.

singular S, singular V
The *audience was* bored.

singular S, singular V
The *jury is examining* the evidence.

A singular verb is used because the group is meeting, or feeling bored, or examining, *as one unit*.

Collective nouns take a plural verb *only* when the members of the group are acting individually, not as a unit.

collective noun with a plural verb:

plural S, plural V
The football *team are arguing* among themselves. (The phrase *among themselves* shows that the team is not acting as one unit.)

Exercise 15   Practice: Making Subjects and Verbs Agree: Using
Collective Nouns

Circle the correct verb in each of the following sentences.

1. The Saddle Club (wants / want) all the members to support the local horse rescue organization.

2. West Valley's student council (has / have) suggested constructing a safety fence around the parking lot.

3. Morrison Tee Shirts Company (designs / design) commemorative tees for birthdays, festivals, and local softball teams.

4. After the plans are approved, a group of volunteers (intends / intend) to begin building a new women's shelter.

5. The tourists from China (was / were) scheduled to visit Disney World in two days.

6. The jury (is / are) quarrelling among themselves; a swift verdict is unlikely.

7. Two generations of millionaire investors recently announced that, because of distrust within the family, several members (was / were) dividing the family assets.

8. After the comedian returned for the second curtain call, the audience (was / were) more appreciative than ever.

MAKING SUBJECTS AND VERBS AGREE: A REVIEW

As you have probably realized, making subjects and verbs agree is not as simple as it first appears. But if you can remember the basic ideas in this section, you will be able to apply them automatically as you edit your own writing. Following is a quick summary of subject–verb agreement.

INFO BOX   Making Subjects and Verbs Agree: A Summary

1. Subjects and verbs should agree in number: singular subjects get singular verbs; plural subjects get plural verbs.

2. When pronouns are used as subjects, they must agree in number with verbs.

3. Nothing in a prepositional phrase can be the subject of a sentence.

4. Questions, sentences beginning with *here* or *there*, and other sentences can change word order.

5. Compound subjects joined by *and* are usually plural.

6. When subjects are joined by *or*, *either . . . or*, *neither . . . nor*, and *not only . . . but also*, the verb form agrees with the subject closest to the verb.

7. Certain indefinite pronouns always take singular verbs.

8. Collective nouns usually take singular verbs.

Exercise 16   **Practice: A Comprehensive Exercise on Subject–Verb Agreement**

This exercise covers all the rules on subject–verb agreement. Circle the correct verb form in the following sentences.

1. If the restless crowd (is / are) pushing and shoving among themselves, then the security staff will have to act.

2. The computer programming company in San Francisco (is / are) thinking of opening a branch office in San Diego.

3. How (was / were) the sound system and lighting at the auditorium?

4. Sometimes, when a bad day at work leaves me frustrated, a good dinner and my boyfriend's sympathy (soothes / soothe) my nerves.

5. Anybody with a taste for deep-fried seafood (loves / love) my cooking.

6. Behind all Simon's jokes and foolish behavior (is / are) an insecure man with a hunger for acceptance.

7. Each of the students attending the library workshop (has / have) a paper to write for a class.

8. Neither a bad cold nor occasional backaches (keeps / keep) Pete from his daily workout.

Exercise 17   **Practice: Another Comprehensive Exercise on Subject–Verb Agreement**

This exercise covers all the rules on subject–verb agreement. Circle the correct verb form in the following sentences.

1. Occasionally, famous celebrities (wants / want) nothing more than privacy.

2. After spring break, everyone in school (was / were) longing for the semester to end.

3. If you want to send your girlfriend a picture of you, either of the photographs from the picnic (is / are) an excellent choice.

4. Where on earth (is / are) the advising and registration offices?

5. Every week, there (is / are) a classic film and a discussion group at the National Cinema.

6. For years, the United States (has / have) offered free public libraries in each state.

7. At the end of the term, the early childhood education class (gives / give) a party for children at a local daycare center.

8. To me, nothing in Mario's apology (seems / seem) sincere.

Collaborate

Exercise 18   **Collaborate: Writing Sentences with Subject–Verb Agreement: A Comprehensive Exercise**

With a partner or group, write two sentences for each of the following phrases. Use a verb that fits and put it in the present tense. Be sure that the verb agrees with your subject. The first one is done for you.

1. A group of Ecuadoran students _visits my high school once a year in the_ _fall._

    A group of Ecuadoran students _corresponds with a group of high school_ _seniors from Milwaukee._

2. Nothing at the movies _____

    _____

    Nothing at the movies _____

    _____

3. My cell phone provider _____

    _____

    My cell phone provider _____

    _____

4. Anyone with common sense _____

    _____

    Anyone with common sense _____

    _____

5. Each of my classes _____

    _____

    Each of my classes _____

    _____

6. Not only my mother but also the neighbors _____

    _____

    Not only my mother but also the neighbors _____

    _____

7. Everyone on the stairs _____

    _____

    Everyone on the stairs _____

    _____

8. The group by the copy machine _____

    _____

    The group by the copy machine _____

    _____

Exercise 19 **Collaborate: Create Your Own Text on Subject–Verb Agreement**

Collaborate

Work with a partner or group to create your own grammar handbook. Following is a list of rules on subject–verb agreement. Write two sentences that are examples of each rule. Write an *S* above the subject of each sentence and a *V* above the verb. After you've completed this exercise, trade it for another group's exercise. Check that group's examples while it checks yours. The first one is done for you.

Rule 1: Subjects and verbs should agree in number: singular subjects get singular verb forms; plural subjects get plural verb forms.

example 1: An apple is a healthy snack.
[S above "apple", V above "is"]
_____

example 2: Runners need large quantities of water.
[S above "Runners", V above "need"]
_____

Rule 2: When pronouns are used as subjects, they must agree in number with verbs.

example 1: _____

_____

example 2: _____

_____

Rule 3: Nothing in a prepositional phrase can be the subject of a sentence.

example 1: _____

_____

example 2: _____

_____

Rule 4: Questions, sentences beginning with *here* or *there*, and other sentences can change word order.

example 1: _____

_____

example 2: _____

_____

Rule 5: Compound subjects joined by *and* are usually plural.

example 1: _____

_____

example 2: _____

_____

Rule 6: When subjects are joined by *or, either . . . or, neither . . . nor,* or *not only . . . but also,* the verb form agrees with the subject closest to the verb.

example 1: _____

_____

example 2: _____

_____

Rule 7: Indefinite pronouns always take singular verbs.

example 1: _____

_____

example 2: _____

_____

Rule 8: Collective nouns usually take singular verbs.

example 1: _____

_____

example 2: _____

_____

Connect

Exercise 20   **Connect: A Comprehensive Exercise: Editing a Paragraph for Subject–Verb Agreement**

The following paragraph has eight errors in subject–verb agreement. Correct the errors in the spaces above the lines.

The City Cares Club are known for giving time and money to various

projects in the community. Last week, third-grade students at Kennedy

Community School were pleasantly surprised to receive a gift from the club

members. The president and five other people involved in the gift arrived at

the school with boxes of goodies. The goodies, however, was not edible. Brain

food arrived in the boxes. Each of the third graders were startled to receive a

dictionary. The students' teacher quickly focused the students' attention by asking

them to look up the meaning of two words: "dangerous" and "enormous." Within minutes, several students quickly found both words; every student in the class

were excited. One of the excited students were anxious to know if she could bring

her dictionary home. "Of course," said the club's president, "The City Cares Club

want every student to own a book." Neither the teacher nor the students was

able to remember a better surprise. The third-grade class at Kennedy Community

School are likely to remember this day for a long time.

Chapter Test **Making Subjects and Verbs Agree**   MyWritingLab™

Some of the sentences below are correct; others have errors in making subjects and verbs agree. Put *OK* next to the correct sentences and *X* next to
the incorrect ones.

1. _____ Where is the advising and student centers?

2. _____ Each of Eva's elaborate hairstyles take her at least an hour
to create.

3. _____ Two instructors or the academic dean is always present for
student elections.

4. _____ There are a large black snake and a speckled lizard relaxing
on the sunny patio.

5. _____ The celebrity chef, with all his television fame and popular
cookbooks, has never cooked red beans and rice.

6. _____ Every time the temperature falls below freezing, not only
my cat but also my dogs crawls into my bed.

7. _____ Something in the taste and texture of the soup makes me
wonder about the ingredients.

8. _____ Our local government must find a way to limit its spending
until the economy improves.

CHAPTER 14

Using Pronouns Correctly: Agreement and Reference

Learning Objectives

In this chapter, you will learn to:

1 Identify pronouns and antecedents.

2 Use a variety of methods to check for pronoun agreement.

3 Use pronouns with clear antecedents.

---

1 Identify pronouns and antecedents.

Pronouns are words that substitute for nouns. A pronoun's **antecedent** is the word or words it replaces.

pronouns and antecedents:

antecedent   pronoun
George is a wonderful father; *he* is loving and kind.

            antecedent   pronoun
Suzanne wound *the clock* because *it* had stopped ticking.

          antecedent   pronoun
Texting on my smartphone is fun, but *it* takes up too much of my time.

antecedent   pronoun
Joanne and David know what *they* want.

antecedent   pronoun
Christopher lost *his* favorite baseball cap.

antecedent   pronoun
The *horse* stamped *its* feet and neighed loudly.

Exercise 1 **Practice: Identifying the Antecedents of Pronouns**

In each of the following sentences, a pronoun is underlined. Circle the word or words that are the antecedent of the underlined pronoun.

1. Elizabeth and her mother loved to shop together; however, <u>they</u> didn't have the same taste in clothes.

2. My brother hates the work in English class; however, <u>it</u> doesn't bother me.

3. Dancing to loud music energizes Sheila; <u>it</u> allows her to shake off her worries and cares.

4. Fortunately, the travelers were able to find <u>their</u> way to a police station and report the incident.

5. Kelly, will you promise me one thing?

6. Over the weekend my girlfriend and I had a new experience; <u>we</u> spent two days at the auto races.

7. Halloween left <u>its</u> mark in my house in the form of bags of extra candy.

8. The students in the chemistry class let out a collective sigh when the instructor returned their exams, and <u>she</u> smiled slightly.

AGREEMENT OF A PRONOUN AND ITS ANTECEDENT

A pronoun must agree in number with its antecedent. If the antecedent is singular, the pronoun must be singular. If the antecedent is plural, the pronoun must be plural.

singular antecedents, singular pronouns:

singular antecedent   singular pronoun
The *textbook* was quite expensive; *it* was not available used.

singular antecedent   singular pronoun
Maria spends most of *her* salary on rent.

plural antecedents, plural pronouns:

plural antecedent   plural pronoun
Carlos and Ronnie went to Atlanta for a long weekend; *they* had a
   good time.

plural antecedent   plural pronoun
Cigarettes are expensive, and *they* can kill you.

2 Use a variety of methods to check for pronoun agreement.

SPECIAL PROBLEMS WITH AGREEMENT

Agreement of pronoun and antecedent seems fairly simple: If an antecedent is singular, use a singular pronoun; if an antecedent is plural, use a plural pronoun. There are, however, some special problems with agreement of pronouns, and these problems will come up in your writing. If you become familiar with the explanations, examples, and exercises that follow, you'll be ready to handle special problems.

Indefinite Pronouns

Certain indefinite pronouns, such as *anybody* and *somebody*, always take a singular verb. Therefore, if an indefinite pronoun is the antecedent, the pronoun that replaces it must be singular. Here are some common indefinite pronouns:

INFO BOX	**Common Indefinite Pronouns: Singular**			
one	everyone	somebody	anything	each
anyone	nobody	everybody	something	either
someone	anybody	nothing	everything	neither

You may think that *everybody* is plural, but in grammatically correct English, it is a singular word. Therefore, if you want to write clearly and correctly, memorize these words as the *-one*, *-thing*, and *-body* words: *everyone, everything, everybody, anyone, anything,* and so on, plus *each, either,* and *neither.* If any of these words is an antecedent, the pronoun that refers to it is singular.

indefinite pronouns as antecedents:

indefinite pronoun antecedent   singular pronoun
Each of the women skaters did *her* best in the Olympic competition.

indefinite pronoun antecedent   singular pronoun
Everyone nominated for Father of the Year earned *his* nomination.

Avoiding Gender Bias

Consider this sentence:

Everybody in the cooking contest prepared _____ best dish.

How do you choose the correct pronoun to fill this blank? You can write:

Everybody in the cooking contest prepared *his* best dish.

if everybody in the contest is male. Or you can write:

Everybody in the cooking contest prepared *her* best dish.

if everybody in the contest is female. Or you can write:

Everybody in the cooking contest prepared *his or her* best dish.

if the contest has male and female entrants.

In the past, most writers used *his* to refer to both men and women when the antecedent was an indefinite pronoun. Today, many writers try to use *his or her* to avoid gender bias. If you find using *his or her* is getting awkward and repetitive, you can rewrite the sentence and make the antecedent plural.

Correct: *The entrants* in the cooking contest prepared *their* best dishes.

But you cannot shift from singular to plural:

Incorrect: ~~Everybody in the cooking contest prepared their best dish.~~

Exercise 2   **Practice: Making Pronouns and Their Antecedents Agree: Simple Agreement and Indefinite Pronouns**

In each of the following sentences, write the appropriate pronoun in the blank space. Look carefully for the antecedent before you choose the pronoun.

1. After Joshua decided to study for a degree in sports management, _____ felt free of stress.

2. Most of my relatives spend _____ vacations at home, doing home repairs or yard work.

3. A female resident in the dorm found _____ student ID in the laundry room.

4. Has anybody from the men's club lost _____ membership card?

5. My daughters are going to a free concert at the park; _____ will enjoy the music and sunshine.

6. Either of my brothers would have offered me _____ support in these tough times.

7. One of the men on the train dropped _____ tablet on the floor and cracked the screen.

8. A divorced father with children in a distant state and little cash may miss _____ children terribly.

Exercise 3   **Connect: Editing a Paragraph for Errors in Agreement: Indefinite Pronouns**

Connect

The following paragraph contains seven errors in agreement where the antecedents are indefinite pronouns. Correct the errors in the space above the lines.

When one of the classroom buildings at my college lost their power yesterday,

a brief period of excitement, uncertainty, and amusement followed. In my math

class, everyone was sitting quietly, listening to the professor explain some new

material, when the lights went out. At first, nobody expressed their surprise.

Then somebody got out of their chair and walked toward the windows. Suddenly

another person began to talk, and soon a wave of conversation spread through the

room. Our teacher remained calm. He called the maintenance department, but nei-

ther an employee in the central maintenance building nor one in our dark building

was able to say much. By this time, several people in our classroom had tried to open the windows and found them hard to unstick. Meanwhile, everyone began to fan themselves with a lightweight textbook or notebook. Next, somebody left their chair and, in near darkness, headed to the hall. Almost immediately, each student grabbed their belongings and stumbled into the windowless third-floor hallway. That area was lighted only by small emergency exit markers. Fortunately, at the same moment when the entire class was stumbling around the hall, electricity was restored. Nobody had to suffer in the darkness and heat anymore, but everybody had to be seated and return their attention to the mathematics lesson.

Collective Nouns

Here are some collective nouns that refer to more than one person or thing:

> **INFO BOX   Common Collective Nouns**
>
> | team | audience | family | government |
> |---|---|---|---|
> | class | company | jury | group |
> | committee | corporation | council | crowd |

Most of the time, collective nouns take a singular pronoun:

collective nouns and singular pronouns:

collective noun   singular pronoun
The *jury* in the murder trial announced *its* verdict.

       collective noun   singular pronoun
The *company* I work for has been in business a long time; *it* started in Atlanta, Georgia.

Collective nouns are usually singular because the group is announcing a verdict or starting a business as one, as a unit. Collective nouns take a plural *only* when the members of the group are acting individually, not as a unit:

collective noun and a plural pronoun:

collective noun plural pronoun
The *team* signed *their* contracts yesterday. (The members of the team sign contracts individually.)

Connect

Exercise 4   Connect: Making Pronouns and Antecedents Agree: Collective Nouns

Circle the correct pronoun in each of the following sentences.

1. The student government is having (its / their) holiday party early this year.

2. My favorite team began to suffer many losses when the players began to quarrel among (itself / themselves).

3. When the featured singer arrived an hour late, the audience lost (its / their) faith in the show.

4. Several of the pharmaceutical corporations agreed to donate part of (its / their) profits to medical research.

5. Over the years, bad feelings broke the family apart; (it / they) never resolved an old feud and lost touch with one another.

6. Aqua Sports created a cheaper version of (its / their) popular personal watercraft.

7. The Helping Hands Club lost (its / their) president last week.

8. The committee that interviewed me for the job will let me know (its / their) decision next week.

9. The Air Force brings (its / their) best jets to the air show.

10. My son's kindergarten class had (its / their) fundraiser yesterday.

Connect

| Exercise 5 | **Connect: Editing a Paragraph for Errors in Agreement: Collective Nouns** |

The following paragraph contains five errors in agreement where the antecedent is a collective noun. Correct the errors in the spaces above the lines.

Last summer, the Student Conduct Committee of our county's school board made a controversial decision. They decided that mandatory school uniforms would bring harmony and better behavior to the county's schools. Of course, families with school-age children had their own reactions to this plan. A small group quickly expressed their approval. On the other hand, a much larger crowd loudly expressed its disapproval and horror. Meanwhile, hundreds of students marched, spoke, and wrote about the issue. Letters to the editor of the local newspaper blasted the Conduct Committee for forcing students into clothing that would suppress their individuality and stifle their creativity. On the other hand, some writers praised the uniforms as a way to place all students, rich and poor, at the same level. These writers argued that low-income students cannot afford the latest "hot" clothing styles and labels and may endure ridicule or bullying from classmates. By the end of the summer, the Student Conduct Committee had not responded to the complaints. Finally, days before the school term began, the committee issued their final decision. Uniforms became the rule. However, the anti-uniform crowd won on a few of their points. Today, school uniforms are simply dark or khaki pants or shorts for males; dark or khaki pants, shorts, or skirts for females; and a variety of solid-colored polo shirts for everyone. Compromise has not made everyone happy, but the students have adjusted. In addition, each class has their share of students who like being freed from the daily decision of what to wear to school.

Collaborate

Exercise 6 **Collaborate: Writing Sentences with Pronoun–Antecedent Agreement**

With a partner or with a group, write a sentence for each of the following pairs of words, using each pair as a pronoun and its antecedent(s). The first pair is done for you.

1. men . . . their

    sentence: _The men at the dance were wearing their best clothes._

    _____

2. The Language and Literature Department . . . its

    sentence: _____

    _____

3. parrot . . . its

    sentence: _____

    _____

4. anyone . . . his or her

    sentence: _____

    _____

5. Graciela and Brandon . . . their

    sentence: _____

    _____

6. nothing . . . its

    sentence: _____

    _____

7. neither . . . her

    sentence: _____

    _____

8. bragging . . . it

    sentence: _____

    _____

PRONOUNS AND THEIR ANTECEDENTS: BEING CLEAR

3 Use pronouns with clear antecedents.

Remember that pronouns are words that replace or refer to other words, and those other words are called **antecedents**.

Make sure that a pronoun has one clear antecedent. Your writing will be vague and confusing if a pronoun appears to refer to more than one antecedent or if a pronoun doesn't have any specific antecedent to refer to. Such confusing language is called a problem with **pronoun reference**.

When a pronoun refers to more than one thing, the sentence can become confusing or silly.

> **pronouns below refer to more than one thing (unclear antecedent):**
> Carla told Elaine that her car had a flat tire. (Whose car had a flat tire? Carla's? Elaine's?)
> Josh woke to the shrieking alarm clock, buried his head in his pillow, and threw it across the room. (What did Josh throw? The pillow? The clock? His head?)

If there is no one, clear antecedent, you must rewrite the sentence to make the reference clear. Sometimes the rewritten sentence may seem repetitive, but a little repetition is better than a lot of confusion.

> **unclear:** Carla told Elaine that her car had a flat tire.
> **clear:** Carla told Elaine that Carla's car had a flat tire.
> **clear:** Carla told Elaine that Elaine's car had a flat tire.
> **clear:** Carla told Elaine, "Your car has a flat tire."
> **clear:** Carla told Elaine, "My car has a flat tire."

> **unclear:** Josh woke to the shrieking alarm clock, buried his head in his pillow, and threw it across the room.
> **clear:** Josh woke to the shrieking alarm clock, buried his head in his pillow, and threw the clock across the room.

Sometimes the problem is a little more confusing. Can you spot what's wrong with this sentence?

> Linda was able to negotiate for a raise, which pleased her. (What pleased Linda? The raise? Or the fact that she was able to negotiate for it?)

Be very careful with the pronoun *which*. If there is any chance that using *which* will confuse the reader, rewrite the sentence and get rid of *which*.

> **clear:** Linda was pleased that she was able to negotiate for a raise.
> **clear:** Linda was pleased by the raise she negotiated.

Sometimes a pronoun has nothing to refer to; it has no antecedent.

> **pronouns with no antecedent:**
> When Mary took the television to the repair shop, they said the television couldn't be repaired. (Who are *they*? Who said the television couldn't be repaired? The television service personnel? The customers? The repairmen?)
> I have always been interested in designing clothes and have decided that's what I want to be. (What does *that* refer to? The only word it could refer to is *clothes*. You certainly don't want to be clothes. You don't want to be a dress or a suit.)

If a pronoun lacks an antecedent, add an antecedent or eliminate the pronoun.

add an antecedent: When Mary took the television to the repair shop and asked *the service personnel* for an estimate, they said the television couldn't be repaired.

eliminate the pronoun: I have always been interested in designing clothes and have decided I want to be a fashion designer.

To check for clear reference of pronouns, underline any pronouns that may not be clear. Then try to draw a line from that pronoun to its antecedent. Are there two or more possible antecedents? Is there no antecedent? In either case, you will need to rewrite.

Exercise 7 **Practice: Rewriting Sentences for Clear Reference of Pronouns**

Rewrite the following sentences so that the pronouns have clear references. You can add, take out, or change words.

1. Alice rarely has a free weekend, which saddens her.

   rewritten: _____

   _____

2. Charlie warned his classmate that his luck was running out.

   rewritten: _____

   _____

3. They didn't tell me that late registration had ended.

   rewritten: _____

   _____

4. Mark dropped a china candlestick on the glass coffee table, but it didn't break.

   rewritten: _____

   _____

5. Natalie quizzed Deanna, trying to find out what Adam had said about her.

   rewritten: _____

   _____

6. My sister stopped speaking to Stephanie because she has a quick temper.

   rewritten: _____

   _____

7. My parents want me to consider the healthcare field, but I don't want to be one.

   rewritten: _____

   _____

8. Bill returned the expensive new laptop, which infuriated his roommate.

   rewritten: _____

   _____

Collaborate: Revising Sentences with Problems in Pronoun Reference: Two Ways

Collaborate

Do this exercise with a partner or group. Each of the following sentences contains a pronoun with an unclear antecedent. Because the antecedent is unclear, the sentence can have more than one meaning. Rewrite each sentence twice to show the different meanings. The first one is done for you.

1. Mrs. Klein told Mrs. Yamaguchi her dog was digging up the flower beds.

   sentence 1: Mrs. Klein told Mrs. Yamaguchi, "Your dog is digging up the flower beds."

   sentence 2: Mrs. Klein told Mrs. Yamaguchi that Mrs. Klein's dog was digging up the flower beds.

2. Jimmy asked Lewis if he could bring a friend to the party.

   sentence 1: _____

   _____

   sentence 2: _____

   _____

3. Patty ran into her mother at her favorite restaurant.

   sentence 1: _____

   _____

   sentence 2: _____

   _____

4. Leonard took a five-dollar bill out of the envelope and gave it to me.

   sentence 1: _____

   _____

   sentence 2: _____

   _____

5. Once the guests had petted the dogs, they left the room.

   sentence 1: _____

   _____

   sentence 2: _____

   _____

6. Pete soon got a new job, which brightened his mood.

sentence 1: _____

_____

sentence 2: _____

_____

7. Yolanda told Melissa she worried too much about little things.

sentence 1: _____

_____

sentence 2: _____

_____

8. After my two roommates met my science and math instructors, they were more compassionate about my studying.

sentence 1: _____

_____

sentence 2: _____

_____

Connect

Exercise 9 **Connect: Editing a Paragraph for Errors in Agreement and Reference**

The following paragraph contains five errors in pronoun agreement and reference. Correct the errors in the space above the lines.

A pet can be a terrible nagger. Although I love my animals, each of the critters can be a torment at various times. If my dog Chance wants to go outside, for instance, he knows how to tell me. Whenever he looks out the window and sees a squirrel playing in the yard, he whines and paws the glass until I let him outside. Chance is sure that whatever I am doing, even if it is studying for a test or standing on a ladder to change a light bulb, cannot be as important as chasing a squirrel. When Chance sees a squirrel, nothing matter. He has to go out and chase that pesky creature. My cat Ethel is equally impatient when she wants to be fed. Unfortunately, she has decided that she wants to be fed at 3:00 a.m. At that ghastly hour, she sits next to my head on the pillow and repeatedly licks my face with her sandpaper tongue, which makes me crazy. When I finally crawl out of bed and stagger to the kitchen, Puffy, my parrot, wakes up. Puffy resents the early wake-up call and begins to scold me. He squawks until my cat and I have left the room and quiet has returned to the kitchen. Everyone who hears about my pets'

little imperfections has their own opinion about animal behavior and training. But

I know that each of my pets has demonstrated their capacity to learn and grow.

Unfortunately, the group of animals in my house have learned how to train *me*.

Chapter Test **Using Pronouns Correctly: Agreement and Reference** MyWritingLab™

Some of the sentences below are correct; others have errors in pronoun agreement or reference. Put *OK* next to the correct sentences and *X* next to the incorrect ones.

1. _____ Drinking too many soft drinks can be bad for your weight; it can also be bad for your teeth.

2. _____ Each of the Clemons brothers had their own brand of charm.

3. _____ Everything in the Florida Keys lost its appeal for me when I experienced a hurricane in Key West.

4. _____ I took Management I and II, but it wasn't very interesting.

5. _____ My mother and her sister met to discuss her recent failing grade.

6. _____ Last week, the Fantastic Toys Company announced their new line of miniature robots.

7. _____ My four-year-old loves to visit the library because they always have new books and videos.

8. _____ Someone in our neighborhood has posted fliers about his or her missing cat.

CHAPTER 15

Using Pronouns Correctly: Consistency and Case

Quick Question MyWritingLab™

Which sentence(s) is/are correct?

A. You can borrow the notes from Darryl or me.
B. We've worked on that paper for hours, but I still haven't finished it.

(After you study this chapter, you will be confident of your answer.)

Learning Objectives

In this chapter, you will learn to:

① Identify first-, second-, and third-person point of view.
② Choose the correct case of pronouns.

① Identify first-, second-, and third-person point of view.

When you write, you write from a **point of view**, and each point of view gets its own form. If you write from the first person point of view, your pronouns are in the *I* (singular) or *we* (plural) forms. If your pronouns are in the second person point of view, your pronouns are in the *you* form, whether they are singular or plural. If you write from the third person point of view, your pronouns are in the *he*, *she*, or *it* (singular) or *they* (plural) forms.

Different kinds of writing may require different points of view. When you are writing a set of directions, for example, you might use the second person (*you*) point of view. For an essay about your childhood, you might use the first person (*I*) point of view.

Whatever point of view you use, be consistent in using pronouns; do not shift the form of your pronouns without some good reason.

not consistent: The last time *I* went to that movie theater, the only seat *you* could get was in the front row.
consistent: The last time *I* went to that movie theater, the only seat *I* could get was in the front row.

not consistent: By the time the shoppers got into the store, *they* were so jammed into the aisles that *you* couldn't get to the sales tables.
consistent: By the time the shoppers got into the store, *they* were so jammed into the aisles that *they* couldn't get to the sales tables.

Exercise 1   **Practice: Consistency in Pronouns**

Correct any inconsistency in point of view in the following sentences. Cross out the incorrect pronoun and write the correct one above it.

1. Many people in my class like to study in the library because you can reserve a study room.

2. On even the sunniest summer day, I always carry an umbrella to work because you could get caught in a thunderstorm without warning.

3. After I spoke briefly to a salesperson making an unsolicited call, I soon realized that allowing one company to make contact left you open to a flood of sales calls.

4. Freshmen who register for classes late have few choices because you have waited too long, and most classes are filled.

5. Twice a year, I went to a giant sale at the local library; it offered used books, magazines, DVDs, CDs, and videos, and you could get as many as ten items for ten dollars.

6. I'm planning to finish school next summer and then look for a job in the city, but you can't make plans too far ahead of time and then expect them to work out.

7. Children trusted the teacher's aide because you would always get a kind word of encouragement from her.

8. Whenever Charlene gives me a compliment, you know she wants something from me.

Collaborate

| Exercise 2 | **Collaborate: Rewriting Sentences with Consistency Problems**

Do this exercise with a partner or group. Rewrite the following sentences, correcting any errors in pronoun consistency. To make the corrections, you may need to change, add, or eliminate words.

1. I don't see why I should give Ella another chance; after she makes new promises, she always hurts you again.

   rewritten: _____

   _____

   _____

2. Once the instructor has explained the assignment, the students work on it, and then you grade it.

   rewritten: _____

   _____

   _____

3. The first time I worked in the kitchen at the pizza place, the pace of the workers was so fast that you could hardly keep up.

   rewritten: _____

   _____

   _____

4. The most rewarding part of my job at the daycare center is seeing the children run to you when they enter the door.

   rewritten: _____

   _____

   _____

5. Customers who want to take advantage of the store's weekly sales and special offers must remember to present your discount cards at the register.

   rewritten: _____

   _____

   _____

6. Samantha isn't going to invite her cousin Rick to her graduation party because he'll just make you want to scream if he keeps following her around with his camera.

   rewritten: _____

   _____

   _____

7. Parents who return to school need support, for you can get lost balancing school, home, and work responsibilities.

    rewritten: _____

    _____

    _____

8. Students parking in the front lot are advised to pay attention to their parking decal because only cars displaying them are allowed to park in that lot.

    rewritten: _____

    _____

    _____

| Exercise 3 | Connect: Editing a Paragraph for Pronoun Consistency |

Connect

The following paragraph has five errors in consistency of pronouns. Correct the errors above the lines.

When I started volunteering at a convalescent and therapeutic center for

veterans, I expected something totally different from the reality I experienced.

I thought that old men would be slouched in wheelchairs and dozing in

hospital beds. I thought that you would rarely see an alert man. I expected to

be depressed. Every one of my expectations was wrong. First of all, you could

see all types of veterans: old, young, male, and female. Many of them were

undergoing grueling physical therapy, and even those in wheelchairs worked

out. The sight of amputees engaged in tough, demanding exercises made me

rethink your image of a wounded warrior. Of course, my first experience of so

many people fighting disability and pain caused me to feel strong emotions.

However, you didn't feel depressed. Instead, admiration and awe led you to a

sense of gratitude for being able to play a minor role at this place for healing

and transformation.

CHOOSING THE CASE OF PRONOUNS

Pronouns have forms that show number and person, and they also have forms that show **case**. Following is a list of three cases of pronouns:

2 Choose the correct case of pronouns.

> **INFO BOX** **Pronouns and Their Case**
>
> **Singular Pronouns**
>
> | | Subjective case | Objective case | Possessive case |
> |---|---|---|---|
> | First person | I | me | my |
> | Second person | you | you | your |
> | Third person | he, she, it | him, her, it | his, her, its |
>
> **Plural Pronouns**
>
> | | Subjective case | Objective case | Possessive case |
> |---|---|---|---|
> | First person | we | us | our |
> | Second person | you | you | your |
> | Third person | they | them | their |

Rules for Choosing the Case of Pronouns

The rules for choosing the case of pronouns are simple:

1. When a pronoun is used as a subject, use the subjective case.
2. When a pronoun is used as the object of a verb or the object of a preposition, use the objective case.
3. When a pronoun is used to show possession, use the possessive case.

Here are some examples of the correct use of pronouns:

pronouns used as subjects:
She calls the office once a week.
Sylvia wrote the letter, and *we* revised it.
When Guy called, *I* was thrilled.

pronouns used as objects:
The loud noise frightened *me*.
The card was addressed to *him*.
Sadie's favorite book always traveled with *her*.

pronouns used to show possession:
The criticism hurt *her* feelings.
Our car is nearly new.
The restaurant changed *its* menu.

Exercise 4   **Practice: Choosing the Correct Pronoun Case: Simple Situations**

Circle the correct pronoun in each of the following sentences.

1. After years of struggle, my mother earned what (she / her) had wanted for years: her citizenship in the United States of America.

2. Dave can text me tomorrow; (he / him) has my number.

3. Three hikers from our town got lost in the mountains; (they / them / their) survived on one bottle of water and three granola bars until searchers in a plane saw (they / them / their) three days later.

4. Don't forget to bring (you / your) laptop to class tomorrow.

5. After my mother put (I / me / my) in bed for the night, (I / me / my) went to sleep within minutes.

6. Uncle Eddie is an artist; (he / him / his) paintings are in galleries throughout the country.

7. Kathleen and Andy took (they / them / their) dog to the veterinarian yesterday.

8. Mohammed told (he / him / his) instructor that (he / him / his) would not be able to attend class on Friday.

PROBLEMS CHOOSING PRONOUN CASE

Choosing the Correct Pronoun Case in a Related Group of Words

You need to be careful in choosing pronoun case when the pronoun is part of a related group of words. If the pronoun is part of a related group of words, isolate the pronoun. Next, try out the pronoun choices. Then decide which pronoun is correct and write the correct sentence. For example, which of these sentences is correct?

Diane had a big surprise for Jack and *I*.

or

Diane had a big surprise for Jack and *me*.

To choose the correct sentence, follow these steps:

Step 1: Isolate the pronoun. Eliminate the related words *Jack and*.

Step 2: Try each case.

Diane had a big surprise for *I*.

or

Diane had a big surprise for *me*.

Step 3: Decide which pronoun is correct and write the correct sentence.

correct sentence: Diane had a big surprise for Jack and *me*.

The pronoun acts as an object, so it takes the objective case.

To be sure that you understand the principle, try working through the steps once more. Which of the following sentences is correct?

Next week, my sister and *me* will start classes at Bryant Community College.

or

Next week, my sister and *I* will start classes at Bryant Community College.

Step 1: Isolate the pronoun. Eliminate the related words *my sister and*.

Step 2: Try each case.

Next week, *me* will start classes at Bryant Community College.
Next week, *I* will start classes at Bryant Community College.

Step 3: Decide which pronoun is correct and write the correct sentence.

correct sentence: Next week, my sister and *I* will start classes at Bryant Community College.

Common Errors with Pronoun Case

In choosing the case of pronouns, be careful to avoid these common errors:

1. *Between* is a preposition. The pronouns that follow it are objects of the preposition: between *us*, between *them*, between *you and me*. It is never correct to write between *you and I*.

   examples:
   not this: The instructor told me, "Your grades are confidential between you and ~~I~~."
   but this: The instructor told me, "Your grades are confidential between you and me."

2. Never use *myself* as a replacement for *I* or *me*.

   examples:
   not this: My family and ~~myself~~ are grateful for your expressions of sympathy.
   but this: My family and I are grateful for your expressions of sympathy.

   not this: The scholarship committee selected Nadine and ~~myself~~.
   but this: The scholarship committee selected Nadine and me.

3. The possessive pronoun *its* has no apostrophe.

   examples:
   not this: The stale coffee lost ~~it's~~ flavor.
   but this: The stale coffee lost its flavor.

Exercise 5 **Practice: Choosing the Correct Pronoun Case: Problems with Pronoun Case**

Circle the correct pronoun in each of the following sentences.

1. Carlos was pleased with the gift from Kate and (me / myself).

2. Rebecca used to have beautiful skin, but too much sunbathing has had (it's / its) effect on her complexion.

3. I told Henry that he could go to town with Tom and (I / me).

4. After Mike finished studying with Thomas and Wen, he drove (they / them) to their dorms.

5. Blinded by sunlight beating against the windshield, Mr. Abbot and (she / her) could not see the fallen tree in the road.

6. On behalf of (me / myself) and Mrs. Kline, I want to thank you for your outstanding work in customer service.

7. One of my neighbors smiles at Sandra and (I / me) whenever we pass him in the street, but I've forgotten his name.

8. My parents and (we / us) have been thinking about renting a cabin in one of the national parks.

Exercise 6   **Practice: More on Choosing the Correct Pronoun Case: Problems with Pronoun Case**

Circle the correct pronoun in each of the following sentences.

1. Did you think that the anniversary party was to be a secret between you and (I / me)?

2. My brother and (I / myself) have hired an accountant to look into the files at the office.

3. I used to enjoy tracking friends on social networking sites, but it has lost (it's / its) appeal.

4. My mother warned me to stay out of the quarrel between my sister and brother or I would end up hurting (me / myself).

5. Without the unpaid labor of Tony and (I / me), my brother's basement would never have been renovated.

6. By midnight, (she / her) and Sal had studied every assigned chapter in their speech communications textbook.

7. Joe's decision to change majors from computer science to culinary arts was a surprise for his advisor and (I / me).

8. At the end of the month, Leon and (he / him) needed to make a decision about renewing their lease.

Exercise 7   **Collaborate: Write Your Own Text on Pronoun Case**

Collaborate

With a partner or group, write two sentences that could be used as examples for each of the following rules. The first one is done for you.

Rule 1: When a pronoun is used as a subject, use the subjective case.

example 1: _They study for tests in the math lab._

example 2: _Caught in the rain, she ran for cover._

Rule 2:   When a pronoun is used as the object of a verb or the object of a preposition, use the objective case. (For examples, write one sentence in which the pronoun is the object of a verb and one in which the pronoun is the object of a preposition.)

example 1: _____

example 2: _____

Rule 3:   When a pronoun is used to show ownership, use the possessive case.

example 1: _____

example 2: _____

Rule 4:   When a pronoun is part of a related group of words, isolate the pronoun to choose the case. (For examples, write two sentences in which the pronoun is part of a related group of words.)

example 1: _____

example 2: _____

Connect

Exercise 8 **Connect: Editing a Paragraph for Pronoun Consistency and Correct Pronoun Case**

The following paragraph has six errors in pronoun consistency and case. Correct the errors above the lines.

I love to go to the movies, but I am disgusted by the condition of the movie theaters. Even before you find a seat, the sticky floors make me wonder what I've just stepped on or into. The mess could be gum, melted candy, or half-dried cola. The noise of a crackle or an oozy texture under your shoe as I make my way down the aisle does not welcome me into the room. The fact that the room is dark makes the search for a seat even more unpleasant. In a theater with stadium seating, you face the possibility of sliding on a slick substance and falling down the stairs. After I find a seat, two more problems confront me. One is more trash. Last week, me and my girlfriend climbed into two seats in the middle of a row and had to fight our way around half-empty boxes of popcorn, huge paper cups, and crumpled paper plates. When we finally got to the center seats, they were covered in another sticky substance. My girlfriend and myself felt as if we were sitting on garbage in a trash heap. On another occasion, I found another problem: broken seats. I sat back, expecting to relax in a rocking-chair seat, but I relaxed a little too far. The seat had no spring attached, and I slid into an endless slope. Feeling like a fool and hoping no one had noticed me, I scrambled to another seat. It, too, was damaged. This time, the armrest fell off the chair. I know that movie theaters get a large, continuous stream of patrons. I also know that the ushers and cleaners work hard and fast between showings so that the theaters will be fresh. But between you and I, I must confess that, after my recent experiences, renting DVDs is looking better than movie-going.

Chapter Test **Using Pronouns Correctly: Consistency and Case**   ·MyWritingLab™

Some of the sentences below are correct; others have errors in pronoun consistency or case. Write *OK* next to the correct sentences and *X* next to the incorrect ones.

1. _____ Vincent likes to go to the city, where you never know what can happen.

2. _____ A string of arguments over silly misunderstandings caused my boyfriend and I to separate for a few months.

3. _____ Working all night has had its effect on Daniella.

4. _____ Sometimes when I try to reason with my father, I feel that you can't change the mind of someone living in the past.

5. _____ When Cara and I were in our teens, we kept a terrible secret between me and her.

6. _____ The teacher reminded us to bring your textbook to class for every class meeting or we would miss some important lessons.

7. _____ My partner and myself are astonished at winning the award for best design.

8. _____ I and my study group worked for four hours in the library last night.

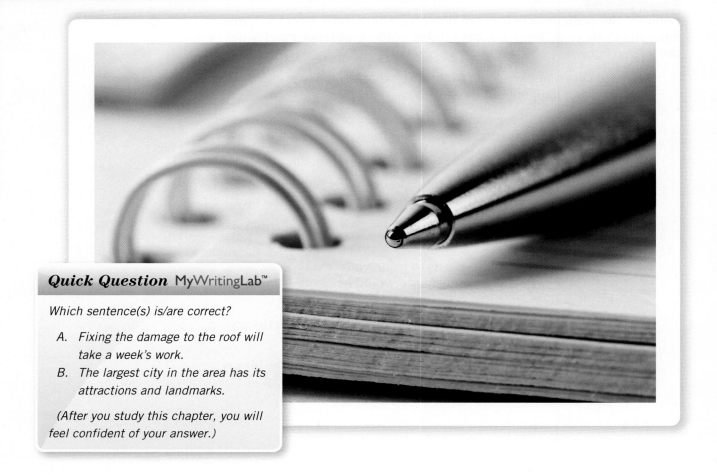

CHAPTER 16 Punctuation

Quick Question MyWritingLab™

Which sentence(s) is/are correct?

A. *Fixing the damage to the roof will take a week's work.*
B. *The largest city in the area has its attractions and landmarks.*

(After you study this chapter, you will feel confident of your answer.)

Learning Objectives

In this chapter, you will learn to:

1. Use the period and question mark correctly.
2. Use the semicolon correctly.
3. Identify the ways to use a comma correctly.
4. Use the apostrophe and colon correctly.
5. Use the colon, exclamation mark, dash, parentheses, hyphen, and quotation marks correctly.
6. Use capital letters, numbers, and abbreviations correctly.

You probably know much about punctuation already. In fact, you probably know many of the rules so well that you punctuate your writing automatically. However, there are times when every writer wonders, "Do I need a comma here?" or "Should I capitalize this word?" The following review of the basic rules of punctuation can help you answer such questions.

THE PERIOD

Periods are used two ways:

1. Use a period to mark the end of a sentence that makes a statement.

   examples:
   My father gave me an exciting new book.
   After the dance, we went to a coffeehouse for a snack.

2. Use a period after abbreviations.

   examples:
   Mr. Vinh
   Carlos Montoya, Sr.
   11:00 a.m.
   Dr. J. T. Mitchell

THE QUESTION MARK

Use a question mark after a direct question.

examples:
Can we exchange cell numbers?
Wasn't that song beautiful?

If a question is not a direct question, do not use a question mark.

examples:
I wonder if it will rain tonight.
Nadine asked whether we had an exam tomorrow.

Exercise 1   **Practice: Punctuating with Periods and Question Marks**

Add the necessary periods and question marks to the following sentences.

1. Why isn't Cecilia at work today

2. Dr. Michalski was appointed to the Water Management Board

3. The instructor wanted to know if Mario had dropped the class

4. When does the plane from LaGuardia Airport arrive

5. My brother was out until 4:00 am, so I don't think he wants to play

   basketball this morning

6. Carmine and Rosanna wondered whether the little dog on the

   street belonged to anyone

7. Mr Sutton has a BA in African History

8. Patrick questioned the truth of Leon's account of the accident

Collaborate

Exercise 2 **Collaborate: Punctuating with Periods and Question Marks**

Do this exercise with a partner. First, by yourself, write a paragraph that needs periods and question marks, but leave out those punctuation marks. Then exchange paragraphs with your partner, and add the necessary periods and question marks to your partner's paragraph. Finally, you and your partner should check each other's punctuation.

Write a paragraph of at least six sentences, using the topic sentence below.

New students have many questions about college, but their questions are soon answered. _____

_____

_____

_____

_____

_____

2 Use the semicolon correctly.

THE SEMICOLON

There are two ways to use semicolons:

1. Use a semicolon to join two independent clauses.

   examples:
   Aunt Celine can be very generous; she gave me fifty dollars for my birthday.

   The ice storm was horrible; our town endured five days without electricity.

   If the independent clauses are joined by a conjunctive adverb, you still need a semicolon. You will also need a comma after the conjunctive adverb if the conjunctive adverb is more than one syllable long.

   examples:
   We went to the coffeehouse; then we studied all night for the exam.

   Stephen forgot about the exam; therefore, he was not prepared for it.

2. If a list contains commas and the items on it need to be clarified, use a semicolon to separate the items. Note how confusing the following lists would be without the semicolons.

   examples:
   The student government presidents at the conference represented Mill Valley High School, Springfield; Longfellow High School, Riverdale; Kennedy High School, Deer Creek; and Martin Luther King High School, Rocky Hills.

   The members of the musical group were Janet Reese, guitar; Richelle Dennison, drums; Sandy Simon, bass; and Lee Vickers, vocalist.

Exercise 3   **Practice: Punctuating with Semicolons**

Some of the following sentences need semicolons; some do not. Add the necessary semicolons. (You may need to change some commas to semicolons.)

1. Bananas are a great snack they are full of potassium and fiber.

2. If you go to the beach tomorrow, be sure to bring heavy sunscreen, a big towel or blanket, several bottles of water, and a hat.

3. Give me your dictionary I need to find the correct spelling of a word.

4. Riding a bicycle to work or school can help you lose weight and can keep you fit.

5. In the summer, my mother took us to free concerts in the park thus we grew up loving all kinds of music.

6. Yesterday, the Neighborhood Crime Watch Association elected these officers: Pierre Nilon, president, Estelle Moreno, vice president, Stanley Rosen, treasurer, and Alan Chang, secretary.

7. Edward spent all afternoon looking for some paint for the kitchen but couldn't decide on the right shade of blue.

8. The mall is hiring Peter and I applied for security jobs.

Exercise 4   **Connect: Punctuating with Semicolons**

Connect

Add semicolons where they are needed in the following paragraph. You may need to change some commas to semicolons.

When Sean started work at the Rose Inn, he struggled to adapt to the personalities and demands of his bosses. At work, Sean had to answer to four people: Alice Lejeune, the head of reservations, Don Davis, the day manager, Catherine Chinn, the night manager, and John Carney, the chief accountant. As a new member of the reservations staff, Sean had to learn how to deal with the hotel guests in addition, he had to learn what each of his superiors required from him. John Carney, for example, cared about money problems he did not want Sean to make any promises of discounts or refunds to customers. If Sean worked the night shift, Catherine Chinn wanted him to be lively and energetic when guests checked in late at night. The day manager was a calm and tolerant man, consequently, Sean learned to relax around Mr. Davis. On the other hand, Alice Lejeune, the head of reservations, expected the best of her staff. Sean worked extra hard to please Ms. Lejeune as a result, he became a competent and confident staff member. For Sean, dealing with the hotel guests was a challenge dealing with

four bosses was an education.

3 Identify the ways to use a comma correctly.

THE COMMA

There are four main ways to use a comma, and there are other, less important ways. Memorize the four main ways. If you can learn and understand these four rules, you will be more confident and correct in your punctuation. That is, you will use a comma only when you have a reason to do so; you will not be scattering commas in your sentences simply because you think a comma might fit, as many writers do. The four main ways to use a comma are as a *lister*, a *linker*, an *introducer*, or an *inserter* (two commas).

1. **Comma as a lister**
   Commas separate items in a series. These items can be words, phrases, or clauses.

   commas between words in a list:
   Charles was fascinated by Doreen because she was smart, creative, and funny.

   commas between phrases in a list:
   I wanted a house on a quiet street, in a friendly neighborhood, and with a school nearby.

   commas between clauses in a list:
   In a single year my uncle joined the army, he fought in the Gulf War, and he was decorated for valor.

> **Note:** In a list, the comma before *and* is optional, but many writers use it.

Exercise 5 **Practice: Using the Comma as a Lister**

Add commas only where they are appropriate in the following sentences.

1. Living on my own turned out to be stressful scary and difficult, but it was also exciting liberating and fun.

2. When registration opened, Margaret saw her advisor, Jonathan stood in line and Herman logged on at home to register.

3. By the time I was ten, my family had lived in four cities: Miami Orlando Atlanta and Charlotte.

4. Babysitting a toddler working in a preschool and volunteering at a children's hospital are all good training for becoming a parent.

5. Brian always checked the tires changed the oil washed the windshield and changed the filters on his sister's old car.

6. With very little money, Aunt Eva serves large tasty and nutritious meals to her family of six.

7. When my grandmother was young, the only good jobs available to most women were secretary nurse and teacher.

8. Get me some shampoo toothpaste deodorant and cough drops when you go to the drug store.

2. Comma as a linker

A comma and a coordinating conjunction link two independent clauses. The coordinating conjunctions are *for, and, nor, but, or, yet, so.* The comma goes before the coordinating conjunction.

comma before coordinating conjunctions:
Norbert was thrilled by the A in Organic Chemistry, for he had studied really hard all semester.

You can pick up the pizza, and I'll set the table.

Our house had no basement, nor did it have much of an attic.

The movie was long, but it was action-packed.

Diane will fly home for summer vacation, or her parents will visit her.

Mr. Weinstein has lived in the neighborhood for a year, yet no one knows him very well.

The front door was open, so I went right in.

> **Note:** Before you use a comma, be careful that the coordinating conjunction is linking two independent clauses.

no comma: Veronica wrote poetry and painted beautiful portraits.
use a comma: Veronica wrote poetry, and she painted beautiful portraits.

Exercise 6 Practice: Using the Comma as a Linker

Add commas only where they are needed in the following sentences.

1. I really need a haircut but I can't afford one right now.

2. Thomas rarely says much yet he always seems quite intelligent.

3. The new neighbors painted the exterior of their house and they planted some bushes in the front yard.

4. Some of my friends from work get together on Fridays and have dinner at a Caribbean restaurant.

5. My new supervisor rarely gives me instructions nor does he criticize my work.

6. Sam is shy so he sometimes appears arrogant or aloof.

7. Many people have dealt with addiction in their own families or have seen friends cope with substance abuse.

8. We have to call an electrician for we need to check the wiring in the basement.

3. Comma as an introducer

Put a comma after introductory words, phrases, or clauses in a sentence.

comma after an introductory word:
No, I can't afford that car.

comma after an introductory phrase:
In my opinion, that car is a lemon.

comma after an introductory clause:
When I earn an A, I am the happiest student around.

Exercise 7   **Practice: Using the Comma as an Introducer**

Add the necessary commas to the following sentences.

1. With no apology the stranger cut ahead of me in the ticket line.
2. Before you go to bed lock the doors.
3. Fortunately I have never had to borrow money from my family.
4. On the first day of the semester I had a difficult time finding all of my classes.
5. Laughing with pleasure Mitchell recognized some old friends at the surprise party in his honor.
6. On a cold winter day I want to stay in my warm bed forever.
7. When my instructor asks me a question I hesitate before answering him.
8. If someone at the college is advertising for a roommate I might call the number on the advertisement.

4. **Comma as an inserter**
   When words or phrases that are not necessary are inserted into a sentence, put a comma on *both* sides of the inserted material.

   commas around inserted material:
   Her science project, a masterpiece of research, won first prize.

   Selena's problem, I believe, is her fear of failure.

   Julio, stuck by the side of the road, waited for the tow truck.

   Artichokes, a delicious vegetable, are not always available at the local market.

Using commas as inserters requires that you decide what is **essential** to the meaning of the sentence and what is **nonessential**.

> **If you do not need material in a sentence, put commas around the material.**
>
> **If you need material in a sentence, do not put commas around the material.**

For example, consider this sentence:

The woman who was promoted to captain was Jack's wife.

Do you need the words *who was promoted to captain* to understand the meaning of the sentence? To answer this question, write the sentence without the words:

The woman was Jack's wife.

Reading the shorter sentence, you might ask, "What woman?" The words *who was promoted to captain* are essential to the sentence. Therefore, you do not put commas around them.

correct: The woman who was promoted to captain was Jack's wife.

Remember that the proper name of a person, place, or thing is always sufficient to identify it. Therefore, any information that follows a proper name is inserted material; it is not essential and gets commas on both sides.

proper names and inserted material:

Margaret Chen, who lives in my apartment building, won the raffle at Dominion High School.

Suarez Electronics, which just opened in the mall, has great deals on flat-screen televisions.

Inserted material often begins with one of these **relative pronouns:** *who, which, that*. If you have to choose between *which* and *that, which* usually begins inserted material that is not essential:

The movie, which was much too long, was a comedy.

That usually begins inserted material that is essential.

The puppy that I want is a miniature poodle.

Note: Sometimes the material that is needed in a sentence is called an **essential** (or **restrictive**) **phrase** or **clause**; material that is not needed is called **nonessential** (or **nonrestrictive**) **phrase** or **clause**.

Exercise 8   Practice: Using Commas as Inserters (Two Commas)

Add commas only where they are needed in the following sentences.

1. The man who identified the suspect was a witness to the crime.

2. One device I would love to own is a new mini tablet.

3. Catherine gave me a DVD of <u>The Incredibles</u> one of my favorite movies to cheer me up.

4. Anyone who can speak a second language has an advantage in this job market.

5. Snickers bars which I first tasted as a child remain my favorite candy.

6. My brother's apology which came a year too late did not change my mind about his character.

7. Professor Gilman taking pity on the class postponed the test for a week.

8. The woman it appears is trying to make friends in a new town.

Exercise 9   Practice: Punctuating with Commas: The Four Main Ways

Add commas only where they are needed in the following sentences.

1. While the instructor lectured Martin took notes.

2. After we eat dinner we'll have some time to look at the old photograph albums and talk about old times.

3. Karen had candles on her coffee table in the kitchen and near her bathtub.

4. I would love to have a piece of coconut cake but I have to watch my weight.

5. It's my brother's birthday tomorrow so I have to find a funny card for him.

6. Isabel found a denim jacket some leather gloves and a red cap at the thrift shop.

7. Sizzling Seafood which is near my apartment offers weekday specials on shrimp dinners.

8. The noisy student chatted during every class but managed to pass the course.

Exercise 10 Practice: More on Punctuating with Commas: The Four Main Ways

Add commas only where they are needed in the following sentences.

1. Until Neal took me out to dinner I had never tasted sushi.

2. Most of my friends don't like to gossip nor do they enjoy constant complaining.

3. Excuse me can I borrow your notes from Thursday?

4. Sarah didn't know anyone at the party yet she quickly made friends with two engineering students.

5. Penelope Greenberg who started a chain of clothing stores is going to speak to our Introduction to Business class next week.

6. Nelson will of course want to spend the long weekend with his family.

7. The house that I wanted was a fishing cabin near a beautiful lake.

8. The girl who won the spelling bee will receive a $10,000 college scholarship.

Collaborate

Exercise 11 Collaborate: The Four Main Ways to Use Commas: Create Your Own Examples

Do this exercise with a partner or group. Below are the rules for the four main ways to use commas. For each rule, write two sentences that are examples. The first one is done for you.

Rule 1: Use a comma as a lister.

example 1: I have old photos stashed in my attic, in my closet, and in the garage.

example 2: The movie was long, dull, and pointless.

_____

Rule 2: Use a comma as a linker.

example 1: _____

_____

example 2: _____

_____

Rule 3: Use a comma as an introducer.

example 1: _____

_____

example 2: _____

_____

Rule 4: Use a comma as an inserter (two commas).

example 1: _____

_____

example 2: _____

_____

| Exercise 12 | Connect: The Four Main Ways to Use Commas |

Connect

Add commas where they are needed in the following paragraph. Do not add or change any other punctuation; just add commas.

When I have achieved some goal I have a secret way of celebrating. Believe it or not I reward myself by making brownies. Last week for example I passed a really difficult chemistry test that had kept me awake for many nights. I had reviewed for the test joined a study group and even worked with a tutor but I was still uncertain about the test. As soon as I saw my passing score I rushed out and bought the ingredients for a pan of brownies. I spent some happy moments in my kitchen for I loved mixing the gooey batter licking the bowl watching the brownies bake and frosting the moist squares of chocolate heaven. Naturally I had to taste a large portion of the frosting and the warm brownies while I prepared them. The chemistry test which had caused me so much misery seemed a distant memory once I enjoyed my reward.

Other Ways to Use a Comma

Besides the four main ways, there are other ways to use a comma. Reviewing these uses will help you feel more confident as a writer.

1. **Use commas with quotations.** Use a comma to set off direct quotations from the rest of the sentence.

    examples:
    Sylvia warned me, "Don't swim there."
    "I can give you a ride," Alan said.

    Note that the comma that introduces the quotation goes before the quotation marks. But once the quotation has begun, commas (or periods) go inside the quotation marks.

2. **Use commas with dates and addresses.** Put commas between the items in dates and addresses.

   examples:

   August 29, 1981, is the day we were married.

   I had an apartment at 2323 Clover Avenue, Houston, Texas, until I was transferred to California.

   Notice the comma after the year in the date, and the comma after the state in the address. These commas are needed when you write a date or an address within a sentence.

3. **Use commas in numbers.** Use commas in numbers of one thousand or larger.

   examples:

   He owed me $1,307.

   That wall contains 235,991 bricks.

4. **Use commas for clarity.** Use a comma when you need to make something clear.

   examples:

   She waltzed in, in a stunning silk gown.

   Whatever you did, did the trick.

   I don't have to apologize, but I want to, to make things right between us.

   Not long after, the party ended.

Exercise 13   **Practice: Other Ways to Use a Comma**

Add commas where they are needed in the following sentences.

1. When Nathan lived in Topeka Kansas he worked at a furniture warehouse.

2. "Money isn't everything" my grandmother used to say.

3. We lived at 307 Orchard Avenue Jackson Mississippi when my father was in the army.

4. A spokesperson from the police department said "We have no suspects at this time."

5. When you meet her her expensive jewelry will be the first thing you notice.

6. In Chicago Illinois you would pay rent of $2500 a month for this apartment.

7. Shortly after the semester ended my classmates and I got together.

8. Priscilla paid $1279 for her living room furniture, but I got similar furniture on sale for $960.

Exercise 14   **Practice: Punctuating with Commas: A Comprehensive Exercise**

Add commas where they are needed in the following sentences.

1. "Don't walk on the wet floor" my mother warned Joel but he paid no attention.

2. Sergei met Noel on the first day of classes and the two became instant friends.

3. After all we've dealt with plenty of bad luck over the years.

4. Amy who would be sending us a package from 770 Taft Boulevard Tulsa Oklahoma?

5. Todd met Dina's brother he spent time with her best friends he visited her cousins yet he never met her parents.

6. Teenagers who have nothing to do are likely to find dangerous ways to pass the time.

7. My parents got engaged on December 25 1979 but didn't get married until June 15 1981 because they waited until my mother had finished school.

8. The students who failed the test never used the textbook nor did they use the online lab.

Exercise 15   **Collaborate: Punctuating with Commas**

Collaborate

Working alone, write a paragraph that is at least six sentences long. The paragraph should require at least five commas, but leave the commas out. Then give your paragraph to a partner; let your partner add the necessary commas. Meanwhile, you punctuate your partner's paragraph. When you are both finished, check each other's answers.

Write your paragraph in the lines below, using the sentence given to you as the topic sentence.

Of all the places I remember from my childhood, one place stands out.

_____

_____

_____

_____

_____

_____

_____

_____

_____

Exercise 16   **Connect: Punctuating with Commas: A Comprehensive Exercise**

Connect

Add commas where they are needed in the following paragraph. Do not add or change any other punctuation; just add commas.

Everyone seems to be short on cash these days and many people are looking for ways to save a few dollars. My cousin Sam, for instance, found a way to save money while he also made some money. Sam is a coffee lover and his weakness is a fancy coffee drink made with cream, foam, special flavors, and a price tag of five dollars. Because his daily trip to a coffee shop was cutting into his budget Sam reluctantly decided to sacrifice his high-priced coffee. After three bad days without his latte, Sam searched for another solution. He applied for and was offered a part-time job at a coffee shop that serves his favorite beverage. Although Sam already had one part-time job he decided the offer was extremely inviting. His decision was based on some new information about the coffee shop. Employees at the place he learned, are permitted free coffee during their working hours. If Sam works at the shop for two years and drinks one latte each day of his three-day work week, he will save $1560 in coffee expenses. Best of all, Sam says "Not many jobs pay a salary and give free drinks, too!"

4 Use the apostrophe and colon correctly.

THE APOSTROPHE

Use the apostrophe in the following ways:

1. Use an apostrophe in contractions to show that letters have been omitted.

   examples:

do not	=	don't
she will	=	she'll
he would	=	he'd
is not	=	isn't
will not	=	won't

   Use an apostrophe to show that numbers have been omitted, too.
   the winter of 2014 = the winter of '14,

Note: Your instructor may want you to avoid contractions in formal assignments. Be sure to follow his or her instructions.

---

2. Use an apostrophe to show possession. If a word does not end in *s*, show ownership by adding an apostrophe and *s*.

   examples:

the car belongs to Maria	=	Maria's car
the tablet is owned by my cousin	=	my cousin's tablet
the hat belongs to somebody	=	somebody's hat

If two people own something, put the *'s* on the last person's name.

Jack and Joe own a car = Jack and Joe's car

If a word already ends in *s* and you want to show ownership, just add an apostrophe.

examples:

The doll belongs to Dolores	=	Dolores' doll
two girls own a cat	=	the girls' cat
Mr. Ross owns a house	=	Mr. Ross' house

3. Use an apostrophe for special uses of time and to create a plural of numbers mentioned as numbers, letters mentioned as letters, and words that normally do not have plurals.

special use of time: It took a *month's* work.
numbers mentioned as numbers: Add the *7's*.
letters mentioned as letters: Dot your *i's*.
words that normally do not have plurals: Give me some more *thank you's*.

> **Caution:** Be careful with apostrophes. Possessive pronouns like *his, hers, theirs, ours, yours,* and *its* do not take apostrophes.

not this: I was sure the dress was ~~her's~~.
but this: I was sure the dress was hers.

not this: The movie has ~~it's~~ highlights.
but this: The movie has its highlights.

Do not add an apostrophe to a simple plural.

not this: Ice cream at this restaurant only comes in three ~~flavor's~~.
but this: Ice cream at this restaurant only comes in three flavors.

Exercise 17 **Practice: Punctuating with Apostrophes**

Add apostrophes where they are needed in the following sentences.

1. One mans lifelong dream of helping others came true when a mens counseling center opened at the hospital.

2. Wed never interfere in other peoples private quarrels.

3. Its silly to buy an expensive hair product just because its advertising is glamorous.

4. The winter of 98 was so cold that my parents thought about moving to Nevada.

5. Frances friend was having trouble with her CDs.

6. My sisters knew that theyd have a long ride ahead of them before they got to Manny and Franks house.

7. You shouldnt have asked Jessica about her job; thats a subject she doesnt want to discuss.

8. Theres a pile of books on the table; you can take the ones that are yours.

Exercise 18 **Connect: Punctuating with Apostrophes**

Edit the following paragraph by correcting the errors related to apostrophes. You will need to add some apostrophes and eliminate the unnecessary ones.

In a time when everybodys complaining about doctors, I was lucky enough to find a great doctor. Since I am rarely sick, I didnt know any doctor's to call when I got a bad case of bronchitis. I asked all my friends about their doctors, but all I heard were horror stories about long hours spent in the waiting room, days spent trying to get an appointment, and one or two minutes spent with a hurried and distracted doctor. Feeling worse, I turned to my mother. "Go to Dr. Morano," she said. "Dr. Moranos wonderful." Within ten minutes, I had reached the doctors office and made an appointment for the next day. The voice on the phone was warm and kind. Still, I was prepared for an hours wait in a room packed with unhappy patients. Thats not what I got. My time in the waiting room was about thirty minutes, for I had to fill out a form for new patient's. Then I prepared myself to sit alone in an examining room while the doctor tended to two or three other patients stacked up in other rooms. Dr. Morano appeared within ten minutes, and she actually sat down to talk. Id never met a doctor like Dr. Morano, and she left only after she had explored my medical history, checked me carefully, and prescribed some medication for my cough. I realized that its possible to find a kind and human atmosphere inside a doctor's office.

THE COLON

A colon is used at the end of a complete statement. It introduces a list or explanation.

5 Use the colon, exclamation mark, dash, parentheses, hyphen, and quotation marks correctly.

colon introducing a list:
When my father went to the Bahamas, he brought me back some lovely gifts: a straw bag, a shell necklace, and some Bahamian perfume.

colon introducing an explanation:
The salesperson was very helpful: he told us about special discounted items and the free gift-wrap service.

Remember that the colon comes after a complete statement. What comes after the colon explains or describes what came before the colon. Look once more at the two examples, and you'll see the point.

When my father went to the Bahamas, he brought me back some lovely gifts: a straw bag, a shell necklace, and some Bahamian perfume. (The words after the colon, *a straw bag, a shell necklace, and some Bahamian perfume*, describe the lovely gifts.)

The salesperson was very helpful: he told us about special discounted items and the free gift-wrap service. (The words after the colon, *he told us about special discounted items and the free gift-wrap service*, explain what the salesperson did to be helpful.)

Some people use a colon every time they put a list in a sentence, but this is not a good rule to follow. Instead, remember that a colon, even one that introduces a list, must come after a complete statement.

not this: ~~If you are going to the drug store, remember to pick up: toothpaste, dental floss, and mouthwash~~.

but this: If you are going to the drug store, remember to pick up these items: toothpaste, dental floss, and mouthwash.

A colon may also introduce a long quotation.

colon introducing a long quotation:
In a speech to the alumni at Columbia University, Will Rogers joked about what a big university it was and said: "There are 3,200 courses. You spend your first two years in deciding what course to take, the next two years in finding the building that these courses are given in, and the rest of your life in wishing you had taken another course."

Exercise 19   **Practice: Punctuating with Colons**

Add colons where they are needed in the following sentences.

1. After my first day of class at the college, I felt bewildered by the crowds of students, the fast pace of the instructors' lectures, and the long lines at the bookstore.

2. After my first day of class at the college, I felt bewildered by three experiences the crowds of students, the fast pace of the instructors' lectures, and the long lines at the bookstore.

3. My niece's bed is piled with bears teddy bears, bears dressed in bride and groom outfits, bears in football jerseys, and even talking bears.

4. To be sure that I had completed everything for my classes, I made a list that included the following readings, essays, homework, lab work, and exams.

5. When my mother told my brother to clean out his closet, he stuffed shoes, socks, empty soda cans, ancient bags of cookies, old magazines, and a broken light bulb under his bed.

6. With a big grin on his face, my boyfriend said he had won fifty dollars in a radio contest.

7. My supervisor's desk was always immaculate all the paper stacked neatly, the pencils placed in a china mug, the computer lined up with the mouse pad, and one personal photograph framed in shiny metal.

8. Since Wednesday is a long day for me at the college, I always bring these snacks an apple, a candy bar, and a large bottle of water.

Connect

Exercise 20   **Connect: Punctuating with Colons**

Edit the following paragraph, correcting the errors related to colons. You need to add some colons and eliminate any unnecessary colons.

Buying furniture can be tricky because so-called bargains can turn out to be deceptive. The other day I saw a newspaper advertisement for a bedroom set that looked like a good deal. It offered a five-piece set for a sale price of $900. The photograph showed an attractive group of furniture a large, queen-sized bed, two nightstands, a large dresser with a mirror, and a tall bureau. Because I desperately needed some new bedroom furniture, I visited the furniture showroom during the sale. The bedroom set was quite impressive the bed was large and sturdy, the dresser and bureau seemed solid, and the nightstands were a good size. I quickly found a salesperson and told him that I wanted to get: the bed, two nightstands, the bureau, and the dresser for the sale price. I was shocked by his reply: the sale price applied to five pieces of furniture, but the pieces were not the ones I had expected. I had failed to read the small print in the advertisement. It said that the five pieces were: the bed, the bed rails, the headboard, the dresser, and its mirror. The other pieces, the bureau and the nightstands, were sold separately and cost between $250 and $400 apiece. Feeling tricked and disappointed, I went home to my decrepit bedroom furniture.

THE EXCLAMATION MARK

The exclamation mark is used at the ends of sentences that express strong emotion.

appropriate:	Mr. Zimmerman, you've just become the father of triplets!
inappropriate:	The dance was fabulous! (*Fabulous* already implies excitement and enthusiasm, so you don't need the exclamation mark.)

Be careful not to overuse the exclamation mark. If your choice of words is descriptive, you should not have to rely on the exclamation mark for emphasis. Use it sparingly, for it is easy to rely on exclamation marks instead of using better vocabulary.

THE DASH

Use a dash to interrupt a sentence; use two dashes to set off words in a sentence. The dash is somewhat dramatic, so be careful not to overuse it.

examples:
Helena's frustration at her job made her an angry woman—a mean, angry woman.
My cousins Celia and Rick—the silly fools—fell off the dock when they were clowning around.

PARENTHESES

Use parentheses to set off words in a sentence.

examples:
The movies he rented (<u>Kung Fu Panda</u>, <u>Blades of Glory</u>, and <u>The Happening</u>) were all too silly for me.

> **Note:** In handwritten student essays, movie titles are underlined.

Simon nominated Justin Lewis (his best friend) as club treasurer.

> **Note:** Commas in pairs, dashes in pairs, and parentheses are all used as inserters. They set off inserted material that interrupts the flow of the sentence. The least dramatic and smoothest way to insert material is to use commas.

THE HYPHEN

A hyphen joins two or more descriptive words that act as a single-word adjective (often called a **phrasal adjective**).

examples:
Mr. Handlesman was wearing a custom-made suit.
My great aunt's hair is a salt-and-pepper color.

Exercise 21   **Practice: Punctuating with Exclamation Marks, Dashes, Parentheses, and Hyphens**

In the following sentences, add exclamation marks, dashes, parentheses, or hyphens where they are needed. Answers may vary because some writers may use dashes instead of parentheses.

1. Artie used to be a good ballplayer one of the best at our college.

2. My old car once known as the Broken Beast has been running fairly well recently.

3. My parents encouraged me to spend the summer at a workshop for student leaders; they called it a once in a lifetime opportunity.

4. Rebecca Richman my best friend is transferring to another college.

5. The Kennerly Lodge a first rate hotel is hiring extra staff for the summer season.

6. I've just seen a ghost

7. If you are self conscious, you may have a hard time speaking in public.

8. There's a spider on your backpack

Connect

Exercise 22   Connect: Punctutating with Exclamation Marks, Dashes, Parentheses, and Hyphens

Edit the following paragraph, correcting the errors related to exclamation marks, dashes, parentheses, and hyphens. You can add, change, or eliminate punctuation. Answers may vary because dashes in pairs and parentheses are both used as inserters. Also, try to use only one exclamation mark in your edited version of this paragraph.

My visit to a fancy and expensive restaurant was not at all what I had expected. A new friend wanted to impress me and took me to Palm Breeze the most popular restaurant in town last Saturday night. We sat in a courtyard decorated with an elegant, bubbling fountain and lush foliage. Bright tropical flowers peeked from behind green palm fronds! The sights and sounds were enticing, but some unpleasant surprises followed! First, my friend ordered oysters for us both. I love seafood and expected a tasty dish of baked, broiled, or steamed shellfish. I recoiled in horror when I realized that the oysters were raw a gooey mess of gray, jelly like tissue. The main course was somewhat better, but the portions were tiny. Because Palm Breeze charges so much, I expected it to serve generous helpings that would cover the plate. Instead, my plate contained a tiny portion of roast pork, thin slivers of red, yellow, and green peppers, and a small spoonful of rice. Unfortunately, my biggest surprise was yet to come. For dessert, I ordered a Palm Breeze specialty a tropical fruit salad filled with guava, pineapple, mangoes, and berries. This dessert called Passion at Sunset was famous for the delicious orange sauce covering the fruit. However, one other item was also covered by that sauce. It was a large, green, scaly lizard. That lizard was a little more of the tropics than I wanted. Clearly, my first visit to Palm Breeze will also be my last.

QUOTATION MARKS

Use quotation marks for direct quotes, for the titles of short works, and for other, special uses.

1. Put quotation marks around direct quotations (a speaker or writer's exact words).

   quotation marks around direct quotations:
   Ernest always told me, "It is better to give than to receive."

   "Nobody goes to that club," said Ramon.

   "We could go to the movies," Christina offered, "but we'd better hurry."

   My mother warned me, "Save your money. You'll need it for a rainy day."

Look carefully at the preceding examples. Note that a comma is used to introduce a direct quotation, and that, at the end of the quotation, a comma or a period goes inside the quotation marks.

   Ernest always told me, "It is better to give than to receive."

Notice how direct quotations of more than one sentence are punctuated. If the quotation is written as one unit, quotation marks go before the first quoted word and after the last quoted word:

   My mother warned me, "Save your money. You'll need it for a rainy day."

But if the quote is not written as one unit, the punctuation changes:

   "Save your money," my mother warned me. "You'll need it for a rainy day."

Caution: Do *not* put punctuation marks around indirect quotations.

---

   indirect quotation: Tyree asked if the water was cold.
   direct quotation: Tyree asked, "Is the water cold?"

   indirect quotation: She said that she needed a break from work.
   direct quotation: She said, "I need a break from work."

2. Put quotation marks around the titles of short works. If you are writing the title of a short work like a short story, an essay, a newspaper or magazine article, a poem, or a song, put quotation marks around the title.

   quotation marks around the titles of short works:
   My father's favorite poem is "The Raven" by Edgar Allan Poe.

   When I was little, I used to sing "Twinkle, Twinkle, Little Star."

   I couldn't think of a good title, so I just called my essay "How I Spent My Summer Vacation."

If you are writing the title of a longer work like a book, movie, magazine, play, television show, or music album, underline the title.

   underlining the titles of longer works:
   My favorite childhood movie was <u>Twilight</u>.

   For homework, I have to read an article called "Children and Reading Skills" in <u>Education Today</u> magazine.

Note: In printed publications such as books or magazines, titles of long works are put in italics. But when you are writing by hand, underline the titles of long works. In formal typed papers, italicizing major works is acceptable.

---

3. There are other, special uses of quotation marks. You use quotation marks around special words in a sentence.

quotation marks around special words:
When you say "sometimes," how often do you mean?

People from New England say "frappe" when they mean "milkshake."

If you are using a quotation within a quotation, use single quotation marks.

a quotation within a quotation:
Janey said angrily, "You took my car without permission, and all you can say is, 'It's no big deal.' "

Aunt Mary said, "You need to teach that child to say 'please' and 'thank you' more often."

Exercise 23   **Practice: Punctuating with Quotation Marks**

Add quotation marks where they are needed in the following sentences.

1. There are so many meanings to the word love that it is hard to define.

2. Rena told her boyfriend, Unless you are willing to say I was wrong, we have no future together.

3. A British child may call his or her mother Mummy, but an American child is likely to say Mommy.

4. I have got to save some money, my sister said. I will have to cut back on expensive haircuts and manicures.

5. I have got to save some money. I will have to cut back on expensive haircuts and manicures, said my sister.

6. We were all shocked when Tara said she was quitting her job and moving out of the state.

7. The Power of Love is a popular song at weddings and at banquets that honor a special person.

8. Did you remember to turn off the stove? Mrs. Bethel asked her husband as they left for work.

Exercise 24   **Practice: More on Punctuating with Quotation Marks**

Add quotation marks where they are needed in the following sentences.

1. Sonya isn't sure whether she has to work late next weekend.

2. I've had enough of your nagging, she said. I'm not going to listen to it any longer, she added.

3. Stephanie once said, I wish my father had been able to say I love you to me at least once.

4. Groovy used to be a popular slang term in the 1960s; in fact, there was even a hit song called Feelin' Groovy about feeling happy.

5. My girlfriend sometimes says she loves a particular gift from me when I know she is just trying not to hurt my feelings.

6. Good idea, my roommate said when I asked him if he wanted to order a pizza.

7. I'm hungry, my five-year-old nephew complained. When can we get out of the car and get something to eat?

8. After I take English 102, stated Rajib, I'm going to take American Literature 104 because I love those old stories.

CAPITAL LETTERS

There are ten main situations when you capitalize.

6 Use capital letters, numbers, and abbreviations correctly.

1. Capitalize the first word of every sentence.

   examples:
   Sometimes we take a walk on the beach.
   An apple is a healthy snack.

2. Capitalize the first word in a direct quotation if the word begins a sentence.

   examples:
   Jensina said, "Here is the money I owe you and a little something extra."

   "Here is the money I owe you," Jensina said, "and a little something extra." (Notice that the second section of this quotation does not begin with a capital letter because it does not begin a sentence.)

3. Capitalize the names of people.

   examples:
   Ingrid Alvorsen and Sean Miller invited me to their wedding.
   I asked Father to visit me.

Do not capitalize words like *mother*, *father*, or *aunt* if you put a possessive in front of them.

   names with possessives:
   I asked my father to visit me.
   She disliked her aunt.

4. Capitalize the titles of people.

   examples:
   I worked for Dr. Mabala.
   She is interviewing Captain Richards.

Do not capitalize when the title is not connected to a name.

   a title not connected to a name:
   I worked for that doctor.
   She is interviewing the captain of the submarine.

5. Always capitalize nationalities, religions, races, months, days of the week, documents, organizations, holidays, and historical events or periods.

   examples:
   In eighth grade, I completed a project on the American Revolution.

   During the month of February, the department presents documentaries on Rosa Parks and Martin Luther King, Jr.

   Every Tuesday night, he goes to meetings at the African Heritage Club.

Use small letters for the seasons.

> **a season with a small letter:**
> I always look forward to the coming of winter.

6. Capitalize the names of particular places.

> **examples:**
> I used to attend Hawthorne Middle School.
> My friends like to stroll through City Center Mall.

Use small letters if a particular place is not given.

> **small letter for no particular place:**
> My friends like to stroll through the mall.

7. Use capital letters for geographic locations.

> **examples:**
> Lisa wanted to attend a college in the South.
> I love autumn in the Midwest.

But use small letters for geographic directions.

> **small letter for a geographic direction:**
> The easiest way to find the airport is to drive south on the freeway.

8. Capitalize the names of specific products.

> **examples:**
> I need some Tylenol for my headache.
> Melanie eats a Snickers bar every day.

But use small letters for a general type of product.

> **small letter for a general product:**
> Melanie eats a candy bar every day.

9. Capitalize the names of specific school courses.

> **examples:**
> My favorite class is Ancient and Medieval History.
> Alicia is taking Introduction to Computers this fall.

But use small letters for a general academic subject.

> **small letter for a general subject:**
> Before I graduate, I have to take a computer course.

10. Capitalize the first and last words in the titles of long or short works, and capitalize all other significant words in the title.

> **examples:**
> I loved the movie <u>Fifty First Dates</u>.
> There is a beautiful song called "You Are the Sunshine of My Life."

Exercise 25   Practice: Punctuating with Capital Letters

Add capital letters where they are needed in the following sentences.

1. My cousin is a captain in the police department of a large city in

the west.

2. I have recently become aunt Hannah to my sister's newborn baby, but I am not really sure what an aunt does.

3. In our introduction to american government class, we studied the parts of the constitution of the united states of america.

4. I have a bad cold, so I can't go anywhere without a box of kleenex and some cough drops.

5. The new professor who teaches education courses is not as friendly as professor Schaeffer.

6. On memorial day my family is going to a ceremony that will commemorate the American soldiers who died in the Vietnam war.

7. "you would make me very happy," my girlfriend said, "if you would finish school."

8. The caribbean art center, north of Miami, is exhibiting a fine collection of haitian art.

Exercise 26   **Collaborate: Punctuating with Capital Letters: Creating Your Own Examples**

Collaborate

Do this exercise with a partner or group. Below is a list giving situations when you should—or should not—use capital letters. Write a sentence at least five words long as an example for each item on the list.

1. Capitalize the names of particular places.

   example: _____

   _____

2. Use capital letters for geographic locations.

   example: _____

   _____

3. Use small letters for geographic directions.

   example: _____

   _____

4. Capitalize historic events or periods.

   example: _____

   _____

5. Capitalize nationalities.

   example: _____

   _____

6. Capitalize the names of persons.

   example: _____

   _____

7. Do not capitalize words like _mother, father,_ or _uncle_ if you put a possessive in front of them.

   example: _____

   _____

8. Capitalize the titles of persons.

   example: _____

   _____

Connect

Exercise 27 **Connect: Punctuating with Quotation Marks, Underlining, and Capital Letters**

Following is a paragraph with some blank spaces. Fill in the blanks, remembering the rules for using quotation marks, underlining, and capital letters. When you have completed the exercise, be ready to share your responses with members of the class.

When I think about last year, I remember some very specific details. I remember that one song I was always listening to was called _____

_____, and the singer I admired most was _____.

The one movie I remember best is _____, and a television

show I recall watching is _____. There are also several

places I associate with last year. Among them is a store called _____

_____, the school nearest to my home, called _____, and a

place I always wanted to go to, but never visited, called _____.

When I think of last year, I realize that I spent many hours eating or socializing at

a fast-food restaurant named _____. My favorite cold drink was

_____. Today, I realize that some of my habits and tastes have

changed, yet I am still very much connected to the places and things of the past.

Exercise 28	Connect: Punctuating with Quotation Marks, Underlining, and Capital Letters

Connect

Edit the following paragraph by correcting the errors related to quotation marks, underlining, and capital letters. You need to add some quotation marks, underlining, and capital letters, and to eliminate the unnecessary or incorrect quotation marks, underlining, and capital letters.

I have recently become interested in ghosts. My interest began when I was flipping through the television channels and then stopped at a grainy black-and-white image of two men in a shadowy room. The men were walking quietly and carefully, and one held a light. The other had a camera. The scene was silent. When the image was replaced by a commercial break, I discovered the show I had been watching was "Ghost Hunters," and this episode was about ghosts in new england. After watching one or two more episodes of this show, I learned that the hunters were believers in ghosts or scientists trying to investigate the reality of ghosts. I have also learned some new vocabulary. The hunters focus on what they call sightings of spirits, or incidents of paranormal activity. Nobody on the show ever seems to wonder "if ghosts are real." I have an open mind on the subject but have become more curious. Recently, I went to my town's Library and asked a librarian "if she would help me search for books and articles about ghosts." I was surprised to find several books about hauntings in my area: "The Spirits Of Western Ghost Towns," "Mountain Mysteries," and "The haunted Mines of Colorado." In fact, I even discovered an article called <u>Paranormal Denver</u>, about the ghosts in my hometown. So far, my ghost-hunting has been limited to the library, and unless there is a spirit hiding among the bookshelves, I will never see a ghost.

NUMBERS

Spell out numbers that take one or two words to spell out.

> **examples:**
> The coat cost seventy dollars.
> Bridget sent two hundred invitations.

Use hyphens to spell out compound numbers from twenty-one to ninety-nine.

> **examples:**
> Clarissa, twenty-three, is the oldest daughter.
> I mailed sixty-two invitations.

Use numerals if it takes more than two words to spell out a number.

> **examples:**
> The company sold 367 toy trains.
> The price of the car was $15,629.

Also use numerals to write dates, times, and addresses.

> **examples:**
> You can visit him at 223 Sailboat Lane.
> I received my diploma on June 17, 2014.
> We woke up at 6:00 a.m., bright and early.

Use numbers with *a.m.* and *p.m.*, but use words with *o'clock*.

> **example:**
> We woke up at six o'clock, bright and early.

ABBREVIATIONS

Although you should spell out most words rather than abbreviate them, you may use common abbreviations like *Mr.*, *Mrs.*, *Ms.*, *Jr.*, *Sr.*, and *Dr.* when they are used with a proper name. Abbreviations may also be used for references to time and for organizations widely known by initials.

> **examples:**
> I gave Dr. Lambert my medical records.
> The phone rang at 3:00 a.m. and scared me out of a sound sleep.
> Nancy got a job with the FBI.

Spell out the names of places, months, days of the week, courses of study, and words referring to parts of a book.

> **not this:** I visited a friend in Philadelphia, ~~Penn~~.
> **but this:** I visited a friend in Philadelphia, Pennsylvania.

> **not this:** My brother skipped his ~~phys. ed~~. class yesterday.
> **but this:** My brother skipped his physical education class yesterday.

> **not this:** Last week, our garbage was not picked up on ~~Weds~~. or ~~Sat~~., so I called the Dept. of Sanitation.
> **but this:** Last week, our garbage was not picked up on Wednesday or Saturday, so I called the Department of Sanitation.

Exercise 29 **Practice: Punctuating with Numbers and Abbreviations**

Correct the errors in punctuating with numbers and abbreviations in the following sentences.

1. Pres. Thurman closed Salton U. yesterday after heavy rains

   flooded parts of the campus.

2. I couldn't sleep last night, so I watched a movie about the CIA until

   one twenty-five a.m.

3. My sister got a scholarship to Penn. State U., and she leaves for her

   first semester on Weds.

4. You can find 5 or 6 topics for your psych. paper if you look on

   p. 323 of the text.

5. Prof. Thomas always gives us too much socio. homework.

6. The last chapt. of our Intro. to Business textbook has a helpful

   section on writing a resume.

7. January 15, 2005, is the day I moved into Carlton Apts. in New

   Bedford, Mass.

8. Thomas started volunteering at the Red Cross during his sr. year in

   high school.

Exercise 30 **Practice: Punctuation: A Comprehensive Exercise**

In the following sentences, add punctuation where it is needed and correct
any punctuation errors.

1. After I pay off my college loans Sam said I can start saving for a

   house.

2. Macaroni and cheese which is my childrens favorite food is an

   easy meal to make when youre in a hurry.

3. Helena doesnt like to fly instead she drives long distances to see

   her son and daughter in law.

4. Lester had a hard time dealing with his puppies energy so he

   enrolled them in an obedience class for young dogs.

5. Prof. Marcus asked Does anyone want to do some work for extra

   credit

6. My boyfriend knows all about Jefferson community hospital

   because he spent two months there last Feb.

7. My father wants me to read a book called The purpose-driven life

   he loved it and wants to pass it on.

8. Boris used to call me from work then his supervisor warned him

   about making too many personal calls.

Connect

Exercise 31 **Connect: Editing a Paragraph for Errors in Punctuation**

Edit the following paragraph for errors in punctuation. You may have to add, eliminate, or change punctuation.

I am a receptionist in the office of a large Physical Therapy Center. My job has brought me many new friends; and each one has a special quality. Among these friends are Lynne Povitch, the manager of the center, Andrew Falzone, an experienced therapist specializing in back injuries, Kristin Wing, a therapist specializing in hand and wrist therapy, Alicia nardello, a therapy student training at the center, and Arthur Connolly, the office custodian. I know when Lynn Povitch has arrived at the office because she always sings the same song: You Had A Bad Day. Although her choice of song is a bit negative, Lynne sings it in a cheery voice. Andrew Falzone arrives each day in worn jeans and a hawaiian shirt; however, he carries a top of the line leather briefcase. He is a serious person dedicated to his work but he has a new joke for me every day. Kristin Wing loves to bake, and brings homemade cookies, muffins, or Banana bread to the office every Friday. Alicia Nardello, the trainee therapist spends most of her day assisting the other therapists. She runs from one piece of equipment to another. Sometimes she distributes fresh, hot towels or lotion at other times, she finds files or charts. Alicia is a tiny woman who scurries like a mouse and always smiles. Everyones favorite staff member is Arthur Connolly. he is respected because he can repair anything without losing his cheerful, calm personality. However, he is loved for his generosity. He has time to listen to every member of the office. I have confided in him many times. Arthur never proposes a solution to my problems but his willingness to listen to my stories allows me to think through my worries and find my own way to deal with them. When I think about the kindness, humor, and spirit of my office friends, I know that I am lucky to work in an environment, with so many special people.

MyWritingLab™ Visit Chapter 16, "Punctuation," in *MyWritingLab* to test your understanding of the chapter objectives.

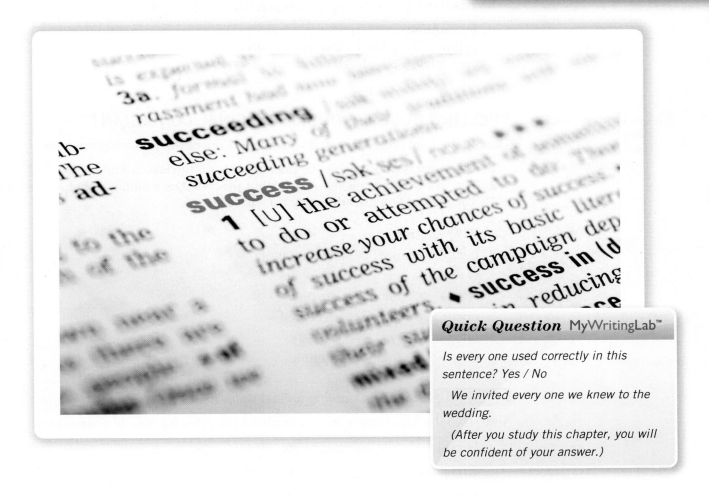

Quick Question MyWritingLab™

Is every one used correctly in this sentence? Yes / No

We invited every one we knew to the wedding.

(After you study this chapter, you will be confident of your answer.)

Learning Objectives

In this chapter, you will learn to:

1. Identify vowels and consonants.
2. Use basic spelling rules to determine correct word endings and variations.
3. Recognize when a one- or two-word spelling applies to certain terms.

No one is a perfect speller, but there are ways to become a better speller. If you can learn a few spelling rules, you can answer many of your spelling questions.

1. Identify vowels and consonants.

VOWELS AND CONSONANTS

To understand the spelling rules, you need to know the difference between vowels and consonants. **Vowels** are the letters *a, e, i, o, u,* and sometimes *y.* **Consonants** are all the other letters.

The letter *y* is a vowel when it has a vowel sound.

examples:
silly (The *y* sounds like *ee* in this example.)
cry (The *y* sounds like *i* in this example.)

The letter *y* is a consonant when it has a consonant sound.

examples:
yellow (The *y* has a consonant sound.)
yesterday (The *y* has a consonant sound.)

2 Use basic spelling rules to determine correct word endings and variations.

SPELLING RULE 1: DOUBLING A FINAL CONSONANT

Double the final consonant of a word if all three of the following are true:

1. The word is one syllable, or the accent is on the last syllable.
2. The word ends in a single consonant preceded by a single vowel.
3. The ending you are adding starts with a vowel.

examples:

begin	+	ing	=	beginning
shop	+	er	=	shopper
stir	+	ed	=	stirred
occur	+	ed	=	occurred
fat	+	est	=	fattest
pin	+	ing	=	pinning

Exercise 1 **Practice: Doubling a Final Consonant**

Add *-ed* to the following words by applying the rules for double consonants.

1. pad _____   5. offer _____

2. scatter _____   6. defer _____

3. scan _____   7. strand _____

4. track _____   8. wander _____

SPELLING RULE 2: DROPPING THE FINAL *E*

Drop the final *e* before you add an ending that starts with a vowel.

examples:

observe	+	ing	=	observing
excite	+	able	=	excitable
fame	+	ous	=	famous
create	+	ive	=	creative

Keep the final *e* before an ending that starts with a consonant.

examples:

love	+	ly	=	lovely
hope	+	ful	=	hopeful
excite	+	ment	=	excitement
life	+	less	=	lifeless

CRITICAL THINKING

Look at the word before the ending (suffix) is added. What is the part of speech? How did the suffix change the part of speech? Do you notice a pattern with a particular suffix? Which part of speech does it represent?

Examples:
The suffix *-able* changes *adore* (verb) to *adorable* (adjective).
The suffix *-ly* changes *active* (adjective) to *actively* (adverb).

Exercise 2   **Practice: Dropping the Final e**

Combine the following words and endings by following the rule for dropping the final *e*.

1. adore   +   able   _____

2. home   +   less   _____

3. active   +   ly   _____

4. name   +   ing   _____

5. adore   +   ing   _____

6. encourage   +   ment   _____

7. promote   +   ion   _____

8. expense   +   ive   _____

SPELLING RULE 3: CHANGING THE FINAL *Y* TO *I*

When a word ends in a consonant plus *y*, change the *y* to *i* when you add an ending.

examples:

try	+ es	=	tries
silly	+ er	=	sillier
rely	+ ance	=	reliance
tardy	+ ness	=	tardiness

Note: When you add *-ing* to words ending in *y*, always keep the *y*.

examples:

cry	+ ing	=	crying
rely	+ ing	=	relying

Exercise 3   **Practice: Changing the Final y to *i***

Combine the following words and endings by applying the rule for changing the final *y* to *i*.

1. sloppy   +   er   _____

2. hardy   +   ness   _____

3. cry   +   er   _____

4. pity   +   less   _____

5. try   +   ing   _____

6. marry   +   ed   _____

7. apply   +   ance   _____

8. plenty   +   ful   _____

SPELLING RULE 4: ADDING -S OR -ES

Add -es instead of -s to a word if the word ends in *ch*, *sh*, *ss*, *x*, or *z*. The -es adds an extra syllable to the word.

examples:

box   +   es   =   boxes
watch   +   es   =   watches
class   +   es   =   classes
brush   +   es   =   brushes

Exercise 4   **Practice: Adding -s or -es**

Add -s or -es to the following words by applying the rule for adding -s or -es.

1. astonish _____   **5.** fix _____

2. perch _____   **6.** fetch _____

3. glass _____   **7.** wonder _____

4. bunch _____   **8.** block _____

SPELLING RULE 5: USING IE OR EI

Use *i* before *e* except after *c*, or when the sound is like *a*, as in *neighbor* and *weigh*.

examples of *i* before *e*:

relief   field   friend   piece

examples of *e* before *i*:

conceive   sleigh   weight   receive

Exercise 5   **Practice: Using *ie* or *ei***

Add *ie* or *ei* to the following words by applying the rules for using *ie* or *ei*.

1. bel__ __ve   **5.** __ __ght

2. dec__ __t   **6.** misch__ __f

3. cr__ __d   **7.** r__ __ns

4. th__ __f   **8.** gr__ __f

Exercise 6   **Practice: Spelling Rules: A Comprehensive Exercise**

Combine the following words and endings by applying the spelling rules.

1. coax   + s *or* es   _____
2. toy   + s *or* es   _____
3. deny   + s *or* es   _____
4. bounty   + ful   _____
5. conserve + ing   _____
6. shape   + less   _____
7. force   + ful   _____
8. confer   + ed   _____

Exercise 7   **Practice: Spelling Rules: Another Comprehensive Exercise**

Combine the following words and endings by applying the spelling rules.

1. ready   + ness   _____
2. commit   + ment   _____
3. commit   + ed   _____
4. forget   + ing   _____
5. hatch   + s *or* es   _____
6. harass   + s *or* es   _____
7. filthy   + er   _____
8. sleigh   + s *or* es   _____

Exercise 8   **Collaborate: Creating Examples for the Spelling Rules**

Collaborate

Working with a partner or group, write examples for the following rules.

Spelling Rule 1: Doubling the Final Consonant
Double the final consonant of a word if all three of the following are true:

1. The word is one syllable, or the accent is on the last syllable.
2. The word ends in a single consonant preceded by a single vowel.
3. The ending you added starts with a vowel.

example:

1. Write a word that is one syllable (or the accent is on the last syllable), and that ends in a consonant preceded by a single vowel: _____

2. Write an ending that starts with a vowel: _____
3. Combine the word and the ending: _____

Spelling Rule 2: Dropping the Final *e*

Drop the final *e* before you add an ending that starts with a vowel.

example:

1. Write a word that ends with an *e:* _____
2. Write an ending that starts with a vowel: _____
3. Combine the word and the ending: _____

Spelling Rule 3: Changing the Final *y* to *i*

When a word ends in a consonant plus *y*, change the *y* to *i* when you add an ending. (Note: When you add *-ing* to words ending in *y*, always keep the *y*.)

example:

1. Write a word that ends in a consonant plus *y:* _____
2. Write an ending (not an *-ing* ending): _____
3. Combine the word and the ending: _____

Spelling Rule 4: Adding *-s* or *-es*

Add *-es* instead of *-s* to a word if the word ends in *ch, sh, ss, x,* or *z.* The *-es* adds an extra syllable to the word.

example:

1. Write a word that ends in *ch, sh, ss, x,* or *z:* _____
2. Add *-es* to the word: _____

Spelling Rule 5: Using *ie* or *ei*

Use *i* before *e* except after *c,* or when the sound is like *a,* as in *neighbor* and *weigh.*

example:

1. Write three words that use *i* before *e:* _____, _____, _____
2. Write one word that uses *ei:* _____

Connect

Exercise 9 **Connect: Editing a Paragraph for Spelling Errors**

Correct the ten spelling errors in the following paragraph. Write your corrections above each error.

Last night, when my neice Ella asked me to help her with her homework,

I suddenly realized how bad my spelling truly is. Here I was, triing hard to help

a nine-year-old child with an essay she had written about a beautyful day at the

beach. While I know something about beachs, I don't know much about puting

a paper together. In fact, I think my writing is hopless, and I will not be surprised

if someday soon Ella catchs me in a mistake or two, especially in spelling. I am

almost ready to spend some time learning to be a better speller. Not only would

Ella respect me more, but I also beleive that all my written work—business letters, job applications, reports, and forms—would be more convinceing if I could remove the sloppyness of bad spelling. In addition, learning to spell could be my first step to better writing.

HOW DO YOU SPELL IT? ONE WORD OR TWO?

Sometimes you can be confused about certain words. You are not sure whether to combine them to make one word or to spell them as two words. Review the following lists of some commonly confused words:

③ Recognize when a one- or two-word spelling applies to certain terms.

Words That Should Not Be Combined

a lot	even though	high school (noun)
all right	every time	good night
dining room	home run	living room
each other	in front	no one

Words That Should Be Combined

another	grandmother	schoolteacher
bathroom	high-school (adjective)	southeast, northwest, etc.
bedroom	nearby	throughout
bookkeeper	nevertheless	worthwhile
cannot	newspapers	yourself, myself,
downstairs	playroom	himself, etc.
good-bye, goodbye, or good-by	roommate	

Words Whose Spelling Depends on Their Meaning

one word: *Already* means "before."
He offered to do the dishes, but I had *already* done them.
two words: *All ready* means "ready."
My dog was *all ready* to play Frisbee.

one word: *Altogether* means "entirely."
That movie was *altogether* too confusing.
two words: *All together* means "in a group."
My sisters were *all together* in the kitchen.

one word: *Always* means "every time."
My grandfather is *always* right about baseball statistics.
two words: *All ways* means "every path" or "every aspect."
We tried *all ways* to get to the beach house.
He is a gentleman in *all ways*.

one word: *Anymore* means "any longer."
I do not want to exercise *anymore*.
two words: *Any more* means "additional."
Are there *any more* pickles?

one word: *Anyone* means "any person at all."
Is *anyone* home?
two words: *Any one* means "one person or thing in a special group."
I'll take *any one* of the chairs on sale.
He offered *any one* of the students a ride home.

one word: *Apart* means "separate."
Liam stood *apart* from his friends.
two words: *A part* is a piece or section.
I read *a part* of the chapter.

one word: *Everyday* means "ordinary."
Tim was wearing his *everyday* clothes.
two words: *Every day* means "each day."
Sam jogs *every day*.

one word: *Everyone* means "all the people."
Everyone has bad days.
two words: *Every one* means "all the people or things in a specific group."
My father asked *every one* of the neighbors for a donation to the Red Cross.

one word: *Maybe* means "perhaps."
Maybe you can go to a college near your home.
two words: *May be* means "might be."
Sam *may be* the right person for the job.

one word: *Thank-you* is an adjective that describes a certain kind of note or letter.
Heather wrote her grandfather a *thank-you* note.
two words: We state our gratitude by saying, "*Thank you.*"
"*Thank you* for lending me your car," Kyle said.

> **Exercise 10** **Practice: How Do You Spell It? One Word or Two?**

Circle the correct word in the following sentences.

1. It was an (everyday / every day) kind of luncheon; (nevertheless / never the less), I was glad to have been invited.

2. Steve saw (apart / a part) of the movie, but he left after ten minutes because the story didn't seem (worthwhile / worth while).

3. In my mother's apartment, the (livingroom / living room) is large and comfortable, but the (bedroom / bed room) is tiny and cramped.

4. I (cannot / can not) figure out how (everyone / every one) of my shirts got stained with blue ink.

5. My best friend lives (nearby / near by), and we see each other (a lot / alot).

6. My son was (already / all ready) to spend more time in the (playroom / play room) at the local mall.

7. Years after he graduated from college, Alonzo sent a (thank-you / thank you) letter to the (schoolteacher / school teacher) who had helped him learn to read.

8. You (always / all ways) nag me about putting gas in the car, (even-though / even though) you know I have never let the gauge get to "Empty."

| **Exercise 11** | **Connect: How Do You Spell It? One Word or Two?** |

Connect

The following paragraph contains ten errors in word combinations. Correct the errors in the space above each line.

I have always been interested in numbers, and math has been my favorite sub-

ject for years, so a career in accounting has been my goal. My mother, who had only

a highschool education, has worked as a book keeper for many years. However,

I have a higher goal for my self and want to be an accountant. I have all ready applied

to several colleges near by and I hope that I will be accepted into one with a good

accounting program. Eventhough I would like to experience college life on my own,

I can not afford the cost of my own apartment, even if I shared with a room mate.

Living in a dormitory would also be expensive. As a person who likes to account for

every penny, I am all ways looking for the most economical way to reach my goal,

even if it means sleeping in my old bed room at home for a few more years.

A LIST OF COMMONLY MISSPELLED WORDS

Below is a list of words you use often in your writing. Study this list and use it as a reference.

1. absence	16. American	31. automobile
2. absent	17. answer	32. autumn
3. accept	18. anxious	33. avenue
4. ache	19. apology	34. awful
5. achieve	20. apparent	35. awkward
6. acquire	21. appetite	36. balance
7. across	22. appreciate	37. basically
8. actually	23. argue	38. because
9. advertise	24. argument	39. becoming
10. again	25. asked	40. beginning
11. a lot	26. athlete	41. behavior
12. all right	27. attempt	42. belief
13. almost	28. August	43. believe
14. always	29. aunt	44. benefit
15. amateur	30. author	45. bicycle

(Continued)

46. bought	99. describe	152. goes
47. breakfast	100. desperate	153. going
48. breathe	101. development	154. government
49. brilliant	102. different	155. grammar
50. brother	103. dilemma	156. grateful
51. brought	104. dining	157. grocery
52. bruise	105. direction	158. guarantee
53. build	106. disappearance	159. guard
54. bulletin	107. disappoint	160. guess
55. bureau	108. discipline	161. guidance
56. buried	109. disease	162. guide
57. business	110. divide	163. half
58. busy	111. doctor	164. handkerchief
59. calendar	112. doesn't	165. happiness
60. cannot	113. don't	166. heavy
61. career	114. doubt	167. height
62. careful	115. during	168. heroes
63. catch	116. dying	169. holiday
64. category	117. early	170. hospital
65. caught	118. earth	171. humorous
66. cemetery	119. eighth	172. identity
67. cereal	120. eligible	173. illegal
68. certain	121. embarrass	174. imaginary
69. chair	122. encouragement	175. immediately
70. cheat	123. enough	176. important
71. chicken	124. environment	177. independent
72. chief	125. especially	178. integration
73. children	126. etc.	179. intelligent
74. cigarette	127. every	180. interest
75. citizen	128. exact	181. interfere
76. city	129. exaggeration	182. interpretation
77. college	130. excellent	183. interrupt
78. color	131. except	184. iron
79. comfortable	132. exercise	185. irrelevant
80. committee	133. excite	186. irritable
81. competition	134. existence	187. island
82. conscience	135. expect	188. January
83. convenient	136. experience	189. jewelry
84. conversation	137. explanation	190. judgment*
85. copy	138. factory	191. kindergarten
86. cough	139. familiar	192. kitchen
87. cousin	140. family	193. knowledge
88. criticism	141. fascinating	194. laboratory
89. criticize	142. February	195. language
90. crowded	143. finally	196. laugh
91. daily	144. forehead	197. leisure
92. daughter	145. foreign	198. length
93. deceive	146. forty	199. library
94. decide	147. fourteen	200. listen
95. definite	148. friend	201. loneliness
96. dentist	149. fundamental	202. lying
97. dependent	150. general	203. maintain
98. deposit	151. generally	204. maintenance

205. marriage
206. mathematics
207. meant
208. measure
209. medicine
210. million
211. miniature
212. minute
213. muscle
214. mysterious
215. naturally
216. necessary
217. neighbor
218. nervous
219. nickel
220. niece
221. ninety
222. ninth
223. occasion
224. o'clock
225. often
226. omission
227. once
228. operate
229. opinion
230. optimist
231. original
232. parallel
233. particular
234. peculiar
235. perform
236. perhaps
237. permanent
238. persevere
239. personnel
240. persuade
241. physically
242. pleasant

243. possess
244. possible
245. potato
246. practical
247. prefer
248. prejudice
249. prescription
250. presence
251. president
252. privilege
253. probably
254. professor
255. psychology
256. punctuation
257. pursue
258. quart
259. really
260. receipt
261. receive
262. recognize
263. recommend
264. reference
265. religious
266. reluctantly
267. remember
268. resource
269. restaurant
270. rhythm
271. ridiculous
272. right
273. sandwich
274. Saturday
275. scene
276. schedule
277. scissors
278. secretary
279. seize
280. several

281. severely
282. significant
283. similar
284. since
285. sincerely
286. soldier
287. sophomore
288. strength
289. studying
290. success
291. surely
292. surprise
293. taught
294. temperature
295. theater
296. thorough
297. thousand
298. tied
299. tomorrow
300. tongue
301. tragedy
302. trouble
303. truly
304. twelfth
305. unfortunately
306. unknown
307. until
308. unusual
309. using
310. variety
311. vegetable
312. Wednesday
313. weird
314. which
315. writing
316. written
317. yesterday

*judgement is an alternate spelling

Connect

Connect: A Comprehensive Exercise on Spelling

The following exercise contains ten spelling errors, including errors related to the spelling rules, one- or two-word errors, and errors related to commonly misspelled words. Correct the errors in the space above each line.

My brother is the only member of our family who reads for pleasure. I can

read, but I am more intrested in math than in English. I don't read books or maga-

zines for enjoyment. In addition, I never read the news paper becose I use the

Internet if I need to find information. My sister is not much of a reader, either.

She wants to be a graphic designer and spends more time looking at cartoons,

games, and videos than enjoying books. However, Adam, my older brother, reads

all the time. In fact, he will read anything, including the cerial box as he eats

breakfast. He is happyest when he comes home from the library with an armful

of books. On many weekends, I have seen him sit on his bed for hours, piles of

books stackked around him. Adam's favorite books are about the unknown or the

imaginery. He dreams of becomming an author who specializes in tales of fantasy

and the supernatural. If reading is good training for that type of writeing, then

Adam should be a tremendous sucess.

Words That Sound Alike/ Look Alike

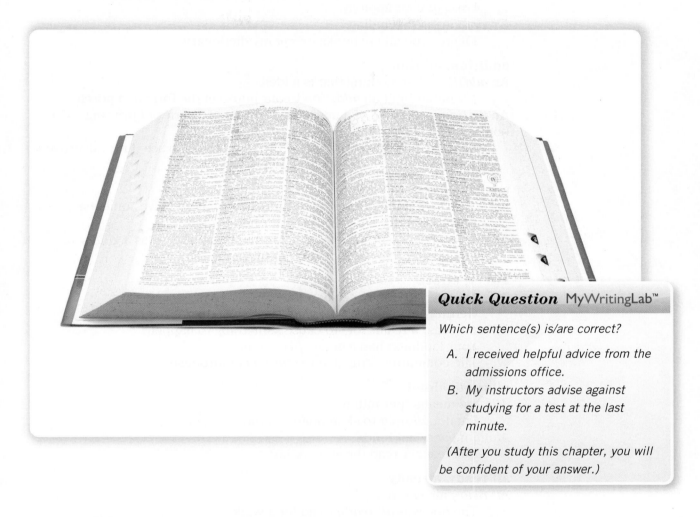

Learning Objectives

In this chapter, you will learn to:

1️⃣ Distinguish among common sound-alike and look-alike words.

WORDS THAT SOUND ALIKE/LOOK ALIKE

1️⃣ Distinguish among common sound-alike and look-alike words.

Words that sound alike or look alike can be confusing. Here is a list of some of the confusing words. Study this list, and make a note of any words that give you trouble.

a, an, and

A is used before a singular noun beginning with a consonant or consonant sound.

> Jason bought *a* car.

An is used before a singular noun beginning with a vowel or vowel sound.

> Nancy took *an* apple to work.

And joins words or ideas.

> Pudding *and* cake are my favorite desserts.
> Fresh vegetables taste delicious, *and* they are nutritious.

accept, except

Accept means "to receive."

 I *accept* your apology.

Except means "excluding."

 I'll give you all my books *except* my dictionary.

addition, edition

An *addition* is something that is added.

 My father built an *addition* to our house in the form of a porch.

An *edition* is an issue of a newspaper or one of a series of printings of a book.

 I checked the latest *edition* of the <u>Daily News</u> to see if my advertisement is in it.

advice, advise

Advice is an opinion offered as a guide; it is what you give someone.

 Betty asked for my *advice* about finding a job.

Advise is what you do when you give an opinion offered as a guide.

 I couldn't *advise* Betty about finding a job.

affect, effect

Affect means "to influence something."

 Getting a bad grade will *affect* my chances for a scholarship.

Effect means "a result" or "to cause something to happen."

 Your kindness had a great *effect* on me.

 The committee struggled to *effect* a compromise.

allowed, aloud

Allowed means "permitted."

 I'm not *allowed* to skateboard on those steps.

Aloud means "out loud."

 The teacher read the story *aloud*.

all ready, already

All ready means "ready."

 The dog was *all ready* to go for a walk.

Already means "before."

 David had *already* made the salad.

altar, alter

An *altar* is a table or place in a church.

 They were married in front of the *altar*.

Alter means "to change."

 My plane was delayed, so I had to *alter* my plans for the evening.

angel, angle

An *angel* is a heavenly being.

 That night, I felt an *angel* guiding me.

An *angle* is the shape formed by two intersecting lines.

 The road turned at a sharp *angle*.

are, our

Are is a verb, the plural of *is*.

 We *are* friends of the mayor.

Our means "belonging to us."

 We have *our* family quarrels.

beside, besides

Beside means "next to."

He sat *beside* me at the concert.

Besides means "in addition."

I would never lie to you; *besides*, I have no reason to lie.

brake, break

Brake means "to stop" or "a device for stopping."

That truck *brakes* at railroad crossings.

When he saw the animal on the road, he hit the *brakes*.

Break means "to come apart or "to make something come apart."

The eggs are likely to *break*.

I can *break* the seal on that package.

breath, breathe

Breath is the air you take in, and it rhymes with "death."

I was running so fast that I lost my *breath*.

Breathe means "to take in air."

He found it hard to *breathe* in high altitudes.

buy, by

Buy means "to purchase something."

Sylvia wants to *buy* a shovel.

By means "near," "by means of," or "before."

He sat *by* his sister.

I learn *by* taking good notes in class.

By ten o'clock, Nick was tired.

capital, capitol

Capital means "a city" or "wealth."

Albany is the *capital* of New York.

Jack invested his *capital* in real estate.

A *capitol* is a building.

The city has a famous *capitol* building.

cereal, serial

Cereal is a breakfast food or type of grain.

My favorite *cereal* is Cheerios.

Serial means "in a series."

Look for the *serial* number on the appliance.

choose, chose

Choose means "to select." It rhymes with "snooze."

Today I am going to *choose* my classes for next semester.

Chose is the past tense of *choose*.

Yesterday I *chose* a new major.

close, clothes, cloths

Close means "near" or "intimate." It can also mean "to end or shut something" when the *s* is pronounced as a *z*.

We live *close* to the train station.

James and Margie are *close* friends.

Noreen wants to *close* her eyes for ten minutes.

Clothes are wearing apparel.

Eduardo has new *clothes*.

Cloths are pieces of fabric.

I clean the silver with damp *cloths* and a special polish.

coarse, course

Coarse means "rough" or "crude."

> The top of the table had a *coarse* texture.
> His language was *coarse*.

A *course* is a direction or path. It is also a subject in school.

> The hurricane took a northern *course*.
> In my freshman year, I took a *course* in drama.

complement, compliment

Complement means "complete" or "make better."

> The colors in that room *complement* the style of the furniture.

A *compliment* is praise.

> Trevor gave me a *compliment* about my cooking.

conscience, conscious

Your *conscience* is your inner, moral guide.

> His *conscience* bothered him when he told a lie.

Conscious means "aware" or "awake."

> The accident victim was not fully *conscious*.

council, counsel

A *council* is a group of people.

> The city *council* meets tonight.

Counsel means "advice" or "to give advice."

> I need your *counsel* about my investments.
> My father always *counsels* me about my career.

decent, descent

Decent means "suitable" or "proper."

> I hope Mike gets a *decent* job.

Descent means "the process of going down, falling, or sinking."

> The plane began its *descent* to the airport.

desert, dessert

A *desert* is a dry land. To *desert* means "to abandon."

> To survive a trip across the *desert*, people need water.
> He will never *desert* a friend.

Dessert is the sweet food we eat at the end of a meal.

> I want ice cream for *dessert*.

do, due

Do means "perform."

> I have to stop complaining; I *do* it constantly.

Due means "owing" or "because of."

> The rent is *due* tomorrow.
> The game was canceled *due* to rain.

does, dose

Does is a form of *do*.

> My roommate *does* his studying at the library.

A *dose* is a quantity of medicine.

> Whenever I had a cold, my mother gave me a *dose* of cough syrup.

fair, fare

Fair means "unbiased." It can also mean "promising" or "good."

> The judge's decision was *fair*.
> José has a *fair* chance of winning the title.

A *fare* is a fee for transportation.
  My subway *fare* is going up.

farther, further
Farther means "at a greater physical distance."
  His house is a few blocks *farther* down the street.
Further means greater or additional. Use it when you are not describing a physical distance.
  My second French class gave me *further* training in French conversation.

flour, flower
Flour is ground-up grain, an ingredient used in cooking.
  I use whole-wheat *flour* in my muffins.
A *flower* is a blossom.
  She wore a *flower* in her hair.

forth, fourth
Forth means "forward."
  The pendulum on the clock swung back and *forth.*
Fourth means "number four in a sequence."
  I was *fourth* in line for the tickets.

hear, here
Hear means "to receive sounds in the ear."
  I can *hear* the music.
Here is a place.
  We can have the meeting *here.*

heard, herd
Heard is the past tense of *hear.*
  I *heard* you talk in your sleep last night.
A *herd* is a group of animals.
  The farmer has a fine *herd* of cows.

hole, whole
A *hole* is an empty place or opening.
  I see a *hole* in the wall.
Whole means "complete" or "entire."
  Silvio gave me the *whole* steak.

isle, aisle
An *isle* is an island.
  We visited the *isle* of Capri.
An *aisle* is a passageway between sections of seats.
  The flight attendant came down the *aisle* and offered us coffee.

its, it's
Its means "belonging to it."
  The car lost *its* rear bumper.
It's is a shortened form of *it is* or *it has.*
  It's a beautiful day.
  It's been a pleasure to meet you.

knew, new
Knew is the past tense of *know.*
  I *knew* Teresa in high school.
New means "fresh, recent, not old."
  I want some *new* shoes.

know, no

Know means "to understand."

  They *know* how to play soccer.

No is a negative.

  Carla has *no* fear of heights.

Exercise 1 **Practice: Words That Sound Alike/Look Alike**

Circle the correct word in the following sentences.

1. When I first saw the (desert / dessert) in a Tucson sunset, the sight was so beautiful that I had to catch my (breath / breathe).

2. Ron and Sandy were (conscience / conscious) of the fact that they would need more (capital / capitol) to start their web design business.

3. Marcy hoped that (buy / by) working extra hours, she would save enough money to (buy / by) her brother a special wedding present.

4. After graduation, the students felt that they could go (forth / fourth) into the world and face (knew / new) challenges.

5. I (heard / herd) that (hole / whole)-grain bread is better for people than white bread.

6. I hate to read (allowed / aloud); (beside / besides), I have a cold today, and my voice is weak.

7. Lee Anne had (all ready / already) eaten all the leftover macaroni and cheese by the time I got home; the only thing left in the cabinet was a box of (cereal / serial).

8. Martin (choose / chose) to make his (decent / descent) into a world of violence and despair instead of fighting for a better life.

Collaborate

Exercise 2 **Collaborate: Words That Sound Alike/Look Alike**

With a partner or a group, write one sentence for each of the words below. When you have completed this exercise, exchange it with another group's completed exercise for evaluation.

1. a. its _____

   b. it's _____

2. a. addition _____

   b. edition _____

3. a. accept _____

   b. except _____

4. a. brake _____

   b. break _____

5. a. farther _____

   b. further _____

6. a. hear   _____

     b. here   _____

7. a. fair   _____

     b. fare   _____

8. a. its   _____

     b. it's   _____

Connect

| Exercise 3 | **Connect: Correcting Errors in Words That Sound Alike/Look Alike** |

The following paragraph has ten errors in words that sound alike or look alike. Correct the errors in the space above each error.

> If someone asked me to chose a perfect day, I would not altar one moment
>
> of yesterday. Twenty-four hours ago, my brother returned from months of military
>
> duty in Iraq. Once I had been informed of his return, I spent the final days of
>
> his overseas service holding my breathe. I was conscience of the many stories
>
> of soldiers being wounded or killed days before their tours of duty were over.
>
> Every time I herd a knock at the door, I feared bad news. Yet the day came when
>
> Carleton was supposed to arrive, and my sisters and I were already to meet are
>
> hero at the airport. Seeing Carleton was better than I had expected. He looked
>
> strong, healthy, and happy. Being able to hug him was pure joy. I felt as if a whole
>
> in my heart had been filled with happiness. Fear had lost it's power over me, and
>
> I new real peace at last.

MORE WORDS THAT SOUND ALIKE/LOOK ALIKE

lead, led
When *lead* rhymes with *need,* it means "to give direction, to take charge."
When *lead* rhymes with *bed,* it is a metal.
> The marching band will *lead* the parade.
> Your bookbag is as heavy as *lead.*
Led is the past form of *lead* when it means "to take charge."
> The cheerleaders *led* the parade last year.

loan, lone
A *loan* is something you give on the condition that it be returned.
> When I was broke, I got a *loan* of fifty dollars from my aunt.
Lone means "solitary, alone."
> A *lone* shopper stood in the checkout line.

loose, lose
Loose means "not tight."
> In the summer, *loose* clothing keeps me cool.

To *lose* something means "to be unable to keep it."

I'm afraid I will *lose* my car keys.

moral, morale

Moral means "upright, honorable, connected to ethical standards."

Students have a *moral* obligation to do their own work.

Morale is confidence or spirit.

After the game, the team's *morale* was low.

pain, pane

Pain means "suffering."

I had very little *pain* after the surgery.

A *pane* is a piece of glass.

The girl's wild throw broke a window *pane*.

pair, pear

A *pair* is a set of two.

Mark has a *pair* of antique swords.

A *pear* is a fruit.

In the autumn, I like a *pear* for a snack.

passed, past

Passed means "went by." It can also mean "handed to."

The happy days *passed* too quickly.

Janice *passed* me the mustard.

Past means "a time before the present." It can also mean "beyond" or "by."

The family reunion was like a trip to the *past*.

Rick ran *past* the tennis courts.

patience, patients

Patience is calm endurance.

When I am caught in a traffic jam, I should have more *patience*.

Patients are people under medical care.

There are too many *patients* in the doctor's waiting room.

peace, piece

Peace is calmness.

Looking at the ocean brings me a sense of *peace*.

A *piece* is a part of something.

Norman took a *piece* of coconut cake.

personal, personnel

Personal means "connected to a person." It can also mean "intimate."

Whether to lease or own a car is a *personal* choice.

That information is too *personal* to share.

Personnel are the staff in an office.

The Digby Electronics Company is developing a new health plan for its *personnel*.

plain, plane

Plain means "simple," "clear," or "ordinary." It can also mean "flat land."

The restaurant serves *plain* but tasty food.

Her house was in the center of a windy *plain*.

A *plane* is an aircraft.

We took a small *plane* to the island.

presence, presents
Your *presence* is your attendance, your being somewhere.
>We request your *presence* at our wedding.
Presents are gifts.
>My daughter got too many birthday *presents*.

principal, principle
Principal means "most important." It also means "the head of a school."
>My *principal* reason for quitting is the low salary.
>The *principal* of Crestview Elementary School is popular with students.
A *principle* is a guiding rule.
>Betraying a friend is against my *principles*.

quiet, quit, quite
Quiet means "without noise."
>The library has many *quiet* corners.
Quit means "stop."
>Will you *quit* complaining?
Quite means "truly" or "exactly."
>Victor's speech was *quite* convincing.

rain, reign, rein
Rain is wet weather.
>We have had a week of *rain*.
To *reign* is to rule; *reign* is royal rule.
>King Arthur's *reign* in Camelot is the subject of many poems.
A *rein* is a leather strap in an animal's harness.
>When Charlie got on the horse, he held the *reins* very tight.

right, rite, write
Right is a direction (the opposite of left). It can also mean "correct."
>To get to the gas station, turn *right* at the corner.
>On my sociology test, I got nineteen out of twenty questions *right*.
A *rite* is a ceremony.
>I am interested in the funeral *rites* of other cultures.
To *write* is to set down words.
>Brian has to *write* a book report.

sight, site, cite
A *sight* is something you can see.
>The truck stop was a welcome *sight*.
A *site* is a location.
>The city is building a courthouse on the *site* of my old school.
Cite means to quote an authority. It can also mean to give an example.
>In her term paper, Christina wanted to *cite* several computer experts.
>When my father lectured me on speeding, he *cited* the story of my best friend's car accident.

sole, soul
A *sole* is the bottom of a foot or shoe. *Sole* can also mean "only."
>My left boot needs a new *sole*.
>Lisa was the *sole* winner of the raffle.
A *soul* is the spiritual part of a person.
>Some people say meditation is good for the *soul*.

stair, stare

A *stair* is a step.

> The toddler carefully climbed each *stair*.

A *stare* is a long, fixed look.

> I wish that woman wouldn't *stare* at me.

stake, steak

A *stake* is a stick driven into the ground. It can also mean "at risk" or "in question."

> The gardener put *stakes* around the tomato plants.

> Keith was nervous because his career was at *stake*.

A *steak* is a piece of meat or fish.

> I like my *steak* cooked medium rare.

stationary, stationery

Stationary means "standing still."

> As the speaker presented his speech, he remained *stationary*.

Stationery is writing paper.

> For my birthday, my uncle gave me some *stationery* with my name printed on it.

than, then

Than is used to compare things.

> For me, writing an essay is easier *than* taking an algebra exam.

Then means "at that time."

> I lived in Buffalo for two years; *then* I moved to Albany.

their, there, they're

Their means "belonging to them."

> My grandparents donated *their* old television to a women's shelter.

There means "at that place." It can also be used as an introductory word.

> Sit *there*, next to Simone.

> *There* is a reason for his happiness.

They're is a short form of *they are*.

> Jaime and Sandra are visiting; *they're* my cousins.

thorough, through, threw

Thorough means "complete."

> I did a *thorough* cleaning of my closet.

Through means "from one side to the other." It can also mean "finished."

> We drove *through* Greenview on our way to Lake Western.

> I'm *through* with my studies.

Threw is the past form of *throw*.

> I *threw* the moldy bread into the garbage.

to, too, two

To means "in a direction toward." It is also a word that can go in front of a verb.

> I am driving *to* Miami.

> Selena loves *to* write poems.

Too means "also." It also means "very."

> Anita played great golf; Adam did well, *too*.

> It is *too* kind of you to visit.

Two is the number.

> Mr. Almeida owns *two* clothing stores.

vain, vane, vein

Vain means "conceited." It also means "unsuccessful."

Victor is *vain* about his dark, curly hair.

The doctor made a *vain* attempt to revive the patient.

A *vane* is a device that moves to indicate the direction of the wind.

There was an old weather *vane* on the barn roof.

A *vein* is a blood vessel.

I could see the *veins* in his hands.

waist, waste

The *waist* is the middle part of the body.

He had a leather belt around his *waist*.

Waste means "to use carelessly." It also means "thrown away because it is useless."

I can't *waste* my time watching trashy television shows.

That manufacturing plant has many *waste* products.

wait, weight

Wait means "to hold oneself ready for something."

I can't *wait* until my check arrives.

Weight means "heaviness."

He tested the *weight* of the bat.

weather, whether

Weather refers to the conditions outside.

If the *weather* is warm, I'll go swimming.

Whether means "if."

Whether you help me or not, I'll paint the hallway.

were, we're, where

Were is the past form of *are*.

Only last year, we *were* scared freshmen.

We're is the short form of *we are*.

Today *we're* confident sophomores.

Where refers to a place.

Show me *where* you used to play basketball.

whined, wind, wined

Whined means "complained."

Paula *whined* about the weather because the rain kept her indoors.

Wind (if it rhymes with *find*) means "to coil or wrap something" or "to turn a key."

Wind that extension cord or you'll trip on it.

Wind (if it rhymes with *sinned*) is air in motion.

The *wind* blew my cap off.

If someone *wined* you, he or she treated you to some wine.

My brother *wined* and dined his boss.

who's, whose

Who's is a short form of *who is* or *who has*.

Who's driving?

Who's been stealing my quarters?

Whose means "belonging to whom."

I wonder *whose* dog this is.

woman, women

Woman means "one female person."

A *woman* in the supermarket gave me her extra coupons.

Women means "more than one female person."

Three *women* from Missouri joined the management team.

wood, would

Wood is the hard substance in the trunks and branches of trees.

I have a table made of a polished *wood*.

Would is the past form of *will*.

Albert said he *would* think about the offer.

your, you're

Your means "belonging to you."

I think you dropped *your* wallet.

You're is the short form of *you are*.

You're not telling the truth.

Exercise 4   **Practice: Words That Sound Alike/Look Alike**

Circle the correct word in the following sentences.

1. (Your / You're) not looking at the good parts of (your / you're) job.

2. Al (wood / would) like to know (weather / whether) Caitlin is selling her car.

3. (Were / We're / Where) at the spot (were / we're / where) that great seafood restaurant used to be.

4. King Henry VIII of England (rained / reigned / reined) for many years and (lead / led) his people during a time of great change.

5. I have to get some good (stationary / stationery) so I can (right / rite / write) letters of application to potential employers.

6. (Their / There / They're) house has a bright and cheerful kitchen, but (their / there / they're) is something gloomy about our small kitchen.

7. Every time Irving (whined / wind / wined) about the long (wait / weight) at the ticket line, Sheila wanted to shout at him.

8. I'm not sure (who's / whose) been making those prank phone calls, but I know (who's / whose) idea it was.

Collaborate

Exercise 5   **Collaborate: Words That Look Alike/Sound Alike**

With a partner or group, write one sentence for each of the words below. When you have completed this exercise, exchange it for another group's completed exercise for evaluation.

1. **a.** waist   _____

   b. waste   _____

2. **a.** principal   _____

   b. principle   _____

3. a. quiet _____

   b. quit _____

   c. quite _____

4. a. passed _____

   b. past _____

5. a. patience _____

   b. patients _____

6. a. pair _____

   b. pear _____

7. a. than _____

   b. then _____

8. a. loose _____

   b. lose _____

Exercise 6   **Connect: Correcting Errors in Words That Sound
Alike/Look Alike**

Connect

The following paragraph has twelve errors in words that sound alike or look alike. Corect the errors in the space above each error.

Amanda is very self-conscious when people stair at her. Her first reaction

is to assume that strangers are looking at her because something is wrong with

her. She wonders if she's wearing to much makeup, or if her outfit is too plane, or

if a peace of spinach is stuck to her teeth. Amanda is not a vane person; in fact,

it's her insecurity that puts her thorough the pane of examining herself for her

flaws. To try to improve her moral, I tell her that others are not staring because

her presents is unattractive. I advise her that everyone enjoys the site of a women

with personnel style.

Exercise 7   **Practice: Words That Sound Alike/Look Alike:
A Comprehensive Exercise**

Circle the correct word in the following sentences.

1. When I am trying to find the (right / rite / write) way to handle a big problem, my brother sometimes (councils / counsels) me.

2. I wonder if my warning had (a / an / and) (affect / effect) on Simon.

3. In my paper on the (rain / reign / rein) of Queen Victoria, I have to (sight / site / cite) at least three historians.

4. Hundreds of years ago, people wore (close / clothes / cloths) made of (coarse / course) wool (close / clothes / cloth).

5. Drive a little (farther / further) down the street, and you will see the (capital / capitol) building in the distance.

6. Train (fair / fare) has increased so much that (its / it's) forced many people to walk to work.

7. Above the (altar / alter) was a huge painting of an (angel / angle).

8. Every day, my grandfather rides his (stationary / stationery) bike; he gets many (complements / compliments) on his trim body.

Connect

Exercise 8 **Connect: Correcting Errors in Words That Sound Alike/Look Alike: A Comprehensive Exercise**

The following paragraph has eleven errors in words that sound alike or look alike. Correct the errors in the space above each line.

One big difference between me and my parents is in the role music plays

in there lives and in mine. I want music to be everywhere in my life. When I am

at home, music channels like MTV or VH1 are on constantly; they are the back-

ground music for my meals, my studies, my chores, and my free time. If I am not

listening to the music on television, I drown out the quite with CDs. In the car, I

have programmed the radio with the stations that are my favorites, and I blast the

music as I drive. My parents, on the other hand, may go threw an entire day with-

out music. My mother and father wood never think of turning on a music channel

like VH1, which appeals to older people. My mother sometimes listens to music on

the car radio, but my father tunes in to talk radio as he drives. To my parents, the

principle purpose of music seems to be to act as a background at large gatherings

like weddings or dances. Perhaps people our destined to brake the habit of living

with music as they grow older. Still, its hard for me to except the idea that one day

I, to, may loose my need for music in every part of the day and night.

MyWritingLab™ Visit Chapter 18, "Words That Sound Alike/Look Alike," in *MyWritingLab* to test your understanding of the chapter objectives.

Using Prepositions Correctly

CHAPTER 19

Which sentence(s) is/are correct?

A. *Margaret is looking for available classes next semester.*

B. *This psychology class is different than my last psychology class.*

(After you study this chapter, you will be confident of your answer.)

Learning Objectives

In this chapter, you will learn to:

① Identify prepositions that show time and prepositions that indicate place.

② Identify expressions that use prepositions.

Prepositions are usually short words that often signal a kind of position, possession, or other relationship. The words that come after the preposition are part of a **prepositional phrase**. You use prepositions often because there are many expressions that contain prepositions.

① Identify prepositions that show time and prepositions that indicate place.

Sometimes it is difficult to decide on the correct preposition. The following pages explain kinds of prepositions and their uses, and list some common prepositions.

PREPOSITIONS THAT SHOW TIME

At a specific time means "then."

> I will meet you *at* three o'clock.
> *At* 7:00 p.m., he closes the store.

By a specific time means "no later than" that time.
> You have to finish your paper *by* noon.
> I'll be home *by* 9:30 p.m.

Until a specific time means "continuing up to" that time.
> I talked on the phone *until* midnight.
> I will wait for you *until* 7:00 p.m.

In a specific time period is used with hours, minutes, days, weeks, months, or years.
> *In* a week, I'll have my degree.
> My family hopes to visit me *in* August.

> **Note:** Write *in* the morning, *in* the afternoon, *in* the evening, but *at* night.

For a period of time means "during" that time period.
> James took music lessons *for* five years.
> I studied *for* an hour.

Since means "from then until now."
> I haven't heard from you *since* December.
> Juanita has been my friend *since* our high school days.

On a specific date means "at that time."
> I'll see you *on* March 23.
> Registration for summer classes will open *on* Saturday.

During means "within" or "throughout" a time period.
> The baby woke up *during* the night.
> Robert worked part time *during* the winter semester.

PREPOSITIONS TO INDICATE PLACE

On usually means "on the surface of," "on top of."
> Put your assignment *on* my desk.
> They have a house *on* Second Avenue.

In usually means "within" or "inside of."
> The markers are *in* the desk.
> They have a house *in* Bolivia.

At usually means "in," "on," or "near to."
> I'll meet you *at* the market.
> The coffee shop is *at* the corner of Second Avenue and Hawthorne Road.
> Jill was standing *at* the door.

❷ Identify expressions that use prepositions.

EXPRESSIONS WITH PREPOSITIONS

angry about: You are *angry about* a thing.
> Suzanne was *angry about* the dent in her car.

angry at: You are *angry at* a thing.
> Carl was *angry at* the cruel treatment of the refugees.

angry with: You are *angry with* a person.
> Richard became *angry with* his mother when she criticized him.

approve of, disapprove of: You *approve* or *disapprove of* a thing or a person or group's actions.

>I *approve of* the smoking ban.
>I *disapprove of* smoking in public places.

argue about: You *argue about* some subject.

>We used to *argue about* money.

argue for: You *argue for* something you want.

>The Student Council *argued for* more student parking.

argue with: You *argue with* a person.

>When I was a child, I spent hours *arguing with* my little sister.

arrive at: You *arrive at* a place.

>We will *arrive at* your house tomorrow.

between, among: You use *between* with two. You use *among* with three or more.

>It will be a secret *between* you and me.
>The work was completed *among* the committee members.

bored by, bored with: You are *bored by* or *bored with* something. Do *not* write *bored of*.

>The audience was *bored by* the long movie.
>The child became *bored with* her toys.
>**not this:** ~~I am bored of school~~.

call on: You *call on* someone socially or to request something of a person.

>My aunt *called on* her new neighbors.
>Our club will *call on* you to collect tickets at the door.

call to: You *call to* someone from a distance.

>I heard him *call to* me from the top of the hill.

call up: You *call up* someone on the telephone.

>When she heard the news, Susan *called up* all her friends.

differ from: You *differ from* someone, or something *differs from* something.

>Roberta *differs from* Cheri in hair color and height.
>Writing an essay in class *differs from* writing an essay outside of class.

differ with: You *differ with* (disagree with) someone about something.

>Theresa *differs with* Mike on the subject of food stamps.

different from: You are *different from* someone; something is *different from* something else. Do *not* write *different than*.

>Carl is *different from* his older brother.
>The movie was *different from* the book.
>**not this:** ~~The movie was different than the book~~.

grateful for: You are *grateful for* something.

>I am *grateful for* my scholarship.

grateful to: You are *grateful to* someone.

>My brother was *grateful to* my aunt for her advice.

interested in: You are *interested in* something.

>The children were *interested in* playing computer games.

look at: You *look at* someone or something.

>Taylor *looked at* the assignment and laughed.

look for: You *look for* someone or something.
>   David needs to *look for* his lost key.

look up: You *look up* information.
>   I can *look up* his address in the phone book.

made of: Something or someone is *made of* something.
>   Do you think I'm *made of* money?
>   The new smartphone was *made of* plastic.

need for: You have a *need for* something.
>   The committee expressed a *need for* better leadership.

object to: You *object to* something.
>   Lisa *objected to* her husband's weekend plans.

obligation to: You have an *obligation to* someone.
>   I feel an *obligation to* my parents, who supported me while I was in
>   college.

opportunity for: You have an *opportunity for* something; an *opportunity*
exists *for* someone.
>   The new job gives her an *opportunity for* a career change.
>   A trip to China is a wonderful *opportunity for* Mimi.

pay for: You *pay* someone *for* something.
>   I have to *pay* the bookstore *for* my textbooks.

pay to: You *pay* something *to* someone.
>   Brian *paid* fifty dollars *to* the woman who found his lost dog.

popular with: Something or someone is *popular with* someone.
>   Jazz is not *popular with* my friends.

prefer . . . to: You *prefer* something *to* something.
>   I *prefer* jazz *to* classical music.

prejudice against: You have a *prejudice against* someone or something.
>   My father finally conquered his *prejudice against* women drivers.
>   He is *prejudiced* against scientists.

> **Note:** Remember to add *-ed* when the word becomes an adjective.

protect against: Something or someone *protects against* something or
someone.
>   A good raincoat can *protect* you *against* heavy rain.

protect from: Something or someone *protects from* something or someone.
>   A good lock on your door can *protect* you *from* break-ins.

qualification for: You have a *qualification for* a position.
>   André is missing an important *qualification for* the job.

qualified to: You are *qualified to* do something.
>   Tim isn't *qualified to* judge the paintings.

quote from: You *quote* something *from* someone else.
>   The graduation speaker *quoted* some lines *from* Shakespeare.

reason for: You give a *reason for* something.
>   He offered no *reason for* his cheating.

reason with: You *reason with* someone.
Sonny tried to *reason with* the angry motorist.

responsible for: You are *responsible for* something.
Luther is *responsible for* the mess in the kitchen.

responsible to: You are *responsible to* someone.
At the restaurant, the waiters are *responsible to* the assistant manager.

rob of: You *rob* someone *of* something.
His insult *robbed* me *of* my dignity.

similar to: Someone or something is *similar to* someone or something.
Your dress is *similar to* a dress I wore yesterday.

succeed in: You *succeed in* something.
I hope I can *succeed in* getting a job.

superior to: Someone or something is *superior to* someone or something.
My final paper was *superior to* my first paper.

take advantage of: You *take advantage of* someone or something.
Maria is going to *take advantage of* the fine weather and go to the beach.

take care of: You *take care of* someone or something.
Will you *take care of* my apartment while I am away?

talk about: You *talk about* something.
We can *talk about* the trip tomorrow.

talk over: You *talk over* something.
The cousins met to *talk over* the plans for the anniversary party.

talk to: You *talk to* someone.
I'll *talk to* my academic advisor.

talk with: You *talk with* someone.
Esther needs to *talk with* her boyfriend.

tired of: You are *tired of* something.
Sylvia is *tired of* driving to work.

wait for: You *wait for* someone or something.
Jessica must *wait for* Alan to arrive.

wait on: You use *wait on* only if you wait on customers.
At the diner, I have to *wait on* too many people.

Exercise 1 **Practice: Choosing the Correct Preposition**

Circle the correct preposition in each of the following sentences.

1. With flowers or cookies in her hands, my aunt (calls on / calls to / calls up) lonely or housebound neighbors.

2. Paul likes shrimp, but he prefers a large steak (over / to) most seafood.

3. You have to be at work (by / during) 8:00 a.m. tomorrow.

4. Mark was never interested (at / in) going to college.

5. Hang your jacket (on / in) the closet.

6. Leo likes to study (in / at) night.

7. My boss said I had all the qualifications (for / to) a promotion to assistant manager.

8. Emilio soon became bored (of / with) the history class.

Exercise 2 **Practice: Choosing the Correct Preposition**

Circle the correct preposition in each of the following sentences.

1. If you go to the mall, be sure to look (up / for) a cheap raincoat.

2. My uncle works in a restaurant (in / at) the north end of Mill Road.

3. I have been waiting (on / for) you (since / for) twenty minutes.

4. Bruce was riding (in / on) a new sports car yesterday.

5. My college English class is different (from / than) my senior English class in high school.

6. At the meeting, several students came to argue (with / for) smaller class sizes.

7. After he saw the movie about starvation in Africa, John became angry (at / with) the hopeless situation of millions.

8. The professor divided the work (between/ among) the four groups.

Collaborate

Exercise 3 **Collaborate: Writing Sentences Using Expressions with Prepositions**

Do this exercise with a partner or group. Below are pairs of expressions with prepositions. Write a sentence that contains each pair. The first one is done for you.

1. **a.** argue with   **b.** object to

   sentence: In college, I used to argue with my roommate whenever he would object to my loud music.

2. **a.** take advantage of   **b.** arrive at

   sentence: _____

   _____

3. **a.** grateful for   **b.** wait on

   sentence: _____

   _____

4. **a.** between   **b.** similar to

   sentence: _____

   _____

5. **a.** popular with   **b.** bored by

   sentence: _____

   _____

6. a. look for   **b.** qualified to

    sentence: _____

    _____

7. a. prejudice against   **b.** reason for

    sentence: _____

    _____

8. a. superior to   **b.** opportunity for

    sentence: _____

    _____

Collaborate

Exercise 4 **Collaborate: Writing Sentences Using Expressions with Prepositions**

Do this exercise with a partner. Review the list of expressions with prepositions in this chapter. Select five expressions that you think are troublesome for writers. Write the expressions below. Then exchange your list for a partner's list. Your partner will write a sentence for each expression on your list; you will write sentences for his or her list. When you have completed the exercises, check each other's sentences.

    1. expression: _____

       sentence: _____

    2. expression: _____

       sentence: _____

    3. expression: _____

       sentence: _____

    4. expression: _____

       sentence: _____

    5. expression: _____

       sentence: _____

Exercise 5 **Connect: Using Prepositions Correctly**

Connect

The following paragraph has ten errors in prepositions. Correct the errors in the space above each error.

    My roommate Bill has a habit of becoming angry with some minor incident,

and then it is impossible to reason for him. Last week, for example, he told me

that he and I needed to talk with my careless behavior. Until the time I was able

to figure out what "behavior" Bill was describing, he had already turned into a

red-faced, shouting monster. He was ranting about my leaving the door unlocked

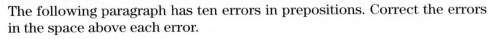

while I went down the hall to check our mailbox. "Someday, you'll be responsible to a burglary when someone sees the unlocked door and walks right on!" he complained. "You'll have to pay to the missing items when some criminal robs the apartment!" Because our apartment door is about twenty feet from the mailboxes, I refused to argue for Bill. I am getting tired by listening to Bill's tantrums. So, instead of arguing, I am going to look on local "Roommate Wanted" ads online. Maybe I'll find someone calmer than Bill.

PHRASAL VERBS

While many of the verbs we have seen are often followed by a preposition, other verbs contain a preposition. These verbs are called **phrasal verbs** and they are informally called *two-word verbs* (and sometimes *three-word verbs*). The meaning of each word by itself is different from the meaning the two words have when they are together. Look at this example:

My friend **dropped by** yesterday.

Drop by means "to visit" while *drop* means "to stop holding something."

Sometimes the verb and the preposition can be separated in phrasal verbs and they are called "separable":

Yesterday, I **took** my brother **out** to dinner.

Here is a list of some common separable and inseparable phrasal verbs:

Common "Separable" Phrasal Verbs

ask out: He *asked* her *out.*
call up: Neil *calls* Marsha *up* on weekends.
drop off: I can *drop* you *off* on my way to school.
think over: Thank you for the offer; I will *think* it *over.*
try on: I like that dress and will *try* it *on.*

Common "Inseparable" Phrasal Verbs

come across: If you *come across* a good mystery, let me know.
get over: I can't seem to *get over* this cold.
look after: She needs to *look after* her nephew tomorrow.
looking forward to: She is *looking forward to* graduation.
take advantage of: You need to *take advantage of* the help session this semester.

> **Note:** Interestingly, some phrasal verbs can be considered both "separable" and "inseparable" depending on their meaning within the sentence. Here are some examples:
>
> **fill in** (separable): Please *fill* me *in* about the arrest today.
> (inseparable): Mike will *fill in* for me at the conference today.
>
> **get ready for** (separable): She needs to *get* her children *ready for* the party.
> (inseparable): She needs to *get ready for* the party.

Exercise 6 **Practice: Writing Sentences with Phrasal Verbs**

Write a sentence for each of the following two- or three-word verbs. Use the examples above as a guide, but consult a dictionary if you are not sure what the verbs mean.

1. grow accustomed to _____

_____

2. come across _____

_____

3. run into _____

_____

4. take advantage of _____

_____

5. looking forward to _____

_____

6. drop off _____

_____

7. keep in mind _____

_____

Exercise 7 **Connect: Using Prepositions Correctly**

Connect

The following paragraph has eleven errors in prepositions. Correct the errors in the space above each error.

Our dog Annabelle was terrified of thunderstorms, and for a long time, we

couldn't do anything to help her. At the first distant rumble of thunder, Annabelle

looked up, with her ears raised, and listened. Then she would look at the family (my

father, my mother, and me) as if to beg us for some comfort. Annabelle wanted the

storm to go away. By the time the lightning and thunder had reached our home, the

dog was hiding under the bed or on a closet. Often she began to wail. Since years,

Annabelle suffered. We didn't know what to do. We couldn't reason for a dog by

explaining that the storm would be gone soon. Between the three of us, we tried

many remedies for Annabelle's pain. My mother sat near the bed or closet, called up

the dog, and, by holding a treat, tried to lure Annabelle out of hiding. Using the Inter-

net, my father looked on information about dogs and thunderstorms, but he couldn't

find much. I tried dragging the dog out of her hiding place, but she shook so pitifully that I let her go back to her safe spot. We felt extremely sorry for our dog and knew

that we could not protect her about inevitable summer storms. Eventually, we did

succeed on helping, but not curing, Annabelle. Our neighbor told us about an herb

that helps to calm anxiety in pets. We found the herb, in capsule form, at a local pet

store. The next time we heard a faint roll of thunder, we slipped the herbal pill into a

spoonful of canned dog food and fed the mixture to our dog. On that thunderstorm,

Annabelle remained anxious, but she was not frightened enough to hide and cry.

Until the day we first gave our dog the herbal remedy, we have continued to rely on it

to calm Annabelle when a storm threatens. We will always be grateful for our neigh-

bor for helping us to ease our dog's suffering.

Collaborate

| Exercise 8 | **Collaborate: Recognizing Prepositional Phrases in a Famous Speech** |

Do this exercise with a group. Following is part of a famous speech by Winston Churchill, prime minister of Great Britain during World War II. When Churchill gave this speech in 1940, the Nazis had just defeated the British troops at Dunkirk, France. In this speech, Churchill explained the events at Dunkirk and then rallied the nation to keep fighting.

To do this exercise, have one member of your group read the speech aloud while the other members listen. Then underline all the prepositional phrases in it. Be ready to share your answers with another group.

We shall not flag* nor fail. We shall go on to the end. We shall fight in France

and on the seas and oceans; we shall fight with growing confidence and growing

strength in the air.

We shall defend our island whatever the cost may be; we shall fight on beaches,

on landing grounds, in fields, in streets and on the hills. We shall never surrender and

even if, which I do not for a moment believe, this island or a large part of it were sub-

jugated* and starving, then our empire beyond the seas, armed and guarded by the

British Fleet,* would carry on the struggle until in God's good time the New World,

with all its power and might, sets forth to the liberation and rescue of the Old.

***flag** means to lose energy
***subjugated** means conquered by the enemy
***the fleet** is a group of warships

MyWritingLab™ Visit Chapter 19, "Using Prepositions Correctly," in *MyWritingLab* to test your understanding of the chapter objectives.

Writing in Stages: The Process Approach

INTRODUCTION

MyWritingLab™
Access the "Writing in Stages" videos in *MyWritingLab*

Learning by Doing

Writing is a skill, and like any skill, writing improves with practice. This part of the book provides you with ample practice to improve your writing through a variety of individual and group activities. Whether you complete assignments at home or in the classroom, just remember that *good writing takes practice:* you can learn to write well by writing.

Steps Make Writing Easier

Writing is easier if you *do not try to do too much at once*. To make the task of writing easier, this section breaks the process into four major stages:

PREWRITING

In this stage, you think about your topic and you *gather ideas*. You *react* to your own ideas and add even more thoughts. You can also react to other people's ideas as a way of expanding your own writing.

PLANNING

In this stage, you examine your ideas and begin to *focus* them around one main idea or point. Planning involves combining, categorizing, and even eliminating some ideas. Placing your specific details in a logical order often involves *outlining*.

DRAFTING AND REVISING

In this stage, the thinking and planning begin to take shape as a piece of writing. You complete a draft of your work, a *rough version* of the finished product. Then you examine the draft and consider ways to *revise* it, a process that may require writing and reworking several versions of your original draft.

EDITING AND PROOFREADING

In this stage, you give your latest revised draft one last, careful review. *Editing* involves identifying and correcting any problems in sentence structure, word choice, spelling, or punctuation you may have missed during revisions. *Proofreading* entails reading your paper one last time to catch any carelessness such as format errors, missing punctuation, spelling mistakes, or even typos.

These four stages in the writing process—**prewriting, planning, drafting and revising**, and **editing and proofreading**—may overlap. You may be changing your plan even as you work on the draft of your paper. There is no rule that prevents you from returning to an earlier stage. In these writing chapters, you will have many opportunities to become familiar with the stages of effective writing. Working individually and with your classmates, you can become a better writer along *all* lines.

Contents   Page

Jumping In

Where do you get your ideas for writing? Do they seem to come at you all at once? Working with a jumble of ideas is a natural part of the writing process. Fortunately, there are several ways to draw on your imagination, experiences, beliefs, and opinions as you sort through these ideas and begin a **paragraph** *that focuses on one idea or point.*

Learning Objectives

In this chapter, you will learn how to:

1 Prewrite to generate specific ideas for a paragraph topic.

2 Select an idea and develop details for it.

3 Create a topic sentence that summarizes the details of your specific idea.

The paragraph is the basic building block of most writing. It is a group of sentences focusing on one idea or one point. Keep this concept in mind: *one idea for each paragraph*. Focusing on one idea or one point gives a paragraph **unity**. If you have a new point, start a new paragraph.

You may ask, "Doesn't this mean a paragraph will be short? How long should a paragraph be, anyway?" To convince a reader of one main point, you need to make it, support it, develop it, explain it, and describe it. There will be shorter and longer paragraphs, but for now, you can assume your paragraph will be between seven and twelve sentences long.

This chapter guides you through the first stage of the writing process, the **prewriting** stage, where you generate ideas for your paragraph.

① Prewrite to generate specific ideas for a paragraph topic.

BEGINNING THE PREWRITING

Suppose your instructor asks you to write a paragraph about family. To write effectively, you need to know your **purpose** and your **audience**. In this case, you already know your purpose: to write a paragraph that makes some point about family. You also know your audience since you are writing this paragraph for your instructor and classmates. Often, your purpose is to write a specific type of paper for a class. However, you may have to write with a different purpose for a particular audience. Writing instructions for a new employee at your workplace, writing a letter of complaint to a manufacturer, and composing a short autobiographical essay for a scholarship application are examples of different purposes and audiences.

Freewriting, Brainstorming, Keeping a Journal

Once you have identified your purpose and audience, you can begin by finding some way to *think* on paper. To gather ideas, you can use the techniques of freewriting, brainstorming, or keeping a journal.

Freewriting Give yourself ten minutes to write whatever comes into your mind on the subject. If you can't think of anything to write, just write, "I can't think of anything to write," over and over until you think of something else. The main goal of **freewriting** is to *write without stopping*. Don't stop to tell yourself, "This is stupid" or "I can't use any of this in a paper." Just write. Let your ideas flow. Write freely. Here's an example:

Freewriting About Family

Family. Family. Whose family? What is a family? What *does* she want me to write about? I'm not married. I don't have a family. Sure, my mother. I guess I have a big <u>other</u> family, too. Cousins, aunts, uncles. But my basic family is my mother and brother, Tito. Is that a family? She's a good mom. Always takes care of me. Family ties. Family matters. How a family treats children.

Brainstorming **Brainstorming** is like freewriting because you write whatever comes into your head, but it is a little different because you can *pause to ask yourself questions* that will lead to new ideas. When you brainstorm alone, you "interview" yourself about a subject. Or you can brainstorm within a group.

If you are brainstorming about family, alone or with a partner or group, you might begin by listing ideas and then add to the ideas by asking and answering questions. Review the example of brainstorming on the next page.

CRITICAL THINKING

When freewriting or brainstorming, applying *who, what, when, where, why,* and *how* questions can help you explore ideas. Such questioning can lead to meaningful reflection and analysis as you gradually narrow your focus and devise suitable topic sentences.

Brainstorming About Family

Family.

Family members.

Who is your favorite family member?

I don't know. Uncle Ray, I guess.

Why is he your favorite?

He's funny. Especially at those family celebrations.

What celebrations?

Birthdays, anniversaries, dinners. I hated those dinners when I was little.

Why did you hate them?

I had to get all dressed up.

What else did you hate about them?

I had to sit still through the longest, most boring meals.

Why were they boring?

All these grown-ups talking. My mother made me sit there, politely.

Were you angry at your mother?

Yes. Well, no, not really. She's strict, but I love her.

If you feel like you are running out of ideas in brainstorming, try to form a question out of what you've just written. For example, if you write, "Families are changing," you could form these questions:

What families? How are they changing? Are the changes good? Why? Why not?

Forming questions helps you keep your thoughts flowing, and you will eventually arrive at a suitable focus for your paragraph.

Keeping a Journal A **journal** is a notebook of your personal writing, a notebook in which you write regularly and often. *It is not a diary, but it is a place to record your experiences, reactions, and observations.* In it, you can write about what you've done, heard, seen, read, or remembered. You can include sayings that you'd like to remember, news clippings, snapshots—anything that you'd like to recall or consider. Journals are a great way to practice your writing and a great source of ideas for writing.

If you were asked to write about family, for example, you might look through your journal entries in search of ideas, and you might see something like this:

Journal Entry About Family

I was at Mike's house last night. We were just sitting around, talking and listening to CDs. Then we were bored, so we decided to go to the movies. When we left, we walked right past Mike's mother in the kitchen. Mike didn't even say goodbye or tell her where we were going. Mike is so rude to his mother. He can't stand her. Lots of my friends hate their parents. I'm lucky. I'm close to my mother.

Finding Specific Ideas

Whether you freewrite, brainstorm, or consult your journal, you end up with something on paper. Follow these first ideas; see where they can take you. You are looking for specific ideas, each of which can focus the general one you started with. At this point, you do not have to decide which specific idea you want to write about. You just want to narrow your range of ideas.

You might ask, "Why should I narrow my ideas? Won't I have more to say if I keep my topic big?" But remember that a paragraph has one main idea, and you want to use convincing and specific details to support it. If you write one paragraph on the broad topic of family, for example, you will probably make only general statements that say very little and that bore your reader.

General ideas are big, broad ones. Specific ideas are narrow. If you scanned the freewriting example on family, you might underline many specific ideas that could be topics.

> Family. Family. Whose family? What is a family? What does she want me to write about? I'm not married. I don't have a family. Sure, <u>my mother</u>. I guess I have a <u>big other family</u>, too. Cousins, aunts, uncles. But <u>my basic family</u> is my mother and brother, Tito. Is that a family? <u>She's a good mom</u>. <u>Always takes care of me</u>. Family ties. Family matters. How a family treats children.

Consider the underlined parts. Many of them are specific ideas about family. You could write a paragraph about one underlined item or about several related items.

Another way to find specific ideas is to make a list after brainstorming, underlining specific ideas. Here is an underlined list about family:

> Family.
>
> Family members.
>
> <u>Uncle Ray</u>.
>
> He's funny. Especially at those <u>family celebrations</u>.
>
> <u>Birthdays, anniversaries, dinners. I hated those dinners when I was little</u>.
>
> <u>I had to get all dressed up</u>.
>
> I had to sit still through the <u>longest, most boring meals</u>.
>
> All these grown-ups, talking. My mother made me sit there, politely.
>
> <u>She's strict, but I love her</u>.

These specific ideas could lead you to specific topics.

If you reviewed the journal entry on family, you would be able to underline many specific ideas:

> I was at Mike's house last night. We were just sitting around, talking and listening to music. Then we were bored, so we decided to go to the movies. When we left, we walked right past Mike's mother in the kitchen. <u>Mike didn't even say goodbye or tell her where we were going. Mike is so rude to his mother. He can't stand her. Lots of my friends hate their parents. I'm lucky. I'm close to my mother</u>.

Remember that following the steps can lead you to specific ideas. Once you have some specific ideas, you can select one idea and develop it.

Exercise 1 **Practice: Brainstorming Questions and Answers**   MyWritingLab™

Following are several general topics. For each one, brainstorm by writing three questions and answers related to the topic that could lead you to specific ideas. The first topic is done for you.

1. **general topic:** home computers

   Question 1: _Do I need my home computer?_

   Answer 1: _Sure. I use it all the time._

   Question 2: _But what do I use it for?_

   Answer 2: _Games. Going online to Facebook and YouTube. E-mail._

   Question 3: _So I don't use it for anything serious, do I?_

   Answer 3: _It helps me do research and type my papers._

2. **general topic:** exercise

   Question 1: _____

   Answer 1: _____

   Question 2: _____

   Answer 2: _____

   Question 3: _____

   Answer 3: _____

3. **general topic:** promises

   Question 1: _____

   Answer 1: _____

   Question 2: _____

   Answer 2: _____

   Question 3: _____

   Answer 3: _____

4. **general topic:** college campus

   Question 1: _____

   Answer 1: _____

   Question 2: _____

   Answer 2: _____

   Question 3: _____

   Answer 3: _____

Exercise 2 **Practice: Finding Specific Ideas in a List**   MyWritingLab™

Following are general topics; each general topic is followed by a list of words or phrases about the topic. It is the kind of list you could make after brainstorming. Underline the phrases that are specific and that could lead you to a specific topic. The first list is done for you.

1. **general topic:** study habits
   where people study
   <u>library</u>
   everyone has his or her own spot
   <u>how often students study</u>
   what students eat when studying

2. **general topic:** sports
   professional sports teams
   baseball heroes through the years
   my hockey injuries
   sports energy drinks
   televised soccer matches

3. **general topic:** employment
   my terrible boss
   bad jobs
   office gossip
   working the night shift
   finding and keeping a suitable job

4. **general topic:** college classes
   choosing a major
   where college classes are
   professors
   differences between high school classes
   types of classes

MyWritingLab™   Exercise 3   **Practice: Finding Specific Ideas in Freewriting**

Following is a sample of freewriting, a written response to a topic. Read the sample, and then underline any words or phrases that could become the focus of a paragraph.

Freewriting on the Topic of Classes on Fridays

<u>Classes on Fridays.</u> <u>Classes on Fridays unpopular with students.</u> They are too tired on Friday. <u>Low enrollment on Fridays.</u> <u>Students work and can't take classes.</u> Who likes Friday classes? I'm not sure anyone really likes Friday classes.

Collaborate

Exercise 4   **Collaborate: Finding Topics Through Freewriting**

Begin this exercise alone; then complete it with a partner or group. First, pick one of the topics and freewrite on it for ten minutes. Then read your freewriting to your partner or group. Ask your listener(s) to jot down any words or phrases that lead to a specific subject for a paragraph.

Your listener(s) should read the words or phrases to you. You will be hearing a collection of specific ideas that came from *your* writing. As you listen, underline the words in your freewriting.

Freewriting Topics (pick one):

a. adventures

b. arguments

c. vacations

Freewriting on _____ (name of topic chosen)

_____

_____

_____

_____

_____

_____

_____

Selecting an Idea

② Select an idea and develop details for it.

After you have a list of specific ideas, you must pick one and try to develop it by adding details. To pick an idea about family, you could survey the ideas you gathered through freewriting. Review the following freewriting in which the specific ideas are underlined:

> Family. Family. Whose family? What is a family? What does she want me to write about? I'm not married. I don't have a family. Sure, <u>my mother</u>. I guess I have <u>a big other family</u>, too. Cousins, aunts, uncles. But <u>my basic family</u> is my mother and brother, Tito. Is that a family? <u>She's a good mom</u>. <u>Always takes care of me</u>. Family ties. Family matters. How a family treats children.

Here are the specific ideas (the underlined ones) in a list:

my mother	She's a good mom.
a big other family	Always takes care of me.
my basic family	

Looking at these ideas, you decide to write your paragraph on the topic, "My Mother." Now you can begin to add details.

Adding Details to an Idea

You can develop the one idea you picked a number of ways:

1. **Check your list** for other ideas that seem to fit the one you've picked.
2. **Brainstorm**—ask yourself more questions about your topic, and use the answers as details.
3. **List any new ideas** you have that may be connected to your first idea.

One way to add details is to go back and check your list for other ideas that seem to fit with the topic, "My Mother." You find these entries:

> She's a good mom. Always takes care of me.

Another way to add details is to brainstorm some questions that will lead you to more details. These questions do not have to be connected to each other; they are just questions that could lead you to ideas and details.

> **Question: What makes your mom a good mom?**
>
> Answer: She works hard.

Question: What work does she do?

Answer: She cooks, cleans.

Question: What else?

Answer: She has a job.

Question: What job?

Answer: She's a nurse.

Question: How is your mother special?

Answer: She had a rough life.

Another way to add details is to list any ideas that may be connected to your first idea of writing about your mother. The list might give you more specific details:

makes great chicken casserole

attractive for her age

lost her husband

went to school at night

If you tried all three ways of adding details, you would end up with this list of details connected to the topic, "My Mother:"

She's a good mom.	She had a rough life.
Always takes care of me.	makes great chicken casserole
She works hard.	attractive for her age
She cooks, cleans.	lost her husband
She has a job.	went to school at night
She's a nurse.	

You now have details that you can work with as you move into the next stage of writing a paragraph.

This process may seem lengthy, but once you have worked through it several times, it will become nearly automatic. When you think about ideas before you try to shape them, you are off to a good start.

INFO BOX **Beginning the Prewriting: A Summary**

The prewriting stage of writing a paragraph enables you to gather ideas. This process begins with four steps:

1. **Think on paper and write down any ideas that you have about a general topic.** You can do this by freewriting, brainstorming, or keeping a journal.

2. **Scan your writing for specific ideas that have come from your first efforts.** List these ideas.

3. **Pick one specific idea.** This idea will be the topic of your paragraph.

4. **Add details to your topic.** You can add details by reviewing your early writing, by questioning, and by thinking further.

FOCUSING THE PREWRITING

Once you have a topic and some ideas about the topic, your next step is to *focus* your topic and ideas around some point.

Two techniques that you can use are

- marking a list of related ideas
- mapping related ideas

Marking Related Ideas

To develop a marked list, take a look at the following marked list developed under the topic, "My Mother." In this list, you'll notice some of the items have been marked with letters that represent categories for related items.

H   marks ideas about your mother at *home*.

J   marks ideas about your mother's *job*.

B   marks ideas about your mother's *background*.

Following is a marked list of ideas related to the topic, "My Mother."

H	She's a good mom.	B	She had a rough life.
H	Always takes care of me.	H	makes great chicken casserole
H & J	She works hard.		attractive for her age
H	She cooks and cleans.	B	lost her husband
H	She has a job.	B	went to school at night
j	She's a nurse.		

You have probably noticed that one item, *She works hard,* is marked with two letters, H and J, because your mother works hard both at home and on the job. One item on the list, *attractive for her age,* isn't marked. Perhaps you can come back to this item later, or perhaps you will decide you don't need it in your paragraph.

To make it easier to see what ideas you have and how they are related, try *grouping related ideas,* giving each list a title, like this:

my mother at home

She's a good mom.	Always takes care of me.
She works hard.	She cooks and cleans.
makes great chicken casserole	

my mother at her job

She has a job.	She's a nurse.
She works hard.	

my mother's background

She had a rough life.	lost her husband
went to school at night	

Mapping

Another way to focus your ideas is to mark your first list of ideas and then cluster the related ideas into separate lists. You can *map* your ideas like this:

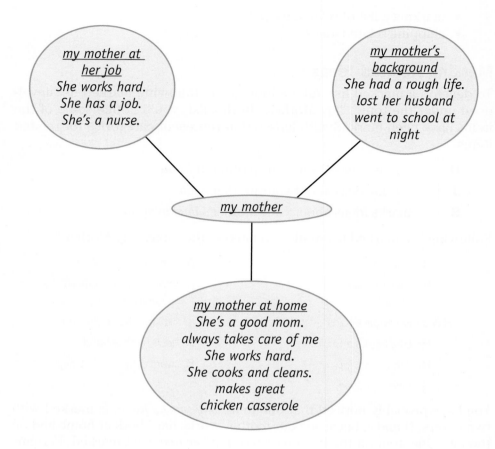

Whatever way you choose to examine and group your details, you are working toward a focus, a point. You are asking and beginning to answer the question, "Where do the details lead?" The answer will be the main idea of your paragraph, which will be stated in the topic sentence.

MyWritingLab™   Exercise 5   **Practice: Grouping Related Items in Lists of Details**

Following are lists of details. In each list, circle the items that seem to fit in one group; then underline the items that seem to belong to a second group. Some items may not belong in either group. The first list is done for you.

1. **topic:** my favorite aunt
   <u>always cheerful</u>
   <u>tells jokes</u>
   gives me compliments
   <u>laughs at her troubles</u>
   (dresses in wild colors)

   (unusual appearance)
   (wild hair)
   an accountant
   (outrageous hats)
   drives a jeep

2. **topic:** summer
   limited classes
   beach

   swimming
   longer days

lots of family time	traffic
summer clothes	more job opportunities
weather reports	ice cream

3. **topic:** accidents

carelessness	plane crash
broken bones	police investigation
fender-bender	bad weather
faulty equipment	truck overturns
sirens blasting	television news reports

4. **topic:** borrowing

home mortgage	not returning clothes
overdue library book	student loan
bankruptcy	foreclosure
credit union	car payments
repossessed car	banks

Forming a Topic Sentence

To form a **topic sentence**, do the following:

1. Review your details and see if you can form some general idea that will summarize the details.

2. Write that general idea in one sentence.

> ③ Create a topic sentence that summarizes the details of your specific idea.

The sentence that summarizes the details is the topic sentence. It makes a general point, and the more specific details you have gathered will support this point.

To form a topic sentence about your mother, you can ask yourself questions about the details. First, there are many details about your mother. You can ask yourself, "What kinds of details do I have?" You have details about your mother's background, about her job, and about her role as a mother. You might then ask, "Can I summarize those details?" You might then summarize those details to get the topic sentence:

> *My mother survived difficult times to become a good parent and worker.*

Check the sentence against your details. Does it cover your mother's background? Yes, it mentions that she survived *difficult times*. Does it cover her job? Yes, it says she is a *good worker*. Does it cover her role as a mother? Yes, it says she is a *good parent*. The topic sentence is acceptable; it is a general idea that summarizes the details.

Hints About Topic Sentences

1. **Be careful. Topics are not the same as topic sentences.** A topic is the subject you will write about. A topic sentence states the main idea you have developed on a topic. Consider the differences between the following topics and topic sentences:

topic:	my mother
topic sentence:	My mother survived difficult times to become a good parent and worker.

topic:	effects of drunk driving
topic sentence:	Drunk driving hurts the victims, their families, and friends.

Exercise 6 **Collaborate: Turning Topics into Topic Sentences**

Do this exercise with a partner or group. The following list contains some topics and some topic sentences. Have someone read the list aloud. As the list is read, decide which items are topics. Put an *X* by those items. On the lines following the list, rewrite the topics into topic sentences.

1. _____ A sound in the night

2. _____ Why choosing a major early is beneficial

3. _____ How to write a thank-you note

4. _____ My instructor is engaging

5. _____ I learned compassion at my job

6. _____ Atlanta is a wonderful place to live

7. _____ Speeding is foolish and selfish

8. _____ The misery and pain of a sore throat

Rewrite the topics. Make each one into a topic sentence.

_____

_____

_____

_____

_____

_____

_____

_____

2. Topic sentences do not announce; they make a point. Look at the following sentences and notice the differences between the sentences that announce and the topic sentences.

announcement: The subject of this paper will be my definition of a bargain.

topic sentence: A bargain is a necessary item that I bought at less than half the regular price.

announcement: I will discuss the causes of depression in my best friend.

topic sentence: My best friend's depression was caused by stress at home, work, and school.

Exercise 7 **Collaborate: Turning Announcements into Topic Sentences**

Do this exercise with a partner or group. The following list contains some topic sentences and some announcements. Have someone read this list aloud. As the list is read, decide which items are announcements. Put an *X* by those items. On the lines following the list, rewrite the announcements, making them topic sentences.

1. _____ My grandfather was the only role model in my childhood.

2. _____ How friendships grow is the subject of this paper.

3. _____ This essay will tell you why some people fly into rages.

4. _____ The drawbacks to constantly changing jobs are the topic of this essay.

5. _____ Why Carson Elementary School needs a longer school day is the issue to be discussed.

6. _____ Riding a bike to work reduces auto emissions, improves the rider's health, and reduces traffic.

7. _____ I will explain why smartphones should be allowed in college classrooms.

8. _____ Parents of a newborn need a 24-hour helpline to advise and reassure them.

Rewrite the announcements. Make each one a topic sentence.

_____

_____

_____

_____

_____

_____

_____

_____

3. Topic sentences should not be too broad to develop in one paragraph. A topic sentence that is too broad may take many pages of writing to develop. Look at the following broad sentences and then notice how they can be narrowed.

too broad: Television violence is bad for children. (This sentence is too broad because "television violence" could include anything from bloody movies to nightly news, and "children" could mean anyone under eighteen. Also, "is bad for children" could mean anything from "causes nightmares" to "provokes children to commit murder.")

**a narrower
topic sentence:** Violent cartoons teach preschoolers that hitting and hurting is fun.

> **too broad:** Education changed my life. (This sentence is so broad that you would have to talk about your whole education and your whole life to support it.)
>
> **a narrower topic sentence:** Studying for my high-school equivalency diploma gave me the confidence to try college.

Collaborate

Exercise 8 **Collaborate: Revising Topic Sentences That Are Too Broad**

Do this exercise with a partner or group. Following is a list of topic sentences. Some are too broad to support in one paragraph. Have someone read this list aloud. As the list is read, decide which sentences are too broad. Put an *X* by those sentences. On the lines following the list, rewrite those sentences, focusing on a limited idea—a topic sentence—that could be supported in one paragraph.

1. _____ When the economy is in trouble, people are reluctant to spend.

2. _____ Alicia found an outlet for her energy in rock climbing.

3. _____ A week at my sister's house introduced me to the challenges of cooking for a large family.

4. _____ My first year in college helped me to gain confidence.

5. _____ When I was sixteen, I believed that smoking cigarettes made me look sophisticated.

6. _____ Children can become spoiled by their parents.

7. _____ Online shopping wastes too much of people's time.

8. _____ Education needs a complete overhaul.

Rewrite the broad sentences. Make each one more limited.

_____

_____

_____

_____

_____

_____

_____

_____

4. Topic sentences should not be too narrow to develop in one paragraph. A topic sentence that is too narrow can't be supported by details. It may be a fact which can't be developed. A topic sentence that is too narrow leaves you with nothing more to say.

too narrow:	We had fog yesterday.
a better, expanded topic sentence:	Yesterday's fog made driving difficult.
too narrow:	I moved to Nashville when I was twenty.
a better, expanded topic sentence:	When I moved to Nashville at age twenty, I learned to live on my own.

Exercise 9 **Collaborate: Revising Topic Sentences That Are Too Narrow**

Collaborate

Do this exercise with a partner or group. Following is a list of topic sentences. Some of them are too narrow to be developed in a paragraph. Have someone read the list aloud. As the list is read, decide which sentences are too narrow. Put an *X* by those sentences. On the lines following the list, rewrite those sentences as broader topic sentences that could be developed in a paragraph.

1. _____ My jacket cost ten dollars on sale, but it was a foolish purchase.

2. _____ Cameron borrowed $123 from his parents.

3. _____ When I ate two huge pieces of chocolate cake, I broke my promise to myself.

4. _____ My advisor's office is small and quiet.

5. _____ Brendan offered to help me with algebra.

6. _____ The dock at the rear of the motel was made of rotten wood.

7. _____ I have a new tablet.

8. _____ Jim threw away his leather necklace.

Rewrite the narrow sentences. Make each one broader.

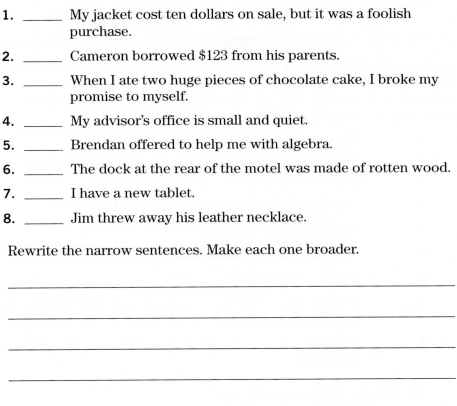

_____

_____

_____

_____

_____

_____

_____

_____

Once you have a topic sentence, you have completed the prewriting stage of writing. This stage begins with free, unstructured thinking and writing. As you work through the prewriting process, your thinking and writing will become more focused.

> ### INFO BOX   Focusing the Prewriting: A Summary
>
> The prewriting stage of writing a paragraph enables you to develop an idea into a topic sentence and related details. You can focus your thinking by working in steps.
>
> 1. Try marking a list of related details or mapping to group your ideas.
>
> 2. Write a topic sentence that summarizes your details.
>
> 3. Check your topic sentence. Be sure that it makes a point and focuses the details you have developed. Also, check that it is not a topic, not too broad or too narrow, and not an announcement.

MyWritingLab™   **Exercise 10**   **Practice: Recognizing and Writing Good Topic Sentences**

Some of the following are good topic sentences. Others are not; they are topics (not topic sentences) or announcements, or they are too broad or too narrow. Put an *X* next to the ones that are not good topic sentences and rewrite them on the blank lines following the list.

1. _____ How you can make extra money in college.

2. _____ Movies about animals appeal to all of my nieces and nephews.

3. _____ Conflicts have always made me nervous.

4. _____ At dusk, I drive to work.

5. _____ Wearing jeans to school is best.

6. _____ Many elderly people are fearful.

7. _____ Several dangers of traveling to parts of Africa will be the subject of this paper.

8. _____ This paper will discuss ways to save money on college textbooks.

Rewrite the faulty topic sentences:

_____

_____

_____

_____

_____

_____

_____

_____

_____

Exercise 11   **Practice: Writing Topic Sentences for Lists of Details**   MyWritingLab™

Following are lists of details that have no topic sentences. Write an appropriate topic sentence for each one.

1. topic sentence: _____

_____

Comforts me when I am sad.
Brings me small treats like brownies.
Always lets me choose the movie we watch.
Saves funny online videos to show me.
Appreciates all my cooking (even microwaved frozen dinners).
Walks the dog on rainy days.
Takes out the garbage.

2. topic sentence: _____

_____

It was a short walk to the beach.
I could open the windows and smell the sea air.
I could study and read on a blanket in the sand.
I could maintain a perfect tan.
It had one bedroom.
The bedroom had a bed and a dresser of fake wood.
The living room was furnished in plastic couches and a wire-
    legged coffee table.
The kitchen was big enough for one person.

3. topic sentence: _____

_____

Ms. Chestnut was my kindergarten teacher.
She was a lively, smiling person.
She welcomed each child every morning.
She sang with us.
She danced in a circle with us.
She frowned only when we misbehaved.
If we didn't pay attention, she noticed and recaptured our
    attention.
If two or three of us fooled around, she gently brought us to the
    center of the group.

4. topic sentence: _____

_____

> Chocolate tastes great.
> It is full of fat and empty calories.
> The sugar in chocolate is bad for a person's teeth.
> Chocolate can also be bad for many people's complexions.
> An apple tastes good.
> It has no fat.
> It is full of fiber, which is healthy for digestion.
> Eating an apple is good for a person's skin and teeth.

MyWritingLab™ Visit Chapter 20, "Writing a Paragraph: Prewriting," in *MyWritingLab* to test your understanding of the chapter objectives.

Writing a Paragraph: Planning

CHAPTER 21

Jumping In

Have you ever noticed how a building's structure helps prevent a collapse? Just like the columns that support the roof of a building, the details you supply in your outline paper will **support** *your* **topic sentence** *and keep your paragraph* **unified** *and* **coherent***.*

Learning Objectives

In this chapter, you will learn to:

1. Provide enough details to support a topic sentence.
2. Provide details that relate to the topic sentence and unify the paragraph.
3. Arrange details in a logical order for coherence.
4. Position your topic sentence correctly.

Once you have a topic sentence, you can begin working on an **outline** for your paragraph. The outline is a *plan* that helps you stay focused in your writing. The outline begins to form when you write your topic sentence and the details beneath it.

Provide enough details to support a topic sentence.

CHECKING YOUR DETAILS

You can now look at your list and ask yourself an important question: "Do I have enough details to support my topic sentence?" Remember, your goal is to write a paragraph of seven to twelve sentences.

Consider this topic sentence and list of details:

topic sentence: Fresh fruit is a good dessert.
details: tastes good
healthy
easy

Does the list contain enough details for a paragraph of seven to twelve sentences? Probably not.

Adding Details When There Are Not Enough

To add details, try brainstorming. Ask yourself some questions:

What fruit tastes good?
What makes fruit a healthy dessert?
Why is it easy? How can you serve it?

By brainstorming, you may come up with these details:

topic sentence: Fresh fruit is a good dessert.
details: tastes good
a ripe peach or a juicy pineapple tastes delicious
crunchy apples are always available and satisfying
plump strawberries are great in summer
healthy
low in calories
rich in vitamins and fiber
easy
served as it is
in a fruit salad
mixed with ice cream or sherbet
no cooking necessary

Keep brainstorming until you feel you have enough details for a paragraph of seven to twelve sentences. Remember, it is better to have too many details than to have too few, for you can always eliminate the extra details later.

Collaborate

Exercise 1 **Collaborate: Adding Details to Support a Topic Sentence**

Do this exercise with a partner or group. The following topic sentences have some—but not enough—details. Write sentences to add details to each list.

1. **topic sentence:** A bad cold can make your life miserable.

   details: 1. A cold means you will have a runny nose.

   2. It means you will sneeze constantly.

   3. _____

   _____

   4. _____

   _____

5. _____

_____

6. _____

_____

2. topic sentence: When Patrick prepares for a test, he follows a strict ritual.

details: 1. He prefers to study alone.

2. However, if someone else organizes a study group, he will join it.

3. _____

_____

4. _____

_____

5. _____

_____

6. _____

_____

3. topic sentence: Stress is hitting me from every part of my life.

details: 1. I am overwhelmed with coursework at school.

2. I need a better work schedule.

3. _____

_____

4. _____

_____

5. _____

_____

6. _____

_____

Eliminating Details That Do Not Relate to the Topic Sentence

2 Provide details that relate to the topic sentence and unify the paragraph.

Sometimes what you thought were good details don't relate to the topic sentence because they don't fit or support your point. Eliminate details that don't relate to the topic sentence. For example, the following list contains details that don't relate to the topic sentence. Those details are crossed out.

topic sentence: My neighbors are making my home life unbearable.
details: play loud music at 3:00 a.m.
I can't sleep
leave garbage all over the sidewalk
~~come from Philadelphia~~

sidewalk is a mess
insects crawl all over their garbage
~~I carefully bag my garbage~~
argue loudly and bang on the walls
my privacy is invaded
park their van in my parking space

MyWritingLab™   **Exercise 2**   **Practice: Eliminating Details That Do Not Relate**

Following are topic sentences and lists of details. Cross out the details that do not relate to the topic sentence.

1. **topic sentence:** Katherine's new apartment needs some work.
   details: The apartment complex is far from campus.
   The toilet is leaking.
   The paint in the kitchen is flaking off one wall.
   The carpet in the bedroom needs cleaning.
   There are no assigned parking spaces.
   The closet door will not shut properly.
   The baseboards are filthy.

2. **topic sentence:** I love city life for a number of reasons.
   details: I am a morning person.
   I like the excitement of crowds.
   In the city, I never run out of things to do or see.
   I can meet all kinds of people in the city.
   I rarely feel alone in the city.
   City people tend to be accepting of nonconformists.
   I was born in the suburbs.

3. **topic sentence:** Although we keep hearing about a paperless world, we still use paper in some critical parts of our daily life.
   details: I need facial tissue.
   It would be hard to find a substitute for toilet paper.
   Paper creates problems with waste disposal.
   Many of our financial transactions can already be paperless.
   It would be difficult to find a substitute for the paper in disposable diapers.
   Tissue paper protects fragile items when they are transported.
   Boxes are generally made of cardboard, a form of paper.

3 Arrange details in a logical order for coherence.

From List to Outline

Take another look at the topic sentence and list of details on the topic, "My Mother:"

topic sentence: My mother survived difficult times to become a good parent and worker.
details: She's a good mom.
always takes care of me
She works hard.
She cooks and cleans.

> makes a great chicken casserole
> She has a job.
> She's a nurse.
> She had a rough life.
> lost her husband
> went to school at night

After you scan the list, you will be ready to develop the outline of a paragraph.

The outline is a plan for writing, and it can be a kind of draft in list form. It sketches what you want to write and the order in which you want to present it. An organized, logical list will make your writing unified because each item on the list will relate to your topic sentence.

When you plan, keep your topic sentence in mind:

My mother <u>survived difficult times</u> to become <u>a good parent</u> and <u>worker</u>.

Notice that the key words are underlined and lead to key phrases:

survived difficult times
a good parent
a good worker

Can you put the details together so that they connect to one of these key phrases?

survived difficult times

She had a rough life, lost her husband, went to school at night

a good parent
She's a good mom, always takes care of me, She cooks and cleans, makes a great chicken casserole

a good worker
She works hard, She has a job, She's a nurse

With this kind of grouping, you have a clearer idea of how to organize a paragraph. You may have noticed that the details grouped under each phrase explain or give examples that are connected to the topic sentence. You may also have noticed that the detail "She works hard" is placed under the phrase "a good worker." It could also be placed under "a good parent," so it would be your decision where to place it.

Now that you have grouped your ideas with key phrases and examples, you can write an outline:

An Outline for a Paragraph on My Mother

topic sentence	My mother survived difficult times to become a good parent and worker.
details	She had a rough life.
difficult times	She lost her husband.
	She went to school at night.
	She's a good mom and always takes care of me.
a good parent	She cooks and cleans.
	She makes a great chicken casserole.
a good worker	She works hard at her job.
	She's a nurse.

As you can see, the outline combines some details from the list. Even with these combinations, the details are very rough in style. As you reread the list of details, you may notice places that need more combining, places where ideas need more explaining, and places that are repetitive. Keep in mind that an outline is merely a rough organization of your paragraph.

As you work through the steps of devising an outline, you can check for the following:

Checklist for an Outline

✓ **Unity:** Do all the details relate to the topic sentence? If they do, the paragraph will be unified.

✓ **Support:** Do I have enough supporting ideas? Can I add to those ideas with more specific details?

✓ **Coherence:** Are the ideas listed in the right order? If the order of the points is logical, the paragraph will be coherent.

Coherence

Check the sample outline again, and you'll notice that the details are grouped in the same order as in the topic sentence: first, details about your mother's difficult life; next, details about your mother as a parent; finally, details about your mother as a worker. Putting details in an order that matches the topic sentence is a logical order for this paragraph. It makes the paragraph **coherent**.

Determining the Order of Details

Putting the details in a logical order makes the ideas in the paragraph easier to follow. The most logical order for a paragraph depends on the subject of the paragraph. If you are writing about an event, you might use **time order** (such as telling what happened first, second, and so forth); if you are arguing some point, you might use **emphatic order** (such as saving your most convincing idea for last); if you are describing a room, you might use **space order** (such as describing from left to right or from top to bottom).

MyWritingLab™ | **Exercise 3** **Practice: Coherence: Putting Details in the Right Order**

These outlines have details that are in the wrong order. In the space provided, number the sentences so that they are in the proper order: 1 would be the number for the first sentence, and so on.

1. **topic sentence:** Drinks that mix alcohol, a sickening sweet flavor, and a large jolt of caffeine are dangerous. (Put the sentences in emphatic order, from the least dangerous effect to the most.)

_____ They make the drinker feel wide awake and energized.

_____ The drinker feels capable of drinking more drinks (full of alcohol) than he or she would consume by drinking a traditional alcoholic beverage.

_____ Consumers of these "energy drinks" do not sense the alcohol's effect on their brains.

_____ Some of these drinkers kill themselves and/or others when they get behind the wheel.

_____ Some of these drinkers believe they can drive home.

_____ Some have car accidents.

2. topic sentence: Yoga class is not for the lazy. (Put the sentences in time order, from first to last.)

_____ The instructor arrived and started us off with some simple stretching exercises.

_____ The stretching exercises hurt me.

_____ Then we moved on to what the instructor called simple yoga positions.

_____ While most people enjoyed themselves in these "simple" positions, I kept falling over.

_____ I went home sore and humiliated after I learned that the instructor was sixty years old.

_____ I decided to enroll in a community center's evening yoga class for adults.

_____ Last year I was looking for an easy way to exercise and maybe lose a little weight.

_____ Because the class was in the evening at a community center, I figured the class would be full of people older and less fit than I am.

_____ On the first evening, while I waited for the instructor to arrive, I looked around and saw older men and women, in great shape, stretching on their mats.

Where the Topic Sentence Goes

4 Position your topic sentence correctly.

The outline format helps you organize your ideas. The topic sentence is written above the list of details. This position helps you remember that the topic sentence is the main idea and that the details that support it are written under it. You can easily check each detail on your list against your main idea. You can also check the **unity** (relevance) and **coherence** (logical order) of your details.

When you actually write a paragraph, the topic sentence does not necessarily have to be the first sentence in the paragraph. Read the following paragraphs, and notice where each topic sentence is placed.

Topic Sentence at the Beginning of the Paragraph

<u>Dr. Chen is the best doctor I have ever had</u>. Whenever I have to visit him, he gives me plenty of time. He does not rush me through a physical examination and quickly hand me a prescription. Instead, he takes time to chat with me and encourages me to describe my symptoms. He examines me carefully and allows me to ask as many questions as I want. After I am dressed, he discusses his diagnosis,

explains what medicine he is prescribing, and tells me exactly how and when to take the medication. He tells me what results to expect from the medication and how long it should take for me to get well. Dr. Chen acts as if he cares about me. I believe that is the most important quality in a doctor.

Topic Sentence in the Middle of the Paragraph

The meal was delicious, from the appetizer of shrimp cocktail to the dessert of strawberry tarts. Marcel had even taken the time to make home-baked bread and fresh pasta. <u>Marcel had worked hard on this dinner, and his hard work showed</u>. Everything was served on gleaming china placed on an immaculate tablecloth. There were fresh flowers in a cut glass bowl at the center of the table, and there was a polished goblet at every place setting. The pale green napkins had been carefully ironed and folded into precise triangles.

Topic Sentence at the End of the Paragraph

I woke up at 5:00 a.m. when I heard the phone ringing. I rushed to the phone, thinking the call was some terrible emergency. Of course, it was just a wrong number. Then I couldn't get back to sleep because I was shaken by being so suddenly awakened and irritated by the wrong number. The day got worse as it went along. My car stalled on the freeway, and I had to get it towed to a repair shop. The repair cost me $250. I was three hours late for work and missed an important training session with my boss. On my way out of work, I stepped into an enormous puddle and ruined a new pair of shoes. <u>Yesterday was one of those days when I should have stayed in bed</u>.

Note: Be sure to follow your own instructor's directions about placement of the topic sentence.

MyWritingLab™   Exercise 4   **Practice: Identifying the Topic Sentence**

Underline the topic sentence in each of the following paragraphs.

1. Autumn is my favorite season of the year. There is a huge sycamore tree outside the front window of my second-floor apartment, and it sheds huge, golden leaves for weeks. They are like a carpet of perfectly shaped, glowing pieces of art. I love the cool nights and the clear days when the sun keeps the wind from chilling me too much. In addition, I associate autumn with all the holidays to come. I dream of Halloween, Thanksgiving, and the long stretch of days for giving and celebration in December and January. For many people, autumn signals the end of the old year, but for me, it means a burst of nature's and human nature's goodness.

2. My friend Amanda got the call early one morning last month. Her boyfriend, Ryan, had been killed in what appeared to be a robbery at his family's home. The police investigators did not know much, but they knew that Ryan and his parents had been at home when it happened. The parents were asleep, and Ryan had gone into the kitchen at about 1:00 a.m. At or shortly after that time, Ryan's father and mother heard a noise, and the father went to the kitchen to investigate. Ryan lay on the floor, dead from a gunshot wound. The back door of the house was open. Amanda could not believe this account. Ryan was a good student and a popular one. He had no criminal record or gang affiliations. She could only speculate that Ryan, who liked to stay up late playing games on his computer, had gone to the kitchen for a snack. In a few minutes of unexplained violence, a beloved son and boyfriend had been taken from this earth.

CHAPTER 22

Writing a Paragraph: Drafting and Revising

Jumping In

Once a project begins to take shape, what comes next? If you were creating a piece of sculpture or writing a song, would you try to rush the project to completion, or would you concentrate on further shaping and refining? Such questions relate to **drafting and revising**, the next phase of the writing process.

Learning Objectives

In this chapter, you will learn to:

1 Create multiple drafts as a part of the writing process.
2 Make structural changes as a part of the revision process.

As you have learned, an outline is a draft of a paragraph in list form. Once you have an outline, you are ready to create a first draft of your paragraph.

1 Create multiple drafts as a part of the writing process.

DRAFTING

The drafting and revising stage of writing is the time to draft, revise, and draft again. You may write several drafts or versions of the paragraph in this stage. Writing several drafts is not an unnecessary chore or a punishment. Rather, it is a way of taking pressure off yourself. By revising several times, you are telling yourself that the first try doesn't have to be perfect.

Review the outline on the topic, "My Mother," on page 263. You can create a first draft of this outline in the form of a paragraph. (Remember that the first line of each paragraph is indented.) In the draft of the following paragraph, the first sentence of the paragraph is the topic sentence.

First Draft of a Paragraph on My Mother

My mother survived difficult times to become a good parent and worker. She had a rough life. She lost her husband. She went to school at night. She's a good mom and always takes care of me. She cooks and cleans. She makes a great chicken casserole. She works hard at her job. She's a nurse.

Revising a Draft

Once you have a first draft, you can begin to think about revising it. **Revising** means rewriting the draft to change the structure, the order of the sentences, and the content (later, as you edit, you can make significant improvements in word choice, specific details, sentence patterns, and punctuation choices). It may also include adding a few **transitions**—words, phrases, or sentences that link ideas.

Below is a list of some common transitional words and phrases and the kinds of connections they express:

2 Make structural changes as a part of the revision process.

INFO BOX   **Common Transitions**

To join two ideas

again	another	in addition	moreover
also	besides	likewise	similarly
and	furthermore		

To show a contrast or a different opinion

but	instead	on the other hand	still
however	nevertheless	or	yet
in contrast	on the contrary	otherwise	

To show a cause-and-effect connection

accordingly	because	for	therefore
as a result	consequently	so	thus

To give an example

for example	in the case of	such as	to illustrate
for instance	like		

To show time

after	first	recently	subsequently
at the same time	meanwhile	shortly	then
before	next	soon	until
finally			

One easy way to begin the revising process is to read your work aloud to yourself. As you do so, listen carefully to your words and concentrate on their meaning. Each question in the following checklist will help you focus on a specific aspect of revising. The name (or key term) for each aspect is in parentheses.

Checklist for Revising the First Draft of a Paragraph (with key terms)

✓ Am I staying on my point? (unity)

✓ Should I eliminate any ideas that do not fit? (unity)

✓ Do I have enough to say about my point? (support)

✓ Should I add any details? (support)

✓ Should I change the order of my sentences? (coherence)

✓ Is my choice of words appropriate? (style)

✓ Is my choice of words repetitive? (style)

If you apply the checklist to the draft of the paragraph, you may notice these rough spots:

- The sentences are very short and choppy.
- Some words are repeated often.
- Some ideas need more details for support.
- The paragraph needs transitions: words, phrases, or sentences that link ideas.

Below is a sample revised draft; you can assume that the writer worked on *several* drafts before reaching this point. Changes from the initial draft are underlined.

Revised Draft of a Paragraph on My Mother

(Changes from the initial draft are underlined; editing and proofreading are still necessary.)

topic sentence ——————— My mother survived difficult times to become a good

sentences combined ——— parent and worker. <u>Her hard times began when she lost</u>

transition ——————— <u>her husband. At his death,</u> she was only nineteen and had

a baby, me, to raise. She survived by going to school at

details added, transition ——— night <u>to train for a career. Even though she lives a stress-</u>

<u>ful life,</u> she is a good mom. She always takes care of me.

<u>She listens to my problems, encourages me to do my best,</u>

details added ——————— <u>and praises all my efforts. She cleans our apartment until</u>

<u>it shines, and she makes dinner every night.</u> She makes

transition ——————— a great chicken casserole. <u>In addition,</u> she works hard at

her job. She is a nurse <u>at a home for elderly people, where</u>

details added ——————— <u>she is on her feet all day and is still kind and cheerful.</u>

When you are revising your own paragraph, you can use the checklist to help you. Read the checklist several times; then reread your draft, looking for answers to the questions on the list. If your instructor agrees, you can work with your classmates. You can read your draft to a partner or group. Your listener(s) can react to your draft by applying the questions on the checklist and by making notes about your draft as you read. When you are finished reading aloud, your partner(s) can discuss their notes about your work.

Exercise 1 **Practice: Revising a Draft for Unity**   MyWritingLab™

Some of the sentences in the following paragraph do not relate to the topic sentence. (The topic sentence is the first sentence in the paragraph.) Cross out the sentences that do not fit.

My husband and I finally found a way to handle our child's nightmares. Our

five-year-old son, Enrique, used to sleep peacefully through the night in his own

room, but recently he has been waking up, screaming. He claims that there is

a ghost in his room. Once he is awake, he cannot go back to sleep and instead

becomes frightened at every ordinary sound. I remember when the sound of

tree branches against the window used to terrify my little sister. At first we took

Enrique into our bed, and he slept fairly well. However, he began to wake up,

startled, and listen for "ghosts." Soon all three of us were awake for most of the

night. The "ghosts" seemed to get worse. Comic books and cartoons often contain

ghosts, but they don't always frighten small children. My husband realized that

Enrique spent each night listening for ghosts, so our son might feel safer if he

couldn't hear strange noises. Enrique returned to his own room where we played

soft music all night. He sleeps much better now.

Exercise 2 **Collaborate: Adding Supporting Details to a Draft**   Collaborate

Do this exercise with a partner or group. The following paragraph needs more details to support its point. Add the details in the blank spaces provided.

Our weekend trip to a beach resort was nearly perfect. First of all, the

weather really cooperated with our plans. (Add two sentences of details.)

_____

_____

The beach and the water could not have been better. (Add two sentences about

the beach and the water.) _____

_____

_____ In addition, our hotel was a pleasant surprise. (Add two sentences

about the unexpected pleasures of the hotel.) _____

_____

_____

Our only complaint was that we couldn't stay longer, but we will soon return.

MyWritingLab™   Exercise 3   **Practice: Revising a Draft for Coherence**

In the following paragraph, one sentence is in the wrong place. Move it to the right place in the paragraph by drawing an arrow from the sentence to its proper place.

      I thought I could get away with parking in a no-parking area for just a few minutes, but I could not escape one vigilant police officer. I had desperately searched the parking lot at a local strip mall, but I couldn't find one empty spot. It was lunch hour, and people were running errands, grabbing fast food, stopping at the bank, and picking up dry cleaning. All I needed was to dash into the pharmacy and pick up my prescription medication. Unfortunately, a man in uniform caught me running back to my illegally parked car. Desperate, I decided to snatch the only available—and tempting—spot: a handicapped spot right in front of the pharmacy. I raced to the store and waited impatiently until a clerk handed me my medication. By the time the electronic doors of the pharmacy parted, I was feeling triumphant. A hefty fine and a well-deserved lecture from the officer made me feel guilty about the nasty, selfish aspects of my behavior.

| Exercise 4 | **Collaborate: Refining a Draft for Style**

Do this exercise with a partner or a group. The following paragraph is repetitive in its word choice. Replace each underlined word with a word that is less repetitive. Write the new word above the underlined one.

    My friend Isaac's tropical pets are all ugly. I expected some of them to be pretty, but I was disappointed to find each one <u>uglier</u> than the next. For example, Isaac has a pet iguana that lives in the yard, and I thought it would be a <u>pretty</u> lizard. Instead, it was a large, <u>ugly</u> lizard with <u>ugly</u> scales on its back. Isaac also rescued an abandoned parrot who had been left in a cage. People usually think of parrots as <u>pretty</u> birds with <u>pretty</u> feathers, but Isaac's parrot is <u>ugly</u>. Isaac's tropical fish were the worst disappointment. They were the <u>ugliest</u> tropical fish I had ever seen. I know Isaac must love his pets, but I wish Isaac had found at least one <u>pretty</u> one.

CHAPTER 23

Writing a Paragraph: Editing and Proofreading

Jumping In

Do you know anyone who is extremely careful about applying the finishing touches to a project such as personalizing a Web page, designing a landscape, or painting a favorite subject? Do you apply the same degree of care when you check your writing, or do you become frustrated and end up rushing the process just to meet a deadline? What approach do you take toward **editing** and **proofreading** your writing?

Learning Objectives

In this chapter you will learn how to:

1. Recognize the importance of editing and proofreading your writing.
2. Use critical thinking in your writing.

1. Recognize the importance of editing and proofreading your writing.

EDITING AND PROOFREADING YOUR PARAGRAPH

After you are satisfied with the latest revised draft of your paragraph, you are ready to edit. **Editing** often involves making improvements or correcting errors you may have overlooked during the revision process. Examining sentence patterns and length, checking appropriate word choice, and ensuring that specific details are linked smoothly are all natural refinements during editing. **Proofreading** entails reading your final version to spot and correct any careless mistakes including formatting errors, missing words or punctuation, and even simple typos. Through careful proofreading when you are alert and rested, you can add finishing touches to make your work the best it can be.

Take a look at the corrections in the following paragraph on "My Mother," and then imagine what would have happened if the writer had submitted this "final" draft for a grade *without* making any refinements or corrections. If you compare this version to the sample revised draft in Chapter 22, page 270, you will notice that *mom* has been changed to *mother*, the vague word *great* has been changed to *delicious*, and a final statement has been added to unify the paragraph. Also, keep in mind that careless spelling and punctuation mistakes, such as the ones corrected below, often go unnoticed without careful proofreading.

A Corrected Final Draft of a Paragraph on My Mother

My mother survived difficult ~~time's~~ times to become a good ~~parrent~~ parent and worker. Her hard times began when she lost her husband. At his death, ~~She~~ she was only nineteen and had a baby, me, to raise. ~~she~~ She survived by going to school at ~~nite~~ night to train for a career. Even though she lives a stressful life, she is a good ~~mom~~ mother. She ~~allways take~~ always takes care of me. She listens to my ~~prolems~~ problems, ~~encourage~~ encourages me to do my best, and praises all my efforts. She cleans our apartment until it ~~shine~~ shines, and she makes dinner every night. She makes a ~~great~~ delicious chicken casserole. In addition, she works hard at her job. She is a nurse at a home for elderly people, where she is on her feet ~~allday~~ all day and is still kind and cheerful. At work or at home, my mother is an inspiration to me.

Exercise 1 Practice: Correcting the Errors in the Final Draft of a Paragraph — MyWritingLab™

Edit the following paragraph by correcting any punctuation and spelling mistakes. Correct the ten errors by crossing out each mistake and writing your correction above it.

I'm not a great athlete, superior student, or son of wealthy parents, but I have 1 asset that makes me popular. I'm a good listener. For some reason, people like to tell me about themselfs. When I travel, strangers on a plane have told me there life stories. In high school, I new more secrets about my classmates then anyone would believe. At my job, my Coworkers and even my boss confide in me. When people confide in me, I don't do much talking but simply nod my head or make other appropriate responses. Maybe I have an honest-looking face. For some reason, people trust me and I have never enjoyed telling other peoples' secrets. Perhaps I should be studying for a career as a counselor. Because I have years of experience in listening.

Before you prepare a final version of your paragraph, edit your latest draft to check for precise word choice, accurate spelling, coherent sentence structure, and appropriate punctuation. Make a clean copy, and then proofread to catch any careless errors in format, spelling, punctuation, and typing. You can then submit a clean, final version to your instructor for evaluation. The following checklist may help you edit and proofread your work more effectively:

Checklist for Editing and Proofreading Your Paragraph

(Note: Items 1–7 relate to editing; items 8–10 relate to proofreading.)

1. Is spelling correct, and are word choices specific?
2. Are sentences complete and coherent?
3. Should any sentences be shortened or combined?
4. Should any sentences be reordered?
5. Should any punctuation be changed, added, or corrected?
6. Are supporting details appropriate, specific, and in logical sequence?
7. Does the title accurately reflect the paragraph's content?
8. Are there any missing words or letters?
9. Are there any missing punctuation marks or careless misspellings/typos?
10. Is the paragraph formatted correctly?

Giving Your Paragraph a Title

When you prepare the final version of your paragraph, you may be asked to give it a title. The title should be short and should fit the subject of the paragraph. For example, an appropriate title for the paragraph on one's mother could be "My Wonderful Mother" or "An Inspiring Mother." Check with your instructor to see if your paragraph needs a title. (In this book, the sample paragraphs do not have titles.)

CRITICAL THINKING

If your instructor requires a title, try to devise one that is both creative and practical. An effective title often captures the reader's attention and subtly relates to a work's main idea.

Collaborate

Exercise 2 **Collaborate: Creating a Title**

With a partner or group, create a title for the following paragraph.

Title: _____

My family left New Jersey when I was seven years old, and I am very happy living in Florida. However, sometimes I feel homesick for the North.

At Christmas, especially, I wish I could see the snow fall and then run outdoors to make a snowman. In December, it feels strange to string outdoor lights on palm trees. I also miss the autumn when the leaves on the trees turn fiery red and gold. Sometimes my aunt in New Jersey sends me an envelope of autumn leaves, and I remember the crackle of leaves beneath my feet and the smell of the burning leaves in the fall bonfires. Life is different in Florida where we enjoy sunshine all year. We are spared the icy gray days of a Northern winter, the slush of melting snow, and the gloomy rain of early spring. I now live in a place that is always warm and bright, but sometimes I miss the changing seasons of my first home.

Reviewing the Writing Process

In four chapters, you have worked through *four important stages* in writing. As you become more familiar with the stages and with working through them, you will be able to work more quickly. For now, try to remember the four stages:

INFO BOX   **The Stages of the Writing Process**

Prewriting: gathering ideas, thinking on paper through freewriting, brainstorming, or keeping a journal

Planning: planning the paragraph by grouping details, focusing the details with a topic sentence, listing the support, and devising an outline

Drafting and Revising: drafting the paragraph; then revising it extensively, which may require several additional drafts to improve organization and coherence

Editing and Proofreading: reviewing the latest draft to improve style and correct serious errors; then giving your work one last check to catch careless errors in format, spelling, punctuation, or typing

---

Now that you have seen how a paragraph can evolve through the stages of the writing process, here are the outline, sample revised draft, and final version in one place for quick reference:

Outline for a Paragraph on My Mother

topic sentence	My mother survived difficult times to become a good parent and worker.
details	She had a rough life.
	She lost her husband.
	She went to school at night.
	She's a good mom and always takes care of me.
	She cooks and cleans.
	She makes a great chicken casserole.
	She works hard at her job.
	She's a nurse.

Revised Draft of a Paragraph on My Mother

My mother survived difficult times to become a good parent and worker. Her hard times began when she lost her husband. At his death, she was only nineteen and had a baby, me, to raise. She survived by going to school at night to train for a career. Even though she lives a stressful life, she is a good mom. She always takes care of me. She listens to my problems, encourages me to do my best, and praises all my efforts. She cleans our apartment until it shines, and she makes dinner every night. She makes a great chicken casserole. In addition, she works hard at her job. She is a nurse at a home for elderly people, where she is on her feet all day and is still kind and cheerful.

Final Version of a Paragraph on My Mother

(Changes from the revised draft are underlined.)

My mother survived difficult times to become a good parent and worker. Her hard times began when she lost her husband. At his death, she was only nineteen and had a baby, me, to raise. She survived by going to school at night to train for a career. Even though she <u>still</u> lives a stressful life <u>today</u>, she is a good <u>mother</u>. She always takes care of me. She listens to my problems, encourages me to do my best, and praises all my efforts. She cleans our apartment until it shines, and she makes dinner every night. She makes a <u>delicious</u> chicken casserole. In addition, she works hard at her job. She is a nurse at a home for elderly people, where she is on her feet all day and is still kind and cheerful. <u>At work or at home, my mother is an inspiration to me.</u>

2 Use critical thinking in your writing.

Critical Thinking and the Writing Process

As you know by now, one of the popular methods of prewriting is called **brainstorming**, the practice of asking yourself key questions that can lead you to new ideas and directions related to your writing topic. During your college career, you will find that such questioning can enable you to engage in **critical thinking**, a type of reasoning that has several meanings and practical uses. For now, just remember that any time you evaluate the relevance of supporting details, determine their order of importance, and attempt to justify their inclusion in your work, you are making judgments that are considered *critical*. Making such judgments will become more common for you as you undertake college writing assignments. You will soon appreciate the crucial role critical thinking plays in effective writing, whether you are recalling an order of events to include in a personal narrative, crafting vivid images for a descriptive paper, choosing the best supporting details for illustrating a point, or clearly explaining the key steps of a specific process.

At the end of this chapter and in subsequent writing chapters, you will find a variety of critical thinking and writing options. These topics may require you to defend a point of view, imagine a certain scenario, or examine a trend. Whether you discuss these topics with classmates, participate in a group assignment, or tackle an issue on your own, keeping an open mind will help you become a better writer and a stronger critical thinker.

Lines of Detail: A Walk-Through Assignment

Write a paragraph about a friend. To write this paragraph, follow these steps:

Step 1: For fifteen minutes, freewrite or brainstorm about a friend.

Step 2: Survey your freewriting or brainstorming and underline any specific ideas you can find. Put these ideas in a list.

Step 3: Pick one idea from your list; it will be your topic. Try to develop it by adding details. Get details by going back to your list for other ideas that fit your topic, by brainstorming for more ideas, and by listing new ideas.

Step 4: Put the ideas on your list into categories by marking them or by mapping them.

Step 5: Write a topic sentence and list your ideas below it.

Step 6: Draft your paragraph by writing the topic sentence and all the ideas on your list in paragraph form. Revise, draft, and revise again until you are satisfied with your paragraph.

Step 7: Edit your latest draft to refine word choice, strengthen transition, combine sentences, and incorporate additional details if necessary. Then proofread it and prepare a final copy free of errors.

Topics for Writing Your Own Paragraph

When you write on any of these topics, be sure to work through the stages of the writing process in preparing your paragraph.

1. This assignment involves working with a group. First, pick a topic from the following list: MyWritingLab™

   texting while driving
   homesickness
   powerful music

   Next, join a group of other students who picked the same topic you did. Brainstorm in a group. Discuss questions that could be asked to get ideas for your paragraph.

   For the texting-while-driving topic, sample questions could include "Is it dangerous to text while driving?" or "How can people stop texting while driving?"

   For the homesickness topic, sample questions could include "When were you homesick?"or "What did you miss most about your former home?"

   For the music topic, sample questions could include "Is music most powerful at sad occasions or at happy ones?" or "Do the words or the rhythm make music powerful?"

   As you brainstorm, write the questions down. Keep them flowing. Don't stop to answer the questions. Don't stop to say, "That's silly," or "I can't answer that." Try to generate at least twelve questions.

Twelve Brainstorming Questions

1. _____

2. _____

3. _____

4. _____

5. _____

6. _____

7. _____

8. _____

9. _____

10. _____

11. _____

12. _____

Once you have the questions, split up. Begin the prewriting step by answering as many questions as you can. You may also add more questions or freewrite. Then pick a specific topic, list the related details, and write a topic sentence.

Work through the planning stage by developing an outline with sufficient details.

After you've written a draft of your paragraph, read it to your writing group, the same people who met to brainstorm. Ask each member of your group to make one positive comment and one suggestion for revision.

Revise your draft after considering the group's ideas for improvement. Prepare a clean copy of your latest draft; then edit for style and proofread carefully.

MyWritingLab™

2. Following are some topic sentences. Select one and use it to write a paragraph.

The best way for me to relax is _____.

Learning a new language is hard because _____.

I still have two unanswered questions about college; they are

_____ and _____.

If I had a hundred extra dollars, I would spend it on _____.

I am most suited for a career in _____.

Collaborate

3. This assignment requires you to interview a partner. Your final goal is to write a paragraph that will inform the class about your partner. Your paragraph should use this topic sentence:

_____ (fill in your partner's name) has had three significant experiences.

Step 1: Before you write the paragraph, prepare to interview a class-mate. Make a list of six questions you want to ask. They can be questions such as, "Have you ever had any interesting experiences?" or "Have you ever been in danger?" Write at least six questions *before* you begin the interview. List the questions below, leaving room to fill in short answers later.

Interview Form

1. Question: _____

    Answer: _____

2. Question: _____

    Answer: _____

3. Question: _____

    Answer: _____

4. Question: _____

    Answer: _____

5. Question: _____

    Answer: _____

6. Question: _____

    Answer: _____

    Additional questions and answers:

    _____

    _____

    _____

Step 2: As you interview your partner, ask the questions on your list and jot down brief answers. Ask any additional questions you can think of as you are talking; write down the answers in the additional lines at the end of the interview form.

Step 3: Change places. Let your partner interview you.

Step 4: Split up. Use the list of questions and answers about your partner as the prewriting part of your assignment. Work on the outline and draft steps.

Step 5: Ask your partner to read the draft version of your paragraph, to write any comments or suggestions for improvement below the paragraph, and to mark any spelling or grammar errors in the paragraph itself.

Step 6: Revise your draft based on your partner's suggestions; then prepare a clean copy.

Step 7: Edit for style and proofread carefully. When you have completed a final version of your paragraph, read it to the class

MyWritingLab™

4. Select one of the following topics. Then narrow it to one aspect of the topic and write a paragraph on that aspect. If you choose the topic of movie trilogies, for example, you might want to narrow it by writing about your favorite movie trilogy.

clothing styles	college rules	tablets
holidays	national heroes	habits
movie trilogies	viral videos	dreams
a dangerous sport	children	transportation

MyWritingLab™

5. Study the photo of the silhouette as a prompt to write a paragraph about the most significant relationship in your life.

Topics for Critical Thinking and Writing

MyWritingLab™

1. Consider how heavily you rely on technology either in school, at work, or with family and friends. Then imagine how your life would be different if you had no access to a cell phone, a computer, or a television. Write about how difficult or easy it would be for you to eliminate these technological devices from your daily life.

MyWritingLab™

2. Think about a controversial change in your neighborhood. Write a paragraph that describes the reactions of the residents, or summarize the specific reasons the change was so controversial.

MyWritingLab™ Visit Chapter 23, "Writing a Paragraph: Editing and Proofreading," in *MyWritingLab* to test your understanding of the chapter objectives.

Writing a Narrative Paragraph

Jumping In

*What do you think happened just before this dramatic scene? Can you imagine what led to the expressions of frustration? There must be a story behind this picture, and if you write the story, you will be writing a **narrative** paragraph.*

Learning Objectives

In this chapter, you will learn to:

1. Identify the characteristics of a narrative paragraph.
2. Prewrite to focus your topic and details.
3. Write a clear topic sentence.
4. Write a narrative paragraph that uses transitions and details effectively.

Paragraphs use different methods to make their points. One kind of paragraph uses *narration*.

WHAT IS NARRATION?

Narration means telling a story. Everybody tells stories; some people are better storytellers than others. When you write a **narrative** paragraph, you can tell a story about something that happened to you or to someone else, or about something that you saw or read.

A narrative covers events in a time sequence because it is always about happenings: events, actions, incidents. However, interesting narratives do more than just tell what happened. They help the reader become involved in the story by providing vivid details. These details come from your memory, your observation, or your reading. Using good details, you don't just tell the story; you *show* it.

1 Identify the characteristics of a narrative paragraph.

283

Give the Narrative a Point

We all know people who tell long stories that seem to lead nowhere. These people talk on and on; they recite an endless list of activities and soon become boring. Their narratives have no point.

The difficult part of writing a narrative is making sure that it has a point. That point will be included in the topic sentence. The point of a narrative is the meaning of the incident or incidents you are writing about. To get to the point of your narrative, ask yourself questions like these:

What did I learn?
What is the meaning of this story?
What is my attitude toward what happened?
Did it change me?
What emotion did it make me feel?
Was the experience a good example of something (like unfairness, or kindness, or generosity)?

The answers to such questions can lead you to a point. An effective topic sentence for a narrative is

not this: This paper will be about the time I found a wallet on the sidewalk. (This is an announcement; it does not make a point.)
but this: When I found a wallet on the sidewalk, my honesty was tested.

not this: Last week my car alarm wouldn't stop screeching. (This identifies the incident but does not make a point. It is also too narrow to be a good topic sentence.)
but this: I lost my faith in fancy gadgets when my car alarm wouldn't stop screeching.

MyWritingLab™   Exercise 1   **Practice: Recognizing Good Topic Sentences for Narrative Paragraphs**

If a sentence is a good topic sentence for a narrative paragraph, write *OK* on the line provided.

1. _____ This is the story of an online rumor.

2. _____ Last week, someone in my class was accused of plagiarism.

3. _____ When my brother stole my phone, he learned the force of my anger.

4. _____ The strength of a person's desire to win one important game will be discussed here.

5. _____ Raising money for a family who suffered in a fire made me feel useful and needed.

6. _____ Temporary employment in a department store gave me an understanding of sales techniques.

7. _____ Reading a disturbing article about child slavery motivated me to take action.

8. _____ A few months ago, my fiancé lost his wallet with all his identification and credit cards.

Exercise 2 **Collaborate: Writing the Missing Topic Sentences in a Narrative Paragraph**

Collaborate

Working with a partner or group, write an appropriate topic sentence for the following paragraph. Be ready to share your answer with another group or with the class.

topic sentence: _____

_____

     Last month I had to renew my driver's license. I had recently moved to a new part of the state, and I was unsure of the procedure to follow. Had I brought sufficient identification? I was not sure. Would I have to pass any kind of test? I did not think so. After a series of long lines and stressful moments, I left the testing site with a new photo and my new address on my updated license. I felt triumphant. Later that afternoon, I returned to my house, put my license in my pocket, and took a short walk. On the next morning, I couldn't find my license. In a panic, I searched my clothes, my house, and even the route where I had walked on the previous day. Furious at myself, I wound up back at the license bureau where I was ashamed to admit the truth: I had lost my new license within twenty-four hours. Later, my story had a somewhat happy ending. Ten days after I had lost the first license, an envelope addressed to me arrived in the mail. In it was my original "new" license. Someone had found it, and, using the address on the new license, mailed it to me. That person is a rare and kind human being.

HINTS FOR WRITING A NARRATIVE PARAGRAPH

Everyone tells stories, but some people tell stories better than others. When you write a story, be sure to follow these guidelines:

- Be clear.
- Be interesting.
- Stay in order.
- Pick a topic that is not too big.

    1. Be clear. Put in all the information the reader needs in order to follow your story. Sometimes you need to explain the time, or place, or the relationships of the people in your story in order to make the story clear. Sometimes you need to explain how much time has elapsed between one action and another. This paragraph is not clear:

      Getting the right textbooks from the campus bookstore was a frustrating experience. First of all, I missed the first two days of classes, so José had to give me the list of books, and I really couldn't understand his writing. Then, when I got there, they didn't have all the books I needed. The book I needed the most, the workbook for my Intermediate Algebra class, wasn't on the shelves, and they said they had run out and wouldn't get more until next week. In addition, I couldn't use a Mastercard, only a Visa card, to pay, and I didn't have a Visa card. I left with only one of my required textbooks.

What is wrong with the paragraph? It lacks all kinds of information. Who is José? Is he a classmate? Someone who works in the bookstore? And what list is *the* list of books? The writer talks about getting "there," but is "there" the campus bookstore or another bookstore, and who are "they"?

2. Be interesting. A boring narrative can make the greatest adventure sound dull. Here is a dull narrative:

> Volunteering with the homebuilders club was great. Last weekend I helped the club members fix up an old house. First, we did some things outside. Then we worked on the inside and cleaned up the kitchen. We did a little painting, too. I particularly liked the end of the project, when the family who owned the house saw the improvements. They were happy.

Specific, vivid details could turn this dull narrative into an interesting one.

3. Stay in order. Put the details in a clear order so that the reader can follow your story. Usually, time order is the order you follow in narration. This narrative has a confusing order:

> Celia was really upset with me yesterday. But that was before I explained about the car accident. Then she forgave me and felt guilty about being so mean. She was angry because I had promised to take her to the movies last night. When I didn't show up, she started calling me on my cell phone. She claims she called seven times and never got an answer. What Celia didn't know was that, on my way to her house, I had skidded on a wet road and hit a tree. I wasn't badly hurt, but the paramedics insisted on taking me to the emergency room. My cell phone was in my car while I rode in an ambulance. By the time I left the hospital and made it to Celia's house, it was midnight, and Celia was not in a good mood.

There's something wrong with the order of events here. Tell the story in the order it happened: First, I promised to take Celia to the movies. Second, I had a car accident. Third, Celia tried to call many times. Fourth, I was taken to the emergency room and then released. Fifth, I went to Celia's house, where she was angry. Sixth, I told my story and she forgave me. A clear time sequence helps the reader follow your narrative.

4. Pick a topic that is not too big. If you try to write about too many events in a short space, you risk being superficial. You cannot describe anything well if you cover too much. This paragraph covers too much:

> Visiting New York City was like exploring a new world for me. It started with a ride on the subway, which was both frightening and exciting. Then my cousin, a native New Yorker, introduced me to Times Square, where I saw people dressed like aliens in a science fiction movie and I learned to navigate through thousands of people all trying to cross the street. After that, we went to a famous New York deli where I ate Greek, Korean, and Italian food. The next day, we walked to Central Park and heard a free concert. That night, we went to a club where the music was loud and wild.

This paragraph would be better if it discussed one shorter time period in greater depth and detail. For example, it could cover one incident—the subway ride, the visit to Times Square, the deli meal, the concert, or the club—more fully.

CRITICAL THINKING TIP

When selecting a topic, sometimes it is difficult to see whether or not a topic is too big. Ask yourself all of the *who, what, when, where, why,* and *how* questions about the topic. If you think you can answer such questions sufficiently within a paragraph, then your topic is probably a good one. If you need more than one paragraph (and your instructor has stated that the assignment should be one paragraph), then your topic is probably too big.

Using a Speaker's Exact Words in Narrative

Narratives often include the exact words someone said. You may want to include part of a conversation in your narrative. To do so, you need to know how to punctuate speech.

A person's exact words get quotation marks around them. If you change the words, you do not use quotation marks.

> **exact words:** "You're acting strangely," he told me.
> **not exact words:** He told me that I was acting strangely.

> **exact words:** My father said, "I can get tickets to the soccer match."
> **not exact words:** My father said he could get tickets to the soccer match.

There are a few other points to remember about punctuating a person's exact words. Once you've started quoting a person's exact words, periods and commas generally go inside the quotation marks. Here are two examples:

> Marcelline said, "My car needs new tires."
> "Eat your breakfast," my grandmother told me.

When you introduce a person's exact words with phrases like "She said" or "The police officer told us," put a comma before the quotation marks. Here are two examples:

> She said, "Take your umbrella."
> The police officer told us, "This road is closed."

If you are using a person's exact words and have other questions about punctuation, check the section on quotation marks in Chapter 16.

WRITING THE NARRATIVE PARAGRAPH IN STEPS

PREWRITING   **NARRATION**

2 Prewrite to focus your topic and details.

Suppose your instructor asks you to write a narrative paragraph on this topic:

My Last _____

You might begin by *freewriting:*

Freewriting on My Last _____

My last _____. My last what? Last chance? Last dance? My last chance at passing Algebra. My last cup of coffee. My last day of high school. That was wild. Seniors are crazy sometimes. Coffee—I love coffee. Quit it suddenly. Last cup of morning coffee. Needed my morning coffee.

You scan your freewriting and realize that you have three possible topics: My Last Day of High School, My Last Chance at Passing Algebra, and My Last Cup of Coffee. Since you do not have any details on passing algebra, and the last day of high school seems like a topic that many students might write about, you decide to be original and work with My Last Cup of Coffee.

MyWritingLab™ | Exercise 3 | **Practice: Finding Topics in Freewriting**

The freewriting example that follows contains more than one possible topic for a paragraph. In the spaces below the freewriting, write the possible topics, and write the one that you think would be the best topic for a narrative paragraph. Briefly explain why it would be the best topic: Is it the one with the most details? Is it the most original topic? Or is it the one that would be the easiest to develop with specific details?

Freewriting on this Topic: My First _____

My first what? My first kiss. How dumb is that? And I can't remember anything anyway. My first day in college. Maybe. Pretty confusing and intimidating. Will everyone write about college? My first taste of Mexican food. Wow. I wasn't ready for the hot sauce. Now I love it. All kinds of Mexican food. My first bike. Riding it on the sidewalk.

possible topics: _____

_____

your choice of the best topic: _____

reason for your choice: _____

Listing Ideas

Now that you have a specific topic, you can scan your freewriting for all your ideas on that topic. You put all those ideas into a list:

My Last Cup of Coffee

I love coffee.
Quit it suddenly.
Last cup of morning coffee.
Needed my morning coffee.

Adding Specific Details by Brainstorming

To add ideas to your list, try brainstorming. Add questions that will lead you to more details. You can start with questions that are based on the details you already have. See where the questions—and their answers—lead you.

Question: **Why do you love coffee?**
Answer: I love the taste.

Question: **Is that the only reason?**
Answer: It picks me up. Gives me energy.

Question: **Why did you quit it suddenly?**
Answer: I figured quitting suddenly would be the best way. Don't drag it out.

Question: **Why was your last cup drunk in the morning? Why not the afternoon or evening?**

Answer: My first cup in the morning was the one I needed the most. To wake up.

Question: **Were there any other times you needed it?**

Answer: I needed it all day.

Question: **Can you be more specific?**

Answer: I craved coffee around 10:00 a.m., and then again around 3:00 or 4:00 p.m., and also after dinner.

Question: **How did you feel after you quit?**

Answer: I felt terrible at first. The next day I felt better.

Question: **What do you mean by saying you felt terrible?**

Answer: I was irritable. Shaky. I had bad headaches.

As you can see, questions can lead you to more details and can help you to decide whether you will have enough details to develop a paragraph on your topic or whether you need to choose another topic. In this case, the details in the answers are sufficient for writing a paragraph.

Exercise 4   Collaborate: Brainstorming for Details

Collaborate

Following are topics and lists of details. With a partner or group, brainstorm at least five questions and answers, based on the existing details, that could add more details. The first one is partly done for you.

1. **topic:** Getting Lost at the University

   It was our first visit.
   We were going to a big football game.
   We had no air conditioning or fans.
   We felt grown up.
   Three of us were driving around.
   We had no idea the place was so big.

   Brainstorming Questions and Answers:

   Question 1:   Who were the three of you?

   Answer 1:   Me (Ryan), Jack, and Marty

   Question 2:   How old were you?

   Answer 2:   We were seventeen.

   Question 3:   _____

   Answer 3:   _____

   Question 4:   _____

   Answer 4:   _____

   Question 5:   _____

   Answer 5:   _____

2. topic: Learning to Ride a Bicycle

I got my first two-wheeler.
I had wanted it so badly.
My mother was worried.
It was a surprise gift.
I got a used bike.
I loved it anyway.

Brainstorming Questions and Answers:

Question 1: _____

Answer 1: _____

Question 2: _____

Answer 2: _____

Question 3: _____

Answer 3: _____

Question 4: _____

Answer 4: _____

Question 5: _____

Answer 5: _____

Focusing the Prewriting

To begin focusing your topic and details around some point, list your topic and all the details you have gathered so far. The list that follows includes all of the details gathered from freewriting and brainstorming.

My Last Cup of Coffee

I love coffee.
Quit it suddenly.
Last cup of morning coffee.
Needed my morning coffee.
I love the taste of coffee.
It picks me up.
Gives me energy.
I figured quitting suddenly would be the best way.
Don't drag it out.
My first cup in the morning was the one I needed the most.
To wake up.
I needed it all day.
I craved coffee around 10:00 a.m., and then again around 3:00 or 4:00 p.m., and also after dinner.
I felt terrible at first.
The next day I felt better.
First I was irritable. Shaky. I had bad headaches.

Coherence: Grouping the Details and Selecting a Logical Order

If you survey the list, you can begin to group the details:

List of Details on My Last Cup of Coffee

Why I Love Coffee

I love the taste.
It picks me up.
Gives me energy.

The Morning I Quit

I quit it suddenly.
I figured quitting suddenly would be the best way.
Don't drag it out.
Drank my last cup in the morning.
My first cup in the morning was the one I needed most.
To wake up.

The Afternoon

I needed it all day.
Around 3:00 or 4:00 p.m., I craved coffee.
I felt terrible at first.
I was irritable and shaky.

The Evening

I craved coffee after dinner.
I was more irritable.
I had a bad headache.

The Next Day

I felt better.

Looking at these groups, you notice one, "Why I Love Coffee," is background for your narrative. Three groups—"The Morning I Quit," "The Afternoon," and "The Evening"—tell about the *stages* of your quitting. And the last group tells how you felt *after* you had your last cup. These groups seem to lead to a **logical order** for the paragraph: a **time order**. A logical order will give your paragraph coherence.

Unity: Selecting a Topic Sentence

To give the paragraph unity, you need a point, a topic sentence. Surveying your topic and detail, you might decide on this topic sentence:

> My last cup of coffee was in the morning.

To be sure that your paragraph has **unity**, check your topic sentence. It should (1) make a point and (2) relate to all your details.

3 Write a clear topic sentence.

Does it make a point? No. It says your last cup of coffee was in the morning. That isn't much of a point. It is too narrow to develop into a paragraph. Does the topic sentence relate to all your details? No. You have details about why you love coffee, when you needed it, how you quit, and how you felt afterward. But with your topic sentence, you can talk only about the morning you quit.

You need a better topic sentence. To find it, ask yourself questions like:

Did I learn anything from this experience?
Did the experience hurt me?
Did it help me?
Was it a sad experience?
Was it a joyful one?
Were the results good or bad?
Is there a lesson in this experience?

Surveying your details, you might realize that they tell of someone who drank a great deal of coffee and who feels better after he or she quit. You might decide on a better topic sentence:

My last cup of coffee was the beginning of better health.

This topic sentence relates to many of the details you have. You can mention why you love coffee and when you drank it so that you can give some background on how hard it was to quit. You can explain quitting and discuss how you felt afterward. This topic sentence will give your paragraph unity.

To check your topic sentence for unity, ask the following questions:

Checklist for Unity and the Topic Sentence

✓ Does the topic sentence make a point?

✓ Is the point broad enough to cover all the details?

✓ Do the details relate to the topic sentence?

If the answer to these questions is yes, you are helping to unify your paragraph.

Now that you have a topic sentence and a list of details, you are ready to begin the planning stage of writing.

MyWritingLab™   **Exercise 5** **Practice: Grouping Details**

Below are topics and lists of details. Group the details of each list, writing them under the appropriate headings. Some details may not fit under any of the headings.

1. topic: Starting Over

details: After one semester, I quit college to find a job.

I didn't see my old friends much because I had dropped out.

I got promoted at my job once in five years.

When I returned to college, I was more of an adult.

Working had taught me a few things about getting stuck in a rut.

I was a bored and restless nineteen-year-old sitting in a lecture hall.

Returning to school, the first thing I did was take a deep breath.

Once I had a job, I felt fairly satisfied at first.

On my first day back at college, I sat in the front row of the lecture hall.

At nineteen, I had no idea what I wanted in life—except some money.

Gradually, I felt stuck, lonely, and bored in my job.

This time, I looked at college as a way to test my limits.

I enjoyed my first day of being an older student.

I knew what I wanted on my second try.

After high school, all my friends were going to college, so I did, too.

List details about the writer's first try at college: _____

_____

_____

_____

List details about the time after his first try at college: _____

_____

_____

_____

List details about his different attitude on his return to college: _____

_____

_____

_____

List details about his first day back in college: _____

_____

_____

_____

2. topic: Choices

details: My parents and I came to America when I was two years old.

My parents could not hold on to their business.

Shortly after they arrived in the United States, my father and mother used all their savings to open a small business.

They worked long, hard hours at their business.

I considered returning to Taiwan because otherwise I would be all alone, without any family.

I wanted to be a loyal son.

The business did fairly well, but then bad times hit my parents hard.

I've never understood the economics of small family businesses.

They had no more money to invest.

They decided to ask me, an adult now, to return to Taiwan with them.

They decided to return to Taiwan where our extended family would help them.

I would be left without my parents' encouragement and care.

I knew no other life than my American life.

I had a steady job in America.

I knew that America was my real home, even without my family.

I chose to stay in America.

List details about the writer's family background in America: _____

_____

_____

_____

_____

_____

List details about the parents' decision: _____

_____

_____

_____

List details about the writer's dilemma: _____

_____

_____

_____

List details about the writer's choice: _____

_____

_____

_____

Exercise 6 **Collaborate: Creating Topic Sentences**

Collaborate

Do this exercise with a partner or a group. Following are lists of details. For each list, write two appropriate topic sentences.

1. topic sentence 1: _____

_____

topic sentence 2: _____

_____

details: On Saturday afternoon, I was returning to my house after a trip to the supermarket.

I felt proud of myself because I had planned for the week ahead.

I had stocked up on supplies for breakfast, dinner, and snacks.

As I approached my garage, I couldn't find the garage door opener.

Quickly, I bent down to check the floor of the car.

Suddenly, there was a loud sound of metal crumbling and glass breaking.

I had taken my foot off the brake just as my car had slowly hit the garage door.

The door had crumpled when my car bumped it.

I was horrified.

Then I was more horrified and ashamed when I thought about the cost of a new garage door.

2. topic sentence 1: _____

_____

topic sentence 2: _____

_____

details: My sister and her husband recently moved out of their old, two-story townhouse into a newer but smaller one.

My sister Abigail is an efficient and organized person.

Her husband Bill is a more spontaneous one.

My sister cleaned her clothes closet, sorting items into boxes labeled "keep," "give away," and "toss."

Then she began on her husband's closet.

Unfortunately, Bill appeared just as she was dumping his favorite t-shirt (full of holes) into the "toss" box.

Bill snatched the shirt and stuffed it in the "keep" box.

He commandeered his closet, grabbing faded jeans and ragged sweaters.

He found beloved shoes he had not seen in years.

Everything went into the "keep" box.

Abigail was unhappy.

Out of desperation, she tried to sneak a pair of Bill's sweatpants into the "give away" box.

At that moment, she found her old college sweatshirt in a corner of Bill's closet.

She decided to put her sweatshirt in the "keep" box.

PLANNING   NARRATION

Once you have a topic sentence and a list of details, you can write them in outline form. Below is an outline for a paragraph on "My Last Cup of Coffee." As you read the outline, you will notice that some of the items on the earlier list have been combined, and the details have been grouped into logical categories.

Outline on My Last Cup of Coffee

topic sentence	My last cup of coffee was the beginning of better health.
details	
why I love coffee	I love the taste of coffee.
	Coffee picks me up and gives me energy.
the morning I quit	I quit it suddenly.
	I figured quitting suddenly would be the best way.
	Don't drag it out.
	Drank my last cup in the morning.
	My first cup in the morning was the one I needed most.
	I needed it to wake up.
the afternoon	I needed it all day.
	Around 3:00 or 4:00 p.m., I craved coffee.
	I felt terrible at first.
	I was irritable and shaky.
the evening	I craved coffee after dinner.
	I was more irritable.
	I had a bad headache.
the next day	I felt better.

Following is a checklist that can help you prepare your outline:

> **Checklist for a Narrative Outline**
>
> ✓ Do all the details connect to the topic sentence?
>
> ✓ Are the details in a clear order?
>
> ✓ Does the outline need more details?
>
> ✓ Are the details specific enough?

With a good outline, you are ready to write a first draft of a narrative paragraph.

Exercise 7 **Practice: Finding Details That Do Not Fit**   MyWritingLab™

Following are outlines. In each outline, there are details that do not relate to the topic sentence. Cross out the details that do not fit.

1. topic sentence: One evening, we had an unexpected visitor from the natural world.

   details: My husband and I live in a first-floor apartment.

   Although it is a large modern complex, it is close to a nature preserve.

   The complex has a large pool and patio area.

   One night after dinner, we were sitting outdoors on our small, screened porch.

   We like to relax as the sun goes down.

   Suddenly, we saw a small creature about fifteen feet away.

   "It's a cat," I said.

   The creature came closer.

   It was a small fox.

   We were thrilled to see the wild fox so close to us.

   We've seen many squirrels, but never a fox.

2. topic sentence: When our plans for Friday night did not work out, we found a great alternative.

   details: A great new movie opened on Friday night.

   We arrived at our local theater where about a hundred people were already in line for the show.

   It was hot and humid in the line.

   The line didn't seem to be moving.

   Everyone wants to be the first to see a certain film so he or she can talk about the film at work.

   Finally, my girlfriend went up to the box office.

   She returned with bad news.

The movie was already sold out for the current showing.

The line was for tickets for the midnight show, and that show was nearly sold out.

We decided to leave.

On the way home, we devised a plan.

We stopped at a Mexican restaurant and ordered take-out fajitas.

There are two Mexican restaurants near our apartment.

We went home, browsed through our DVDs, and found one comedy that we love.

Comedies are good when people need to lift their moods.

We turned down the air conditioner, lit candles, ate our fajitas, and laughed through the video.

MyWritingLab™ Exercise 8 **Practice: Recognizing Details That Are Out of Order**

Each outline below has one detail that is out of order. Indicate where it belongs by drawing an arrow from it to the place where it should go.

1. **topic sentence:** In the future, I will eat only take-out pizza.

   details: Yesterday I was feeling both lazy and hungry.

   I decided to eat whatever I could find at home.

   Given a choice between wilted lettuce and pizza, I picked the pizza.

   My refrigerator held only a bag of wilted salad, a bottle of Diet Sprite, and a frozen pizza.

   I checked the required baking temperature on the pizza box.

   Then I set the oven for the correct temperature.

   When the oven had reached the correct temperature, I took the pizza out of the freezer.

   I ripped open the pizza box and tore off the plastic covering.

   I placed the pizza on a metal pan, set the oven timer, and popped the pizza in the oven.

   When the timer sounded, I pulled the pizza from the oven, set my meal on a plate, and cut the pizza into slices.

   Hungrily I bit into the first slice.

   It had a burnt flavor, and the texture was a bit strange.

   Examining the slice more carefully, I studied the bottom of the piece.

I had baked the pizza without removing the cardboard that separates the bottom of the pizza from the box.

2. topic sentence: Two children made my long wait at the doctor's office into an amusing afternoon.

details: I arrived on time for my 2:00 p.m. doctor's appointment.

When I arrived, there were four other people in the waiting room.

"The doctor is running a little late," said the receptionist a few minutes later when a sixth person arrived.

At 2:30 p.m., a mother with a little girl arrived.

The little girl sat next to her mother but soon began to fidget.

By 2:45, the mother had warned the little girl, scolded, and even grabbed the child when the little girl began to wander.

The receptionist replied that the doctor had been handling an emergency.

At about ten minutes past three, a little boy and his mother entered the waiting room.

For the little boy, one look at the little girl led to instant love.

He ran to the little girl and kissed her.

Everyone in the room laughed.

After an hour of waiting, I asked the receptionist why no one had been called in to see the doctor.

For a few minutes, all of us in the waiting room forgot to be impatient as we watched the toddlers play together.

Exercise 9   Collaborate: Putting Details in the Correct Order

Collaborate

Do this exercise with a partner or a group. In each of the outlines below, the list of details is in the wrong order. Number the details in the correct order, writing *1* next to the detail that should be listed first, and so on.

1. topic sentence: My dream of a quiet evening at home turned into a nightmare.

details: _____ During a busy week at work, I promised myself a quiet, luxurious Saturday night at home alone.

_____ Once I stashed my goodies in the kitchen, I prepared for a long, hot bath.

_____ I was about to sink into a warm, bubble-filled bathtub when the phone rang.

_____ My former boyfriend was calling, was back in town, and wanted to know if he could stop by.

_____ Even though I knew I was being stupid, I agreed that he could come over.

_____ I was shocked to see him arrive with friends: two beautiful girls and a man.

_____ I rushed to dress, do my hair, and put on makeup before he arrived.

_____ I arrived home with all the necessities: two DVDs, fresh French bread from the bakery, cheese, a bottle of wine, and chocolates.

_____ The visitors sipped my wine, ate the bread, and savored my chocolate.

_____ As they feasted, I fumed and tried to determine the relationships among these visitors.

2. **topic sentence:** Getting my four-year-old ready for preschool yesterday became a mission I swore to accomplish.

details: _____ Miranda woke up in a bad mood.

_____ As I coaxed her out of bed, she grumbled.

_____ She resisted as I tried to wash her.

_____ After the battle of the bathroom, she could not decide what to eat.

_____ Dressing her proved to be worse than feeding her.

_____ She rejected her princess outfit, her pink dress and leggings, and all her other favorite styles.

_____ We left the house with Miranda still sulking but feeling somewhat victorious in her choice of clothes: a flowered hat, a fleece pajama top, sparkly jeans, and bunny slippers.

_____ I offered hot cereal, cold cereal, sliced bananas, sliced and diced peaches, milk, and two kinds of juice.

_____ She refused all my offerings.

_____ Desperate, I whipped up a smoothie in the blender.

_____ She agreed to drink a little but slipped most of the smoothie to our dog.

④ Write a narrative paragraph that uses transitions and details effectively.

DRAFTING AND REVISING   **NARRATION**

Once you have a good outline, you can write a draft of your paragraph. Once you have a first draft, you can begin to think about revising extensively. The checklist below may help you revise your draft.

Checklist for Revising the Draft of a Narrative Paragraph
✓ Is my narrative vivid?
✓ Are the details clear and specific?
✓ Do all the details relate to the topic sentence?
✓ Are the details written in a clear order?
✓ Do the transitions make the narrative easy to follow?
✓ Have I made my point?

Transitions

Transitions are *words*, *phrases*, or even *sentences* that link ideas. Sometimes they tell the reader what he or she has just read and what is coming next. Every kind of writing has its own transitions. When you tell a story, you have to be sure that your reader can follow you as you move through the steps of your story. Most of the transitions in narration relate to time. Below is a list of transitions writers often use in writing narratives:

INFO BOX	Transitions for a Narrative Paragraph			
after	at the same time	immediately	now	until
again	before	in the meantime	soon	when
always	during	later	soon after	while
at first	finally	later on	still	
at last	first (second, etc.)	meanwhile	suddenly	
at once	frequently	next	then	

Following is a revised draft that evolved from the outline on page 296. You can assume that the writer worked through *several* drafts to get to this point. As you read it, you will notice that it adds some specific details and incorporates effective transitional phrases. (More work, however, will still be necessary.)

Revised Draft of a Paragraph on My Last Cup of Coffee

(Changes from the outline are underlined; editing and proofreading are still needed.)

My last cup of coffee was the beginning of better health. It was hard for me to stop drinking coffee because I love the taste of coffee. *transition added* — In addition, coffee picks me up and gives me energy. I quit it suddenly. *added details* — I figured that a sharp break would be better than dragging out the process. I drank my last cup in the morning. It was the cup I needed *added details, transition added* — most, to wake up, so I decided to allow myself that cup. By afternoon, I saw how much I needed coffee all day. Around 3:00 or 4:00 p.m., I craved it. I felt terrible. I was shaky and irritable. After dinner, my coffee craving was worse. I was *details added, transition added* — more irritable, and I had a pounding headache. The next day, I felt better.

MyWritingLab™ | Exercise 10 | **Practice: Recognizing Transitions**

Underline all the transitions—words and phrases—in the paragraph below.

Desperation led to humiliation for Andrew. We had an important exam in our Introduction to Business class, and we were both nervous. In fact, we had spent most of the previous night studying for that test. I went to Andrew's house, and we crammed for hours. First, we skimmed the assigned reading and asked each other questions. Then we reviewed our lecture notes. Meanwhile, we drank plenty of coffee. When I couldn't stuff another piece of information into my head, I went home and caught a few hours of sleep. Next morning, I made it to the classroom just before the exam was to begin. Soon after, Andrew stumbled in, bleary-eyed. "I'd better do well on this exam," he whispered as he passed me. "I stayed up after you left and kept reviewing." He found a seat near the front and fell into it. I finished the test ahead of time and took a breath before I submitted my test booklet and answer sheet. While I sat calmly, I looked around. Andrew had his head in his hands. Then his head began to fall toward the desk. His head fell softly into his folded arms. At once, Andrew began to snore. It was a loud snore, and at the same time that I heard it, the other students heard it, too. When our professor walked quietly to Andrew's seat, Andrew was still snoring over his test booklet.

MyWritingLab™ | Exercise 11 | **Practice: Adding the Appropriate Transitions**

In the following paragraph transitions are shown in parentheses. Circle the appropriate transitions.

Getting to college and getting home again are complicated processes for me. I don't have a car, and my house is too far from college for me to walk or ride a bike. (After / While) I eat breakfast and pack my book bag, I walk about a mile to the nearest bus stop. There is a bench at the bus stop but no covered area. (Until / When) it rains, I get wet unless I remember to carry a small umbrella. The bus gets me to school an hour and a half (before / while) my classes start.

The campus is not very crowded (during / next) this time so I can find a quiet place

to read or study. (Later / When) my classes begin, they are scheduled one after

the other. If the last class runs a few minutes overtime, I have to run to catch a

bus home. If I miss that bus, I have to wait another hour (soon / until) another bus

appears. Someday I will be rewarded for my long journeys to and from campus,

but (at first / in the meantime), I just accept these trips as part of my education.

Exercise 12   **Collaborate: Using Transitions**

Collaborate

Do this exercise with a partner or a group. Write a sentence for each item
below. Be ready to share your answers with another group or with the
entire class.

1. Write a sentence with *frequently* in the middle of the sentence

2. Write a sentence that begins with *Before.*

3. Write a sentence with *at last* in the middle of the sentence.

4. Write a sentence that begins with *At first.*

5. Write a sentence with *later on* in the middle of the sentence.

6. Write a sentence with *when* in the middle of the sentence.

7. Write a sentence with *always* in the middle of the sentence.

8. Write a sentence that begins with *Then.*

EDITING AND PROOFREADING   NARRATION

The revised draft of the paragraph on "My Last Cup of Coffee" (page 301) still
has some rough spots:

- One idea is missing from the paragraph: Why did you decide to give
  up coffee? How was it hurting your health?
- Added details could make it more vivid.
- The paragraph needs transitions to link ideas.
- To make its point, the paragraph needs a final sentence about
  better health.

Following is the final version of the paragraph on "My Last Cup of Coffee." As you review the final version, you will notice several refinements the writer made through careful **editing**:

- A new idea, about why you wanted to stop drinking coffee, has been added.
- To avoid repetition, one use of the word *coffee* has been replaced with *it*.
- Sentence combining and more transitions have been incorporated.
- Some vivid details have been added.
- The verbs in the first few sentences of the paragraph have been changed to the past tense because those sentences talk about the time when you drank coffee.
- A final sentence about better health has been added.

Final Version of a Paragraph on My Last Cup of Coffee

(Key changes from the revised draft are underlined.)

My last cup of coffee was the beginning of better health. It was hard for me to stop drinking coffee because I <u>loved</u> the taste of <u>it</u>. In addition, I <u>thought that</u> coffee <u>picked</u> me up and <u>gave</u> me energy. <u>However, I decided to quit drinking coffee when I realized how much I needed it to keep going and to keep from feeling low</u>. I quit it suddenly because I figured that a sharp break from my habit would be better than dragging out the process. I drank my last cup in the morning. It was the cup I needed most, to wake up, so I decided to allow myself that <u>final</u> cup. By afternoon, I saw how much I needed coffee all day. Around 3:00 or 4:00 p.m., I craved it. I felt terrible. I was shaky, <u>nervous</u>, and irritable. After dinner, <u>when I used to have two or three cups of strong coffee</u>, my craving was worse. I was more irritable, <u>I was ready to snap at anyone who asked me a question</u>, and I had a pounding headache. <u>Soon, the worst was over, and</u> by the next day, I felt better. <u>Now, free of my coffee-drinking habit, I have a steady flow of energy, few crashing lows, and pride in my achievement</u>.

Before you prepare your final copy of your paragraph, edit your latest draft to improve word choice, strengthen transition, and combine sentences if necessary. Then proofread carefully to spot any careless errors in punctuation, spelling, or format.

Connect

Exercise 13 Connect: Correcting Errors in the Final Draft of a Narrative Paragraph

Proofread the following paragraph. Correct any careless errors in spelling, punctuation, and proper word endings. There are eight errors. Write your corrections in the space above each error.

Last Saturday, I tried and failed to convince my father to change his diet.

My effort's began when my Father and I went shopping together. After we had

finished looking for a good used car to replace his old Nissan, he offered to take

me to lunch. I agreed and suggest a nearby restaurant that is known for it's fresh

salads and homemade soup's. My father laughed and insisted that we go to his favorite barbecue place. As soon as we arrived, my father was ready to order.

He always eats the same meal of steak fries, ribs covered with a thick, sugary bar-

becue sauce, and a tub of cole slaw swimming in mayonnaise. Of course, flaky bis-

cuits shiny with grease come with this meal. My father teased me when I choose

to eat a few items from the salad bar. He warned me that the salad dressings were

as unhealthy as butter or grease. My only response was to show him the raw

vegetables and low-fat dressing I had on my plate. After he had gobbled his meal,

I gave him a lecture about heart disease and stroke. Then I scolded him about high

blood pressure. he did not become annoyed. Instead, he said I had made some

good points. Then he ordered a piece, of key lime pie.

Lines of Detail: A Walk-Through Assignment

For this assignment, write a paragraph on My First _____. (You
fill in the blank. Your topic will be based on how you complete Step 1 below.)

> **Step 1:** To begin the prewriting part of writing this paragraph, com-
> plete the following questionnaire. It will help you think of
> possible topics and details.

Collaborative Questionnaire for Gathering Topics and Details Answer
the following questions as well as you can. Then read your answers to a group.
The members of the group should then ask you follow-up questions, based on
your answers. For example, if your answer is "I felt nervous," a group member
might ask, "Why were you nervous?" or "What made you nervous?" Write your
answers on the lines provided; the answers will add details to your list.

Finally, tear out the page and ask each member of your group to circle
one topic or detail that could be developed into a paragraph. Discuss the
suggestions.

Repeat this process for each member of the group.

Questionnaire

1. Have you ever been interviewed for a job? When? _____

   _____

   Write four details you remember about the interview:

   a. _____

   b. _____

   c. _____

   d. _____

   Additional details to add after working with the group:

   _____

   _____

   _____

2. Do you remember your first day of school (in elementary school, middle school, high school, or college)? Write four details about that day.

   a. _____

   b. _____

   c. _____

   d. _____

Additional details to add after working with the group:

_____

_____

_____

3. Do you remember your first visit to a special place? Write four details about that place.

   a. _____

   b. _____

   c. _____

   d. _____

Additional details to add after working with the group:

_____

_____

_____

Step 2: Select a topic from the details and ideas on the questionnaire. Brainstorm and list ideas about the topic.

Step 3: Group your ideas in time order.

Step 4: Survey your grouped ideas and write a topic sentence. Check that your topic sentence makes a point and is broad enough to relate to all the details.

Step 5: Write an outline of your paragraph, putting the grouped details below the topic sentence. Check your outline. Be sure that all of the details relate to the topic sentence and that the details are in a clear and logical order.

Step 6: Write a first draft of your paragraph; then revise it extensively. You may need to write *several* drafts until you are satisfied with the content and structure.

Step 7: Edit your latest revised draft and be sure that your details are specific and your word choice is precise.

Step 8: Prepare a clean copy of your paragraph and proofread to catch any careless errors in format, spelling, punctuation, and typing.

Topics for Writing Your Own Narrative Paragraph

When you write on any of the following topics, be sure to follow the stages of the writing process in preparing your paragraph.

1. Interview someone who has an enviable job. Ask the person why he or she chose that career. You can ask questions such as, "How did you decide to become a _____?" or "What most interested you in working as a _____?" Take notes. If you have a recording device, you can record the interview, but take notes as well.

   When you have finished the interview, review the information with the person you've interviewed. Would he or she like to add anything? If you wish, ask follow-up questions.

   Next, on your own, find a point to the story. Use that point in your topic sentence. In this paragraph, you will be writing about another person, not about yourself.

   MyWritingLab™

2. Visit the Web site of your local newspaper and find a news story about an unusual crime. Summarize the details of the story in time order and focus your summary with a topic sentence that states what type of crime was committed as well as the most unusual aspect of the crime. Be aware that newspaper accounts of a crime are not always written in time order, so you may have to determine the sequence of events.

   MyWritingLab™

3. Following are some topic sentences. Complete one of them and use it to write a paragraph.
   When _____, I was thrilled because _____.
   Apologizing to _____ was one of the hardest things I have ever done.
   One encounter _____ taught me _____.
   The biggest surprise in my life came when _____.
   The longest day of my life was the day I _____.
   My best day at my first job was the day I _____.

   MyWritingLab™

4. To write on this topic, begin with a partner. Ask your partner to tell you about a day that turned out unexpectedly. It can be a day that included a good or bad surprise.
   As your partner speaks, take notes. Ask questions. When your partner has finished speaking, review your notes. Ask your partner if he or she has anything to add.
   On your own, outline and draft a paragraph on your partner's day. Read your draft to your partner, adding comments and suggestions. Check the final draft of your paragraph for errors in punctuation, spelling, and word choice.
   Your partner can work through this same process to write a paragraph about a day that turned out unexpectedly for you.

   Collaborate

Topics for Critical Thinking and Writing

> **Note:** Critical thinking often involves examining an encounter or issue from perspectives other than your own.

MyWritingLab™

1. Think of a recent frustrating incident with a family member or friend. Write a narrative paragraph detailing what happened, but imagine that you are the family member or friend relating what happened. You will be writing what happened strictly from his or her perspective.

MyWritingLab™

2. After studying the body language of the couple in the middle of the street, write a paragraph that tells a story about them. Imagine who they are, why they are together on a deserted street, what he and she are thinking, and where they are headed. Be sure your details are arranged in a clear sequence.

Writing a Descriptive Paragraph

CHAPTER 25

Jumping In

*What is your strongest impression of this scene? Does it stir up feelings of power? Excitement? Fear? Examining the scene carefully, along with your reactions, will help you **describe** it effectively.*

Learning Objectives

In this chapter, you will learn to:

1. Identify the characteristics of a descriptive paragraph.
2. Prewrite to focus your topic and details.
3. Write a clear topic sentence.
4. Write a descriptive paragraph that uses transition, support, and details effectively.

WHAT IS DESCRIPTION?

Description *shows, not tells,* a reader what a person, place, thing, or situation is like. When you write a description, you want your reader to have a vivid picture of what you are describing. Your description may even make your reader think about or act upon what you have shown.

① Identify the characteristics of a descriptive paragraph.

HINTS FOR WRITING A DESCRIPTIVE PARAGRAPH

Using Specific Words and Phrases

Your description will help the reader see if it uses specific words and phrases. If a word or phrase is *specific*, it is *exact and precise*. The opposite of specific language is language that is vague, general, or fuzzy. Think of the difference between specific and general in this way:

> Imagine that your mother asks you what gift you want for your birthday.
> "Something nice," you say.
> "What do you mean by 'nice'?" your mother asks.
> "You know," you say. "Not the usual stuff."
> "What stuff?" she asks.
> "Like the usual things you always give me," you reply. "Don't give me that kind of stuff."
> "Well, what would you like instead?" she asks.

The conversation could go on and on. You are being very general in saying that you want "something nice." Your mother is looking for specific details: What do you mean by "nice"? What is "the usual stuff"? What are "the usual things"?

In writing, if you use words like "nice" or "the usual stuff," you will not have a specific description or a very effective piece of writing. Whenever you can, try to use a more precise word instead of a general term. To find a more explicit term, ask yourself such questions as "What type?" or "How?" The examples below show how a general term can be replaced by a more specific one.

general word: sweater (Ask "What type?")
more specific words: pullover, vest, cardigan

general word: science class (Ask "What type?")
more specific words: chemistry, physics, biology

general word: walked (Ask "How?")
more specific words: stumbled, strutted, strode

general word: funny (Ask "How?")
more specific words: strange, comical, entertaining

MyWritingLab™   **Exercise 1**   **Practice: Identifying General and Specific Words**

Below are lists of words. Put an *X* by the one term in each list that is a more general term than the others. The first one is done for you.

List 1

___X___ silverware

_____ knife

_____ soup spoon

_____ teaspoon

_____ fork

List 2

_____ cousin

_____ uncle

_____ relative

_____ brother

_____ grandmother

List 3

_____ lab packet

_____ algebra book

_____ textbook

_____ Chinese-English dictionary

_____ novel

List 4

_____ beans

_____ carrots

_____ peas

_____ vegetables

_____ celery

Exercise 2   **Practice: Ranking General and Specific Items**   MyWritingLab™

Below are lists of items. In each list, rank the items from the most general _1_ to the most specific _4_.

List 1

_____ college

_____ community college

_____ community colleges in
the Northeast

_____ community colleges with
nursing programs in the
Northeast

List 2

_____ law enforcement

_____ local law enforcement

_____ sheriff's deputy

_____ local law enforcement
officer

Exercise 3   **Collaborate: Interviewing for Specific Answers**   **Collaborate**

To practice being specific, interview a partner. Ask your partner to answer the questions below. Write his or her answers in the spaces provided. When you have finished, change places. In both interviews, your goal is to find specific answers, so both you and your partner should be as explicit as you can in your answers.

Interview Questions

1. What is your favorite classroom activity? _____

_____

2. Name three objects that are in your wallet or purse right now. _____

_____

3. What is your favorite television commercial? _____

_____

4. What actor or actress do you like most? _____

_____

5. If you were buying a car, what color would you choose? _____

_____

6. What sound do you think is the most irritating? _____

_____

7. When you think of a beautiful woman or man, who comes to mind? _____

_____

8. When you think of a vacation getaway, what place do you picture?

_____

MyWritingLab™   **Exercise 4**   **Practice: Finding Specific Words or Phrases**

List four specific words or phrases beneath each general one. You may use brand names where they are appropriate. The first word on List 1 is done for you.

List 1:
general word: green
specific word or phrase: *olive green* _____

_____

_____

_____

List 2:
general word: student
specific word or phrase: _____

_____

_____

_____

List 3:
general word: cell phone
specific word or phrase: _____

_____

_____

_____

MyWritingLab™   **Exercise 5**   **Practice: Identifying Sentences That Are Too General**

Below are lists of sentences. In each group put an *X* by one sentence that is general and vague.

1. a. _____ She is afraid to go out at night.
   b. _____ She can't fall asleep until she has checked every door and window twice.
   c. _____ She is a nervous person.

2. a. _____ Michael is a great guy.
   b. _____ Michael lends me money often.
   c. _____ Michael volunteers at a homeless shelter.

3. a. _____ The advising office is interesting.
   b. _____ The advising office has purple and green walls.
   c. _____ The advising office is the size of the ladies' restroom.

Using Sense Words in Your Descriptions

One way to make your description specific and vivid is to use **sense words**. As you plan a description, ask yourself,

> What does it **look** like?
> What does it **sound** like?
> What does it **smell** like?
> What does it **taste** like?
> What does it **feel** like?

The sense details, also called **sensory details**, can make a description vivid, and carefully selected adjectives can appeal to the reader's imagination (examples: *leaping* flames; *musty* odor; *bitter* taste; *screeching* brakes). In your description, try to include specific details related to the senses. As you brainstorm sense details, refer to the box to help you focus your thinking.

INFO BOX Devising Sense Details

For the sense of	Think about
sight	colors, light and dark, shadows, or brightness.
hearing	noise, silence, or the kinds of sounds you hear.
smell	fragrance, odors, scents, aromas, or perfume.
taste	bitter, sour, sweet, or compare the taste of one thing to another.
touch	the feel of things: texture, hardness, softness, roughness, smoothness.

Exercise 6 **Collaborate: Brainstorming Sense Details for a Description Paragraph**

Collaborate

With a partner or a group, brainstorm the following ideas for a paragraph. That is, for each topic, list at least six questions and answers that could help you find sense details. Be prepared to read your completed exercise to another group or to the class.

1. **topic:** The fire fascinated and horrified the crowd.
   Brainstorm questions and answers:

Question: _____

Answer: _____

Question: _____

Answer: _____

Question: _____

Answer: _____

Question: _____

Answer: _____

Question: _____

Answer: _____

Question: _____

Answer: _____

2. **topic:**   The final exam was a nightmare.
Brainstorm questions and answers:

Question: _____

Answer: _____

Question: _____

Answer: _____

Question: _____

Answer: _____

Question: _____

Answer: _____

Question: _____

Answer: _____

Question: _____

Answer: _____

MyWritingLab™   Exercise 7   **Practice: Writing Sense Words**

Write sense descriptions for the items below.

1. Write four words or phrases to describe what a new pair of sneakers feels like:

_____

_____

2. Write four words or phrases to describe what a sleeping baby looks like:

_____

_____

3. Write four words or phrases to describe the sounds of a traffic jam:

_____

_____

4. Write four words or phrases to describe the taste of a slice of lemon:

_____

_____

2 Prewrite to focus your topic and details.

WRITING THE DESCRIPTIVE PARAGRAPH IN STEPS

PREWRITING **DESCRIPTION**

Suppose your instructor asks you to write about this topic: "An Outdoor Place." You might begin by **brainstorming**.

Sample Brainstorming on an Outdoor Place

Question: What place?

Answer: Outside somewhere.

Question: Like the outside of a building?

Answer: Maybe.

Question: The beach?

Answer: That would be OK. But everybody will write on that.

Question: How about a park?

Answer: Yes. A park would be good.

Question: How about the park near your workplace—the city park?

Answer: I could do that. I go there at lunchtime.

You scan your brainstorming and realize you have three possible topics: the outside of a building, the beach, or a city park. You decide that you can write the most about the city park, so you brainstorm further:

Brainstorming on a Specific Topic: A City Park

Question: What does the park look like?

Answer: It's small.

Question: How small?

Answer: Just the size of an empty lot.

Question: What's in it?

Answer: Some trees. Benches.

Question: What else is in it?

Answer: A fountain. In the middle.

Question: Any swing sets or jungle gyms?

Answer: No, it's not that kind of park. Just a green space.

Question: Why do you like this park?

Answer: I just like it. It's near the store where I work. I go there at lunchtime.

Question: But why do you go there?

Answer: It's nice and green. It's not like the rest of the city.

Question: What's the rest of the city like?

Answer: The rest of the city is dirty, gray, and noisy.

By asking and answering questions, you can (1) choose a topic and (2) begin to develop ideas on that topic. Each answer can lead you to more questions and thus to more ideas.

MyWritingLab™ **Exercise 8** **Practice: Identifying Topics in Brainstorming**

Following are examples of early brainstorming. In each case, the brainstorming is focused on selecting a narrow topic from a broad one. Imagine that the broad topic is one assigned by your instructor. Survey each example of brainstorming and list all the possible narrower topics within it.

1. **broad topic:** Describe a place that made you feel uncomfortable.

   brainstorming:

   Question: **What does "uncomfortable" mean? Physically uncomfortable?**

   Answer: It could be. It could mean emotionally out of place.

   Question: **What about being crowded in an elevator with too many people?**

   Answer: That would be physically uncomfortable.

   Question: **Couldn't it be emotionally stressful, too?**

   Answer: If it made me feel trapped, and once, when I got stuck in an elevator, it did.

   Question: **Did you ever feel emotionally uncomfortable in another place?**

   Answer: The first prom I attended made me feel nervous and foolish.

   Question: **Why did you feel uncomfortable?**

   Answer: I barely knew the girl I took to the prom.

   Question: **Did you feel physically crowded in another space?**

   Answer: Once. On a subway in a big city.

   possible topics: _____

   _____

   _____

2. **broad topic:** Write about a powerful person.

   brainstorming:

   Question: **Who is powerful?**

   Answer: The president. A sports star. A rich person.

   Question: **Can it be a different kind of power?**

   Answer: Somebody with a powerful personality.

   Question: **What's a powerful personality?**

   Answer: A strength that can change lives. Or maybe someone who just changed his or her life.

   Question: **What do you mean when you say "changed"?**

   Answer: Changed attitudes, changed bad habits, or maybe just improved life for one or more people.

   possible topics: _____

   _____

   _____

Focusing the Prewriting

To begin focusing your topic and details around some point, list the topic and all the details you've gathered so far. The following list includes all the details you've gathered from both sessions of brainstorming on a city park.

3 Write a clear topic sentence.

> **topic: A City Park**
>
> park near my workplace
> I go there at lunchtime.
> It's small.
> just the size of an empty lot
> Some trees. Benches.
> A fountain. In the middle.
> a green space
> I like it.
> It's near the store where I work.
> It's nice and green.
> It's not like the rest of the city.
> The rest of the city is dirty, gray, and noisy.

Grouping the Details

If you survey the list, you can begin to group the details:

> **What It Looks Like**
>
> It's small.
> just the size of an empty lot
> it's nice and green.
> a green space
> Some trees. Benches.
> A fountain.
> In the middle.

> **Where It Is**
>
> park near my workplace
> It's near the store where I work.

> **How I Feel About It**
>
> I like it.
> I go there at lunchtime.
> It's not like the rest of the city.
> The rest of the city is dirty, gray, and noisy.

Surveying the details, you notice that they focus on the look and location of a place you like. You decide on this topic sentence:

> A small city park is a nice place for me because it is not like the rest of the city.

You check your topic sentence to decide whether it covers all your details. Does it cover what the park looks like and its location? Yes, the words *small* and *city* relate to what it looks like and its location. Does it cover how you feel about the park? Yes, it says the park is "a nice place for me because it is not like the rest of the city."

Now that you have a topic sentence and a list of details, you are ready to begin the planning stage of writing.

Exercise 9 **Practice: Grouping Details**

Following is a topic and a list of details. Group the details, writing them under the appropriate headings. Some details may not fit.

topic: A Cluttered Desk

details: It is an old, scratched, and dented desk.

One of the drawers has an old packet of microwave popcorn peeping out.

The floor beneath the desk is covered in dust bunnies.

The top of the desk is stacked with folders and papers.

The drawers overflow with manila envelopes, notebooks, and crumpled documents.

Ballpoint pens without tops and stubs of pencils lie under the desk.

A box crammed with markers, pens, pencils, and erasers has been pushed to the edge of the desktop.

The desk drawers are always open; they are too full to shut.

List details about what is on the desk: _____

_____

_____

_____

List details about what is inside the desk drawers: _____

_____

_____

_____

List details about what is under the desk: _____

_____

_____

_____

PLANNING **DESCRIPTION**

Once you have a topic sentence, a list of details, and some grouping of the details, you can write them in outline form. Before you write your details in outline form, check their order. Remember that when you write a description, you are trying to make the reader *see*. It will be easier for the reader to imagine what you see if you put your description in a simple, logical order. You might want to put descriptions in order by **time sequence** (first to last), by **spatial position** (e.g., top to bottom, right to left, or outside to inside), or by **similar types** (e.g., all about the flowers, then all about the trees in a garden).

If you are describing a house, for instance, you may want to start with the outside of the house and then describe the inside. You do not want the details to shift back and forth, from outside to inside and back to outside. If you are describing a person, you might want to group all the details about his or her face before you describe the person's body. You might want to describe a meal from the first course to dessert.

Look again at the grouped list of details on a city park. To help make the reader see the park, you decide to arrange your details in **spatial order**: First, describe where the park is located; second, describe the edges and the middle of the park. The final lines of your paragraph can describe your feelings about the park. The following outline follows this order:

Outline for a Paragraph on A City Park

topic sentence	A small city park is a nice place for me because it is not like the rest of the city.
details	
location	It is near the store where I work.
appearance from edges to the middle	It is just the size of an empty lot. It is nice. It is a green space. It has some trees and benches. It has a fountain in the middle.
how I feel about it	I like it. I go there at lunchtime. It is not like the rest of the city. The rest of the city is dirty, gray, and noisy.

Once you have an outline, you can begin writing your descriptive paragraph.

Exercise 10 **Practice: Putting Details in Order**   MyWritingLab™

Following are lists that start with a topic sentence. The details under each topic sentence are not in the right order. Put the details in the right order by labeling them, with *1* being the first detail, *2* the second, and so forth.

1. topic sentence: The children's choir quickly found its rhythm.
(Arrange the details in time order.)

details: _____ By their second selection, they and their audience were having fun.

_____ As they entered the stage, the children awkwardly stumbled into their places.

_____ The music director calmly extended his hands to the children as they stood waiting to sing.

_____ Family and friends waited eagerly for the children to appear.

_____ They began their first number a little hesitantly.

_____ The children's power grew until they left the stage with a standing ovation.

2. topic sentence: When I was young, the attic in my grandmother's old house was my fantasy land.

(Arrange the details from outside to deeper and deeper inside the attic.)

details: _____ I could reach the attic by climbing a set of narrow, creaking stairs.

_____ Once I had entered the attic, I could see an old mirror covered in cobwebs.

_____ At the top of the stairs was a door.

_____ The door opened to the attic itself, a wide area with a sloping roof.

_____ Beyond the mirror were countless boxes full of treasures such as old toys, tools, and clothes.

Collaborate

Exercise 11 **Collaborate: Creating Details Using a Logical Order**

The following list includes a topic sentence and indicates a required order. With a partner or group, write five sentences of details in the required order.

topic sentence: Jenna dressed appropriately for her job interview.
(Describe the person from head to foot.)

a. _____

b. _____

c. _____

d. _____

e. _____

④ Write a descriptive paragraph that uses transition, support, and details effectively.

DRAFTING AND REVISING **DESCRIPTION**

After you have an outline, the next step is creating a first draft of the paragraph. Once you have the initial draft, review it by using the following checklist:

Checklist for Revising a Descriptive Paragraph

✓ Are there enough details?

✓ Are the details specific?

✓ Do the details include sense words?

✓ Are the details in order?

✓ Is the description easy to follow?

✓ Have I made my point?

If you look at the outline about a city park on page 319, you'll notice that it has some problems:

- The details are not very specific. Words like *nice* do not say much, and *nice* is used twice, in the topic sentence and in the details.

- Some parts of the outline need more support. The description of the inside of the park needs more details.

- The description would also be easier to follow if it had some effective transitions.

These weak areas can be improved in the drafting and revising stage of the writing process.

Transitional Words and Phrases

As you revise your descriptive paragraph, you may notice places in the paragraph that seem choppy or abrupt. That is, one sentence may end and another may start, but the two sentences don't seem to be connected. Reading your paragraph aloud, you may sense that it is not very smooth. Effective transitions can help to make smooth connections between your ideas. Here are some transitions you may want to use in writing a description:

INFO BOX **Transitions for a Descriptive Paragraph**

To show ideas brought together

and	also	in addition	next

To show a contrast

although	however	on the contrary	unlike
but	in contrast	on the other hand	yet

To show a similarity

all	each	like	similarly
both			

To show a time sequence

after	first	next	then
always	second (etc.)	often	when
before	meanwhile	soon	while

To show a position in space

above	beside	in front of	over
ahead of	between	inside	there
alongside	beyond	near	toward
among	by	nearby	under
around	close	next to	underneath
away	down	on	up
below	far	on top of	where
beneath	here	outside	

Note: There are many other transitions you can use, depending on what you need to link your ideas.

The following is a revised draft of the paragraph on "A City Park." You can assume that the writer worked through *several* drafts to get to this point. If you compare it to the outline on page page 319, you will notice additional details, transitions, and better wording. Note that the writer added a final sentence of detail to end the paragraph logically.

Revised Draft of a Paragraph on A City Park

(Changes from the outline are outlined; editing and proofreading are still necessary.)

specific detail	A small city park is a <u>pleasant</u> place for me because it is not like the rest of the city. The park is near the
added specific details	store where I work. It is only a ten-minute walk. <u>It is just the size of an empty lot, yet it is an attractive green space.</u> <u>Under</u> the trees are <u>weathered wooden</u>
transition, added detail, transition, sense details	benches <u>where people of every age sit and enjoy the calm.</u> The only sound is the <u>splash</u> of the fountain
added detail	at the center of the park. <u>I enjoy the park</u> and visit it at lunchtime. It is not like the rest of the city, which
sense words and specific details	is dirty, gray, and <u>filled with the noise of screeching brakes, rumbling trucks, and blaring horns. The park</u>
final sentence, transition, and sense words	<u>is a quiet, clean spot where the sun filters through the leaves of trees.</u>

Although it is important to work on specific details and sense words in each stage of your writing, it is easiest to focus on revising for details in the drafting stage when you have a framework for what you want to say. With that framework, you can concentrate on the most vivid way to express your ideas.

MyWritingLab™   **Exercise 12** **Practice: Adding the Appropriate Transitions**

In the following paragraph, transitions are shown in parentheses. Circle the appropriate transitions.

Mrs. Gallagher served me and her son an unforgettable breakfast. (First / Before) she gave each of us a huge glass of fresh-squeezed orange juice. (After / While) we were enjoying the juice, she was whisking a huge bowl of raw eggs, milk, and spices into a frothy mix for scrambled eggs. (Soon / Often,) the egg mixture was slowly cooking in a buttered pan. As it cooked, Mrs. Gallagher focused on popping some homemade cinnamon buns into the oven. (Always / When) the scrambled eggs began to gel, Mrs. Gallagher stirred them softly with a wooden spoon. (Then / Second) the scent of cinnamon filled the room. With perfect timing, Mrs. Gallagher pulled the buns from the oven and spooned the scrambled eggs onto our plates. The eggs were the creamiest I had ever tasted. (Until / In addition,) the cinnamon buns were the softest, sweetest, and most cinnamon-infused of my life. (After / Before) my first taste of Mrs. Gallagher's breakfast, I had no idea how good breakfast could be.

Exercise 13 **Practice: Using Specific Details or Sense Words**   MyWritingLab™

In the following paragraph, replace each underlined word or phrase with more specific details or sense words. Write your changes in the space above the underlined items.

I had a difficult time finding a shirt to wear. I wanted to look <u>nice</u> at my cousin's graduation party, but I couldn't find a shirt that would look right on me. I looked at <u>lots of</u> shirts in <u>a bunch of</u> stores, but most of the shirts were either <u>funny-looking</u> or <u>wrong</u>. One came in <u>a weird color</u>, another had a <u>stupid</u> stripe, and another <u>wouldn't fit me right</u>. I became <u>fed up with</u> looking at <u>stuff</u> that I would never want to wear. Just as I was leaving the mall, I saw one <u>nice</u> shirt on a sale rack. I grabbed the shirt, paid for it, and left the mall, feeling <u>good</u>.

EDITING AND PROOFREADING   DESCRIPTION

Additional Focus on Supporting Details and Word Choice

Before you prepare the final version of your paragraph, **edit** your latest draft, focusing on your supporting details and word choice. Then you can **proofread** a clean copy to correct any careless errors in spelling, punctuation, format, or typing.

Following is the final version of the paragraph on "A City Park." As you review it, you'll notice several changes from the revised draft on the previous page.

- The name of the park has been added to make the details more specific.
- Some sentences have been combined.
- A sensory detail, "ringed with maple trees," has been added.
- There were too many repetitions of "it" in the paragraph, so "it" has frequently been changed to "the park," "Sheridan Park," and so forth.
- An introductory sentence has been added to make the beginning of the paragraph smoother.

Final Version of a Paragraph on A City Park

(Changes from the revised draft are underlined.)

<u>Everyone has a place where he or she can relax.</u> A small city park is a pleasant place for me because it is not like the rest of the city. <u>Sheridan Park is near the store where I work; in fact, it is only a</u> ten-minute walk. <u>The park</u> is just the size of an empty lot, yet it is an attractive green space <u>ringed with maple trees</u>. Under the trees are weathered wooden benches where people of every age sit and enjoy the calm. The only sound is the splash of the fountain at the center of the park. I enjoy the park and visit it at lunchtime. <u>This special place</u> is not like the rest of the city, which is dirty, gray, and filled with the noise of screeching brakes, rumbling trucks, and blaring horns. The park is a clean, quiet spot where the sun filters through the leaves of trees.

Connect

Exercise 14 **Connect: Correcting Errors in the Final Draft of a Descriptive Paragraph**

Proofread the following paragraph. Correct any errors in spelling, punctuation, or word choice. There are eleven errors in the paragraph. Write your corrections in the space above the errors.

My first steady boyfriend had a decrepit car, and I am surprised that it didnot fall into pieces as we drove around town. The car was so old that I never really knew the make, or model of the automobile. We called it the Green Beast, for it had a faded hint of mint green paint on its battered body. On the passenger's side of the front seat, parts of the floor had rusted thru two the pavement. As a result, I had to be carful where I put my feet when my boyfriend drove me to class the mall, and the movies. The car radio could find only two stations within a three-mile area, so we usually gave up on music. The back seat area of the car had lost it's cushions long ago but the empty space was good for storage. The catch on the car's trunk was holded together by rope. With all it's faults, the car gave us a chance to explore and to escape the restrictions of depending on some one else for transportation. It made us feel grown up and free.

Lines of Detail: A Walk-Through Assignment

For this assignment, write a paragraph about your classroom, the one in which you take this class.

Step 1: To begin, freewrite about your classroom for ten minutes. In your freewriting, focus on how you would *describe* your classroom.

Step 2: Next, read your freewriting to a partner or a group. Ask your listener(s) to write down any ideas in your freewriting that could lead to a specific topic for your paragraph. (For example, maybe your freewriting has several ideas about how you feel when you are in the classroom, how others behave, or how the furniture and decor of the room create a mood.)

Step 3: With a specific topic in mind, list all the ideas in your freewriting that might fit that main topic.

Step 4: Now, brainstorm. Write at least ten questions and answers based on your list of ideas.

Step 5: Group all the ideas you've found in freewriting and brainstorming. Survey them and write a topic sentence for your paragraph. Your topic sentence may focus on the atmosphere of the classroom, the look of the classroom, how you feel in the classroom, the activity in the classroom, and so forth.

Step 6: Write an outline. Be sure that your outline has enough supporting points for you to write a paragraph of seven to twelve sentences.

Step 7: Write your draft and revise it extensively. Check each draft for sufficient support for your topic sentence and use specific sensory details.

Step 8: Share your best draft with a partner or the group. Ask for suggestions or comments. Revise once more.

Step 9: Edit your latest draft to refine word choice, combine sentences, and incorporate additional details if necessary.

Step 10: Prepare a clean copy and proofread it carefully to spot and correct any careless errors in spelling, punctuation, format, and typing.

Topics for Writing Your Own Descriptive Paragraph

When you write on any of the following topics, be sure to follow the stages of the writing process in preparing your paragraph.

1. Write about your most comfortable piece of clothing. In your topic sentence, focus on what makes it so comfortable.   MyWritingLab™

2. Interview a partner so that you and your partner can   MyWritingLab™
   gather details and write separate paragraphs with the title
   "My Dream Job."
      First, prepare a list of at least six questions to ask your partner. Write down your partner's answers and use these answers to ask more questions. For example, if your partner says she wants to work in a large office building, ask her where the office building is. If your partner says he would like to work overseas, ask which country.
      When you have finished the interview, switch roles. Let your partner interview you.
      Finally, give your partner his or her interview responses; take your own responses and use them as the basis for gathering as many details as you can. In this way, you are working through the prewriting stage of your paragraph. Then go on to the other stages. Be prepared to read your completed paragraph to your partner.

3. Write a paragraph that describes one of the following: MyWritingLab™
      the place where you work
      the contents of your backpack
      people in the express lane at the supermarket
      an advisor in the advising center
      the contents of the glove box of your car
      your college library or information commons
      Be sure to focus your paragraph with a good topic sentence.

4. Write a paragraph about the messiest classroom, office, or closet   MyWritingLab™
   you've ever seen.

5. Imagine a place that would bring you a sense of peace. In a para-   MyWritingLab™
   graph, describe that place.

6. Following are some topic sentences. Complete one of them and use it to write a paragraph.

The happiest place I know is _____.

_____ is the most comfortable place in my home.

Whenever I visit _____, I feel a sense of _____.

7. Write about the sensations of riding in a crowded elevator. You might begin by brainstorming all the details you recall.

Topics for Critical Thinking and Writing

1. Visit your school's home page and describe its appearance. Consider what you feel is attractive about the page, whether the descriptions of your schools are accurate, and whether the page would attract a potential student. Pay close attention to such details as the use of color, size and style of print, and use of space as you make your judgments.

2. Write a paragraph about the photograph below. Describe the scene; be sure to include a description of the track, the runner's expression, the use of colors, and what you imagine to be the reaction of the crowd.

Writing an Illustration Paragraph

CHAPTER 26

Jumping In

*Have you ever volunteered to help out in your community? Often, people who volunteer their time, resources, or companionship find that everyone benefits. People who are hungry are fed, sick people and their families are comforted, and homeless animals are adopted. In addition, volunteers derive a feeling of satisfaction from helping out. When you write about how everyone wins when people volunteer in the community, you are developing a topic by **illustration**.*

Learning Objectives

In this chapter, you will learn to:

1. Identify the characteristics of an illustration paragraph.
2. Prewrite to focus your topic and details.
3. Write a clear topic sentence.
4. Write an illustration paragraph that uses transitions, support, and details effectively.

WHAT IS ILLUSTRATION?

Illustration uses specific examples to support a general point. In your writing, you often use illustration because you frequently want to explain a point with a specific example.

① Identify the characteristics of an illustration paragraph.

HINTS FOR WRITING AN ILLUSTRATION PARAGRAPH

Knowing What Is Specific and What Is General

A **general statement** is a broad point. The following statements are general:

College students are constantly short of money.
Nursing is a flexible career.
Pictures can brighten up a room.

You can support a general statement with **specific examples**:

general statement: College students are constantly short of money.
specific examples: They need gas money, or bus or subway fare.
They need cash for snacks, lunch, or dinner.

general statement: Nursing is a flexible career.
specific examples: You can work in a hospital.
You can also work in a physician's office.

general statement: Pictures can brighten up a room.
specific examples: I love to look at my grandmother's family photos, which cover a whole living room wall.
My dentist has framed cartoons on the walls of his waiting room.

When you write an illustration paragraph, be careful to support a general statement with specific examples, not with more general statements:

not this: general statement: Essay tests are difficult.
more general statements: ~~I find essay tests to be hard.~~
~~Essay tests present the most challenges.~~

but this: general statement: Essay tests are difficult.
specific examples: They test organizational skills.
They demand a true understanding of the subject.

If you remember to illustrate a broad statement with specific examples, you will have the key to this kind of paragraph.

MyWritingLab™   **Exercise 1**   Practice: Recognizing Broad Statements

Each list below contains one broad statement and three specific examples. Underline the broad statement.

1. A quilt is filled with warm material but feels light.

   On a cold night, nothing is more comfortable than a quilt.

   A quilt will conform to any person's size and shape.

   A blanket can be itchy, but a quilt is always smooth.

2. Toddlers like to explore, not to sit in one place.

   Small children have short attention spans.

   Kindergartners don't like to play any game for an hour.

   Five-year-olds can't listen to music for long unless they can sing or dance.

3. Studying for a test involves time and patience.

   I always review my class notes when I prepare for a test.

   Studying for a test isn't easy.

   Rereading sections of the textbook helps me when I prepare for a test.

Exercise 2 **Practice: Distinguishing the General Statement from the Specific Example**   MyWritingLab™

Each general statement below is supported by three items of support. Two of these items are specific examples; one is too general to be effective. Underline the one that is too general.

1. **general statement:** Most television reality programs focus on contests.

   support: Contestants often compete to be the best model.

   Competition is at the heart of most television reality shows.

   Some contestants fight to become the most outstanding chef.

2. **general statement:** Staying up all night to study doesn't work very well.

   support: People who try to cram too much material into one evening can panic and lose their ability to concentrate.

   It is not a good idea to rely on one desperate study session.

   The all-night study technique substitutes a few desperate hours for a calm, regular regimen of reading and reviewing.

3. **general statement:** Listening to people talk on their smartphones can be irritating.

   support: Standing in line at the supermarket and listening to someone else's conversation is annoying.

   Smartphones ringing during the movies is one of the most annoying things.

   Smartphones buzzing everywhere is annoying.

Exercise 3 **Collaborate: Adding Specific Examples to a General Statement**   Collaborate

With a partner or group, add four specific examples to each general statement below.

1. **general statement:** People can fall asleep almost anywhere.

   examples: _____

   _____

   _____

   _____

2. **general statement:** Babies are used in many television commercials.

   examples: _____

   _____

   _____

   _____

   _____

3. **general statement:** In any home, we use water for more than just drinking.

examples: _____

_____

_____

_____

② Prewrite to focus your topic and details.

WRITING THE ILLUSTRATION PARAGRAPH IN STEPS

PREWRITING   ILLUSTRATION

Suppose your instructor asks you to write a paragraph about some aspect of cars. You can begin by listing ideas about your subject to find a focus for your paragraph. Your first list might look like the following:

Listing Ideas About Cars

cars in my neighborhood
my brother's car
car prices
drag racing
cars in the college parking lot
parking at college
car insurance

This list includes many specific ideas about cars. You could write a paragraph about one item or about two related items on the list. Reviewing the list, you decide to write your paragraph on cars in the college parking lot.

Adding Details to an Idea

Now that you have a narrowed topic for your paragraph, you decide to write a list of ideas about cars in the college parking lot:

Cars in the College Parking Lot: Some Ideas

vans
cars with strollers and baby seats
beat-up old cars, some with no bumpers
a few new sports cars, gifts from rich parents
some SUVs
older people's cars, Volvos and Fiats
racing cars, modified, brightly striped
elaborate sound systems
bumper stickers
some stickers have a message
some brag

③ Write a clear topic sentence.

Creating a Topic Sentence

If you examine this list and look for **related ideas**, you can create a topic sentence. The ideas on the list include (1) details about the kinds of cars, (2) details about what is inside the cars, and (3) details about the bumper stickers. Not all the details fit into these categories, but many do.

Grouping the related ideas into the three categories can help you focus your ideas and create a **topic sentence**.

Kinds of Cars

beat-up old cars, some with no bumpers
vans
a few new sports cars, gifts from rich parents
some SUVs
older people's cars, Volvos and Fiats
racing cars, modified, brightly striped

Inside the Cars

elaborate sound systems
strollers and baby seats

Bumper Stickers

some stickers have a message
some brag

You can summarize these related ideas in a topic sentence:

Cars in the college parking lot reflect the diversity of people at the school.

Check the sentence against your details. Does it cover the topic? Yes. The topic sentence begins with "Cars in the college parking lot." Does it make some point about the cars? Yes. It says the cars "reflect the diversity of people at the school."

Because your details are about old and new cars, what is inside the cars, and what is written on the bumper stickers, you have many details about differences in cars and some hints about the people who drive them.

Exercise 4 **Practice: Finding Specific Ideas in Lists**   MyWritingLab™

Following are two lists. Each is a response to a broad topic. Read each list, and then underline any phrases that could become a more specific topic for a paragraph.

topic: crime

criminals in our state
prison guards in danger
a local rape crisis center
bullies at Lincoln High School
the death penalty in the
   United States

probation and parole
safety precautions at student
   apartments
drug dealing
an effective burglar alarm
an inefficient court system

topic: health

getting a flu shot
health insurance
nursing around the world
staying healthy
mental illness

home remedies for a cold
heart attacks
healthy snacks for children
a silly high school health class
medical school

Exercise 5 **Practice: Grouping Related Ideas in Lists of Details**   MyWritingLab™

Following are lists of details. In each list, circle the items that seem to fit into one group; then underline the items that seem to fit into a second group. Some items may not fit into either group.

1. **topic:** appropriate times to be good to yourself

you've achieved a difficult goal
a loved one has died

you have an unexpected
holiday at work or school

financial losses are hurting	a distant cousin calls for a long talk
happy memories of an old friend	
satisfying an urge to overeat	giving small gifts to yourself
shopping sprees	depression hits you

2. **topic:** marrying young: pros and cons

sharing new adventures	wedding anniversaries
increased responsibilities	coping with another person's needs
constant source of support	
role of friends	new demands on each other's time
emotional closeness	
freedom from parental control	financial stresses

3. **topic:** losing weight through exercise and diet

mail-order devices for losing weight	eating fresh fruits and vegetables
replace soft drinks with water	
going to a gym	realistic goals
avoid desserts, unhealthy snacks	a regular bike ride
a walk every day	weight-loss contests on television
the struggle to lose weight	

MyWritingLab™   Exercise 6   **Practice: Writing Topic Sentences for Lists of Details**

Following are lists of details that have no topic sentences. Write an appropriate topic sentence for each one.

1. **topic sentence:** _____

_____

details: There are thirty people in our English class.

There are only thirty desks in our classroom.

We often sit in a circle.

Everyone helps one another.

Study groups meet after class and on the weekends.

Peer reviewing is common in our English class.

2. **topic sentence:** _____

_____

details: At the age of four, my brother used his plastic blocks to build little forts.

By six, he could tell long, exciting stories about the friendly monsters in his room.

In fourth grade, he wrote a long story about space travel.

That year, he drew intricate maps of a planet he created.

At ten, he won a school contest for the best-designed robot.

3. topic sentence: _____

_____

    details: A young family owns the Pine Tree Café.

The panels behind the counter are covered with children's art.

Sometimes the owners' children, ages six and eight, help their parents.

The children get to push the buttons on the cash register.

The children hand bags of takeout food to the customers.

Families with small children like to come to the café for weekend breakfasts.

The restaurant gives a free cookie to each child.

`PLANNING` **ILLUSTRATION**

When you plan your outline, keep your topic sentence in mind:

Cars in the college parking lot reflect the diversity of people at the school.

Remember the three categories of related details:

Kinds of Cars
Inside the Cars
Bumper Stickers

These three categories can give you an idea for how to organize the outline.
Below is an outline for a paragraph about cars in the college parking lot. As you read the outline, you will notice that details about the insides of the cars and about bumper stickers and license plates have been added. Adding details can be part of the outlining stage.

Outline on Cars in the College Parking Lot

topic sentence	Cars in the college parking lot reflect the diversity of people at the school.
details	There are beat-up old cars.
	Some have no bumpers.
	There are vans.
	There are a few new sports cars.
kinds of cars	Maybe these are gifts from rich parents.
	There are some SUVs.
	Older people's cars, like Volvos and Fiats, are there.
	There are a few racing cars, modified and brightly striped.
	Some cars have elaborate sound systems.
inside the cars	Some have a baby stroller or baby seat.
	Some have empty paper cups and food wrappers.
	Some have stickers for a club.
bumper stickers	There are stickers with a message.
	There are stickers that brag.

As you can see, the outline uses the details from the list and includes other details. You can add more details, combine some details to eliminate repetition, or even eliminate some details as you draft your paragraph.

Collaborate

Exercise 7 **Collaborate: Adding Details to an Outline**

Below are three partial outlines. Each has a topic sentence and some details. Working with a partner or group, add more details that support the topic sentence.

1. **topic sentence:** Many people suffer from allergies to certain plants, animals, or food.

   details:
   a. Some people sneeze when ragweed blooms.

   b. Pollen from flowers or trees provoke other people's allergic reactions.

   c. Cats can cause allergies in people who react to cat hair or dander.

   d. _____

   _____

   e. _____

   _____

   f. _____

   _____

   g. _____

   _____

2. **topic sentence:** For a number of reasons, parents may give their child an unusual first name.

   details:
   a. Some parents choose an old family name.

   b. Some parents pick the name of a celebrity.

   c. Other parents name their child after a wealthy relative.

   d. _____

   _____

   e. _____

   _____

   f. _____

   _____

   g. _____

   _____

3. **topic sentence:** Many college students have similar hopes.

   details:
   a. They hope to finish their college courses according to their timeline.

   b. They hope for good grades.

   c. They hope they will find a good job after college.

   d. _____

      _____

   e. _____

      _____

   f. _____

      _____

   g. _____

      _____

Exercise 8   **Practice: Eliminating Details That Are Repetitive**   MyWritingLab™

In the following outlines, some details use different words to repeat an example given earlier on the list. Cross out the repetitive details.

1. topic sentence: Many hungry students on a budget rely on a few inexpensive foods.

   details: Toaster pastries are popular at any time of day.

                     Microwave popcorn can fill an empty stomach.

                     Cereal makes up a large part of many students' diet.

                     Frozen pizzas fill many students' freezers.

                     Frozen dinners, such as chicken pot pies and beef with rice, satisfy student appetites.

                     If a product such as popcorn can be microwaved, it is attractive.

                     Students also buy ramen noodles.

                     Some students resort to the sugary cereals they enjoyed as children.

                     No student can resist potato chips.

                     Dinners that can be reheated are often stacked in students' freezers.

2. topic sentence: Mrs. Galliano saved my college career.

   details: I met with Mrs. Galliano when I needed to choose the classes for my third semester of college.

                     She was cheerful, welcoming, and patient.

                     She quickly surveyed my transcript, and then we talked.

                     I knew I had some bad grades and dropped classes on my records.

                     I expected a lecture.

                     Mrs. Galliano did not lecture me.

Instead of making me feel ashamed, she asked about my plans.

I told her that I wanted to be a nurse.

I also told her about my problems in math classes.

We talked about my options.

Mrs. Galliano was patient with me.

She and I designed a class schedule that included one attractive class and one challenging one.

We focused on my options.

I waited for her to lecture me about my responsibilities, but she never did.

I left with a sense that I would have to work hard but had someone in my corner.

④ Write an illustration paragraph that uses transitions, support, and details effectively.

DRAFTING AND REVISING **ILLUSTRATION**

Review the outline on page 333 about cars in the college parking lot. Assume you can create a first draft of a paragraph from this outline. As you consider what revisions to make in your draft, you may decide that some points can be combined and more details should be added. You can revise your draft by using the following checklist:

Checklist for Revising an Illustration Paragraph

✓ Do all of your major points and supporting details relate to your topic sentence?

✓ Are the details specific?

✓ Are the sentences arranged in a logical order?

✓ Is the paragraph unified?

Using Effective Transition

As you work through revisions, which may involve *several* drafts, you will be focusing primarily on improving the organization and content of your paragraph. However, you may notice places where one idea ends and another begins abruptly. If so, you will need to use effective **transition**, the words, phrases, or sentences that link ideas smoothly. Following are some transitions you may want to use in writing an illustration paragraph:

INFO BOX **Transitions for an Illustration Paragraph**

a second example	in addition	other examples
another example	in the case of	other kinds
another instance	like	such as
for example	one example	the first instance
for instance	one instance	to illustrate

Look carefully at the following revised draft of the paragraph about cars in the college parking lot, and compare it to the outline on page 333. You can assume the writer worked through *several* drafts to get to this point. Notice that this version contains additional details and uses transitions to move logically from one example to the next. (Also, keep in mind that when it is time to edit your paragraph, you may find additional ways to use transition and refine your work.)

Revised Draft of a Paragraph on Cars in the College Parking Lot

(Changes from the outline are underlined; editing and proofreading are still necessary.)

details added	Cars in the college parking lot reflect the diversity of people at the school. There are beat-up old cars. Some cars have no bumpers. There are also several vans. There are one or two sports cars like BMWs; they might belong to the few lucky stu-
transition added	dents with rich and generous parents. <u>Other kinds</u>
transition added	include SUVs and older people's cars <u>such as</u> Volvos
transition added	and Fiats. <u>In addition</u>, the parking lot holds a few racing cars, modified and brightly striped. Some cars have elaborate sound systems for <u>music lovers</u>.
details added	<u>Others must belong to parents</u> because they have a baby stroller or baby seat inside. Many are filled
detail added, transition, detail added	with empty paper cups or food wrappers <u>since busy students have to eat on the run.</u> Many cars <u>also</u> have <u>bumper</u> stickers; some are for clubs, like
detail, transition added	<u>Morristown Athletic Club</u>, <u>while</u> others have a mes- sage <u>such as "Give Blood, Save Lives" or "Animals: It's Their World, Too."</u> Some stickers brag that <u>the driver</u>
details added	<u>is the "Proud Parent of an Honor Roll Student at Grove Elementary" or is "Single—and Loving It."</u>

Exercise 9   Practice: Revising a Draft by Adding Transitions

MyWritingLab™

The paragraph below needs some transitions. Add appropriate transitions (words or phrases) to the blanks.

I have a hard time understanding my boyfriend. Sometimes Charles emphasizes his need for freedom and takes off with his friends. Then he suddenly becomes a family man. _____ he will return from a weekend with the boys and spend two days taking me and my daughter to a water park. _____ he will treat my daughter like a princess at the park, snapping endless photographs and buying her expensive souvenirs. _____ he will say he loves me and, ten minutes later, will talk about an old girlfriend. Money is related to _____ of mixed signals. Charles sometimes buys me expensive clothes. He has given me some valuable jewelry. However, he has also been known to ask me to split the bill for dinner at a drive-in burger place. Feeling close to Charles can also be difficult for me. _____ conversation, Charles will sometimes talk all night about his dreams for the future. Yet at other times, Charles does not want to talk at all. I am torn between hoping to know Charles better or giving up on his dual personality.

Collaborate

Exercise 10 **Collaborate: Adding Details to a Draft**

The following paragraph lacks the kind of details that would make it more interesting. Working with a partner or group, add details in the blank spaces provided. When you are finished, read the revised paragraph to the class.

Until a few weeks ago, I lived with my parents, but now I am learning the costs of living independently. I expected the basic costs of rent, food, and _____. However, I am suddenly responsible for kitchen items such as paper towels, _____, and _____. At home, my parents paid for basic bathroom products, including _____ and _____, but now I have to spend money on these and other items like deodorant and _____. Even doing my laundry means I have to pay for using the washer, dryer, and for _____ and _____. I am tempted to make a quick trip to my parents' house for two more items: _____ and a doormat.

EDITING AND PROOFREADING ILLUSTRATION

When you **edit** the latest draft of your illustration paragraph, you may be making changes in word choice, sentence structure, or even transitions to refine your style. After you prepare a clean copy of your paragraph, be sure to **proofread** it carefully to spot and correct any careless errors in spelling, punctuation, format, and typing. As you read the following final version and compare it with the revised draft on the previous page, you will notice these effective changes:

- Some details have been added.
- Some sentences have been combined.
- Several long transitions have been added. The paragraph needed to signal the shift in subject from the kinds of cars to what was inside the cars; then it needed to signal the shift from the interior of the cars to bumper stickers.
- A concluding sentence has been added to reinforce the point of the topic sentence: A diverse college population is reflected in its cars.

Final Version of a Paragraph on Cars in the College Parking Lot

(Changes from the draft are underlined.)

Cars in the college parking lot reflect the diversity of people at the school. <u>There are beat-up old cars, some with no bumpers, near several vans. There are one or two new sports cars like BMWs; they might belong to the few lucky students with rich and generous parents.</u> Other kinds include SUVs and older people's cars such as Volvos and Fiats. In addition, the parking lot holds a few racing cars, modified and brightly striped. <u>What is inside the cars is as revealing as the cars themselves.</u> Some cars have elaborate sound systems for music lovers <u>who can't drive without pounding sound.</u> Others must belong to parents because they have a baby stroller or baby seat inside. Many are filled with empty paper cups or food wrappers since busy students have to eat on the run. <u>Bumper stickers also tell a story.</u> Many cars have stickers; some are for clubs, like Morristown Athletic Club, while others have a message, such as "Give Blood: Save Lives" or "Animals: It's Their World, Too." Some stickers brag that the driver is the "Proud Parent of an Honor Student at Grove Elementary School" or is "Single—and Loving It." <u>A walk through the parking lot hints that this college is a place for all ages, backgrounds, and interests.</u>

Exercise 11 **Practice: Editing a Draft by Combining Sentences**   MyWritingLab™

The paragraph below has many short, choppy sentences which are underlined. Wherever you see two or more underlined sentences clustered next to each other, combine them into one clear, smooth sentence. Write your edited version of the paragraph in the spaces above the lines.

In the summer, I want to enjoy every minute of sunshine. I live in an area

with a cold climate. <u>Winter starts early. Also, winter lasts a long time</u>. Although

we do have spring ahead of us, spring is generally cold. <u>People cannot put away</u>

<u>their coats during the spring. Jackets are also necessary</u>. As a result of all this

bad weather, I celebrate summer. When I am at my job, I spend every minute of

each break sitting in the sun. <u>At college, I study between classes. I find a sunny</u>

<u>bench. Sitting on the grass is also a possibility</u>. Instead of spending my time off

at a mall or at the movies, I choose outdoor activities. <u>I run in my neighborhood.</u>

<u>Barbecuing on my tiny balcony before sunset also offers the benefit of sunshine</u>.

I am not obsessed with sunbathing or looking good in summer clothes. I crave sun

for other reasons. Sunny days are actually brighter days. <u>Sunny days improve my</u>

<u>mood. People look better in sunlight. Even buildings and trees are more attractive</u>

<u>when the sky is clear and the air warm</u>. In sunshine, I like my life better.

MyWritingLab™ [Exercise 12] **Practice: Proofreading the Final Draft of an Illustration Paragraph**

Following is an illustration paragraph with the kinds of errors it is easy to overlook when you prepare the final version of an assignment. Correct the errors by writing above the lines. There are ten errors.

Growing up is full of dangers, and younger childs should be keeped from exposure to frightening situations or stories. Halloween can be a thrilling time for small children, but it can easily bring to many grotesque images or threatening moments. During that holiday, for example, the youngest children should not be confronted by masked adults or older children jumping out from a dark space. Haunted house attractions are fun for teens or grown-ups, and small children may beg to visit these places. How ever, the fear and shock can haunt a second-grader for a long time Similarly, children of seven or 8 do not belong in the audience at horror movies designed to scare teenagers At home, children may here more than adults my think. As a result, a five-year-old sitting on the floor and playing with an electronic toy may be absorbing adult tales of ghosts and monsters. Adults may enjoy seeing a young boy's eyes widen as he hears about Frankenstein. However, the child is not likely to enjoy replaying that story when he is alone in bed that night. Worst of all, boys and girls of preschool or kindergarten age will remember an overherd conversation about a local robbery or assault. A child who listens to such a frightening tale can develop long-lasting irrational fears.

Lines of Detail: A Walk-Through Assignment

Your assignment is to write an illustration paragraph about change.

Step 1: List all your ideas on this broad topic for ten minutes. You can list ideas on any aspect of change, such as a change of attitude, changing schools, a new job, a change in a daily routine, and so forth.

Step 2: Review your list. Underline any parts that are specific ideas related to the broad topic: change.

Step 3: List all the specific ideas. Choose one as the narrowed topic for your paragraph.

Step 4: Add related ideas to your chosen, narrowed topic. Do this by reviewing your list for related ideas and by brainstorming for more related ideas.

Step 5: List all your related ideas and review their connection to your narrowed topic. Then write a topic sentence and an outline for your paragraph.

Step 6: Write your first draft and revise it extensively through several additional drafts.

Step 7: Edit your latest draft to refine word choice, combine sentences, and incorporate additional details if necessary.

Step 8: Prepare a clean copy and proofread it carefully to spot any careless errors in spelling, punctuation, format, and typing.

Topics for Writing Your Own Illustration Paragraph

When you write on any of these topics, be sure to work through the stages of the writing process in preparing your paragraph.

1. Select one of the topics listed. Narrow the topic and write a paragraph on it. If you choose the topic of money, for example, you might narrow it by writing about credit cards for college students or about paying bills.

   MyWritingLab™

basketball	exercise	sleep
driving	movies	children
songs	smartphones	worrying
books	style	social networks
money	celebrities	travel

2. Following are topic sentences. Select one and use it to write a paragraph.

   MyWritingLab™

   The best advice I've ever been given is _____.

   There are several parts of my college experience that I dislike.

   There are several parts of my college experience that I like.

   The most hurtful word in the English language is

   _____.

   The most overused word in the English language is

   _____.

   Three teams represent the best in _____ (baseball, football, basketball, hockey, soccer—choose one).

   Several people illustrate what it means to be a hero.

MyWritingLab™

3. Look carefully at the following photographs. Use them as a way to begin thinking about a paragraph with this topic sentence: The best kind of pet is a _____. Draw on your experience with any kind of pet (from a cat to an iguana) to write an illustration paragraph.

Topics for Critical Thinking and Writing

MyWritingLab™

1. Imagine that you are at a job interview, and your interviewer asks you to think of a motto that guides your life. For example, would you state, "Treat other people the way you would like to be treated," "Always do your best," or some other motto? Write a paragraph that illustrates why a particular motto best describes your work ethic or your core values.

MyWritingLab™

2. Assume that you are a member of a student advisory board at your college, and the administration has asked the board to identify potential safety hazards on campus. Make a list of potential dangers, and then identify what you believe to be the most severe hazard. For this assignment, illustrate why this safety hazard poses such a serious threat to the campus population.

Writing a Process Paragraph

CHAPTER 27

Jumping In

*Finding the right apartment takes planning and careful investigation. What should you do before, during, and after the process to ensure a successful move? How would you share what you've learned about finding a great apartment? Understanding the steps in a **process** helps us share our experiences with others who face similar challenges.*

Learning Objectives

In this chapter, you will learn to:

1 Identify the characteristics of a process paragraph.

2 Prewrite to focus your topic and details.

3 Write a clear topic sentence.

4 Write a process paragraph that uses transitions effectively.

WHAT IS PROCESS?

1 Identify the characteristics of a process paragraph.

Process writing explains how to do something or describes how something happens or is done. When you tell the reader how to do something (a **directional process**), you speak directly to the reader and give him or her clear, specific instructions about performing some activity. Your purpose is to explain an activity so that a reader can do it. For example, you may have to leave instructions telling a new employee how to close the cash register or use the copy machine.

When you describe how something happens or is done (an **informational process**), your purpose is to explain an activity without telling a

343

reader how to do it. For example, you can explain how a boxer trains for a fight or how the special effects for a movie were created. Instead of speaking directly to the reader, an informational process speaks about *I, he, she, we, they*, or about a person by his or her name. A directional process uses *you* in the way it gives directions, or the word *you* is understood.

A Process Involves Steps in Time Order

Whether a process is directional or informational, it describes something that is done in steps, and these steps are in a specific order: a **time order**. The process can involve steps that are followed in minutes, hours, days, weeks, months, or even years. For example, the steps in changing a tire may take minutes, whereas the steps taken to lose ten pounds may take months.

You should keep in mind that a process involves steps that *must follow a certain order*, not just a range of activities that can be placed in any order. This sentence *signals a process*:

> Planting a rose garden takes planning and care. (Planting a rose garden involves following steps in order; that is, you cannot put a rose bush in the ground until you dig a hole.)

This sentence *does not signal a process*:

> There are several ways to build your confidence. (Each way is separate; there is no time sequence here.)

Telling a person in a conversation how to do something or how something is done gives you the opportunity to add important points you may have overlooked or to include details you may have skipped at first. Your listener can ask questions if he or she does not understand you. Writing a process, however, is more difficult. Your reader is not there to stop you, to ask you to explain further, or to question you. In writing a process, you must be organized and very clear.

HINTS FOR WRITING A PROCESS PARAGRAPH

1. In choosing a topic, find an activity you know well. If you write about something familiar to you, you will have a clearer paragraph.

2. Choose a topic that includes steps that must be done in a specific time sequence.

> **not this:** I find lots of things to do with old photographs.

> **but this:** I have a plan for turning an old photograph into a special gift.

3. Choose a topic that is fairly small. A complicated process cannot be covered well in one paragraph. If your topic is too big, the paragraph can become vague, incomplete, or boring.

> **too big:** There are many steps in the process of an immigrant becoming an American citizen.

> **smaller and manageable:** Persistence and a positive attitude helped me through the stages of my job search.

4. Write a topic sentence that makes a point. Your topic sentence should do more than announce. Like the topic sentence for any paragraph, it should have a point. As you plan the steps of your process and gather details, ask yourself some questions: What point do I want to make about this process? Is the process hard? Is it easy? Does the process require certain tools? Does the process require certain skills, like organization, patience, or endurance?

>**an announcement:** This paragraph is about how to register for classes.

>**a topic sentence:** You do not have to be a computer expert to register for classes online, but you do have to follow a few simple steps.

5. Include all of the steps. If you are explaining a process, you are writing for someone who does not know the process as well as you do. Keep in mind that what seems clear or simple to you may not be clear or simple to the reader, and be sure to tell what is needed before the process starts. For instance, what ingredients are needed to cook the dish? Or what tools are needed to assemble the toy?

6. Put the steps in the right order. Nothing is more irritating to a reader than trying to follow directions that skip back and forth. Careful planning, drafting, and revision can help you get the time sequence right.

7. Be specific in the details and steps. To be sure you have sufficient details and clear steps, keep your reader in mind. Put yourself in the reader's place. Could you follow your own directions or understand your steps?

If you remember that a process explains, you will focus on being clear. Now that you know the purpose and strategies of writing a process, you can begin the prewriting stage of writing one.

Exercise 1   **Practice: Recognizing Good Topic Sentences for Process Paragraphs**

MyWritingLab™

If a sentence is a good topic sentence for a process paragraph, put *OK* on the line provided. If a sentence has a problem, label that sentence with one of these letters:

>**A**   This is an announcement; it makes no point.

>**B**   This sentence covers a topic that is too big for one paragraph.

>**S**   This sentence describes a topic that does not require steps.

1. _____ I've learned a better, shorter system for giving myself a manicure.

2. _____ The best way to study for a test is the subject of this paragraph.

3. _____ There are several places you can find used textbooks online.

4. _____ The steps required to set a person's broken leg are intricate.

5. _____ Finding a deal on a phone plan takes a little research.

6. _____ This paper shows a way to curl long, straight hair.

7. _____ The role of the governor in this state evolved in several stages.

8. _____ A few hints can help you make a good impression at a job interview.

Collaborate

Exercise 2   Collaborate: Including Necessary Materials in a Process

Below are three possible topics for a process paragraph. For each topic, work with a partner or a group and list the items (materials, ingredients, tools, utensils, supplies) the reader would have to gather before he or she began the process. When you've finished the exercise, check your lists with another group to see if you've missed any items.

1. topic: getting a campus parking permit

needed items: _____

_____

2. topic: doing your laundry

needed items: _____

_____

2 Prewrite to focus your topic and details.

WRITING THE PROCESS PARAGRAPH IN STEPS

PREWRITING   PROCESS

The easiest way to start writing a process paragraph is to pick a small topic, one that you can cover well in one paragraph. Then you can gather ideas by listing or freewriting or both.

If you decided to write about how to adopt a shelter dog, you might begin by freewriting. Then you might check your freewriting, looking for details that have to do with the process of adopting a shelter dog. You can underline those details, as in the example that follows.

Freewriting for a Process Paragraph

Topic: How to Adopt a Shelter Dog

What kind of dog do you want? It's difficult to walk through an animal shelter and see all those dogs begging for a home. Be realistic. A purebred or a mixed breed? A puppy? Can you afford it? There's a fee at the shelter. You have to be willing to take care of a dog for a long time.

Next, you can put what you've underlined into a list, in correct time sequence:

before you decide on any dog

Can you afford it?
You have to be willing to take care of a dog for a long time.

considering the right dog

What kind of a dog do you want?
A purebred or a mixed breed? A puppy?
Be realistic.

at the shelter

It's difficult to walk through a shelter.
A fee at the shelter.

Check the list. Are some details missing? Yes. A reader might ask, "How do you decide what kind of dog is best for you?" or "What's so expensive about getting a dog at a shelter?" or "How much does it cost to own a dog, anyway?" Answers to questions like these can give you the details needed to write a clear and interesting informational process.

Writing a Topic Sentence for a Process Paragraph

Freewriting and a list can now help you focus your paragraph by identifying the point of your process. You already know that the subject of your paragraph is how to adopt a shelter dog. But what's the point? Is it easy to adopt a shelter dog? Is it difficult? What does it take to find the right dog?

Looking at your list of steps and details, you notice that most of the steps come before you actually select a dog. Here is a possible topic sentence:

> You have to do your homework if you want to find the shelter dog that's right for you.

Once you have a topic sentence, you can think about adding details that explain your topic sentence, and you can begin the planning stage of writing.

3 Write a clear topic sentence.

| Exercise 3 | **Practice: Finding the Steps of a Process in Freewriting** |

MyWritingLab™

Read the following freewriting, then reread it, looking for all the words, phrases, or sentences that have to do with steps. Underline all those items. Then once you've underlined the freewriting, put what you've underlined into a list in a correct time sequence.

How to Make Brewed Coffee: Freewriting

I love coffee in the morning. Especially brewed. Instant tastes awful once you've had brewed coffee. Don't forget to fill the glass carafe with the right amount of water for the number of cups. Start it all with a clean carafe. Use a spoon or plastic scoop to put the coffee in the brew basket. After you put a clean paper filter in the brew basket, get ready to add coffee. Don't turn on the coffeemaker until all the other steps have been completed. If you forget the paper filter, you'll have a mess. Make sure you measure out the right amount of coffee. The tempting smell of coffee brewing. Pour the water from the carafe into the water-heating compartment. Coffee tastes funny if it comes from a dirty carafe. Decide how many cups of coffee you want to make.

Your List of Steps in Time Sequence

_____

_____

_____

_____

_____

_____

_____

_____

_____

_____

_____

PLANNING **PROCESS**

Using the freewriting and topic sentence on how to adopt a shelter dog, you could make an outline. Then you could revise it, checking the topic sentence and improving the list of details where you think they could be better. Here is a sample revised outline on adopting a shelter dog:

Outline for a Paragraph on How to Adopt a Shelter Dog

topic sentence
You have to do your homework if you want to find the shelter dog that's right for you.

details
Decide whether you can afford a dog.

before you decide on any dog
Dogs cost money for food, regular veterinary care, and grooming.
Decide if you are willing to take care of a dog for a long time.
Dogs can live ten to fifteen years.
They need exercise, attention, and training.
Think carefully about what kind of dog you want.
You have to decide whether you want a purebred or mixed breed.

considering the right dog
You can get both types at a shelter.
Puppies are adorable and fun.
They need more training and attention.
The size and temperament of the dog are important, too.
Do some research and talk to friends who own dogs.
It is difficult to walk through an animal shelter and see all the dogs begging for a home.

at the shelter
Remember the kind of dog you've decided to adopt.
Look around carefully.
Make your selection, pay the adoption fee, and look forward to giving your dog the best years of its life.

You probably noticed that the outline follows the same stages as the list but has many new details. Such details can be added as you create your own outline.

The following checklist may help you revise an outline for your process paragraph:

Checklist for Revising a Process Outline

✓ Is my topic sentence focused on some point about the process?

✓ Does it cover the entire process?

✓ Have I included all of the steps?

✓ Are they in the right order?

✓ Have I explained clearly?

✓ Do I need better details?

Exercise 4   **Practice: Revising the Topic Sentence in a Process Outline**   MyWritingLab™

The topic sentence below doesn't cover all the steps of the process. Read the outline several times; then write a topic sentence that covers all the steps of the process and has a point.

topic sentence: On a chilly autumn day, you can stay warm.

details: First, step outdoors and feel the temperature.

If the sun is shining and you are not shivering, you probably don't want to wear a heavy coat.

Instead, survey the contents of your closet.

Choose a t-shirt or other cotton shirt for the first layer of your clothing.

Finish this layer with a fairly heavy pair of jeans.

For the next layer, look for something warm such as a heavy pullover or sweatshirt.

Then cover it all with a jacket that is large enough to hold the layers in place.

As the day goes by and the temperature rises, you can shed the jacket.

Later in the day, you can remove the second layer of your clothing.

At each time of the day, the number of layers you wear will keep you as warm or as cool as you want to be.

In addition, you will not have to drag a heavy coat around when the weather becomes warm.

revised topic sentence: _____

_____

Exercise 5   **Practice: Revising the Order of Steps in a Process Outline**   MyWritingLab™

The steps in the following outline are out of order. Put numbers in the spaces provided, indicating what step should be first, second, and so forth.

topic sentence: From Monday through Friday, I follow the same morning schedule.

details: _____ Finally, I grab my coffee, lead my twins to the car, and I drive first to my boys' pre-school and second to my job.

_____ My alarm rings at 6:00 a.m. and I do not dare to linger in bed and fall back to sleep.

_____ In the kitchen, l give them juice, cereal, milk, and fruit while I make myself instant coffee.

_____ While they eat breakfast, they chatter and play.

_____ Soon I take them away from the remains of their breakfast.

_____ They resist getting dressed, but I finally manage to tug them into some wrinkled clothes.

_____ I force myself out of bed and stagger to my sons' room.

_____ Nagging my twin four-year-old sons, Zachary and Marshall, I manage to get them up.

_____ While they use the toilet and wash their sleepy faces, I dress.

MyWritingLab™   Exercise 6   **Practice: Listing All of the Steps in an Outline**

Following are two topic sentences for process paragraphs. Write all of the steps needed to complete an outline for each sentence. After you've listed all of the steps, number them in the correct time order.

    1. topic sentence: Anyone can cook spaghetti and tomato sauce.

        steps: _____

_____

_____

_____

_____

_____

_____

_____

_____

_____

_____

_____

_____

    2. topic sentence: When you have ten minutes between classes, you can find an easy way to make the most of your time.

        steps: _____

_____

_____

_____

_____

_____

_____

_____

_____

| DRAFTING AND REVISING | **PROCESS**

By arranging the points of the outline in paragraph form, you'll have a **first draft** of the process paragraph. As you write the initial draft, you can combine some of the short sentences from the outline. (Later, during the editing and proofreading stage, you can improve word choice, strengthen transition, evaluate punctuation choices, and check for careless errors.)

④ Write a process paragraph that uses transitions effectively.

Using the Same Grammatical Person

Remember that the _directional_ process speaks directly to the reader, calling him or her "you." Sentences in a directional process use the word _you_, or they imply _you_.

>**directional:** _You_ need a good skillet to get started.
>Begin by cleaning the surface. ("You" is implied.)

Remember that the _informational_ process involves somebody doing the process. Sentences in an informational process use words such as _I, we, he, she_, or _they_ or a person's name.

>**informational:** Dave needed a good skillet to get started.
>First, I can clean the surface.

One problem in writing a process is shifting from describing how somebody did something to telling the reader how to do an activity. When that shift happens, the two kinds of processes get mixed. That shift is called a **shift in person**. In grammar, the words _I_ and _we_ are considered to be in the first person, _you_ is in the second person, and _he, she, it_, and _they_ are in the third person.

    If these words refer to one, they are _singular_; if they refer to more than one, they are _plural_. The following list may help.

INFO BOX **A List of Persons**

First person singular:	I
Second person singular:	you
Third person singular:	he, she, it, or a person's name
First person plural:	we
Second person plural:	you
Third person plural:	they, or the names of more than one person

---

In writing your process paragraph, decide whether your process will be directional or informational, and stay with one kind.

    Following are two examples of a shift in person. Look at them closely and study how the shift is corrected.

shift in person: After *I* preheat the oven to 350 degrees, *I* mix the egg whites and sugar with an electric mixer set at high speed. *Mix* until stiff peaks form. Then *I* put the mixture in small mounds on an ungreased cookie sheet. ("Mix until stiff peaks form" is a shift to the "you" person.)

shift corrected: After *I* preheat the oven to 350 degrees, *I* mix the egg whites and sugar with an electric mixer set at high speed. *I* mix until stiff peaks form. Then *I* put the mixture in small mounds on an ungreased cookie sheet.

shift in person: A *salesperson* has to be very careful when a customer tries on clothes. The *clerk* can't hint that a suit may be a size too small. *You* can insult a customer with a hint like that. (The sentences shifted from "salesperson" and "clerk" to "you.")

shift corrected: A *salesperson* has to be very careful when a customer tries on clothes. The *clerk* can't hint that a suit may be a size too small. *He or she* can insult a customer with a hint like that.

Using Transitions Effectively

As you revise your draft, you can add **transitions**. Transitions are particularly important in a process paragraph because you are trying to show the steps in a *specific sequence*, and you are trying to show the *connections* between steps. Effective transitions will also keep your paragraph from sounding like a choppy, boring list.

Following is a list of some of the transitions you can use in writing a process paragraph. Be sure that you use transitional words and phrases only when logical to do so, and try not to overuse the same transitions in a paragraph.

INFO BOX **Transitions for a Process Paragraph**

after	during	later	then
afterward	eventually	meanwhile	to begin
as	finally	next	to start
as he/she is	first, second, etc.	now	until
as soon as	first of all	quickly	when
as you are	gradually	sometimes	whenever
at last	in the beginning	soon	while
at the same time	immediately	suddenly	while I am
before	initially	the first step	
begin by	last	the second step, etc.	

When you write a process paragraph, you must pay particular attention to clarity. As you revise, keep thinking about your audience to be sure your steps are easy to follow. The following checklist can help you revise your draft:

Checklist for Revising a Process Paragraph
✓   Does the topic sentence cover the whole paragraph?
✓   Does the topic sentence make a point about the process?
✓   Is any important step left out?
✓   Should any step be explained further?
✓   Are the steps in the right order?
✓   Have I avoided a shift in person throughout my explanation of the process?
✓   Have I used transitions effectively?

Exercise 7   **Practice: Correcting Shifts in Person in a Process Paragraph**   MyWritingLab™

Below is a paragraph that shifts from being an informational to a directional process in several places. Those places are underlined. Rewrite the underlined parts, directly above the underlining, so that the whole paragraph is an informational process.

Eddie has an efficient system for sorting and organizing his mail. As soon as he picks up his mail, he begins sorting it. Any junk mail, such as advertisements and offers for credit cards or phone plans, never reaches the kitchen table. <u>You</u> immediately <u>toss</u> it into the garbage. Then Eddie sits at the table and sorts the remaining mail. Eddie opens all the bills. He puts the ones that <u>you need</u> to pay right away in one stack; he places the ones he can pay later in another stack. Next, Eddie places each stack in its own compartment in a plastic tray. Finally, he looks at what mail is left: cards from friends, a reminder from the dentist about his next appointment, a bank statement. By sorting his mail every day, Eddie never has to face a mountain of old mail that can take <u>you</u> hours to sort.

Exercise 8   **Practice: Revising Transitions in a Process Paragraph**   MyWritingLab™

The transitions in this paragraph could be better. Rewrite the underlined transitions, directly above each one, so that the transitions are smoother.

Packing glassware for a move can be tricky, but a few steps can save you stress and broken glass. <u>First</u>, get a sturdy cardboard box that can be sealed across the top. <u>Second</u>, gather a stack of old newspapers or a pile of tissue paper. <u>Third</u>, place a roll of strong, wide packing tape and a pair of scissors near the box and the paper. <u>Fourth</u>, line the box with paper so that the glasses will be cushioned. <u>Fifth</u>, pick up one glass. Wrap it tightly in paper, making sure that the paper protects the inside, outside, and any stem or base on the glass. <u>Sixth</u>, place the first wrapped glass in the bottom of the box. <u>Seventh</u>, continue the packing process, using paper to separate each wrapped glass from the others. <u>Eighth</u>, close the box, cut large lengths of tape, and tape the top openings. <u>Ninth</u>, breathe deep, relax, and feel sure that your glasses will arrive intact at your destination.

Revised Draft of a Process Paragraph

Below is a revised draft of the process paragraph on adopting a shelter dog. This draft has more details than the outline on page 348, and you can assume that the writer worked through *several* drafts to get to this point. Notice that some details and transitions have been added but that editing will still be necessary to improve the paragraph's style:

Revised Draft of a Paragraph on How to Adopt a Shelter Dog

(Changes from the outline are underlined; editing and proofreading are still necessary.)

transition added —

details added —

transition added —

detail added —

transition added —

transition sentence added —

transition added —

transition added —

You have to do your homework if you want to find the shelter dog that's best for you. <u>Begin by</u> deciding whether you can afford a dog. <u>Most shelters spay and neuter their animals</u>, but dogs cost money for food, regular veterinary care, and grooming. Then decide if you are willing to take care of a dog for ten to fifteen years. That is the lifespan of a dog. Remember that dogs need <u>regular</u> exercise, attention, and training. <u>If you are ready to make the personal and financial commitment</u> of owning a pet, you can begin thinking carefully about the kind of dog you want. You have to decide whether you want a purebred or a mixed breed. You can get both types at a shelter. <u>At the same time, think about the age of the dog you want</u>. Puppies are adorable and fun. They need training and attention. The size and temperament of the dog are important, too. Do some research and talk to friends who own dogs. It is difficult to walk through an animal shelter and see all the dogs begging for a home. <u>When you make your adoption visit</u>, remember the kind of dog you decided to adopt. Look around carefully. <u>Finally</u>, make your selection, pay the adoption fee, and look forward to giving your dog the best years of its life.

EDITING AND PROOFREADING PROCESS

Before you prepare a final version of your process paragraph, **edit** your latest draft to improve transition, word choice, and sentence structure. Then **proofread** a clean copy to spot and correct any careless errors in spelling, punctuation, format, or typing.

Following is the final version of the process paragraph on adopting a shelter dog. You'll notice that it contains these changes from the revised draft:

- A sentence of introduction has been added; it begins the paragraph and creates a smoother opening.
- Two more transitions ("However" in line 2 and "Later" in line 14) have been added.
- Some sentences have been combined.
- "Look around" has been changed to "look" to emphasize that this is not a quick or casual glance but an examination.
- The second use of "carefully" has been changed to "thoroughly" to avoid repetition.

Final Version of Paragraph on How to Adopt a Shelter Dog

(Changes from the draft are underlined.)

Most people who love animals and have big hearts have thought about adopting a dog with no home, a shelter dog. However, you have to do your homework if you want to find the shelter dog that's best for you. Begin by deciding whether you can afford a dog. Most shelters spay and neuter their animals, but dogs cost money for food, regular veterinary care, and grooming. Then decide if you are willing to take care of a dog for the ten to fifteen years that is its likely lifespan. Remember that dogs need regular exercise, attention, and training. If you are ready to make the personal and financial commitment of owning a pet, you can begin thinking carefully about the kind of dog you want. You have to decide whether you want a purebred or a mixed breed, for you can get both types at a shelter. At the same time, think about the age of the dog you want. Puppies are adorable and fun, but they need more training and attention. The size and temperament of the dog are important, too. To make all these decisions, do some research and talk to friends who own dogs. Later, as you prepare to go to the shelter, be aware that it is difficult to walk through an animal shelter and see all the dogs begging for a home. When you make your adoption visit, remember the kind of dog you've decided to adopt and look thoroughly. Finally, make your selection, pay the adoption fee, and look forward to giving your dog the best years of its life.

Exercise 9   **Practice: Editing to Combine Sentences in a Process Paragraph**   MyWritingLab™

The paragraph below has many short, choppy sentences, which are underlined. Wherever you see two or more underlined sentences clustered next to each other, combine them into one clear, smooth sentence. Write your edited version of the paragraph in the spaces above the lines.

My uncle has come up with a smart way to avoid standing in line at popular

restaurants. His first step was to do a little research. He looked into which restau-

rants issue pagers to their waiting customers. Next, he drove around town and sur-

veyed those restaurants. He was looking for specific ones. He wanted ones near a

bookstore. He also wanted ones near a discount store. Once he was familiar with these restaurants, he began to put his plan into action. When he wants to eat at a restaurant, he always chooses one on his new list. <u>If there is a long wait at the restaurant, my uncle knows what to do. He takes the pager. He leaves for the nearby bookstore. Sometimes he leaves for the nearby discount store.</u> He browses in the bookstore or picks up a few items at the discount store. When his pager tells him his table is ready, he walks a few steps and has a good dinner.

MyWritingLab™   Exercise 10 **Practice: Proofreading the Final Draft of a Process Paragraph**

Following is a process paragraph with the kinds of errors it is easy to overlook in a final draft. Proofread carefully, and make necessary corrections above the line. There are ten errors.

Their is a right way to brush your teeth, and brushing correctly can save you many unpleasant moments in the dentists office. One of the first lessons I learned in the dental hygiene Program at my college is, that millions of people make mistakes during the simple process of brushing their teeth. You may be one of them. First of all, you need to brush with the proper toothbrush. Many people think a hard toothbrush is the best because it will be tough on tooth decay. However, a soft toothbrush is better at massaging your gums and covering the surface of your teeth. Second, don't waste your money on fancy new toothpastes. Most toothpastes contain the same cavity-fighting ingredients so a inexpensive one will do. Once you have put a small amount of toothpaste on your brush, you should brush gently. Don't scrub your teeth as if they were a dirty pot or pan. Softly massage them near the gum line. Last, brush for a long time. A long time don't mean hours, but it does mean two minutes. You may think that you all ready brush for two minutes, but you probably don't. The next time you brush, time yourself. Two minutes feels like a long time. However, if you spend thirty seconds one each part of your teeth (the upper teeth on the inner surface, the upper teeth on the outer surface, and so forth), you will be on your way to healthier teeth.

Lines of Detail: A Walk-Through Assignment

Your assignment is to write an informational process on how you found the perfect gift for your best friend or parent. Follow these steps:

Step 1: Decide whether to write about a gift for your friend or for your parent. Then think about a time when you found a gift that made that person very happy.

Step 2: Now freewrite. Write anything you can remember about the gift, how you decided what to give, how you found it and gave it.

Step 3: When you've completed the freewriting, read it. Underline all the details that refer to steps in finding the gift. List the underlined details in time order.

Step 4: Add to the list by brainstorming. Ask yourself questions that can lead to more details. For example, if an item on your list is, "I realized my mother likes colorful clothes," ask questions such as "What colors does she like?" "What is her favorite color?" or "What kind of clothes does she like to wear?"

Step 5: Survey your expanded list. Write a topic sentence that makes some point about your finding this gift. To reach a point, think of questions like, "What made the gift perfect?" or "What did I learn from planning, finding, and giving this gift?"

Step 6: Use the topic sentence to prepare an outline. Be sure that the steps in the outline are in the correct time order.

Step 7: Write a first draft of the paragraph; then revise it through several drafts to ensure that you have sufficient content, organization, and unity.

Step 8: Edit your latest revised draft to refine word choice, incorporate additional transition, and improve sentence structure.

Step 9: Prepare a clean copy, and proofread it carefully to catch and correct any careless errors in spelling, punctuation, format, or typing.

Topics for Writing Your Own Process Paragraph

When you write on one of these topics, be sure to work through the stages of the writing process in preparing your process paragraph. MyWritingLab™

1. Write a **directional or informational process** about one of these topics:

painting a chair

training for a marathon

setting up an advising appointment

choosing a roommate

avoiding morning traffic jams

handling a customer's complaint

setting up a social network identity

getting to school on time

asking a professor for help in a college course

fixing a leaky pipe

installing speakers in a car

buying airline tickets online

getting or giving a manicure

fighting a traffic ticket

getting ready for moving day

staying on an exercise program

2. Imagine that one of your relatives has never used a smartphone but wants to know how to text. Explain how to create and send a text by describing the steps you use in sending one through your smartphone.

3. Interview someone who always seems to be organized at school or at work. Ask that person to tell you how he or she manages to be so efficient. Narrow the question by asking how the person always manages to get all his work done at the store or how she always submits her assignments on time. Ask whether the person has developed a system and what steps are involved in that system. Take notes or tape the interview.

    After the interview, write a paragraph about that system, explaining how to be organized for a particular task at college or at work. Your paragraph will explain the process to someone who needs to be more organized.

4. The children in the photograph below are playing tug-of-war. Use the photograph to think about a childhood game you used to play that was popular with boys and girls. Write a paragraph explaining how to play that game.

Topics for Critical Thinking and Writing

1. Imagine that a friend is about to register for classes at your college, but he cannot visit the campus during regular business hours to register in person. This will be your friend's first term at the college. Write a paragraph giving your friend clear directions for registering online. For each step, explain what is involved and emphasize its importance to the overall process.

2. Interview one of the counselors at your college. Ask him or her to tell you the steps in applying for a scholarship. Take notes or record the interview, obtain copies of any forms that may be included in the application process, and be sure to ask questions about these forms if they appear confusing to you. After the interview, write a paragraph explaining the application process, and assume that your audience is a current student who has never applied for any scholarship or financial aid.

MyWritingLab™ Visit Chapter 27, "Writing a Process Paragraph," in *MyWritingLab* to test your understanding of the chapter objectives.

Moving from Paragraphs to Essays

CHAPTER 28

Jumping In

*A well-built house begins with proper framing and quality building blocks. Similarly, a well-constructed **essay** relies on logical organization as its frame and on effective paragraphs as its building blocks. Keep this analogy in mind as you move from the paragraph to the essay.*

Learning Objectives

In this chapter, you will learn to:

1. Identify the basic components of an essay.
2. Recognize the difference between a topic sentence and a thesis statement.
3. Prewrite to narrow your essay topic.
4. Write a multi-paragraph essay that sufficiently incorporates unity, support, and coherence.

WHAT IS AN ESSAY?

An essay's main point is called the **thesis** (also referred to as the **thesis statement** or **thesis sentence**). It is commonly found in the first paragraph, or **introductory paragraph**, of the essay. The main section of the essay, called the **body**, contains the topic sentences and paragraphs that support the thesis. In fact, each paragraph in the body of an essay is similar in format to the ones you've already written. All of the body paragraphs of an essay should support the thesis, just as all of the details in a paragraph should support the topic sentence.

1 Identify the basic components of an essay.

COMPARING THE SINGLE PARAGRAPH AND THE ESSAY

Read the paragraph and the essay that follow, both about sharing happy moments. You will notice many similarities.

A Single Paragraph

When I am happy, I want to share my happiness. When my wife gave birth to our son, for example, I couldn't wait to tell everyone. I started by calling my parents, my wife's parents, and every other relative I could think of. After I had run out of family members, I told friends, coworkers, and even a few total strangers. In another instance, I had to share the news about my dream of getting a college education. As soon as I opened the letter announcing my college loan, I wanted to spread the informa-tion. Just seeing the look on my wife's face increased my happiness. Later, telling my best friend, who had encouraged me to apply for the loan, was a pleasure. When good comes into my life, I figure, why not share it?

An Essay

Everybody has special moments of pure joy when a dream suddenly becomes a reality or a goal is finally in sight. These rare times mark the high points in life, and some people like to experience them alone. However, I am not one of these people. When I am happy, I want to share my happiness.

When my wife gave birth to our son, for example, I couldn't wait to tell everyone. I started by calling my parents, my wife's parents, and every other relative I could think of. By the time I found myself calling my second cousin in New Zealand, I realized I had run out of relatives. I prolonged my happiness by calling all my friends, the people at the bakery where I work, and even a few strangers. One poor man nearly tripped when I ran into him as he tried to get out of the hospital elevator. "Oh, I'm so sorry," I said, "but I've just had a baby boy." I even told the mail carrier on my street.

In another instance, I had to share the news about my dream of get-ting a college education. As soon as I opened the letter announcing my college loan, I wanted to spread the information. Just seeing the look on my wife's face increased my happiness. She knew what I was thinking: With the loan, I wouldn't have to take a second job in order to attend college. Later, telling my best friend, who had encouraged me to apply for the loan, was a pleasure. My getting the loan was his victory, too, for without him, I would have given up on going to college.

I suppose I could have told my friend about my financial aid a few days later, over lunch. As for the birth of my son, I could have saved hefty long-distance phone charges by sending birth announcements to aunts, uncles, and cousins who live far away. But I chose not to hold back. When good comes into my life, I figure, why not share it?

If you read the two selections carefully, you noticed that they make the same main point, and they support that point with two subpoints.

main point: When I am happy, I want to share my happiness.

subpoints: 1. When my wife gave birth to our son, I couldn't wait to tell everyone.
2. I had to share the news about my dream of getting a college education.

You noticed that the essay is longer because it has more details and examples to support the points.

ORGANIZING AN ESSAY

When you write an essay of more than one paragraph, the **thesis** is the focus of your entire essay; it is the major point of your essay. The other important points that relate to the thesis are in topic sentences.

> **thesis:** Working as a salesperson has changed my character.
>
> > **topic sentence:** I have had to learn patience.
> >
> > **topic sentence:** I have developed the ability to listen.
> >
> > **topic sentence:** I have become more tactful.

Notice that the thesis expresses a bigger idea than the topic sentences below it, and it is supported by the topic sentences. The essay has an introduction, a body, and a conclusion.

1. **Introduction:** The first paragraph is usually the introduction. The thesis goes here.

2. **Body:** This central part of the essay is the part where you support your main point (the thesis). Each paragraph in the body of the essay has its own topic sentence.

3. **Conclusion:** The final component of an essay, the conclusion, re-emphasizes the essay's thesis. It can be shorter than a body paragraph.

WRITING THE THESIS

There are several characteristics of a thesis:

1. **It is expressed in a sentence.** A thesis is *not* the same as the topic of the essay or the title of the essay:

> **topic:** learning to ski
> **title:** Why I Learned to Ski
> **thesis:** I learned to ski because all my friends ski, I needed more exercise in the winter, and I wanted to meet girls.

2. **A thesis does not announce; it makes a point about the subject.**

> **announcement:** This essay will explain the reasons why street racing is popular with teens.
> **thesis:** Street racing is popular with teens because it gives them a sense of power and identity.

3. **A thesis is not too broad.** Some ideas are just too big to cover well in an essay. A thesis that tries to cover too much can lead to a superficial or boring essay.

> **too broad:** The world would be a better place if everyone would just be more tolerant.
> **acceptable thesis:** The diversity celebration at our school spread good feelings among many groups.

2 Recognize the difference between a topic sentence and a thesis statement.

4. A thesis is not too narrow. Sometimes, writers start with a thesis that looks good because it seems specific and precise. Later, when they try to support such a thesis, they can't find anything to say.

> **too narrow:** Academic advisors help students schedule classes.
> **acceptable thesis:** Academic advisors have a variety of tools to help students plan practical class schedules.

Hints for Writing a Thesis

1. Your thesis can mention the specific subpoints of your essay. For example, your thesis might be like the following:

> Boundaries are important because they make children feel safe, connected, and loved.

With this thesis, you have indicated the three subpoints of your essay: (1) Boundaries make children feel safe, (2) boundaries make children feel connected, and (3) boundaries make children feel loved.

2. Another way to write your thesis is to make a point without listing your subpoints. For example, you can write a thesis like the following:

> Children need boundaries in order to grow.

With this thesis, you can still use the subpoints stating that boundaries make children feel safe, boundaries make children feel connected, and boundaries make children feel loved. You just don't have to mention all your subpoints in the thesis.

MyWritingLab™ **Exercise 1** **Practice: Recognizing Good Thesis Sentences**

Review the entries below and determine which ones are suitable thesis sentences. Note that some entries are too broad or narrow, and one is not a sentence. Write a *G* next to the "good" thesis sentences.

1. _____ How rumors spread on college campuses will be discussed.

2. _____ On Saturday, a local police officer stopped my brother for speeding.

3. _____ Family support influences all future relationships.

4. _____ Cartoons with sophisticated humor appeal to many adults.

5. _____ Sustainable living practices are becoming increasingly popular.

6. _____ A married college student with a job and family juggles many responsibilities.

7. _____ Shopping online is not always convenient.

8. _____ Brazil is a large South American nation with many natural resources.

MyWritingLab™ **Exercise 2** **Practice: Selecting a Good Thesis Sentence**

In each pair of thesis statements below, put a *G* next to the good thesis sentence.

1. a. _____ The most stressful times for me.

   b. _____ My most stressful times come during final exams.

2. a. _____ Photographing red-light violations has positive and negative effects.

   b. _____ Our country must do something to stop the epidemic of texting while driving.

3. a. _____ The difficulties of learning English as a second language will be discussed in this essay.

   b. _____ Students learning English as a second language have difficulties with fast-talking native speakers and confusing grammar rules.

4. a. _____ What to do if a tornado threatens your neighborhood.

   b. _____ If a tornado threatens your neighborhood, act fast and sensibly.

5. a. _____ I quit my job because the working conditions were terrible.

   b. _____ The terrible working conditions and what I did about them will be the subject of this essay.

6. a. _____ Dancing is a great way to stay in shape.

   b. _____ What dancing can do for people.

7. a. _____ The hidden story of bottled water and its origins.

   b. _____ Bottled water can have the same risks and come from the same sources as tap water.

8. a. _____ Tri-City College has several academic programs.

   b. _____ Studying at Tri-City College has created several opportunities for me.

Exercise 3 **Practice: Writing a Thesis That Relates to the Subpoints**   MyWritingLab™

Following are lists of subpoints that could be discussed in an essay. Write a thesis for each list. Remember that there are two ways to write a thesis: you can write a thesis that includes the specific subpoints, or you can write one that makes a point without listing the subpoints. As an example, the first one is done for you, using both kinds of topic sentences.

1. **one kind of thesis:** Children need to leave their computers and televisions and play some outdoor sports.

   another kind of thesis: For children, playing sports outdoors burns more energy, creates more friendships, and stimulates more interest than playing indoors.

   subpoints: a. Sitting at a computer or in front of a television burns very little energy; playing sports burns more energy.
   b. Playing indoors is often solitary; sports involve other children and may lead to friendships.
   c. Children playing indoors can easily become bored, but outdoor sports require more involvement.

2. **thesis:** _____

_____

subpoints: a. Prospective buyers think a cluttered house is smaller than it really is.

b. To potential buyers, a cluttered house appears messy or even dirty.

3. **thesis:** _____

_____

subpoints: a. Too great a need to win can take the pleasure out of friendly games.

b. An obsessive need to win encourages some people to cheat.

c. When winning becomes the only goal, people in professional sports may damage their bodies in order to win.

d. Corporations that are competing for financial success have been known to break laws.

WRITING THE ESSAY IN STAGES

In an essay, you follow the same stages you learned in writing a paragraph—prewriting, planning, drafting and revising, and editing and proofreading—but you adapt them to the longer essay form.

3 Prewrite to narrow your essay topic.

PREWRITING AN ESSAY

Often you begin by **narrrowing a topic**. Your instructor may give you a large topic so you can find something smaller, within the broad one, that you would like to write about.

Some students think that because they have several paragraphs to write, they should pick a big topic, one that will give them enough to say. But big topics can lead to boring, superficial, general essays. A smaller topic can challenge you to find the specific, concrete examples and details that make an essay effective.

If your instructor asked you to write about student life, for instance, you might **freewrite** some ideas as you narrow the topic:

Narrowing the Topic of Student Life

Student activities—how boring!

Maybe how to meet people at college, except how <u>do</u> you meet people? I don't really know. I have my friends, but I'm not sure how I met them.

The food on campus. Everyone will do that topic.

The classrooms in college. The tiny chairs and the temperature.

Yes!

In your freewriting, you can consider your **purpose**—to write an essay about some aspect of student life—and **audience**—your instructor and classmates.

Your narrowed topic will appeal to this audience because both college teachers and students spend a good part of their time in classrooms.

Listing Ideas

Once you have a narrow topic, you can use whatever process works for you. You can brainstorm by writing a series of questions and answers about your topic, you can freewrite on the topic, you can list ideas on the topic, or you can do any combination of these processes.

Following is a sample **listing of ideas** on the topic of classrooms.

College Classrooms: A List

the tiny chairs	the temperature
the awful desks	all the graffiti
the carvings in the desks	too hot in the room
freezing on some days	cramped rooms
blinds on windows don't close	the teacher's desk
no one cares	

By **clustering** related items on the list, you'll find it easier to see the connections between ideas. The following items have been clustered (grouped), and they are listed under subtitles.

College Classrooms: Ideas in Clusters

the furniture	**student damage**
the tiny chairs	the carvings in the desks
the awful desks	all the graffiti
the teacher's desk	

the temperature
freezing on some days
too hot in the room
blinds on windows don't close

When you surveyed the clusters, you probably noticed that some of the ideas from the original list were left out. These ideas on the cramped rooms and no one caring could fit into more than one place and might not fit anywhere. You might come back to them later.

When you name each cluster by giving it a subtitle, you move toward a focus for each body paragraph of your essay. And by beginning to focus the body paragraphs, you start thinking about the main point, the thesis of the essay. Concentrating on the thesis and on focused paragraphs helps you to **unify** your essay.

Reread the clustered ideas. When you do so, you'll notice that each cluster is about a different kind of problem in the college classroom. You can incorporate that concept into a thesis statement like this:

The typical classroom at my college is unwelcoming because of its tiny furniture, uncomfortable temperature, and student damage.

Once you have a thesis and a list of details, you can begin working on the planning part of your essay.

Collaborate

Exercise 4 **Collaborate: Narrowing Topics**

Working with a partner or a group, narrow these topics so that the new topics are related but smaller and suitable for short essays between four and six paragraphs long. The first topic is narrowed for you.

1. **topic:** your college major
   smaller, related topics:
   a. *courses of study* _____
   b. *possible future jobs* _____
   c. *why you chose this major* _____

2. **topic:** nature
   smaller, related topics:
   a. _____
   b. _____
   c. _____

3. **topic:** employment
   smaller, related topics:
   a. _____
   b. _____
   c. _____

MyWritingLab™   **Exercise 5** **Practice: Clustering Related Ideas**

Mark all the related items on the list with the same number (1, 2, or 3). Some items might not get any number. When you've finished marking the list, write a title for each number that explains the cluster of ideas.

1. **topic:** why friendships end

   _____ one friend joins the army and is sent overseas

   _____ one friend betrays the other friend's secret

   _____ one friend works at two full-time jobs

   _____ one friend spends all his time trying to save the family business

   _____ one friend dies in a car accident

   _____ one friend borrows money and never repays it

   _____ the friends share mutual goals

   _____ family members accept and act kindly toward the friends

   _____ one is sent to prison and is unable to prove his innocence

   _____ one marries someone who hates the old group of friends

   The ideas marked 1 can be titled _____

   The ideas marked 2 can be titled _____

   The ideas marked 3 can be titled _____

PLANNING **AN ESSAY**

In the next stage of writing your essay, draft an outline. Use the thesis to focus your ideas. There are many kinds of outlines, but all are used to help a writer organize ideas. When you use a **formal outline**, you show the difference between a main idea and its supporting detail by *indenting* the supporting detail. In a formal outline, Roman numerals (numbers) and capital letters are used. Each Roman numeral represents a paragraph, and the letters beneath the numeral represent supporting details.

The Structure of a Formal Outline

first paragraph	I. Thesis
second paragraph	II. Topic sentence
details	A. B. C. D. E.
third paragraph	III. Topic sentence
details	A. B. C. D. E.
fourth paragraph	IV. Topic sentence
details	A. B. C. D. E.
fifth paragraph	V. Conclusion

Hints for Outlining

Developing a good, clear outline now can save you hours of confused, disorganized writing later. The extra time you spend to make sure that your outline has sufficient details and that *each paragraph stays on one point* will pay off in the long run.

1. Check the topic sentences. Keep in mind that each topic sentence in each body paragraph should support the thesis sentence. If a topic sentence is not carefully connected to the thesis, the structure of the essay will be confusing. Here are a thesis and a list of topic sentences; the topic sentence that does not fit is crossed out:

thesis: I. Designing a playlist of a person's favorite songs is a creative act and a thoughtful gift.

topic sentences: II. Selecting just the right songs takes insight.
III. Assembling the playlist requires imagination.
IV. ~~MP3 players are getting cheaper all the time.~~
V. Whoever receives the playlist will be flattered that someone took the time to design such a personal gift.
VI. A personally crafted playlist challenges the mind of the giver and opens the heart of the receiver.

Because the thesis of this outline is about the creative challenge of designing a personal playlist as a gift and the pleasure of receiving one, topic sentence IV doesn't fit: it isn't about making the gift or receiving it. It takes the essay off track. A careful check of the links between the thesis and the topic sentences will help keep your essay focused.

2. Include enough details. Some writers believe that they don't need many details in the outline. They feel they can fill in the details later, when they actually write the essay. Even though some writers do manage to add details later, others who are in a hurry or who run out of ideas run into problems.

For example, imagine that a writer has included very few details in an outline such as in this outline for a paragraph:

II. Vandalism of cars takes many forms.
  A. Most cars suffer external damage.
  B. Some are hit in their interiors.

The paragraph created from that outline might be too short and lack specific details, like this:

> Vandalism of cars takes many forms. First of all, most cars suffer external damage. However, some are hit in their interiors.

If you have difficulty thinking of ideas when you write, try to tackle the problem in the outline. The more details you put into your outline, the more detailed and effective your draft essay will be. For example, suppose the same outline on the vandalism topic had more details, like this:

II. Vandalism of cars takes many forms.

more details about exterior damage
  A. Most cars suffer external damage.
  B. The most common damage is breaking off the car antenna.
  C. "Keying" a car, scratching its surface with a key, is also widespread.
  D. Some vandals slash or take the air out of the tires.
  E. Others pour paint on the body of the car.

more details about interior damage
  F. Some are hit in their interiors.
  G. Interior damage ranges from ripped upholstery to torn carpet.

You will probably agree that the paragraph will be more detailed, too.

3. Stay on one point. It is a good idea to check the outline of each body paragraph to see if each paragraph stays on one point. Compare each topic sentence, which is at the top of the list for the paragraph, against the details indented under it. Staying on one point gives each paragraph unity.

Below is the outline for a paragraph that has problems staying on one point. See if you can spot the problem areas.

III. Charles is a fun-loving and cheerful person.

  A. Every morning at work, he has a new joke for me.
  B. He even makes our boss, who is very serious, smile.
  C. One day when a customer was extremely rude to him, he kept his temper.
  D. On weekends, when our job gets hectic, Charles never becomes irritable.

E. Most of our customers love him because he always greets them with, "How are you on this beautiful day?"

F. When we all took a pay cut, he looked on the positive side.

G. "At least we still have our jobs," he said.

The topic sentence of the paragraph is about Charles' love of fun and cheerfulness. But sentences C and D talk about Charles' ability to remain calm. When you have a problem staying on one point, you can solve the problem two ways:

1. Eliminate details that do not fit your main point.
2. Change the topic sentence to cover all the ideas in the paragraph.

For example, you could cut out sentences C and D about Charles' calm nature, getting rid of the details that do not fit. As an alternative, you could change the topic sentence in the paragraph so that it relates to all the ideas in the paragraph. A better topic sentence is "Charles is a fun-loving, even-tempered, and cheerful person."

Revisiting the Prewriting Stage

Writing an outline for your essay can help you identify places where your body paragraphs will need more details. You can generate more details in two ways:

1. Go back to the writing you did in the prewriting stage. Check whether items on a list or ideas from freewriting can lead you to more details for your outline.

2. Brainstorm for more details by using a question-and-answer approach. For example, if your outline includes "My little sister is greedy," you might ask, "When is she greedy? How greedy is she?" Or if your outline includes the point, "There is nothing to do in this town," you might ask, "What do you mean? Sports? Clubs? Parties?"

The time you spend writing and revising your outline will make it easier for you to write an essay that is well developed, unified, and coherently structured. The checklist below may help you revise:

Checklist for Revising the Outline of an Essay

✓ **Unity:** Do the thesis and topic sentences all lead to the same point? Does each paragraph make one, and only one, point? Do the details in each paragraph support the topic sentence? Does the conclusion unify the essay?

✓ **Support:** Do the body paragraphs have enough supporting details?

✓ **Coherence:** Are the paragraphs in the most effective order? Are the details in each paragraph arranged in the most effective order?

A sentence outline on college classrooms follows. It includes the thesis in the first paragraph. The topic sentences have been created from the titles of the ideas clustered earlier. The details have been drawn from ideas in the clusters and from further brainstorming. The conclusion's final statement unifies the essay because it re-emphasizes the thesis.

Outline for an Essay

paragraph 1

I. Thesis: The typical classroom at my college is unwelcoming because of its tiny furniture, uncomfortable temperature, and student damage.

paragraph 2: topic sentence

II. Child-size furniture makes it difficult to focus on adult-level classes.
   A. The student chairs are tiny.
   B. I am six feet tall, and I feel like I am crammed into a kindergarten chair.
   C. The chairs are attached to miniature desks, which are just slightly enlarged armrests.

details

   D. I cannot fit my legs under the desk.
   E. I cannot fit my textbook and a notebook on the surface of the desk.
   F. In some classrooms, the teacher has no desk and is forced to use one of the miniature student versions.

paragraph 3: topic sentence

III. The temperature in the classrooms is anything but pleasant.
   A. I have been at the college for both the fall and winter terms.
   B. In the early fall, the rooms were too hot.
   C. The air conditioning feebly pumped hot air.
   D. The sun beat through the glass windows because the blinds were broken.

details

   E. On some days in the winter, we froze.
   F. Two of my teachers have reported the problems to maintenance, but nothing changed.
   G. It is hard to concentrate when you are sweating or shivering.

paragraph 4: topic sentence

IV. Student damage to the classrooms makes them seedy and ugly.
   A. There is graffiti all over the desks.
   B. There are messages, slogans, and drawings.
   C. They are all childish.
   D. Half the desks and chairs have gum stuck to their undersides.

details

   E. Some students carve into the desks and chairs.
   F. Others have stained the carpet with spilled coffee or soft drinks.
   G. It's depressing to think that my fellow students enjoy damaging the place where they come to learn.

paragraph 5: conclusion

V. When I started college, I knew I would face many challenges, but I didn't expect them to include squeezing into the chairs, dressing for a blizzard or a heat wave, and picking gum off my desk.

Exercise 6   **Practice: Completing an Outline for an Essay**   MyWritingLab™

Following is part of an outline that has a thesis and topic sentences, but no details. Add the details and write them in complete sentences. Write one sentence for each capital letter. Be sure that the details are connected to the topic sentence.

  I. **Thesis:** Money has a different meaning for different people.

 II. When some people think of money, they think of the freedom to spend it on whatever they want for themselves.

    A. _____

    B. _____

    C. _____

    D. _____

    E. _____

III. To others, money means security.

    A. _____

    B. _____

    C. _____

    D. _____

    E. _____

IV. Some people think of money as something to share.

    A. _____

    B. _____

    C. _____

    D. _____

    E. _____

  V. The way people perceive money reveals what matters to them.

Exercise 7   **Practice: Focusing an Outline for an Essay**   MyWritingLab™

The outline below has a thesis and details, but it has no topic sentences for the body paragraphs. Write the topic sentences.

  I. **Thesis:** My girlfriend and I will never eat at the The Bridge Restaurant again.

 II. _____

    _____

    A. We had to stand in line for a table.

    B. The restaurant's hostess promised us the waiting time would be short.

    C. The wait lasted half an hour.

    D. The line of people grew longer as time passed.

E. There was no place to sit as we all crowded into a small front room.

F. No one seemed to be led from the line to the dining room.

III. _____

_____

A. The shrimp salad that I ordered had tiny canned shrimp.

B. Steak is supposed to be the specialty of the house.

C. My steak was gristly and tough.

D. An order of grilled vegetables was cold and mushy.

E. My girlfriend's chicken was not thoroughly cooked.

F. The key lime pie we both ordered for dessert appeared to be a pie crust filled with lime pudding.

IV. _____

_____

A. My shrimp salad appetizer cost me ten dollars.

B. The steak that The Bridge Restaurant features cost me more than my weekly food budget.

C. I paid extra money for a side order of grilled vegetables.

D. My girlfriend's request for an iced tea cost $2.50.

E. For dessert, I ordered a "special" cup of coffee flavored with amaretto that cost five dollars.

F. Worst of all, I could have bought an entire pie at the local bakery for the price of our two slices.

V. Our visit to The Bridge Restaurant was our first—and last.

4 Write a multi-paragraph essay that sufficiently incorporates unity, support, and coherence.

DRAFTING AND REVISING   AN ESSAY

When you are satisfied with your outline, you can begin your drafting and then revising of the essay. Start by writing a first draft of the essay which includes these parts: introduction, body paragraphs, and conclusion.

WRITING THE INTRODUCTION

Where Does the Thesis Go?

The **thesis** should appear in the introduction of the essay, in the first paragraph. But most of the time it should not be the first sentence. In front of the thesis, write a few (three or more) sentences of introduction. These sentences are called your **lead-in** because they lead your reader to the essay's thesis. Generally, the thesis is the *last sentence* in the introductory paragraph.

Why put the thesis at the end of the first paragraph? First of all, writing several sentences in front of your main idea gives you a chance to lead into it, gradually and smoothly. This will help you build interest and gain the reader's attention. Also, by placing the thesis after a few sentences of introduction, you will not startle the reader with your main point.

Finally, if your thesis is at the end of the introduction, it states the main point of the essay just before that point is supported in the body paragraphs. Putting the thesis at the end of the introduction is like putting an arrow pointing to the supporting ideas in the essay.

Hints for Writing the Introduction

There are several ways to write an effective lead-in to your thesis:

1. You can begin with some general statements that gradually lead to your thesis:

general statements	My mother has two framed pictures in the living room. They are sketches of a town square. In the pictures, people are sitting and talking, shopping in the small stores around the square, and strolling through the friendly streets. I envy the people in these scenes, for they seem to enjoy a calm, central gathering place, far from busy highways and enormous parking lots. Unfortunately, my community has no such place.
thesis at end	My town needs a neighborly, accessible town center

2. You can begin with a quote that leads smoothly to your thesis. The quote can be a quote from someone famous, or it can be an old saying. It can be something your mother always told you, a slogan from an advertisement, or the words of a song.

quotation	A song tells us, "It's a small, small, small, small world." There are days when I wish my world were smaller. Sometimes I get sick of driving to a huge supermarket for my groceries, then dashing to a giant mall for new shoes, and finally making a quick stop at a drive-through restaurant for a hamburger. As I make this journey, I rarely meet anyone I know. At these times, I wish my life were different: I'd like to get off the highway, forget the fast food and the huge malls, and run into a few friends as I do my errands. Then
thesis at end	I realize that my town needs a neighborly, accessible town center.

> **Note:** Remember that you can add transitional words or phrases that lead into your thesis, as in the sample above.

3. You can tell a story as a way of leading into your thesis. You can open with the story of something that happened to you or to someone you know, a story you read about or heard on the news.

story	Yesterday my best friend called, and we got into a lengthy conversation. After we had talked for half an hour, we realized we wanted to continue our conversation face to face. "Let's meet for coffee," my friend said. He suggested a coffee shop near the interstate highway. I suggested another place, which he said was "in the middle of nowhere." Then we ran out of ideas.
thesis at end	There was no easy, central place. At that moment, it occurred to me that my town needs a neighborly, accessible town center.

4. You can explain why this topic is worth writing about. Explaining could mean giving some background on the topic, or it could mean discussing why the topic is an important one.

explain　　Almost everyone feels lonely at some time. Teens feel left out by the many cliques that make up high school society. Older people, often suffering the loss of a spouse, need human contact. Singles try to find a comfortable place in what seems to be a world of married couples. As for couples, each partner needs to feel part of a world outside of marriage. In my community, there is no friendly place where all types

thesis at end　of people can feel accepted. <u>My town needs a neighborly, accessible town center</u>.

5. You can use one or more questions to lead into your thesis. You can open with a question or questions that will be answered by your thesis. Or you can open with a question or questions that catch the reader's attention and move toward your thesis.

question　　Have you ever seen an old movie called <u>It's a Wonderful Life?</u> It's about George Bailey, a small-town husband and father whose life changes on Christmas Eve when an angel visits to teach George a lesson. Although I enjoy the plot of the movie, what I like most about the film is the small town George lives in, where everyone seems to know everyone else and life centers on a few streets of stores, homes, and businesses. I sometimes wish that I had a little of

thesis at end　that simple life. Then I conclude that <u>my town needs a neighborly, accessible town center</u>.

6. You can open with a contradiction of your main point as a way of attracting the reader's interest and leading to your thesis. You can begin with an idea that is the opposite of what you will say in your thesis. The opposition of your opening and your thesis creates interest.

contradiction　My town appears to have every shopping and entertainment attraction of an ideal community. It has two giant malls, a movie theater with sixteen screens and stadium seating, cafes, restaurants, popular clubs, a water park, a skating rink, and a bowling alley. However, it doesn't offer what people want most: the comfort of a small-town gathering place that invites shoppers, strollers, people with their dogs, and people

thesis at end　who like to sit, talk, and drink coffee. <u>My town needs a neighborly, accessible town center</u>.

Note: Always check with instructor regarding thesis statement placement for your assignments.

MyWritingLab™　**Exercise 8**　**Practice: Writing an Introduction**

Following are five thesis statements. Pick one. Then write an introductory paragraph on the lines provided. Your last sentence should be the thesis statement. If your instructor agrees, read your introduction to others in the class who wrote an introduction to the same thesis, or read your introduction to the entire class.

Thesis Statements

1. Digital textbooks are becoming increasingly common in college classrooms.

2. Technology has revolutionized the music industry.

3. Today's tattoos can be art, fashion, or personal statements.

4. Many parents try to give their children what the parents never had.

5. A million dollars would/would not change the way I live my life.

(Write an introduction) _____

_____

_____

_____

_____

_____

_____

WRITING THE BODY OF THE ESSAY

In the body of the essay, the paragraphs *explain, support,* and *develop* your thesis. In this part of the essay, each paragraph has its own topic sentence. The topic sentence in each paragraph does two things:

1. It focuses the sentences in the paragraph.
2. It makes a point connected to the thesis.

The thesis and the topic sentences are ideas that need to be supported by details, explanations, and examples. You can visualize the connections among the parts of an essay like this:

Introduction with Thesis

Body
{
Topic Sentence
    Details
Topic Sentence
    Details
Topic Sentence
    Details
}

Conclusion

When you write topic sentences, you can organize your essay by referring to the following checklist.

> **Checklist for the Topic Sentences of an Essay**
>
> ✓ Does the topic sentence convey the point of the paragraph?
>
> ✓ Does the topic sentence support (or relate to) the thesis of the essay?

HOW LONG ARE THE BODY PARAGRAPHS?

Remember that the body paragraphs of an essay are the places where you explain and develop your thesis. Those paragraphs should be long enough to explain, not just list, your points. To do this well, try to make your body paragraphs *at least seven sentences* long. As you develop your writing skills, you may find that you can support your ideas in fewer than seven sentences.

DEVELOPING THE BODY PARAGRAPHS

You can write well-developed body paragraphs by following the same steps you used in writing single paragraphs for the earlier assignments in this course. By working through the stages of gathering ideas, outlining, drafting, revising, editing, and proofreading, you can create clear, effective paragraphs.

To focus and develop the body paragraphs, ask the questions below as you revise:

> **Checklist for Developing Body Paragraphs for an Essay**
>
> ✓ Do all of the details in the paragraph support, develop, or illustrate the topic sentence's point (or idea)?
>
> ✓ Do I have sufficient details to support the topic sentence?

MyWritingLab™   Exercise 9   **Practice: Creating Topic Sentences**

Following are thesis sentences. For each thesis, write topic sentences (as many as indicated by the numbered blanks). The first one is done for you.

1. **thesis:** Many families have traditions for celebrating special occasions.

   topic sentence 1: *Family birthdays can involve special rituals.*
   _____

   topic sentence 2: *At weddings, many family traditions appear.*
   _____

   topic sentence 3: *Some families have customs for celebrating New Year's Day.*
   _____

2. **thesis:** Daytime college classes are different from evening college classes.

   topic sentence 1: _____
   _____

topic sentence 2: _____

_____

3. thesis: Studying in groups is more beneficial than studying alone.

topic sentence 1: _____

_____

topic sentence 2: _____

_____

topic sentence 3: _____

_____

4. thesis: Working at night has its good and bad points for college students.

topic sentence 1: _____

_____

topic sentence 2: _____

_____

topic sentence 3: _____

_____

topic sentence 4: _____

_____

WRITING THE CONCLUSION

The last paragraph in the essay is the **conclusion**. It does not have to be as long as a body paragraph, but it should be long enough to tie the essay together and remind the reader of the thesis. You can use any of these strategies in writing the conclusion:

1. You can restate the thesis in new words. Go back to the first paragraph of your essay and reread it. For example, this could be the first paragraph of an essay:

introduction

I recently moved to a city that is a thousand miles from my hometown. I drove the long distance with only one companion, my mixed-breed dog Casey. Casey was a wonderful passenger: he kept me company, never asked to stop or complained about my driving, and was happy to observe the endless stretches of road. By the end of our trip, I loved Casey even more than I had when we started. Unfortunately, I found that landlords do not appreciate the bonds between dogs and their owners. In fact,

thesis at end

renting a decent apartment and keeping a dog is nearly impossible.

The thesis is the sentence you can rephrase in your concluding paragraph. Your challenge is to re-emphasize the thesis but in different words. You can work that restatement into a short paragraph, like this:

<table>
<tr><td>**restating the thesis**</td><td>Most dogs can adapt to apartment living. They will not bark too much, destroy property, or threaten the neighbors. They can adjust to being alone indoors as long as their owners provide time for fun, exercise, and affection. But most landlords refuse to give dogs the benefit of the doubt. <u>The landlords pressure dog owners to make a choice between an apartment and a pet.</u></td></tr>
</table>

2. You can make a judgment, valuation, or recommendation. Instead of simply restating your point, you can end by making some comment on the issue you've described or the problem you've illustrated. If you were looking for another way to end the essay on finding an apartment that allows pets, for example, you could end with a recommendation.

<table>
<tr><td>**ending with a recommendation**</td><td>I understand that landlords need to make a profit on their property and that some dogs and dog owners damage that property. However, not all dogs go wild, and not all dog owners let their pets destroy an apartment. <u>If landlords made an individual judgment about each applicant with a pet, instead of following a hard, cold policy, they might realize that dogs can be model apartment dwellers.</u></td></tr>
</table>

3. You can conclude by framing your essay. You can tie your essay together neatly by *using something from your introduction* as a way of concluding. When you take an example, a question, or even a quote from your first paragraph and refer to it in your last paragraph, you are "framing" the essay. Take another look at the sample introduction to the essay on finding an apartment that will allow a dog. The writer talks about driving a thousand miles away from home, about his or her dear companion, Casey. The writer also mentions the difficulties of finding a decent place to live when landlords will not allow dogs. Now consider how the ideas of the introduction are used in this conclusion:

<table>
<tr><td>**frame**
frame

frame

frame
frame
frame</td><td>When <u>I drove into this city a thousand miles from my home, I brought my dear friend and loyal companion with me.</u> That friend, <u>my dog Casey</u>, made me smile as he sat in the passenger seat, a tall, proud traveler. He fell asleep on my feet when I stopped at a lonely rest stop. <u>Many cruel landlords told me I would have to give Casey up if I wanted a comfortable place to live.</u> But I refused, for Casey brings me more comfort than any fancy apartment ever could.</td></tr>
</table>

Exercise 10 **Practice: Choosing a Better Way to Restate the Thesis**   MyWritingLab™

Following are five clusters. Each cluster consists of a thesis sentence and two sentences that try to restate the thesis. Each restated sentence could be used as part of the conclusion to an essay. Put *B* next to the sentence in each pair that is a better restatement. Remember that the better choice repeats the same idea as the thesis but does not rely on too many of the same words.

1. **thesis:** When you are upset about a problem, take a long walk.

    restatement 1:_____ A long walk can help you when you are upset about a problem.

    restatement 2:_____ When something is troubling you, a long walk can bring you some relief.

2. **thesis:** If you are not sure of your major, you should talk to an advisor.

    restatement 1:_____ Talking to an academic advisor about your career options is a good way to start your academic career.

    restatement 2:_____ A good way to discover what you want to study is to talk with an academic advisor.

3. **thesis:** Alexandra has a talent for buying low-cost groceries, combining them in unusual ways, and producing delicious meals.

    restatement 1:_____ Alexandra produces delicious meals after she buys low-cost groceries and combines the food in unusual ways.

    restatement 2:_____ Alexandra can find bargain groceries, mix them creatively, and serve tasty meals.

Revising Your Draft

Once you have a rough draft of your essay, you can begin **revising** it. The following checklist may help you make the necessary changes in your draft:

Checklist for Revising the Draft of an Essay

✓ Does the essay have a clear, unifying thesis?

✓ Does the thesis make a point?

✓ Does each body paragraph have a topic sentence?

✓ Is each body paragraph focused on its topic sentence?

✓ Are the body paragraphs roughly the same size?

✓ Do any of the words need to be changed?

✓ Are the ideas linked smoothly?

✓ Does the introduction catch the reader's interest?

✓ Is there a definite conclusion?

✓ Does the conclusion re-emphasize or remind the reader of the thesis?

Transitions Within Paragraphs

In an essay, you can use two kinds of **transitions**: those within a paragraph and those between paragraphs.

Transitions that link ideas within a paragraph are the same kinds you've used earlier. Your choice of words, phrases, or even sentences depends on the kind of connection you want to make. Here is a list of some common transitions and the kinds of connections they express:

INFO BOX **Common Transitions Within a Paragraph**

To join two ideas

again	another	in addition	moreover
also	besides	likewise	similarly
and	furthermore		

To show a contrast or a different opinion

but	instead	on the other hand	still
however	nevertheless	or	yet
in contrast	on the contrary	otherwise	

To show a cause-and-effect connection

accordingly	because	for	therefore
as a result	consequently	so	thus

To give an example

for example	in the case of	such as	to illustrate
for instance	like		

To show time

after	first	recently	subsequently
at the same time	meanwhile	shortly	then
before	next	soon	until
finally			

Transitions Between Paragraphs

When you write something that is more than one paragraph long, you need transitions that link each paragraph to the others. There are several effective ways to link paragraphs and remind the reader of your main idea and of how the smaller points connect to it. Here are two ways:

1. **Restate an idea from the preceding paragraph at the start of a new paragraph.** Look closely at the following two paragraphs and notice how the second paragraph repeats an idea from the first paragraph and provides a link.

Buying clothes for their designer labels is expensive. A t-shirt marked with the name of a popular designer can cost twenty or thirty dollars more than a similar t-shirt without the name. More expensive items like fleece jackets can be as much as seventy or eighty dollars higher if they carry a trendy name. For each designer jacket a person buys, he or she could probably buy two without a trendy logo or label. If a person decides to go all the way with fashion, he or she can spend a hundred dollars on designer socks and underwear.

transition restating an idea 　　Creating a wardrobe of designer clothes is not only expensive; it is also silly. While designers want buyers to think the designer label means quality, many trendy clothes are made in the same factories as less fashionable clothes. And after all, how much "design" can go into a pair of socks to make them worth four times what an ordinary pair costs? The worst part of spending money on designer labels has to do with style. The hot designer of today can be out of style tomorrow, and no one wants to wear that name across a shirt, a jacket, or a pair of socks.

2. Use synonyms and repetition as a way of reminding the reader of an important point. For example, in the two paragraphs below, notice how certain repeated words, phrases, and synonyms all remind the reader of a point about kindness and generosity. The repeated words and synonyms are underlined.

　　Often the kindest and most generous people are the ones who don't have much themselves. When I was evicted from my apartment, my Aunt Natalie, who has three children under ten, took me into her two-room apartment. Her heart was too big for her to leave me homeless. Another giving person is my best friend. He is a security guard trying to pay for college, but he regularly donates his time and money to the local Police Athletic League. One of the most compassionate people I know is a grandmother living on Social Security. Every day, she gets up at 5:00 a.m. to make sandwiches at the local food bank. She swears she isn't doing anything special, that she gets more than she gives by taking care of others.

　　Not everyone can be a hero working in a food bank at 5:00 a.m. But everyone can perform small acts of generosity and humanity, and most people do. Many are thoughtful and caring enough to leave a large tip for the server who lives on tips. Most people are decent on the highways; they let desperate drivers merge lanes. In the mall, shoppers routinely help lost children, hold the door for the shoppers behind them, and give directions to strangers. Without feeling at all heroic, people give blood at a blood drive, walk in a walk-a-thon, take in lost pets, and sell candy bars for their children's school. But even if they are not thinking about it, these people are acting for others and giving to others.

Revised Draft of the Essay

Below is a revised draft of the essay on college classrooms, and you can assume the writer worked through *several* drafts to get to this point. (Keep in mind that editing and proofreading are still necessary to improve this essay.) If you compare this draft to the outline on page 370, you'll notice the following changes:

- An introduction has been added, phrased in the first person, "I," to unify the essay.
- Transitions have been added within and between paragraphs.
- Details have been added.
- General statements have been replaced by more specific ones.
- Word choice has been improved.
- A conclusion has been added. The conclusion uses one of the ideas from the lead-in (the idea that the outside and inside of National College are different). In addition, one of the other ideas in the conclusion, the point that no one seems to care about the condition of the classrooms, comes from the original list of ideas about the topic of college classrooms. It did not fit in the body paragraphs, but it works well in the conclusion.

Revised Draft of an Essay

(Thesis and topic sentences are underlined; editing and proofreading are still necessary.)

National College, which I attend, has impressive buildings of glass and concrete. It has covered walkways, paved patios, and large clusters of trees and flowers. From the outside, the college looks great. However, on the inside, National College has some problems. The most important rooms in the institution do not attract the most important people in the institution, the students. <u>The typical classroom at my college is unwelcoming because of its tiny furniture, uncomfortable temperature, and student damage</u>.

First of all, <u>child-size furniture makes it difficult to focus on adult-level classes</u>. The student chairs are tiny. They are too small for anyone over ten years old, but for large or tall people, they are torture. For example, I am six feet tall, and when I sit on one of the classroom chairs, I feel like I am crammed into a kindergarten chair. They are attached to miniature desks, which are the size of slightly enlarged armrests. As I sit in class, I cannot fit my legs under the desk. I cannot fit my textbook and a notebook on the surface of the desk. Something always slips off and makes a noise that disrupts the class. In some classrooms, the instructor has no desk and is forced to use one of the miniature student versions.

As students twist and fidget in their tiny desks, they face another problem. <u>The temperature in the classroom is anything but pleasant</u>. I have been at the college for both fall and winter terms, and I have seen both extremes of temperature. In the early fall, the rooms were hot. The air conditioner feebly pumped hot air, which, of course, made the heat worse. Meanwhile, the sun beat through the glass windows because the blinds were broken. Winter did not bring any relief because in winter we froze. On some days, we wore our winter coats during class. Two of my teachers reported the problems to the maintenance department, but nothing changed. I wish the maintenance manager understood how hard it is for students to concentrate when they are sweating or shivering.

Heat and cold create an uncomfortable learning place, but students create a shabby one. <u>Student damage to the classrooms makes them seedy and ugly</u>. There is graffiti all over the desks. There are also messages, slogans, and drawings. They

(Continued)

are all childish. In addition, half the desks have gum stuck to their undersides. Some students even carve their initials and artwork into the plastic and wood of the desks and chairs. Others have stained the carpet with spilled coffee or soft drinks. Sometimes I have to be careful where I walk so that my shoes don't stick to the mess. It's depressing to think that my fellow students enjoy damaging the place where they come to learn.

National College is impressive outside, but no one seems to care about the problems inside. The classrooms seem to be designed without a thought for adult learners who need to sit in adult-size seats and take lecture notes at adult-size desks. The maintenance department does not maintain a comfortable temperature so that students can learn, and students do not respect their learning environment. These problems surprise me. <u>When I started college, I knew I would face many challenges, but I didn't expect them to include squeezing into the chairs, dressing for a blizzard or heat wave, and picking gum off my desk.</u>

Exercise 11   **Practice: Identifying the Main Points in the Draft of an Essay**   MyWritingLab™

Below is the draft of a four-paragraph essay. Read it; then reread it and underline the thesis and the topic sentences in each body paragraph and in the conclusion.

During my high school years, I held several part-time jobs that involved dealing with the public. I once worked as an activities director for an after-school program where ten-year-olds started giving me orders. In my senior year, I worked at a local sandwich shop and learned how to smile at hungry, impatient customers waiting for their twelve-inch submarine orders. I am now a sophomore in college and work at Cook's Place, a small but popular family restaurant. I have learned much while working at this family establishment, first as a waiter and now as the restaurant's first night manager.

The restaurant's owner, Dan Cook, hired me a year ago to be a waiter for what he humorously calls "the dinner crowd shift." I learned several essential business skills in a short time. Although the restaurant has only ten tables (each seating four), I quickly learned how to keep track of multiple orders, how to work the computerized cash register, how to verify active credit card numbers, and how to use certain abbreviations while taking orders. Dan also showed me how to fill out weekly orders for our food and beverage suppliers. Many of our customers are regulars, and I also learned that maintaining a positive attitude and friendly manner can make my job enjoyable, even on slow nights. After a few weeks, I felt confident about my skills as a waiter and looked forward to going to work.

After I had been a waiter for five months, Dan told me he'd like to start spending more time visiting his grown children who live in another state. He asked me if I would like to become the restaurant's "first official night manager." I accepted his offer immediately, and I have acquired even more business skills in this position. I now manage the restaurant three nights each week and one Saturday evening each month. I plan the dinner specials with the cook, negotiate with suppliers to get the best bulk-order prices, and make calls to customers who fill out an evaluation form Dan and I devised. I have learned that if I treat people respectfully, they will usually treat me professionally. Over the past year, I've had to interview applicants whenever a server position became available, and I've learned how important it is to be tactful and encouraging even when I've had to turn someone down. Finally, I've even met with Dan's accountant several times. She showed me the forms various business owners have to fill out, and I've learned about the importance of accurate records for tax purposes. Dan says he's proud of my progress and jokes that I "work well with people and work the numbers well."

At Cook's Place, I was fortunate to have on-the-job training that was both educational and enjoyable. I've gained many business skills, but most importantly, I've learned the value of encouragement, teamwork, respect, and friendship. They are my ingredients for success in any relationship.

MyWritingLab™   Exercise 12   **Practice: Adding Transitions to an Essay**

The essay below needs transitions. Add the transitions where indicated, and add the kind of transition—word, phrase, or sentence—indicated.

When I registered for my college classes at the beginning of the term, I was a little upset by a new problem. Because I had waited so long to sign up for classes, I had few choices of time slots. One problem particularly troubled me. In order to get into one required course, I had to take it as an evening class. _____ (add a word or phrase) while the time of the class is not my first choice, I have found some advantages to taking an evening class.

_____ (add a word) I began the class, I was certain that I would not be able to absorb all the information of a three-hour session. I had never had to focus on that much material in one long session instead of in shorter classes that met two or three times a week. _____ (add a word or a phrase) three hours just seemed too long to sit. _____ (add a word) I began the class, I learned to adjust to the differences in a long session. _____ (add a word or phrase) my instructor varied the pace of the class by using several teaching methods _____ lecture, discussion, and small group work. _____ (add a word or phrase) she allowed us a short break halfway through class time.

The length of each class session became manageable because of my instructor's ability to change the pace, and she shifted the pace by mixing methods of instruction. Another benefit of the class is related to the students. Although a few students, including me, signed up for the evening class because the time slot was the only one left for the course they needed, others had other motives. Some of the students worked full time during the day; _____ (add a word or phrase) they needed to take evening classes. Many of these students came to class directly from their workplace or from their hectic roles as mothers and fathers.

Other students had taken this teacher before and enjoyed her organized, energetic

teaching style. Both types of students had chosen this class at this time. I felt that

this evening class had a larger percentage of lively, committed students than many

daytime classes, and _____ (add a word or phrase) those students

made the class lively for everyone.

_____

_____ After

a few weeks, I learned to appreciate having seven days to complete a long reading

assignment. Writing assignments also were easier when I had more time to plan,

draft, revise, and proofread them. Best of all, I discovered the benefits of doing a

little each day instead of racing to prepare for a test or scratch together an essay,

This method of starting early and breaking my assignments into small steps can

also work in my other classes.

I now recognize that the benefits of my evening class outweigh its

disadvantages. Several hours is a long time to spend in one place _____

(add a word or a phrase) the time is not as dull or as deadly as I expected it to be.

_____ (add a word or a phrase), the atmosphere in the class is lively

because of the students enrolled in it. _____ I have realized that the

method of breaking assignments into small steps can work in many of my classes.

My night class has introduced me to a good teacher, motivated students, and a

better way to learn.

Exercise 13   **Practice: Recognizing Synonyms and Repetition Used to
Link Ideas in an Essay**   MyWritingLab™

In the following essay, underline all the synonyms and repetition (of words
or phrases) that help remind the reader of the thesis statement. (To help you,
the thesis is underlined.)

　　　Some people have artistic talent. They become famous painters, musicians,
or actors. Others are known for their athletic abilities, and they are seen on television in tournaments, matches, games, or other sports contests. My brother will
never be on stage or in a tournament, yet he has a special talent. <u>My brother Eddie
has a gift for making friends.</u>

Our family has moved six times in the past ten years, and every time, Eddie was the first to get acquainted with the neighbors. There is something about his smile and cheerful attitude that draws strangers to him. On one of our moves, Eddie had met our neighbors on both sides of the house and directly across the street by the time we unloaded the van. Within a week, Eddie had made the acquaintance of almost every family on the block. Eddie's ability to connect with others helped our whole family to feel comfortable in a new place. As Eddie formed links within the area, he introduced us to the community. Thanks to my brother, we all got to know Mrs. Lopez next door, the teenagers down the street, and even the mail carrier. Soon familiarity turned into deeper friendships.

One of the most amazing examples of Eddie's talent occurred when he and I took a long bus trip. Twenty-four hours on a bus can be exhausting and depressing, but Eddie made the trip fun. He began by talking to the man seated across from us. Soon the couple behind us joined in. When Eddie passed around a bag of potato chips, he drew four more passengers into this cluster of newfound buddies. Eddie and I didn't sleep during the entire trip. We were too busy talking, laughing, and swapping life stories with the other travelers. Some of the toughest-looking passengers turned out to be the kindest, warmest companions.

Only Eddie could transform a dreary bus ride into a cheerful trip with new friends. And thanks to Eddie, our family's many moves became opportunities to meet new people. If I am with my brother, I know we will never be lonely, for Eddie's real talent is his ability to draw others to him.

EDITING AND PROOFREADING AN ESSAY

Before you prepare a final version of your essay, **edit** your latest draft to improve word choice, strengthen transition between sentences and paragraphs, and combine sentences for better style.

Creating a Title

When you are satisfied with the final content, structure, and style of your essay, you can begin preparing your version. Your essay will now need a title, so try to devise a short title that is connected to your thesis. Because the title is the reader's first contact with your essay, an imaginative title can create a good first impression. If you can't think of anything clever, try using a key phrase from your essay.

The title is placed at the top of your essay, about an inch above the first paragraph. Always capitalize the first word of the title and all other words except *the, an, a*, prepositions (like *of, in, with*), and coordinating conjunctions (*for, and, nor, but, or, yet, so*). *Do not* underline or put quotation marks around your title.

The Final Version of an Essay

Following is the final version of the essay on college classrooms. When you compare it to the revised draft on pages 382–383, you will notice some changes:

- A title has been added.
- Transitions have been added; one is a phrase and one is a sentence.
- The word choice has been changed so that descriptions are more precise and repetition (of the word "problems") is avoided.
- Some sentences have been combined.
- Specific details have been added.

Final Version of an Essay

(Changes from the revised draft are underlined.)

A Look Inside One College's Classrooms

National College, which I attend, has impressive buildings of glass and concrete. It has covered walkways, paved patios, and large clusters of trees and flowers. From the outside, the college looks <u>distinguished</u>. However, on the inside, National College has some problems. The most important rooms in the institution do not <u>appeal to</u> the most important people in the institution, the students. The typical classroom at my college is unwelcoming because of its tiny furniture, uncomfortable temperature, and student damage.

First of all, child-size furniture makes it difficult to focus on adult-level classes. The student chairs are tiny. They are too small for anyone over ten years old, but for large or tall people, they are torture. For example, I am six feet tall, and when I sit on one of the classroom chairs, I feel like I am crammed into a kindergarten chair. They are attached to miniature desks, which are the size of slightly enlarged armrests. As I sit in class, I cannot fit my legs under the desk. I cannot fit my text-book and a notebook on the surface of the desk. Something always slips off and makes a noise that disrupts the class. <u>The child-friendly atmosphere even affects the instructors</u>. In some classrooms, the instructor has no desk and is forced to use one of the miniature student versions.

As students twist and fidget in their tiny desks, they face another problem. The temperature in the classrooms is anything but pleasant. I have been at the college for both fall and winter terms, and I have seen both extremes of temperature. In the early fall, the rooms were <u>sweltering</u>. The air conditioner feebly pumped hot air, which, of course, made the heat worse. Meanwhile, the sun beat through the glass windows because the blinds were broken. Winter did not bring any relief because in winter we froze. On some days, we wore our winter coats during class. <u>At different times during the semester</u>, two of my teachers reported the problems to the maintenance department, but nothing changed. I wish the maintenance manager understood how hard it is for students to concentrate when they are sweating or shivering.

Heat and cold create an uncomfortable learning place, but students create a shabby one. Student damage to the classrooms makes them seedy and ugly. <u>Graffiti covers the desks with childish messages, slogans, and drawings</u>. In addition, half the desks have gum stuck to their undersides. Some students even carve their initials and artwork into the plastic and wood of the desks and chairs. Others have stained the carpet with spilled coffee or soft drinks <u>and left crumbs and ground-in food behind</u>. Sometimes I have to be careful where I walk so that my shoes don't stick to the mess. It's depressing to think that my fellow students enjoy damaging the place where they come to learn.

National College is impressive outside, but no one seems to care about the <u>flaws</u> inside. The classrooms seem to be designed without a thought for adult learners who need to sit in adult-size seats and take lecture notes at adult-size desks. The maintenance department does not maintain a comfortable temperature so that students can learn, and students do not respect their learning environment. These problems surprise me. When I started college, I knew I would face many challenges, but I didn't expect them to include squeezing into the chairs, dressing for a blizzard or heat wave, and picking gum off my desk.

Remember to proofread your final copy to catch and correct any careless errors in spelling, punctuation, typing (or recopying), and format.

MyWritingLab™   Exercise 14   **Practice: Proofreading to Prepare the Final Version**

Following is an essay with the kinds of errors it is easy to overlook when you prepare the final version of an assignment. Correct the errors, writing above the lines. There are sixteen errors.

"Why Tina Upsets Me"

I have a cousin who is about my age. Tina is an attractive young women with an interesting job, a good education, and a loving family. Because the members of my family meet often for meal's and celebrations, I see Tina frequently. Everytime Tina and I meet, I leave the gathering frustrated and angry. Tina has ways of coping and negative attitudes that make me want to avoid her. Tina's most common state of mind is misery. On the outside, Tina appears to be surrounded by love, happiness, and success. her parent's are proud of her. She has a loving, thoughtful, faithful partner. Her years at collage enabled her to find a good job as a pediatric nurse. Yet Tina cannot focus on her advantages. Instead, she concentrates on the sorrows and disappointments in her life. If her parents praise her for getting a promotion at work, Tina wonders why they expect so much of her? Her boyfriend is a constant source of support in her life. Unfortunately, Tina worries whether he may be sticking with her only because he feels pity for her Even her beautiful and pampered pet, a Siamese cat that her boyfriend gave her, makes her sad. She cannot forget that the cat came from an animal shelter, and she dwells on the cat's previous life of misery.

Worrying is Tina's hobby. Each morning, she worries about traffic jams on the way to work. At work, Tina worries that her job may be in jeopardy if a day goes by without some praise from her supervisor. On the other hand, if her supervisor or the parents of one of Tina's patients note Tina's patience or skill, Tina prepares for a problem. She is sure that anyone who expresses appreciation is secretly feeling sorry for her. When she leaves work and head's for home, she worries about making dinner. She obsesses about what to make and whether she has time to cook it. At night, Tina lays awake, worrying about the problems of the next day.

Tina's toughest challenge is coping with her fear. In her life, fear is almost as natural as breathing. She have always been afraid of the dark. Driving at night, hearing a strange sound in the night, and loosing electric power in an evening thunderstorm, all terrify her. Tina rarely travels because she dreads a plane crash. Even through she is a nurse, she is nervous before every visit to her own doctor. Unfortunately, her training as a nurse has made her too conscious of many symptoms that could mean danger to her health, and she dwells on these possibilities.

I pity Tina, and I would like, to help her. Unfortunately, I do not have enough insight or patience to deal with her misery. perhaps I have one significant fear myself: I may be afraid that Tina's anxiety is contagious, and I do not want to be infected by her fears and miseries.

Lines of Detail: A Walk-Through Assignment

Write a five-paragraph essay about three things in your life you would like to discard. These things must be tangible objects like an old car, a bicycle, a uniform, and so forth. They cannot be people or personal traits (or habits) such as shyness or poor study habits. To write the essay, follow these steps:

Step 1: Freewrite a list of all the things you would like to get rid of in your life. To get started, think about what is in your room, car, purse, wallet, house, apartment, garage, basement, and so forth.

Step 2: Select the three items you would most like to toss out. Then prepare a list of questions you can ask yourself about these three items. You can ask questions such as the following:

> Why do I want to get rid of the following?
> Is it useless to me?
> Does it remind me of an unpleasant part of my life?
> Is it ugly? Broken? Out of style?
> Does it remind me of a habit I'd like to break?
> Can I get rid of it? If so, why don't I get rid of it? If not, why can't I get rid of it?

Answer the questions. The answers can lead you to details and topic sentences for your essay. For instance, you might hate the uniform you have to wear because it represents a job you would like to leave. However, you might not be able to get rid of the uniform because you need the job. Or maybe you'd like to toss out your cigarettes because you want to stop smoking.

Step 3: Survey your answers. Begin by listing the three things you would like to get rid of. Then list the details (the answers to your questions) beneath the item they relate to. For example, under the item "uniform," you could list the reason you hate it and the reason you cannot get rid of it.

Step 4: Once you have clustered the three items and the details related to each, you have the beginnings of a five-paragraph essay. Each item will be the focus of one of the body paragraphs, and its details will develop the paragraph.

Step 5: Focus all your clusters around one point. To find a focus, ask yourself whether the things you want to throw away have anything in common. If so, you can make that point in your thesis. For instance, you could write a thesis like one of these:

The things I would like to get rid of in my life are all related to a _____ part of my life.

My weaknesses are reflected in three items I would like to get rid of in my life.

If I could get rid of _____, _____, and _____, I would be _____

If the things you would like to be rid of are not related, then you can use a thesis like one of the following:

Three items I'd like to throw out reflect different aspects of my life.

I'd like to get rid of _____, _____, and _____ for three different reasons.

Step 6: Once you have a thesis and clustered details, draft your outline. Then revise your outline until it is unified, expresses the ideas in a clear order, and has enough supporting details.

Step 7: Write your draft and revise it extensively (you may have to work through *several* drafts).

Step 8: Edit your latest draft to be sure you have a smooth lead-in to your thesis, precise wording, effective transition between sentences and paragraphs, and a satisfying conclusion.

Step 9: Proofread a clean copy of your final version to catch and correct any careless errors in spelling, punctuation, format, or typing.

MyWritingLab™ ## Topics for Writing Your Own Essay

When you write on any of these topics, be sure to work through the stages of the writing process in preparing your essay.

1. Take any paragraph you wrote for this class and develop it into an essay of four or five paragraphs. If your instructor agrees, read the paragraph to a partner or group, and ask your listener(s) to suggest points inside the paragraph that can be developed into paragraphs of their own.

2. Narrow down one of the following topics, and then write an essay on it.

parents	relationships	cities
pleasures	success	digital age
fitting in	childhood	unemployment
heroes	types of classes	responsibilities

3. Write an essay on any one of the following topics:

My Three Favorite Places

Three People Who Changed My Life

Three Mistakes in Using the Internet

Three Songs I Will Always Remember

Three Memories That I Cherish

My Three Best/Worst Experiences Playing _____ (name a sport)

4. Write a four-paragraph essay about a dream you had. In your first body paragraph, describe the dream in detail. In your second body paragraph, explain what you think the dream means: Does it connect to one of your fears or hopes? Is it related to a current problem in your life? Does it suggest an answer to a problem? What does the dream tell you about yourself?

5. Study Photographs A, B, C, and D. Use them to think about this topic for an essay: *The three best part-time jobs for college students.*

A.

B.

C.

D.

Topics for Critical Thinking and Writing: Essay Options

MyWritingLab™

1. Examine your place in your family. Are you an only child? The oldest child? The middle child? Do you have brothers? Sisters? Both? Think about how your position in the family has affected your self-image and the roles you play within the family. Then write an essay about the way(s) you and other family members interact.

2. Find an advertisement (in print or online). It should be one that you find effective and attention-getting. Study it carefully. Then write an essay about what the advertisement depicts, what product it advertises, and what makes this advertisement powerful.

Topics for a Narrative Essay

MyWritingLab™

1. Write about a time when you were surprised. It can be a positive or negative experience.

2. Write about your first day of college.

3. Write about the time you lost something or someone.

4. Write about your first day in a new home, at a new job, or in a new town.

Topics for Critical Thinking and Writing: Narrative Essay

MyWritingLab™

1. Write about the most frustrating experience of your life. As you tell the story of this incident, analyze what parts of the incident annoyed, upset, or infuriated you, and why.

2. Tell the story of an incident in which you were involved and which you regret today. Be sure to discuss what particular parts of this incident and its consequences seem humiliating, foolish, reckless, or unkind today.

Topics for a Descriptive Essay

MyWritingLab™

1. Describe the best social event you ever attended. It can be a wedding, a dance, a holiday party, a graduation celebration, or any other special event. Describe the people at the event, the place where it happened, the food and refreshments served, and the activity (dance, music, awards ceremony) connected to the event. Be sure to include effective sensory details in your description.

2. Write an essay describing any of the following:

> your two favorite childhood toys
> your two (or three) favorite places to relax
> your two favorite subjects
> any scene at sunset

3. Go to a place you visit regularly, but on this visit, study the place carefully. You may choose to visit a supermarket, service station, coffee shop, convenience store, and so forth. As soon as you leave, take notes about what you noticed. Then write an essay describing that place.

MyWritingLab™ **Topic for Critical Thinking and Writing: Descriptive Essay**

1. Imagine your ideal home or apartment. In a five-paragraph essay, describe the three rooms that would be most important to you. As you describe each room's appearance and contents (such as furniture, accessories, equipment, and appliances), explain why the room itself also holds special significance for you.

2. Describe a place or situation that frightened you when you were young. The source of your fear could be a dark cellar (place) or a visit to a relative (situation). In your description, explain what the experience felt like to the child you were. Then describe how the place or situation affects you today.

MyWritingLab™ **Topics for an Illustration Essay**

1. Make a statement about yourself and illustrate it with examples. You can use a thesis like one of the following:

   When faced with a problem, I am a person who _____.

   Everyone who knows me thinks I am too _____.

   I have always felt satisfied with my _____.

   My greatest strength is _____.

   My greatest weakness is _____.

2. Write about a person who has been kind to you. In the body paragraphs, give examples of this person's kindness to you.

3. Here are some general statements that you may have heard:

   Teenage marriages never work out.

   Hard work will get you where you want to be.

   Children these days are too spoiled.

   Old people have an easy life; all they do is sit around all day.

   Pick one of these statements and, in an essay, give examples (from your own experience and observation) of the truth or inaccuracy of the statement.

MyWritingLab™ **Topics for Critical Thinking and Writing: Illustration**

1. Think about a famous person (a political or spiritual leader, celebrity, performer, athlete, and so forth) whom you believe is misunderstood. Illustrate the ways in which he or she is misunderstood. Include examples of incidents in which the person has been misjudged, and arrange your examples in emphatic order. You may want to do some research into this person's background to support your thesis.

2. Have you ever received criticism that you felt was unfair? In an essay, give examples of this criticism and then challenge the criticism by using specific examples illustrating why the criticism is not valid.

MyWritingLab™ **Topics for a Process Essay**

1. Think of some process you perform often. It could be something as simple as studying for a test or setting your DVR to record a program. Now, pretend that you must explain this process

to someone who has no idea how to perform it. Write an essay explaining the process to that person.

2. Observe someone perform a task you've never looked at closely. You can watch your boss close up the store, for instance, or watch a friend complete a science experiment. Then write an essay on how the person works through the steps of that process.

3. Interview a law enforcement officer, asking him or her what steps a person should take to protect a home from crime. Use the information you learned from the interview to write an essay on how to protect a home from crime.

Topics for Critical Thinking and Writing: Process

MyWritingLab™

1. Think of a routine in your life. It could be something as simple as getting ready for work or cleaning out the inside of your car. List the steps of this process and the necessary materials. Next, write about a quicker, easier way to complete the same process.

2. Imagine that you need a big favor from a friend or family member. This favor will involve either money, a written recommendation of your character for a prospective employer, or another important form of generosity or support. In an essay, describe the steps you would take to ask for, and receive, this favor.

Jumping In

Your conversations with good friends no doubt cover a wide spectrum of topics. As you voice your opinions, ask questions, and respond to others' comments, you become actively engaged. Similarly, writing-from-reading assignments may require that you engage in active, focused "conversations" with authors. Whenever you summarize key points, question content, or react strongly to a reading selection's premise, you sharpen your critical-thinking skills and become an active learner.

Learning Objectives

In this chapter, you will learn to:

1. Apply prereading strategies to assigned readings.
2. Prewrite to find the main idea for your summary.
3. Write an effective summary paragraph.
4. Apply critical thinking skills and form an opinion of an assigned reading.
5. Prewrite to find a topic for your reaction paragraph.
6. Write an effective reaction paragraph.
7. Apply critical thinking skills to agree or disagree about a point made in an assigned reading.
8. Write an effective agree or disagree paragraph.
9. Use the steps of reading and the stages of writing to compose an effective answer to an essay test.

WHAT IS WRITING FROM READING?

One way to find topics for writing is to draw from your ideas, memories, and observations. Another way is to write from reading you've done. You can react to something you've read; you can agree or disagree with it. You can summarize what you've read. Many college assignments ask you to write about an assigned reading such as an essay, a chapter in a textbook, or an article in a journal. This kind of writing requires an active, involved attitude toward your reading. Such reading is done in steps:

1. Preread.
2. Read.
3. Reread with a pen or pencil to identify main ideas and understand new vocabulary terms.

Attitude

Before you begin the first step of this reading process, you have to have a certain **attitude**. That attitude involves thinking of what you read as half of a conversation. The writer has opinions and ideas; he or she makes points just as you do when you write or speak. The writer supports his or her points with specific details. If the writer were speaking to you in conversation, you would respond to his or her opinions or ideas. You would agree, disagree, or question. You would jump into the conversation, linking or contrasting your ideas with those of the other speaker.

The right attitude toward reading demands that you read the same way you converse—you become *involved*. By doing so, you talk back as you read, and later, you may react in your own writing. Reacting as you read will keep you focused on what you are reading. If you are focused, you will remember more of what you read. With an active, involved attitude, you can begin the step of prereading.

Prereading

Before you actually read an assigned essay, a chapter in a textbook, or an article in a journal, magazine, or newspaper, be ready to answer the questions in the following checklist:

1 Apply prereading strategies to assigned readings.

Checklist for Prereading

✓ What is the title of the reading?

✓ What can you determine about the reading from the title?

✓ Are there any subheadings? Do they give hints about the reading?

✓ Is there any introductory material about the reading or its author? What can you learn about the reading?

✓ Are there any photographs, illustrations, charts, graphs, or other visuals? Do they give you any hints about the reading?

✓ Are any words or phrases in bold, italic, or underlined? How do these words or phrases connect to the title or subheadings?

Why Preread?

Prereading takes very little time, but it helps you immensely. Some students believe it's a waste of time to scan an assignment; they think they should just jump right in and get the reading over with. However, spending just a few minutes on preliminaries can save hours later. Most importantly, prereading helps you become a **focused reader**.

If you scan the length of an assignment, you can pace yourself. And if you know how long a reading is, you can alert yourself to its plan. For example, a short reading has to come to its point soon. A longer essay may take more time to develop its point and may use more details and examples.

Subheadings, charts, graphs, and boxed or other highlighted materials are important enough that the author wants to emphasize them. Looking over that material before you read gives you an overview of the important points the reading will contain.

Introductory material or introductory questions also help you know what to look for as you read. Background on the author or on the subject may hint at ideas that will emerge in the reading. Sometimes the title of the reading will give you the main idea.

You should preread so that you can start reading the entire assignment with as much knowledge about the writer and the subject as you can find during this preliminary step. When you then read the entire assignment, you will be **reading actively** for more knowledge.

Forming Questions Before You Read

If you want to read with a focus, it helps to ask questions before you read. Form questions by using the information you gained from prereading.

Start by noting the title and turning it into a question. If the title of your assigned reading is, "Causes of the Civil War," ask, "What were the causes of the Civil War?"

You can turn subheadings into questions. If you are reading an article about self-esteem, and one subheading is "Influence of Parents," you can ask, "How do parents influence a person's self-esteem?"

You can also form questions from graphics and illustrations. If a chapter in your economics textbook includes a photograph of Wall Street, you can ask, "What is Wall Street?" or "What is Wall Street's role in economics?" or "What happens on Wall Street?"

You can list these questions, but it's not necessary. Just forming questions and keeping them in the back of your mind helps you read actively and stay focused.

An Example of the Prereading Step

Take a look at the article that follows. Don't read it; *preread* it.

Part-Time Job May Do Teenagers More Harm Than Good

Gary Klott

Gary Klott served as a personal finance consultant for the National Newspaper Syndicate. In this article, he explores the effects of part-time jobs on high school students.

Words You May Need to Know (Corresponding paragraph numbers are in parentheses.)

extracurricular activities (2): activities outside the regular academic course, like clubs and sports
assume (3): suppose, take for granted

menial (4): of a low level, degrading
instant gratification (4): immediate satisfaction

G iven today's high cost of auto insurance, dating, video games, music   **1**
CDs and designer clothing, it shouldn't come as any surprise that a
growing number of high school students are taking part-time jobs
during the school year. Most parents have done little to discourage their
children from working after school. In fact, many parents figure that part-
time jobs can help teach their children about responsibility and the value of
a dollar and better prepare them for life in the adult workaday world. But
there is growing evidence to suggest that parents ought to sharply restrict
the number of hours their children work during the school year.

Academic studies over the past decade have found that high school stu-   **2**
dents who work—particularly those who work long hours during the school
week—tend to do less well in school, miss out on the benefits of extracurricular activities and have more behavioral problems. Most recently, a study
of 12th-graders by Linda P. Worley, a high school counselor in Marietta,
Georgia, indicated that grades suffer when students work more than ten
hours during the school week. The highest grade-point averages were found
for students who worked only on weekends, 3.07, and for those who baby-sat
or did yard work, 3.13. Students who didn't work at all had an average GPA
of 3.02, while those who worked up to ten hours a week earned an average
GPA of 2.95. Students working ten to twenty hours a week averaged 2.77,
twenty to thirty hours per week 2.53 and thirty or more hours 2.10.

Even if a student manages to maintain good grades, parents shouldn't   **3**
automatically assume that long work hours aren't harming their child's
education. Several studies found that many students kept up their grades
by choosing easier courses. A 1993 study of 1,800 high-school sophomores
by researchers at Temple University and Stanford University found that students who worked more than twenty hours a week spent less time on homework, cut class more often, cheated more on tests and assignments, had less
interest in formal education, had a higher rate of drug and alcohol use and
had lower self-esteem.

Researchers also note that some of the perceived benefits of after-   **4**
school jobs are often overrated. For example, many of the jobs high school
students take on are menial and provide few skills that will prove useful after
high school. And many students learn the wrong lessons about the value of a
dollar since they tend to spend all of their job earnings on cars, clothes, and
other purchases that provide instant gratification without saving a penny.

By prereading the article, you might notice the following:

- The title of the article is "Part-Time Job May Do Teenagers More
  Harm Than Good."
- The article is short and can be read in one sitting.
- The author writes about money, and he writes for newspapers.
- The introductory material says the article is about teenagers with
  part-time jobs.
- There are several vocabulary words you may need to know.

You might begin reading the article with these questions in mind:

- Why are part-time jobs harmful to teens?
- What are the harmful effects?
- Why is a writer who writes about money arguing that it is bad for teens to make money?
- Should teens have full-time jobs instead of part-time ones?

Reading

The first time you read, try to *get a sense of the whole piece* you are reading. Reading with questions in mind can help you do this. If you find that you are confused by a certain part of the reading selection, go back and reread that part. If you do not know the meaning of a word, check the vocabulary list to see if the word is defined for you. If it isn't defined, try to figure out the meaning from the way the word is used in the sentence.

If you find that you have to read more slowly than usual, don't worry. People vary their reading speed according to what they read and why they are reading it. If you are reading for entertainment, for example, you can read quickly; if you are reading a chapter in a textbook, you must read more slowly. The more complicated the reading selection, the more slowly and carefully you should read it.

An Example of the Reading Step

Now read "Part-Time Job May Do Teenagers More Harm Than Good." When you've completed your first reading, you will probably have some answers to the prereading questions that you formed.

Answers to Prereading Questions:

Part-time jobs can hurt teens' grades and other areas of their lives such as their behavior and attitudes.
The writer, who writes about money, says part-time jobs give students bad spending habits.
Full-time work would be worse than part-time work.

Rereading with Pen or Pencil

The second reading is the crucial one. At this point, you begin to think on paper as you read. In this step, you make notes or write about what you read. Some students are reluctant to do this because they are not sure what to note or write. *Think of making these notes as a way of learning, thinking, reviewing, and reacting.* Reading with a pen or pencil in your hand keeps you alert. With that pen or pencil, you can do the following:

- mark the main point of the reading
- mark other points
- define words you don't know
- question parts of the reading that seem confusing
- evaluate the writer's ideas
- react to the writer's opinions or examples
- add ideas, opinions, or examples of your own

There is no single system for marking or writing as you read. Some readers like to underline the main idea with two lines and to underline other important ideas with one line. Some students like to put an asterisk (a star) next to important ideas, while others like to circle key words.

Some people use the margins to write comments like "I agree!" or "Not true!" or "That's happened to me." Sometimes readers put questions in the margin; sometimes they summarize a point in the margin, next to its location in the essay. Some people list important points in the white space above the reading; others use the space at the end of the reading.

Every reader who writes as he or she reads has a personal system; what these systems share is an attitude. *If you write as you read, you concentrate on the reading selection, get to know the writer's ideas, and develop ideas of your own.*

As you reread and write notes, don't worry too much about noticing the "right" ideas. Instead, think of rereading as the time to jump into a *conversation* with the writer.

An Example of Rereading with Pen or Pencil

For "Part-Time Job May Do Teenagers More Harm Than Good," your marked article might look like the following:

Part-Time Job May Do Teenagers More Harm Than Good

Gary Klott

Given today's high cost of auto insurance, dating, video games, music CDs and designer clothing, it shouldn't come as any surprise that a growing number of high school students are taking part-time jobs during the school year. Most parents have done little to discourage their children from working after school. In fact, many parents figure that part-time jobs can help teach their children about responsibility and the value of a dollar and better prepare them for life in the adult workaday world. But there is growing evidence to suggest that parents ought to sharply restrict the number of hours their children work during the school year.

I agree!

What parents believe

What parents should do

Academic studies over the past decade have found that high school students who work—particularly those who work long hours during the school week—tend to do less well in school, miss out on the benefits of extracurricular activities and have more behavioral problems. Most recently, a study of 12th-graders by Linda P. Worley, a high school counselor in Marietta, Georgia, indicated that grades suffer when students work more than ten hours during the school week. The highest grade-point averages were found for students who worked only on weekends, 3.07, and for those who baby-sat or did yard work, 3.13. Students who didn't work at all had an average GPA of 3.02, while those who worked up to ten hours a week earned an average GPA of 2.95. Students working ten to twenty hours a week averaged 2.77, twenty to thirty hours per week 2.53 and thirty or more hours 2.10.

*

example
The more you work, the lower the grades

Even if a student manages to maintain good grades, parents shouldn't automatically assume that long work hours aren't harming their child's education. Several studies found that many students kept up their grades by choosing easier courses. A 1993 study of 1,800 high-school sophomores by researchers at Temple University and Stanford University found that *other harm to education*

self-respect, pride

students who worked more than twenty hours a week spent <u>less time on homework, cut class</u> more often, <u>cheated</u> more on tests and assignments, had <u>less interest</u> in formal education, <u>had a higher rate of drug and alcohol use</u> and had lower (self-esteem.)

 Researchers also note that <u>some of the perceived benefits of after-school jobs are often overrated.</u> For example, many of the jobs high school students take on are menial and provide few skills that will prove useful after high school. <u>And many students learn the wrong lessons about the value of a dollar since they tend to spend all of their job earnings on cars, clothes, and other purchases that provide instant gratification without saving a penny.</u>

What the Notes Mean

In the sample above, much of the underlining indicates sentences or phrases that seem important. The words in the margin are often summaries of what is underlined. In the first paragraph, for example, the words "what parents believe" and "what parents should do" are like subtitles in the margin.

 An asterisk in the margin signals an important idea. When "example" is written in the margin, it notes that a point is being supported by a specific example. Sometimes, what is in the margin is the reader's reaction, like "I agree!" One item in the margin is a definition. The word "self-esteem" is circled and defined in the margin as "self-respect, pride."

 The marked-up article is a flexible tool. You can go back and mark it further. You may change your mind about your notes and comments and find other, better, or more important points in the article.

 You write as you read to involve yourself in the reading process. Marking what you read can help you in other ways, too. If you are to be tested on the reading selection or are asked to discuss it, you can scan your markings and notations at a later time for a quick review.

MyWritingLab™   **Exercise 1**   **Practice: Reading and Making Notes for a Selection**

Following is a paragraph from "Part-Time Job May Do Teenagers More Harm Than Good." First, read it. Then reread it and make notes on the following:

 1. Underline the first eight words of the most specific example in the paragraph.

 2. Circle the phrase "formal education" and define it in the margin.

 3. At the end of the paragraph, summarize its main point.

Paragraph from "Part-Time Job May Do Teenagers More Harm Than Good"

 Even if a student manages to maintain good grades, parents shouldn't automatically assume that long work hours aren't harming their child's education. Several studies found that many students kept up their grades by choosing easier courses. A 1993 study of 1,800 high-school sophomores and juniors by researchers at Temple University and Stanford University found that students who worked more than twenty hours a week spent less time on homework, cut class more often, cheated more on tests and assignments, had less interest in formal education, had a higher rate of drug and alcohol use and had lower self-esteem.

Main point of the paragraph (in your own words): _____

_____

_____

WRITING A SUMMARY OF A READING

One way to write about a reading is to write a **summary**. A summary of a reading tells the important ideas in brief form and in your own words. It includes (1) the writer's main idea, (2) the ideas used to explain the main idea, and (3) some examples or details. When you write a summary, you should include only the author's ideas and key details.

| PREWRITING | **MARKING A LIST OF IDEAS: SUMMARY**

When you preread, read, and make notes on the reading selection, you have already begun the prewriting stage for a summary. You can think further, on paper, *by listing the points* (words, phrases, sentences) you've already marked on the reading selection.

To find the main idea for your summary and the ideas and examples connected to the main idea, you can *mark related ideas* on your list. For example, the list below was made from "Part-Time Job May Do Teenagers More Harm Than Good." Three symbols are used to mark the following:

S   the effects of part-time jobs on **schoolwork**

O   **other** effects of part-time jobs

P   what **parents** think about part-time jobs

Some items on the list don't have a mark because they do not relate to any of the categories.

❷ Prewrite to find the main idea for your summary.

A Marked List of Ideas for a Summary of "Part-Time Job May Do Teenagers More Harm Than Good"

high cost of car insurance, dating, video games, music CDs, and designer clothing
P   parents think part-time jobs teach responsibility, money, and job skills
parents should restrict teens' work hours
S   working students do less well in school
S   study of 12th-graders by Linda P. Worley said grades suffer if students work more than ten hours in school week
S   students who work long hours choose easier courses
S   they spend less time on homework
S   they cut class more
S   they cheat
S   they are less interested in school
O   they use drugs and alcohol more
O   they have lower self-esteem
some perceived benefits are overrated
O   students spend money foolishly

The marked list could then be reorganized, like this:

the effects of part-time jobs on schoolwork

- working students do less well in school
- study of 12th-graders by Linda P. Worley said grades suffer if students work more than ten hours in the school week
- students who work long hours choose easier classes
- they spend less time on homework
- they cut class more
- they cheat
- they are less interested in school

other effects of part-time jobs

- if they work over twenty hours, they use drugs and alcohol more
- they have lower self-esteem
- working students spend money foolishly

what many parents think about part-time jobs

- parents think part-time jobs teach responsibility and money and job skills

Selecting a Main Idea

The next step in the process is to select the idea you think is the writer's main point. If you look again at the list of ideas, you see one category that has only one item: what many parents think about part-time jobs. In this category, the only item is that parents think part-time jobs teach responsibility and money and job skills.

Is this item the main idea of the article? If it is, then all of the other ideas support it. However, the other ideas contradict this point.

It is not the main idea, but it *is* connected to the main idea. The author is saying that parents *think* part-time jobs are good for high school students, but they may not be, especially if students work long hours.

You can write a simpler version of this main idea:

> Parents should know that working long hours at part-time jobs is not good for teens.

Once you have a main idea, check it to see if it fits with the other ideas in your organized list. *Do the ideas in the list connect to the main idea?* Yes. The ideas about the effects of jobs on schoolwork show the negative impact of part-time work, and so do the ideas about the other effects. Even the part about what some parents think can be used to contrast what jobs *really* do to teens.

Now that you have a main point that fits an organized list, you can move to the *planning* stage of a summary.

MyWritingLab™   Exercise 2   **Practice: Marking a List and Finding the Main Idea for a Summary**

Following is a list of ideas from an article called "Binge Nights: The Emergency on Campus" by Michael Winerip. It tells the true story of Ryan Dabbieri, a senior at the University of Virginia, who nearly died from binge drinking at a tailgating party before a football game. Read the list, and then mark each item with one of these symbols:

    L   **lessons learned** from the experience

    P   **personal background** on the binge drinker

    S   **steps** leading to the emergency

    E   the life-and-death **emergency**

After you've marked all the ideas, survey them and think of one main idea. Try to focus on a point that connects to what Ryan Dabbieri, the binge drinker, learned.

_____ Ryan Dabbieri was a 22-year-old senior at the University of Virginia.

_____ Ryan did not think he was a binge drinker.

_____ About once a week, he would drink five to seven drinks in two hours.

_____ Before one big football game, he drank five or six very big shots of bourbon in fifteen minutes at a party.

_____ At the stadium, he straightened up to get by security.

_____ Inside, he passed out.

_____ His friends carried him outside.

_____ They couldn't revive him.

_____ In the emergency room, he stopped breathing for four minutes.

_____ His friends were terrified.

_____ The doctors did a scan for brain damage.

_____ Ryan's father flew in from Atlanta.

_____ Ryan awoke the next day in intensive care.

_____ Ryan says he won't drink again.

_____ He says he is lucky to be alive.

main idea: _____

_____

_____

PLANNING   SUMMARY

Following is an **outline** for a summary of "Part-Time Job May Do Teenagers More Harm Than Good." As you read it, you'll notice that the main idea of the prewriting stage has become the topic sentence of the outline, and most of the other ideas have become details.

Outline for a Summary of "Part-Time Job May Do Teenagers More Harm Than Good"

topic sentence	Parents should know that working long hours at part-time jobs is not good for teens.
details	Working students do less well in school.
	A study of 12th-graders by Linda P. Worley showed this.
effects on schoolwork	It showed that grades suffer if students worked more than ten hours in the school week.
	Students who work long hours choose easier classes.
	They spend less time on homework.
	They cut class more.
	They are less interested in school.
other effects	They use drugs and alcohol more.
	They have lower self-esteem.
	They spend money foolishly.

In the outline, the part about what many parents think about part-time jobs has been left out. Since it was an idea that contrasted with the topic sentence, it didn't seem to fit. That kind of selecting is what you do in the planning stage of writing a summary. In the drafting and revising stage, you may change your mind and decide to use the idea later.

DRAFTING AND REVISING   ATTRIBUTING IDEAS IN A SUMMARY

③ Write an effective summary paragraph.

The **first draft** of your summary paragraph is your first try at *combining* all the material into one paragraph. The draft is much like the draft of any other paragraph, with one exception: *When you summarize another person's ideas, be sure to say whose ideas you are writing.* That is, **attribute** the ideas to the writer. Let the reader of your paragraph know the following:

- The author of the selection you are summarizing
- The title of the selection you are summarizing

You may want to *attribute ideas by giving your summary paragraph a title*, such as:

A Summary of Gary Klott's "Part-Time Job May Do Teenagers More Harm Than Good" (Note that the title of Klott's article is in quotation marks.)

Here is a sample draft that still needs some work:

Draft of a Summary of "Part-Time Job May Do Teenagers More Harm Than Good"

(Editing and proofreading are still necessary.)

"Part-Time Job May Do Teenagers More Harm Than Good" by Gary Klott says that parents should know that working long hours at part-time jobs is not good for teens. Working students do less well in school. A study of 12th-graders by Linda P. Worley showed that grades suffer if students work more than ten hours during the school week. Students who work long hours choose easier courses, spend less time on homework, cut class more often, and cheat. They are less interested in school. They use drugs and alcohol more and have lower self-esteem. They spend money foolishly.

After reviewing the draft and reading it aloud, you may have noticed these problems:

- The draft is very choppy; it needs transitions.
- In some places, the word choice could be better.
- The beginning of the paragraph could use an introduction.
- Linda P. Worley completed a study about grades and working students, but the additional information about effects on schoolwork came from other studies. This difference should be made clear.
- The paragraph ends abruptly.

EDITING AND PROOFREADING SUMMARY

After you are satisfied with the latest revised draft of your paragraph, you are ready to edit. **Editing** often involves making improvements or correcting errors you may have overlooked during the revision process. Examining sentence patterns and length, checking appropriate word choice, and ensuring that specific details are linked smoothly are all natural refinements during editing. **Proofreading** entails reading your final version to spot and correct any careless mistakes including formatting errors, missing words or punctuation, and even simple typos. Through careful proofreading when you are alert and rested, you can add finishing touches to make your work the best it can be.

Look carefully at the final version of the summary. Notice how the idea about what parents think has been added to an introduction and how transitions and word choice have improved the summary. You can assume that this version is the result of *several* drafts as well as careful editing and proofreading. Also notice how one phrase, "Other studies indicate that," clarifies the ideas in the summary and how an added conclusion clinches the paragraph.

Final Version of a Summary of "Part-Time Job May Do Teenagers More Harm Than Good"

(Changes from the draft are underlined.)

Many parents think part-time jobs teach their children responsibility and money and job skills, but they may be wrong. An article called "Part-Time Job Do Teenagers More Harm Than Good" by Gary Klott says that parents should know that working long hours at part-time jobs is not good for teens. First of all, working students do less well in school. A study of 12th-graders by Linda P. Worley showed that grades suffer if students work more than ten hours during the school week. Other studies indicate that students who work long hours choose easier courses, spend less time on their homework, and are likely to cheat and cut classes. In addition, such students are less interested in school. Their problems extend outside of school, too, where they use drugs and alcohol more than other students and have lower self-esteem. Finally, they do not learn financial responsibility from their jobs since they spend money foolishly. Parents must consider all these drawbacks before they allow their teens to work long hours.

Writing summaries is good writing practice, and it also helps you develop your reading skills. Even if your instructor does not require you to turn in a polished summary of an assigned reading, you may find it helpful to summarize what you have read. In many classes, midterms or other exams cover many assigned readings. If you write a short summary of each reading as it is assigned, you will have a helpful collection of focused, organized material to review.

④ Apply critical thinking skills and form an opinion of an assigned reading.

THE ROLE OF CRITICAL THINKING AS YOU READ

When you start forming opinions based on what you observe, hear, read, or discuss, you are applying **critical thinking skills**. Thinking critically as you read involves examining an issue from different sides as well as evaluating the validity, or truthfulness, of the information presented. Applying the critical thinking process to evaluate what you are reading requires that you ask yourself the following questions:

- What is the writer's main idea or proposal?
- Is the main idea supported by facts? Personal experience? Expert opinion(s)?
- Does the writer reach logical conclusions based on his or her evidence?

Sharpening critical thinking skills by using this type of questioning as you read can enable you to form reasonable opinions and express them confidently. Reading critically can help you succeed in all of your college classes, and it will be especially beneficial in your future composition classes.

WRITING A REACTION TO A READING SELECTION

A summary is one kind of writing you can do after reading, but there are other kinds. Your instructor might ask you to **react** by writing about some idea you got from your reading. If you read "Part-Time Job May Do Teenagers More Harm Than Good," your instructor might have asked you to react by writing about this topic:

> Gary Klott says that parents may have the wrong idea about their children's jobs. Write about another part of teen life that parents may not understand.

You may begin to gather ideas by freewriting.

⑤ Prewrite to find a topic for your reaction paragraph.

PREWRITING   **REACTION TO A READING: FREEWRITING**

You can **freewrite** in a **reading journal**, if you wish. This kind of journal is a special journal in which you write about selections that you've read. To freewrite, you can

- write key points made by the author,
- write about whatever you remember from the reading selection,
- write down any of the author's ideas that you think you might want to write about someday,
- list questions raised by what you've read, and
- connect the reading selection to other things you've read, heard, or experienced.

A freewriting that reacts to "Part-Time Job May Do Teenagers More Harm Than Good" might look like this:

Freewriting for a Reaction to a Reading

"Part-Time Job May Do Teenagers More Harm Than Good"—Gary Klott

Jobs can be bad for teens. Author says parents should stop teens from working too many hours. But how? Most parents are afraid of their teens. Or they don't want to interfere. They figure teens want to be independent. I know I wanted to be independent when I was in high school. Did I? I'm not so sure. I think I wanted some attention from my folks. Maybe parents don't know this. Why didn't I say anything?

Selecting a Topic, Listing, and Developing Ideas

Once you have your freewriting, you can survey it for a **topic**. You might survey the freewriting above and decide you can write about how parents don't know that their teens want attention. To gather ideas, you begin a list:

teens want attention and parents don't know

sometimes teens look independent

they act smart

no real self-confidence

friends aren't enough

I wanted my father's approval

teens can't say what they need

to get attention, they break rules

I would have liked some praise

Next, you organize, expand, and develop this list until you have a main point, a topic sentence, and a list of details. You decide on this topic sentence:

Some parents are unaware that their teenage children need attention.

With a topic sentence and a list of details, you are ready to begin the planning stage of writing.

PLANNING   **REACTION TO A READING**

Review the following sample outline based on the list of details generated during the prewriting stage. As you read it, notice that the topic sentence and ideas are the student's opinions, not those of the article's author. The student is reacting, in writing, to the article. Also notice that the outline builds on the prewriting list of ideas and organizes them in a clear order.

Outline of a Reaction to a Reading

topic sentence	Some parents are unaware that their teenage children need attention.
details	Teens act independent.
	They act smart.
what parents see	They break rules.
	Parents think that rule-breaking means teens want to be left alone.
	Teens do it to get attention.
what teens want	Teens can't say what they need.
	They have no real self-confidence.
	Their friends aren't enough.
personal example	I wanted my father's approval.
	I would have liked some praise.

6 Write an effective reaction paragraph.

DRAFTING AND REVISING REACTION TO A READING

If your outline provides you with several good ideas to develop, you are on your way to writing a thoughtful reaction paragraph. If you are writing a reaction paragraph based on the points in the outline, your initial draft would probably look much like the following:

Draft of a Reaction to a Reading

(Editing and proofreading are still necessary.)

Some parents are unaware that their teenage children need attention. Teens act independent and smart. They break their parents' rules, so their parents think teenage rule-breaking is a sign the children want to be left alone. Teens break rules to get attention. They can't say what they need; therefore, they act out their needs. Teens have no real self-confidence. Friends aren't enough. I wanted my father's approval. I would have liked some praise.

EDITING AND PROOFREADING REACTION TO A READING

When you reviewed the draft, you probably noticed that it needed improvement in several places. Here is a list of problems the writer resolved through careful editing:

- The word choice could be better.
- There is too much repetition of words like *need*, *needs*, *their parents*, and *children*.
- The paragraph needs many transitions.
- Since the ideas are reactions related to a point by Gary Klott, he needs to be mentioned.
- The ending is a little abrupt.

Following is the final version of the paragraph, and you can assume that the writer worked on *several* drafts, edited thoroughly, and proofread carefully to get to this point:

Final Version of a Reaction to a Reading

(Changes from the draft are underlined.)

<u>Gary Klott says that many parents do not understand the impact of their teenagers' part-time jobs. There is another part of teen life that parents may not understand</u>. Some parents are unaware that their teenage children need attention. Teens act independent and <u>self-assured</u>. They will break their parents' rules, so their parents think the rule-breaking is a sign the children want to be left alone. However, <u>adolescents</u> break rules to get attention. They can't say what they <u>crave;</u> therefore, they act out their needs. Teens have no real self-confidence. <u>While friends help adolescents develop self-confidence</u>, friends aren't enough. <u>My own experience is a good example of what adolescents desire</u>. I wanted my father's approval. I would have liked some praise, <u>but I couldn't ask for what I needed. My father was a parent who was unaware</u>.

WRITING ABOUT AGREEMENT OR DISAGREEMENT

PREWRITING **AGREE OR DISAGREE PARAGRAPH**

7 Apply critical thinking skills to agree or disagree about a point made in an assigned reading.

Another way to write about a reading selection is to find a point in it and *agree or disagree with that point.* To begin writing about agreement or disagreement, you can review the selection and jot down any statements that provoke a strong reaction in you. You are looking for statements with which you can agree or disagree. If you reviewed "Part-Time Job May Do Teenagers More Harm Than Good," you might list these statements as points of agreement or disagreement:

Points of Agreement or Disagreement from a Reading

Grades suffer when students work more than ten hours during the school week.—agree

High school students who work many hours "have less interest in formal education"—disagree

---

Then you might *pick one of the statements and react to it in writing.* If you disagreed with the statement that high school students who work many hours "have less interest in formal education," you might begin by brainstorming.

Brainstorming for an Agree or Disagree Paragraph

Question: **Why do you disagree that high school students who work long hours "have less interest in formal education"?**

Answer: I worked long hours. I was interested in getting a <u>good</u> education.

Question: **If you were interested in school, why were you so focused on your job?**

Answer: To make money.

Question: **Then wasn't money more important than school?**

Answer: No. I was working to make money to pay for college. Working was the only way I could afford college.

Question: **Do you think it <u>looked</u> as if you didn't care about education?**

Answer: Yes, sure.

Question: **Why?**

Answer: I used to be so tired from working I would fall asleep in class.

Once you have some ideas from brainstorming, you can list them, group them, and add to them by more brainstorming. Your topic sentence can be a way of stating your disagreement with the original point, like this:

> Although Gary Klott says that high school students who work long hours tend to lose interest in school, my experience shows the opposite.

With a topic sentence and details, you can work on the planning stage of your paragraph.

PLANNING **AGREE OR DISAGREE PARAGRAPH**

An outline might look like the following. Notice that the topic sentence is the student's personal opinion and that the details stem from his experience.

Outline for an Agree or Disagree Paragraph

topic sentence — Although Gary Klott says that high school students who work long hours may lose interest in school, my experience shows the opposite.

details — While I was in high school, I worked long hours.
I was very interested in getting a good education.

my experience — I wanted to graduate from college.
To save money for college, I was working long hours.
Working was the only way I could pay for college.

why I appeared uninterested — I probably looked as if I didn't care about school.
I fell asleep in class.
I was tired from working.

---

8 Write an effective agree or disagree paragraph.

DRAFTING AND REVISING **AGREE OR DISAGREE PARAGRAPH**

Once you are satisfied with your outline, you can develop an initial rough draft of your agree or disagree paragraph. Here is a sample draft based on the outline you just reviewed:

Draft of an Agree or Disagree Paragraph

(Editing and proofreading are still necessary.)

Although Gary Klott says that high school students who work long hours lose interest in school, my experience shows the opposite. When I was in high school, I worked long hours. I endured my job and even increased my hours because I was interested in getting a good education. I wanted to graduate from college. I was working long hours to save money for college. Working was the only way I could pay tuition. I know that, to my teachers, I probably looked like I didn't care about school. I was tired from working. I fell asleep in class.

EDITING AND PROOFREADING **AGREE OR DISAGREE PARAGRAPH**

After reading the preceding draft, you probably noticed that details could be more precise and that sentences could be combined. During the editing and proofreading stage, the writer realized the following:

- The paragraph could use more specific details.
- Some sentences could be combined.
- It needs a last sentence, reinforcing the point that students who work long hours may be very interested in school.

As you read the following final version, notice how the changes improve both the content and style of the paragraph.

Final Version of an Agree or Disagree Paragraph

(Changes from the draft are underlined.)

     Although Gary Klott says that high school students who work long hours lose interest in school, my experience shows the opposite. When I was in high school, I worked long hours. <u>Sometimes I worked twenty-five hours a week at a fast-food restaurant</u>. I endured my job and even increased my hours because I was interested in getting a good education. I wanted to graduate from college. <u>I was working long hours to save money for college since working was the only way I could pay tuition</u>. I know that, to my teachers, I probably looked like I didn't care about school. I was so tired from working that <u>I came to school in a daze</u>. I fell asleep in class. <u>But my long, hard hours at work made me determined to change my life through education</u>.

WRITING FOR AN ESSAY TEST

Another kind of writing from reading involves the essay test. Most essay questions require you to write about an assigned reading. Usually, an essay test requires you to write from memory, not from an open book or notes. Such writing can be stressful, but breaking the task into steps can eliminate much of the stress.

Before the Test: The Steps of Reading

If you work through the steps of reading days before the test, you are halfway to your goal. Prereading helps to keep you focused, and your first reading gives you a sense of the whole selection. The third step, rereading with a pen or pencil, can be particularly helpful when you are preparing for a test. Most essay questions will ask you either to summarize or react to a reading selection. In either case, you must be familiar with the reading's main idea, supporting ideas, examples, and details. If you note these by marking the selection, you are teaching yourself about the main point, supporting ideas, and structure of the reading selection.

     Shortly before the test, review the marked reading assignment. Your notes will help you focus on the main point and the supporting ideas.

9 Use the steps of reading and the stages of writing to compose an effective answer to an essay test.

During the Test: The Stages of Writing

Answering an essay test question may seem very different from writing at home. After all, on a test, you must rely on your memory and write within a time limit, and these restrictions can make you feel anxious. However, by following the stages of the writing process, you can meet that challenge calmly and confidently.

PREWRITING   **ESSAY TEST**

Before you begin to write, think about these questions: Is the instructor asking for a summary of a reading selection? Or is he or she asking you to react to a specific idea with examples or by agreeing or disagreeing? For example, in an essay question about the article, "Part-Time Job May Do Teenagers More Harm Than Good," by Gary Klott, you might be asked to (1) explain why Klott thinks a part-time job can be bad for a teenager (a summary), (2) explain what Klott means when he says that students who work long hours may keep their grades up but still miss out on the best education (a reaction, in which you develop and explain one part of the reading), or (3) agree or disagree that after-school jobs teach the wrong lesson about the value of money (a reaction, so you have to be aware of what Klott said on this point).

Once you have thought about the question, list or freewrite your first ideas. At this time, do not worry about how "right" or "wrong" your writing is; just write your first thoughts.

PLANNING ESSAY TEST

Your writing will be clear if you follow a plan. Remember that the audience for this writing is your instructor and that he or she will be evaluating how well you stick to the subject, make a point, and support it. Your plan for making a point about the subject and supporting it can be written in a brief outline.

First, reread the question. Next, survey your list or freewriting. Does it contain a main point that answers the question? Does it contain supporting ideas and details?

Next, write a main point and then list supporting ideas and details under the main point. Your main point will be the topic sentence of your answer. If you need more support, try brainstorming.

DRAFTING AND REVISING ESSAY TEST

Write your point and supporting ideas in paragraph form. Be as specific as possible as you develop your details.

EDITING AND PROOFREADING ESSAY TEST

You will probably not have time for significant refinements during an in-class essay test, but you can edit for a few minutes to make improvements in word choice and transitions that link sentences. Also, save a couple of minutes for proofreading just to catch any missing words, punctuation lapses, or careless spelling errors.

Organize Your Time

Some students skip important stages of the writing process. Without thinking or planning, they immediately begin writing their answer to an essay question. Sometimes they find themselves stuck in the middle of a paragraph, panicked because they have no more ideas. At other times, they find themselves writing in a circle, repeating the same point over and over. Occasionally, they even forget to include a main idea.

You can avoid these hazards by spending time on each of the stages. Planning is as important as writing. For example, if you have half an hour to write an essay, you can divide your time as follows:

    5 minutes thinking, freewriting, listing
    10 minutes planning, outlining
    10 minutes drafting
    5 minutes editing and proofreading

Writing from Reading: A Summary of Options

Reading can give you many opportunities for your own writing. You can summarize a writer's work, use it as a springboard for your own related writing, or agree or disagree with it. However you decide to write from reading, you must still work through the same writing process. Following the stages of prewriting, planning, drafting and revising, and editing and proofreading will help you develop your work into an effective paragraph.

Lines of Detail: A Walk-Through Assignment

Here are three ideas from "Part-Time Job May Do Teenagers More Harm Than Good":

  a. Students who work long hours miss out on extracurricular activities at school.

  b. Parents should prevent their teenage children from working long hours.

  c. Teens who work spend their money foolishly.

Pick *one* of these ideas with which you agree or disagree. Write a paragraph explaining why you agree or disagree. To write your paragraph, follow these steps:

Step 1: Begin by listing at least three reasons or examples why you agree or disagree. Make your reasons or examples as specific as you can, using your experiences or the experiences of friends and family.

Step 2: Read your list to a partner or group. With the help of your listener(s), add reasons, examples, and details.

Step 3: Once you have enough ideas, transform the statement you agreed or disagreed with into a topic sentence.

Step 4: Write an outline by listing your reasons, examples, and details below the topic sentence. Check that your list is in a clear and logical order.

Step 5: Write a first draft of your paragraph and revise it thoroughly. Be sure to check that you have attributed Gary Klott's statement, you have sufficient details, and that your points are logical and clearly stated. (Remember that several drafts may be necessary before you are satisfied with your content.)

Step 6: Edit your latest draft to ensure effective sentence combining and variation, precise word choice, and appropriate transition.

Step 7: Prepare a clean copy and proofread it carefully to catch and correct any careless errors in spelling, punctuation, format, or typing.

WRITING YOUR OWN PARAGRAPH

Writing from Reading "Part-Time Job May Do Teenagers More Harm Than Good"

When you write on any of these topics, be sure to work through the stages of the writing process in preparing your paragraph.

  1. Klott talks about high school students who work to pay for car insurance, dates, video games, music, and designer clothes. However, students might not have to work so hard if they learned to do

MyWritingLab™

without things they don't really need: the latest clothes, the newest smartphone, their own car, and so on. Write a paragraph about the many things high school students buy that they don't really need.

MyWritingLab™

2. Work can interfere with high school. Write about something else that interferes with high school. You can write about social life, extracurricular activities, sports, family responsibilities, or any other part of a student's life that can prevent him or her from focusing on school.

As you plan this paragraph, think about details that could fit these categories:

Why students choose this activity/responsibility over school

The effects on students' schoolwork

How to balance school and other activities or responsibilities

Collaborate

3. Many parents believe that a part-time job is beneficial for high school students, but the job can be harmful. Write a one-paragraph letter to parents, warning them about some other part of teen life (not jobs) that parents may think is good but that may be harmful. You can write about the dangers of their child being popular, or having a steady boyfriend or girlfriend, or always being number one in academics.

Once you've chosen the topic, brainstorm with a partner or group: ask questions, answer them, add details. After you've brainstormed, work by yourself and proceed through the stages of preparing your letter to parents.

MyWritingLab™

4. Some parents have misconceptions (incorrect ideas) about their teenage children; for instance, they may believe the teen with a part-time job is automatically learning how to handle money. On the other hand, teenage children have misconceptions about their parents. Write about some misconception that teens have about their parents. You might, for instance, write about some teens' mistaken belief that (1) the best parents are the ones who give their children the most freedom, or (2) parents who love you give you everything you want, or (3) parents do not remember what it is like to be young.

To begin, freewrite on one mistaken idea that teens might have about their parents. Focus on your own experiences, memories, and so forth—as a teen or as a parent of teenagers. Use your freewriting to find details and a focus for your paragraph.

Writing from Reading

To practice the skills you've learned in this chapter, follow the steps of prereading, reading, and rereading with a pencil as you read the following selection.

New Directions

Maya Angelou

Maya Angelou (1928–2014) was born Marguerite Annie Johnson in St. Louis, Missouri. She survived family hardships to become one of the most famous and beloved writers in America. Angelou is best known for her seven autobiographies, starting with her internationally acclaimed book, I Know Why the Caged Bird Sings *(1969). She was also an accomplished poet, composer, screenwriter, professor, and civil rights activist.*

In 1993, she recited her poem, "On the Pulse of Morning," at the inaugu-
ration of President William Jefferson Clinton. In 2011, President Barack
Obama awarded Angelou the Presidential Medal of Freedom, the country's
highest civilian honor. In the following essay, Angelou tells the uplifting
story of a woman who "stepped from the road which seemed to have been
chosen for her and cut herself a brand-new path."

Words You May Need to Know (Corresponding paragraph numbers are in parentheses.)

burdensome (1): troublesome, heavy

conceded (2): admitted

domestic (3): a household worker

meticulously (4): very carefully

cotton gin (4): a factory with a machine for separating cotton fibers from seeds

brazier (6): a container that holds live coals covered by a grill, used for cooking

savors (6): food that smells and tastes good

lint (6): cotton fibers

specters (6): ghosts

balmy (9): mild and soothing

hives of industry (9): places swarming with busy workers

looms (11): rises in front of us

ominous (11): threatening

resolve (11): determination

unpalatable (11): not acceptable

In 1903, the late Mrs. Annie Johnson of Arkansas found herself with two   1
toddling sons, very little money, and a slight ability to read and add simple numbers. To this picture add a disastrous marriage and the burdensome fact that Mrs. Johnson was a Negro.

When she told her husband, Mr. William Johnson, of her dissatisfac-   2
tion with their marriage, he conceded that he too found it to be less than he
expected, and had been secretly hoping to leave and study religion. He added
that he thought God was calling him not only to preach but to do so in Enid,
Oklahoma. He did not tell her that he knew a minister in Enid with whom
he could study and who had a friendly, unmarried daughter. They parted
amicably, Annie keeping the one-room house and William taking most of the
cash to carry himself to Oklahoma.

Annie, over six feet tall, big-boned, decided that she would not go to   3
work as a domestic and leave her "precious babes" to anyone else's care.
There was no possibility of being hired at the town's cotton gin or lumber
mill, but maybe there was a way to make the two factories work for her. In
other words, "I looked up the road I was going and back the way I come,
and since I wasn't satisfied, I decided to step off the road and cut me a new
path." She told herself that she wasn't a fancy cook but that she could "mix
groceries well enough to scare hungry away from starving a man."

She made her plans meticulously and in secret. One early evening to see if   4
she was ready, she placed stones in two five-gallon pails and carried them three
miles to the cotton gin. She rested a little, and then, discarding some rocks, she
walked to the sawmill five miles farther along the dirt road. On her way back
to her house and her babies, she dumped the remaining rocks along the path.

5   That same night she worked into the early hours boiling chicken and frying ham. She made dough and filled the rolled-out pastry with meat. At last she went to sleep.

6   The next morning she left her house carrying the meat pies, lard, an iron brazier, and coal for a fire. Just before lunch she appeared in an empty lot behind the cotton gin. As the dinner noon bell rang, she dropped the savors into boiling fat, and the aroma rose and floated over the workers who spilled out of the gin, covered with white lint, looking like specters.

7   Most workers had brought their lunches of pinto beans and biscuits or crackers, onions, and cans of sardines, but they were tempted by the hot meat pies which Annie ladled out of the fat. She wrapped them in newspapers, which soaked up the grease, and offered them for sale at a nickel each. Although business was slow, those first days Annie was determined. She balanced her appearances between the two hours of activity.

8   So, on Monday if she offered hot fresh pies at the cotton gin and sold the remaining cooled-down pies at the lumber mill for three cents, then on Tuesday she went first to the lumber mill presenting fresh, just-cooked pies as the lumbermen covered in sawdust emerged from the mill.

9   For the next few years, on balmy spring days, blistering summer noons, and cold, wet, and wintry middays, Annie never disappointed her customers, who could count on seeing the tall, brown-skin woman bent over her brazier, carefully turning the meat pies. When she felt certain the workers had become dependent on her, she built a stall between the two hives of industry and let the men run to her for their lunchtime provisions.

10   She had indeed stepped from the road which seemed to have been chosen for her and cut herself a brand-new path. In years that stall became a store where customers could buy cheese, meat, syrup, cookies, candy, writing tablets, pickles, canned goods, fresh fruit, soft drinks, coal, oil, and leather soles for worn-out shoes.

11   Each of us has the right and responsibility to assess the roads which lie ahead, and those over which we have traveled, and if the future road looms ominous or unpromising, and the roads back uninviting, then we need to gather our resolve and, carrying only the necessary baggage, step off that road into another direction. If the new choice is also unpalatable, without embarrassment, we must be ready to change that as well.

MyWritingLab™ **Reading Comprehension**

1. What is the main idea of Angelou's essay? Explain it in one to three sentences and include a comment about how the title of the reading—"New Directions"—relates to the main idea.

2. Describe what happened after Annie built a stall between the lumber mill and the cotton gin and her customers started coming to her, rather than she going to them. Include a brief discussion of how these new developments represented a new direction for Annie.

Topics for Writing from Reading: "New Directions"

When you write on any of the following topics, be sure to work through the stages of the writing process in preparing your paragraph.

1. Using the ideas and examples you gathered by prereading, reading, and, with a pen or pencil, rereading "New Directions," write a summary of Maya Angelou's essay.

2. Write about someone who had many strikes against him or her but who succeeded. Be sure that you include some of the difficulties this person faced.

3. Maya Angelou says, "Each of us has the right and responsibility to assess the roads which lie ahead, and those over which we have traveled," and if an old road or a future road looks dark, we must "step off that road into another direction."

    Write a paragraph that agrees or disagrees with that statement.

    Begin by working with a group. First, discuss what you think the statement means. Then ask at least six questions about the statement. You may ask such questions as, "Does everyone have the courage or talent to choose a new road?" or "What keeps some people from choosing a new direction?" or "Do you know anyone who has done what Angelou advises?"

    Use the questions and answers to decide whether you want to agree or disagree with Angelou's statement.

4. There is an old saying, "When the going gets tough, the tough get going," and Mrs. Annie Johnson's story seems to prove the saying is true. She was faced with poverty, lack of job opportunities, raising two children alone, and yet through hard work, creativity, and determination, she triumphed.

    Write a paragraph that tells a story and proves the truth of another old saying. You can use a saying like, "Take time to stop and smell the roses," or "You never know what you can do until you try," or any other saying.

    Begin by freewriting about old sayings and what they mean to you. Then pick one that connects to your experience or the experience of someone you know. Use that saying as the focus of your paragraph.

Critical Thinking and Writing Topics

1. Mrs. Annie Johnson, the woman who found a "new direction" to success, identified a need (a fresh lunch for workers at the cotton gin and the lumber mill) and filled that need. Write about someone else who found success by meeting a need that others had not recognized. Before writing your paragraph, you may want to do a little research about a well-known inventor or entrepreneur.

2. If you could be a well-known inventor or entrepreneur, who would you choose to be? What do you admire about this person? What do you envy?

Appendix: Readings for Writers

Note: Writing topics based on readings can be found at the end of each selection.

Marjory Stoneman Douglas: Patron Saint of the Everglades

Varla Ventura

Varla Ventura, a self-confessed connoisseur of all things unusual, is a writer living in San Francisco. She is the author of Sheroes *(1998) and* Wild Women Talk About Love *(2007), among other books. In the following 1998 essay, Ventura pays tribute to Marjorie Stoneman Douglas (1890–1998) who, at age seventy-eight, "blind and armed with little more than a big floppy hat and a will of iron, founded Friends of the Everglades." Today, the organization has thousands of members spanning thirty-eight states.*

Words You May Need to Know (Corresponding paragraph numbers are in parentheses.)

habitat (1): home environment
unmoored (2): insecure; lost
scruffy (3): messy, shabby
boom town (3): a town experiencing sudden growth
merit (3): value
niche (3): suitable place
soapbox (3): platform for making a political speech
cub (3): inexperienced beginner
unswerving (3): unchanging
soapbox (3): platform

ghastly (3): upsetting, horrifying
ecosystem (4): an interactive system of organisms and their environment
denizens (4): inhabitants
extinction (4): the dying-out of an organism or species so that it no longer exists
fetid (5): having an offensive smell
raze (6): destroy, demolish
garnered (7): acquired by effort

Although not native to the southernmost state, Marjory Stoneman Douglas took to the Florida Everglades like "a duck to water," becoming, since 1927, the great champion of this rare habitat. She was born to lake country, in Minnesota in 1890, during one of her father's many failed business ventures which kept the family moving around the country. On a family vacation to Florida at the age of four, Marjory fell in love with the Floridian light and vowed to return.

Marjory escaped her unstable home life in the world of books. An extremely bright girl, she was admitted to Wellesley College when higher education for women was still quite uncommon. Her mother died shortly after her graduation in 1911. Feeling unmoored, she took an unrewarding

1

2

job at a department store and shortly thereafter married a much older man, Kenneth Douglas, who had a habit of writing bad checks.

3   Leaving for Florida with her father for his latest business pursuit seemed like the perfect way to get away from her petty criminal husband and sad memories. Frank Stoneman's latest ideas, however, seemed to have more merit: founding a newspaper in the scruffy boom town of Miami (the paper went on to become the *Miami Herald*). Marjory eagerly took a job as a cub reporter. Opinionated, forward-thinking, and unafraid to share unpopular views, both Stonemans found their niche in the newspaper trade. One of the causes they were in unswerving agreement on was Governor Napoleon Bonaparte Broward's plan to drain the Everglades to put up more houses. Father and daughter used the paper as their soapbox to cry out against this ghastly idea with all their might.

4   Roused to action, Marjory educated herself about the facts surrounding the Everglades issue and discovered many of the denizens of Florida's swampy grassland to be in danger of extinction. The more she learned, the more fascinated she became. When, decades later, she decided to leave the newspaper to write fiction, she often wove the Everglades into her plots. Marjory learned that the Everglades were actually not a swamp, but rather wetlands. In order to be a swamp, the water must be still, whereas the Everglades water flows in a constant movement. Marjory coined the term "river of grass" and in 1947 wrote a book about this precious ecosystem entitled *The Everglades: River of Grass*.

5   More than anything else, Marjory's book helped people to see the Everglades not as a fetid swamp, but as a natural treasure without which Florida might become desert. After the publication of her book, President Harry Truman declared a portion of the Florida wetlands as Everglades National Park. The triumph was short-lived, however. The Army Corps of Engineers began tunneling canals all over the Florida Everglades, installing dams and floodgates. As if that weren't enough, they straightened the course of the Kissimmee River, throwing the delicate ecosystem into complete shock.

6   At the age of seventy-eight, Marjory Stoneman Douglas joined in the fight, stopping bulldozers ready to raze a piece of the Everglades for an immense jetport. Almost blind and armed with little more than a big floppy sun hat and a will of iron, Marjory founded Friends of the Everglades, going on the stump to talk to every Floridian about this rare resource and building the organization member by member to thousands of people in thirty-eight states. "One can do so much by learning, reading, and talking to people," she noted. "Students need to learn all they can about animals and the environment. Most of all, they need to share what they have learned."

7   Marjory Stoneman Douglas and "Marjory's Army," as her group came to be known, stopped the jetport in its tracks, garnered restrictions on farmers' use of land and chemicals, saw to the removal of the Army's "improvements,"

and enjoyed the addition of thousands of acres to the Everglades National Park where they could be protected from land-grabbing developers. In 1975 and 1976, Marjory was rewarded for her hard work by being named Conservationist of the Year two years in a row. In 1989, she became the Sierra Club's honorary vice president. Protecting the Everglades became Marjory's life's work, a job she loved. She has never considered retiring and in her 107th year, is still living in the same house she's been in since 1926 and working every day for Friends of the Everglades.

Reading Comprehension   MyWritingLab™

1. In Paragraph 3, Ventura mentions a disturbing plan proposed by the governor of Florida at the time. How did Marjory Stoneman Douglas feel about this plan, and how did fighting it represent a turning point in her life?

2. Explain how Douglas' writings served to change public opinion about the Florida Everglades, listing examples from the reading.

Discussion Prompts/Writing Options   MyWritingLab™

If you write on any of the following topics, work through the stages of the writing process in preparing your assignment.

1. Explore the Friends of the Everglades Web site at *www.everglades .org*. Write a paragraph summarizing your findings to share with the rest of the class.

2. Marjory Stoneman Douglas is quoted in Paragraph 6. Do you agree or disagree with her comments about students? Why or why not? Be specific in your reason.

3. Conduct an Internet search on the topic of *wetlands*. In what ways are these so-called "rivers of grass" valuable to us? In what ways are they endangered? Discuss your findings with the class. Compose a letter to a state or national government official (or some other audience) defending (or arguing against) the need for wetlands preservation.

Topics for Critical Thinking and Writing   MyWritingLab™

If you write on any of the following topics, work through the stages of the writing process in preparing your assignment.

1. If you live in a region where there is controversy or disagreement about the danger a local plant, landfill, factory, or other business poses to the environment, investigate the nature of the disagreement with two or three classmates. Conduct an Internet search for local newspaper articles, contact reporters, and find out why there is a controversy. Based on your group's findings, write individual summaries of the case for or against the continued operation of this business.

2. What is your favorite natural environment—the beach, the mountains, some other? Imagine that you are describing this environment for someone who has never seen or experienced it. Write a brief essay describing what you love about it and why, using sensory details such as smells and sounds to make the scene come alive. Create a dominant impression, such as tranquility, for the reader.

NARRATION

Hunger

Nilsa Mariano

Nilsa Mariano is a poet, teacher, and spoken-word performance artist. In the following narrative, Mariano recalls her visit to an elementary school to entertain students on Latino Heritage Day. The author describes the joyful pride of students who were satisfying their "hunger to be recognized as real people, with gifts and talents that the world needs."

Words You May Need to Know (Corresponding paragraph numbers are in parentheses.)

castanets (1): handheld rhythm instrument

maracas (1): rattles used as percussion instruments

***cuentos folklóricos* (2):** folktales told aloud by a storyteller in front of an audience

caciques (6): pre-Columbian leaders of the Taíno tribes

güiro (6): a musical instrument made out of a gourd

vivacious (7): lively, cheerful

pollo fricassee (9): seasoned chicken

guineos verdes (9): green bananas

arroz con coco (9): coconut rice

frijoles negros (9): black beans

The gym floor gleamed. Tables were set up on each side of the room with books and projects assembled by the children and the staff. There were handmade maps of Puerto Rico and Cuba and glossy maps of Latin America. The children had proudly contributed examples of cultural items that were relevant to their backgrounds. There were colorful shawls, castanets, plates, pictures. And there were maracas: maracas made of wood, maracas honed out of gourds, maraca earrings, maracas made out of paper cups and seeds, and even plastic maracas.

Nate is a musician, and I am a storyteller. Nate set up the instruments as I looked over my notes. I tell *cuentos folklóricos* with an emphasis on multicultural stories, especially stories of the Caribbean, where I was born. I am the Taína Storyteller, descendent of the Taíno Indians of Puerto Rico. To the dismay of my parents, I chose to feature this aspect of my heritage and not just the Spanish great-grandparents on both sides of my family. I wanted to honor this long-ignored part of our greater heritage, and the more I learned, the more joy I felt.

As we were setting up, several teachers and staff stopped by to admire the conga drums and meet the "artists." We shook hands, smiled, and chatted with each visitor. Not one was a person of color. A blonde, tall woman of solid build and thick glasses introduced herself. She told us how pleased she was to have us here. She explained that she worked with these children every day. The school was about 30 percent Latino or from Spanish-speaking homes. Another 20 percent were black or Asian, and the rest were "white non-Hispanic." She told us how the children had been looking forward to this day and how creative and artistic they were. She wanted to expand on this, she said, because after all, "We're not raising rocket scientists here."

4   Nate and I were stunned by her comment. He hit the conga drum softly at first and slowly began a drumbeat, a stiff smile on his handsome Dominican/African-American face. I, who was usually fast on my feet and even quicker with my mouth, stammered something akin to, "I am sure that the children enjoy their artistic side, as I enjoy mine in addition to my work as a teacher and scholar."

5   The children began to arrive. The first session was for the kindergarten through third-grade classes. The gym filled up with over a hundred kids, their teachers, teacher aides, the "grandmothers" who helped out during class time, and parents. I took a deep breath and eyed the children. They were beautiful. I saw brown faces, tan faces, black faces, white faces; most with smiles and lively chatter. A few shy children barely looked up. I tried to make eye contact with them, to smile, to get the audience on my side. I especially tried to search out the more obvious Latino faces.

6   We were introduced, and the stories began. Stories of brave caciques, lovelorn Taínas, and the Taíno gods. Nate drummed a beat; I scraped some musical sounds on my güiro. I asked the children to raise their hands if they spoke English. They all laughed at what seemed like a ridiculous question to them. I then asked who spoke Spanish, and the excitement grew—some of the children were not content to raise their hands so they jumped to their feet to make sure they got my attention. "Me, too," I said, "me, too." Their excitement soared. I went on with stories of animals that speak Spanish, of a talking donkey, a story about my name and what it meant to me, and of boys named Juan Bobo. They listened, some with mouths open, as if they were being fed. They laughed, clapped, and asked for more. We gathered for an interactive story, and in the front row, a red-haired girl named Yolanda and a boy named José competed with other students to be the first ones to hold my hand.

7   The afternoon session brought in another hundred children who were older and seemed determined to be low-key. But I would not allow it. Soon, they were laughing and calling out the names of the countries their people were from. I was loud and barely needed the mic. I was vivacious and funny, and I even danced. They drank it up. Nate was musical, funky and electric; his bald head glistened with sweat as he smiled through it all. They loved it, and we loved them.

8   But it was later, wandering the halls looking for a bathroom, when my heart almost burst. I could not walk five feet without children stepping in my path, telling me proudly that they were "Spanish." The moment I said, "I knew you were because you're beautiful," they raised their arms to hug me. Some almost jumped into my arms. As we were going down the hall to the cafeteria for a "Latino" luncheon prepared by the kids and their parents,

more children came. They mobbed around our table as we ate. They brought us food to try, and they pointed out what they had made. A large fifth-grade girl with curly dark hair came over and asked me to taste her cookies. She firmly took my arm and led me to the table. Putting a cookie in my mouth, she watched carefully as I chewed and swallowed. I told her it was just delicious, as it truly was. She beamed and, with tears in her eyes, whispered "Thank you." Struck by her emotion, I hugged this girl who was taller than me, and she clung to me. Nate brought out his drums, and the boys and girls stood in line to get their turn to play. The joy was intense.

We were surrounded by food of all kinds. Rice and beans, pollo fricassee, guineos verdes, arroz con coco, tacos, burritos, frijoles negros—all of which looked and smelled like heaven. Our hunger was quickly satisfied as we savored the foods of our ancestors, the foods of our living cultures.   9

But the children were satisfying another hunger that day: 10

The hunger to see themselves in us and to know we are like them.

The hunger to be recognized as real people, with gifts and talents that the world needs.

The hunger to feel that they, too, could speak, dream, dance, and eat in Spanish, without fear of being seen as different or less.

The hunger to be *proud*.

Reading Comprehension

1. The author uses the first two paragraphs to set the stage before beginning her narrative. Using the five Ws (*who, what, when, where, why*), list answers to these questions using the information Mariano provides in Paragraphs 1 and 2 before her story unfolds.

2. Interpret what the school staff member means by her comments. How are those comments received by the Taína storyteller and her partner Nate? How does this conversation relate to the reading's title?

Discussion Prompts/Writing Options

If you write on any of the following topics, work through the stages of the writing process in preparing your assignment.

1. The author explores various types of hungers in Paragraph 10. Have you experienced any of these hungers? Choose one and write a paragraph describing the specifics, and include details about the course of action you took to satisfy that hunger. If you took no action, explain why not.

2. Write a brief narrative (200–300 words) describing a time when you worked with or interacted with young children, or write about a time when you were a child and participated in a program led by adults, either in school or at another setting. Keep your story focused on one event, and be sure your narrative has a point that will be clear for your readers.

3. Consider the comment, "We're not raising rocket scientists here" (Paragraph 3). How do you interpret the tall, blonde woman's remark? Is it thoughtless, condescending, well meaning, racist, or something else entirely? Discuss or write about a time when you heard someone make a similar comment. What were your thoughts at the time? Did you respond? Were you satisfied with your response? Why or why not? If applicable, what did you wish you had said instead?

MyWritingLab™ **Topics for Critical Thinking and Writing**

If you write on any of the following topics, work through the stages of the writing process in preparing your assignment.

1. Write a narrative essay that reflects the "hunger" to be proud of one's heritage or the importance of maintaining a positive self-image. You can write about an experience that helped raise your awareness of your heritage, or you can make someone you know the subject of your narrative. In your introductory paragraph, define *positive self-image*, and devise a thesis statement that makes a point about the importance of cultural identity. Be sure your details and the sequence of events in your body paragraphs relate to your thesis statement.

2. Cultural rituals and customs can be confusing and/or misunderstood if one is unaware of the history behind them and the purpose they serve. If you have ever wondered why certain cultural celebrations have become annual traditions in some cities, research one of these customs. Then, in your own words, write a paragraph or short essay describing the custom, its origin, and its purpose. Alternatively, describe one of your own family or cultural traditions, and then explain why someone from another family or culture would probably have difficulty understanding (or relating to) its significance.

NARRATION

Bullet to Blue Sky

Yesenia De Jesus

Yesenia De Jesus won First Place in the 2010 Pearson Education Writing Rewards Contest, a national competition for college students enrolled in basic composition classes. At the time, De Jesus was a Developmental English student at Palm Beach State College in Palm Beach Gardens, Florida. This essay is about an experience that changed her life, and thanks is extended to Professor Marilyn R. Tiedemann for encouraging Ms. De Jesus to enter the writing contest.

Words You May Need to Know (Corresponding paragraph numbers are in parentheses.)

flippantly (2): treating serious things lightly

feudal (4): a system of the Middle Ages in which powerful landowners ruled peasants with few rights

Al Capone, Bonnie and Clyde (5): Al Capone was a famous American gangster of the 1920s; Bonnie and Clyde were well-known bank robbers of the same period

double-dutched (6): verb form of jump-rope style

The sun was in the process of its morning stretch. While the residents of gated communities came alive to be greeted by the tropical heat of South Florida, the stragglers of the universe awoke to the sound of a 9mm dispersing its gunpowder to the blue sky. The ghetto houses that sheltered these citizens were painted different colors; some exposed faded paint, and others told stories in graffiti, inspired by gang artists marking their territories. Roll bars protected the windows covered by filthy bed sheets that not even dogs would lie on. The lanky, dark-haired girl lay in her bed twisting and turning, trying to catch a cool wave from the ceiling fan that spun and thumped overhead all night. She always heard the same dogs barking; her ears still rang from the sound of that gun. She still felt the warm, thin blood that stained her hands. She still felt a sharp, pounding pain along her left side; for every breath she took, the pain reminded her that she was human. She had witnessed many shootings before; she had seen more blood in her days. Why was this shooting any different? It was because for the first time, she was the victim. I understood her pain, for I was that girl.

It all started with Mr. Tangye in the fall of 2004. He was an inspiring math teacher who convinced me that I had more to offer this world than I thought. As the bell rang at Conniston Middle School, the students and I marched like zombies to our classes. I passed through the dark hallways of vandalized lockers with torn papers and ripped books scattered over the ground like a dump. I made my way past the miserable teachers and devilish students. The administrators surrounded the hallways like a S.W.A.T. team, commanding everyone to go to class. I walked into Mr. Tangye's math class; he had a bright, white smile that hurt my eyes every time I looked at him. Before I could make it to my seat, Mr. Tangye handed me a paper that itched my fingers; it was a math test. I stared at the test, and I begged my brain to wake up! The other kids shuffled the paper back and forth on top of their desks or used it as a pillow on which to lay their heads. I secretly tried my best at every problem and flippantly turned it in.

3   As the bell rang, I dashed for the exit. I swiftly dropped off my homework, but Mr. Tangye caught me and pulled me aside to show me my test. He said I was the only one who had passed the test. Mr. Tangye told me I was on the borderline of failing the class but that I could pass. I listened to every word he said because I was tired of being perceived as an idiot.

4   For the rest of the day, all I could think about was whether to study or not to study. I hated being stuck between a world that offered happiness and stability, whose proverb was "anything is possible" and a world that followed the theory of Charles Darwin's "survival of the fittest." My world struggled for everything—money, power, respect, even for the last piece of fried chicken. My world had an underground feudal system to follow with rules to be respected, lines not to be crossed. Although this world was violent, senseless, crazy, it was my world. This unmerciful, savage world . . . I was comfortable in it. I felt connected to this world but also felt guilty leaving it behind, like a crackhead quitting dope. I silenced that voice which begged to stay. I was going to make it out of my world of hardship and struggle and bullets.

5   When I got home, I was greeted by a warm aroma from the kitchen, where I always found my mother. We greeted each other in our usual exchange. After I gave my mother a brief overview of how school went, I rushed to my room to study. I was tired of the struggles, fights, and problems which by birth, I did not deserve. I was going to be somebody; I was going to do something with my life. I was not going to be another Al Capone or Bonnie with a Clyde. I was going to be somebody the way God intended. I was going to earn a living the right, clean way, but in order to be somebody, I needed an education. I would have to get an "A" on my chapter test in Mr. Tangye's math class. I had to do it. I would!

6   Four gruesome weeks passed. I slept, ate, and studied. The morning of the test, I woke up early. I studied some more, for I wanted to be alert in case an unusual math problem was on the test. I left early that day to ask a few questions. Usually, I took a longer route to school to avoid crossing enemy lines, but I rushed through a shortcut. The shortcut led me to the back of the school where boys played basketball and girls double-dutched after school, but the recess court was empty. No one stood in the courtyard but me. My eyes locked on the formula sheet I memorized. Suddenly, I heard

a familiar sound as gunshots sliced the morning air; tires screeched. As I walked toward the school building, I felt something drizzle down the side of my torso. I grabbed my shirt; something slightly tickled me. It was wet. It was not sweat; it was blood. It happened so quickly. I threw my paper and books, bloody from my handprint, on the ground. I screamed at the top of my lungs, not because I had been shot but because I knew I could not take my math test, the test I had studied so damn hard for. My memory faded before I collapsed. A former fire rescuer spotted me on the ground and got help.

As I lay in my bed at home, I dwelled on my secrets. I tried to crawl around my brain; I wanted a reason why God led me to this path. I was not connected to these savages who shot me. These thugs just wandered around the neighborhood trying to find an ordinary person to become a victim whose fate would carry a dark message.   7

When I was shot, it did not overpower my life; it empowered my spirit. As I got out of bed, I tried to convince myself I should stay there, but I could not find any good reason. My injuries were three-days fresh, but I was determined to make that math test. I reached to find the strength from deep within my soul to move. The pain gripped my side like five hundred needles repeatedly stabbing my ribs. I grabbed a chair so deeply that I bent my nails backwards. My arms and legs shook. I screamed with every movement I made, yet the agonizing pain only intensified. I gripped my book as I walked out the door. Slow steps minimized the pain. I gave my mother a kiss as the bus approached the curb. She touched my arm and reassured me I could make up the test after I healed completely. I objected because I was ready for this test.   8

That morning, I told my mother I had tried to better myself. This neighborhood, this ghetto, this hardship-world I lived in had tried to bring me down; it had tried to kill me. The shooting event that took place seven years ago answered the one question I had been asking myself since I was old enough to comprehend the world around me. Through the support of my mother and the leap-of-faith decisions I made, and even by beating death, God kept me alive to respond to a call. God wants me to be somebody. Even though I am excelling in life today, I will never forget who I am, where I came from, and how hard I have worked to get to this point. God gave me life again, for just like that morning in the courtyard, I stood out to those gang bangers because I was born to stand out. I will always stand out.   9

I dropped my coins into the bus depositor, found a seat, and quietly, painfully moaned along the ride. My mother waved to me as the bus drove off. She was staring at me with a satisfied expression upon her face, for she knew she was raising a fighter, a winner, and a believer. She was raising a somebody.   10

MyWritingLab™ ## Reading Comprehension

1. Paragraph 6 marks the turning point of this narrative essay. Summarize the incident. What makes the exact day of this incident so important?

2. What do you think De Jesus means when she tell readers, "When I was shot, it did not overpower my life; it empowered my spirit" (Paragraph 8)? In the last sentence of the essay, the author writes, "She was raising a somebody." Restate this sentence in your own words.

MyWritingLab™ ## Discussion Prompts/Writing Options

When you write on any of the following topics, be sure to work through the stages of the writing process in preparing your paragraph.

1. What does the title of this essay mean? There is definitely a bullet in this story, but what does the reference to blue sky mean? How does the "blue sky" connect to the changes in Yesenia De Jesus' life? You can consider the changes that took place in one day or the changes that De Jesus *chose* to make before and after that day.

2. De Jesus writes vivid descriptions of her neighborhood, her school, and her suffering. These descriptions make her story convincing and hold a reader's attention. Discuss or write about a time when (a) you were forced to make a choice that could change your life or (b) you suffered great pain. Be sure to use sensory details to enhance your narrative.

3. De Jesus writes that she "was going to make it out" of her "world of hardship and bullets," and she explains how a bullet "empowered" her spirit. Write a story about an incident that caused you to feel (a) empowered or (b) powerless.

Topics for Critical Thinking and Writing

MyWritingLab™

1. Do a little research about a well-known person who made his or her way from poverty, illness, or abuse to a life that held meaning and emotional peace. Find several accounts of the transformation in the person's life. Then write a narrative of this person's journey from a dark past to a powerful present.

Collaborate

2. Begin this assignment with a partner or group. De Jesus' essay was based on the topic, "Write about a true experience that changed your life." Working with a partner or group, share at least one personal experience that changed you. Then answer any questions the member(s) of the group may ask, and be ready to provide details. After each person has shared his or her experiences, write separate narratives on the life-changing incident.

DESCRIPTION

El Hoyo

Mario Suárez

Mario Suárez grew up in Tucson, Arizona, in El Hoyo. He wrote this essay in 1947 for an English class at the University of Arizona, and it was published in Arizona Quarterly, *a literary journal. A long and distinguished writing career focusing on the Chicano perspective followed. Suárez's stories have been collected and reissued in the anthology* Chicano Sketches, *published by the University of Arizona Press in 2004.*

Words You May Need to Know (Corresponding paragraph numbers are in parentheses.)

inundated (1): flooded
solace (2): comfort, relief from misery or disappointment
indifference (3): lack of interest in something

conquistador (3): a leader of the Spanish conquest of the Americas in the sixteenth century

From the center of downtown Tucson, the ground slopes gently away to 1 Main Street, drops a few feet, and then rolls to the banks of the Santa Cruz River. Here lies the section of the city known as El Hoyo. Why it is called El Hoyo is not very clear. In no sense is it a hole as its name would imply; it is simply the river's immediate valley. Its inhabitants are Chicanos who raise hell on Saturday night and listen to Padre Estanislao on Sunday morning. While the term chicano is the short way of saying Mexicano, it is not restricted to the paisanos who came from old Mexico with the territory or the last famine to work for the railroad, labor, sing, and go on relief. Chicano is the easy way of referring to everybody. Pablo Gutierrez married the Chinese grocer's daughter and now runs a meat department; his sons are chicanos. So are the sons of Killer Jones who threw a fight in Harlem and fled to El Hoyo to marry Cristina Mendez. And so are all of them. However, it is doubtful that all these spiritual sons of Mexico live in El Hoyo because they love each other—many fight and bicker constantly. It is doubtful they live in El Hoyo because of its scenic beauty—it is everything but beautiful. Its houses are simple affairs of unplastered adobe, wood, and abandoned car parts. Its narrow streets are mostly clearings which have, in time, acquired names. Except for some tall trees which nobody has ever cared to identify, nurse, or destroy, the main things known to grow in the general area are weeds, garbage piles, dark-eyed chavalos, and dogs. And it is doubtful that the Chicanos live in El Hoyo because it is safe—many times the Santa Cruz has risen and inundated the area.

In other respects, living in El Hoyo has its advantages. If one is born 2 with weakness for acquiring bills, El Hoyo is where the collectors are less likely ro find you. If one has acquired the habit of listening to Octavio

Perea's Mexican Hour in the wee hours of the morning with the radio on at full blast, El Hoyo is where you are less likely to be reported to the authorities. Besides, Perea is very popular and sooner or later to everyone "Smoke in the Eyes" is dedicated between the pinto beans and white flour commercials. If one, for any reason whatsoever, comes on an extended period of hard times, where, if not in El Hoyo, are the neighbors more willing to offer solace? When Teofila Malacara's house burned to the ground with all her belongings and two children, a benevolent gentleman carried through the gesture that made tolerable her burden. He made a list of 500 names and solicited from each a dollar. At the end of a month, he turned over to the tearful but grateful señora $100 in cold cash and then accompanied her on a short vacation. When the new manager of a local store decided that no more Chicanas were to work behind the counters; it was the Chicanos of El Hoyo who, on taking their individually small but collectively great buying power elsewhere, drove the manager out, and the girls returned to their jobs. When the Mexican Army was en route to Baja California and the Chicanos found out that the enlisted men ate only at infrequent intervals, it was El Hoyo's Chicanos who crusaded across town with pots of beans and trays of tortillas to meet the train. When someone gets married, celebrating is not restricted to the immediate friends of the couple. Everybody is invited. Anything calls for a celebration and a celebration calls for anything. On Memorial Day, there are no less than half a dozen good fights at the Riverside Dance Hall. On Mexican Independence Day, more than one flag is sworn allegiance to amid cheers for the queen.

3   And El Hoyo is something more. It is this something more which brought Felipe Suárez back from the wars after having killed a score of Japanese with his body resembling a patchwork quilt to marry Julia Armijo. It brought Joe Zepeda, a gunner, back to compose boleros. He has a metal plate for a skull. Perhaps El Hoyo is proof that those people exist, and perhaps exist best, who have as yet failed to observe the more popular modes of human conduct. Perhaps the humble appearance of El Hoyo justifies the indifferent shrug of those made aware of its existence. Perhaps El Hoyo's simplicity motivates an occasional Chicano to move away from its narrow streets, babbling compadres, and shrieking children to deny the bloodwell from which he springs and to claim the blood of a conquistador while his hair is straight and his face beardless. Yet El Hoyo is not an outpost of a few families against the world. It fights for no causes except those which soothe its immediate angers. It laughs and cries with the same amount of passion in times of plenty and of want.

4   Perhaps El Hoyo, its inhabitants, and its essence can best be explained by telling a bit about a dish called *capirotada*. Its origin is uncertain. But, according to the time and the circumstance, it is made of old, new or hard bread. It is softened with water and then cooked with peanuts, raisins,

onions, cheese, and panocha. It is fired with sherry wine. Then it is served hot, cold, or just "on the weather" as they say in El Hoyo. The Sermenõs like it one way, the Garcias another, and the Ortegas still another. While it might differ greatly from one home to another, nevertheless it is still capirotada. And so it is with El Hoyo's Chicanos. While being divided from within and from without, like the capirotada, they remain Chicanos.

Reading Comprehension   MyWritingLab™

1. In Paragraph 2, Suárez presents the reader with several examples of the advantages of living in El Hoyo. Are these advantages unusual or surprising? How so? What do these examples have in common? Explain.

2. At the beginning of Paragraph 3, Suárez writes, "And El Hoyo is something more." What does this statement mean? Be as specific as possible in your answer.

Discussion Prompts/Writing Options   MyWritingLab™

If you write on any of the following topics, work through the stages of the writing process in preparing your assignment.

1. In the last paragraph of the essay, the author compares El Hoyo to the dish known as *capirotada*. What do the residents of the El Hoyo neighborhood and capirotada, as described by Suárez, have in common? Provide several reasons to support your observations.

2. Describe a neighborhood you know very well. What makes it unique? What are its advantages and disadvantages? Evaluate whether it is a good or bad place to live overall. Use specific examples as evidence.

3. Consider the following statement by Suárez in Paragraph 3: "Yet El Hoyo is not an outpost of a few families against the world." What do you think the author means by that statement? Is it a positive or negative statement? Write a paragraph about your opinion(s) of El Hoyo, and be sure to incorporate specific examples from the essay.

Topics for Critical Thinking and Writing   MyWritingLab™

If you write on any of the following topics, work through the stages of the writing process in preparing your assignment.

1. This essay is far from a sentimental look back at an idealized childhood neighborhood. For example, the author criticizes the neighborhood's lack of beauty and mentions that residents often engage in physical fights. However, Suárez praises the way the neighbors stick together, maintain their identity, and appreciate simple pleasures. Imagine if you had to spend a year in El Hoyo, and all of your preparation and expectations would be based on this essay. What do you think you would appreciate or enjoy about

El Hoyo's culture, how would you try to adjust, and what would you hope to learn from the experience? Incorporate specific details from Suárez's essay to support your points.

2. Evaluate the author's capsule definition of the term *Chicano* in Paragraph 1: "Chicano is the easy way of referring to everybody." What else does the author seem to believe constitutes being Chicano? In what way is the author's description of El Hoyo also a definition of the idea of being Chicano, and what does that mean to the author? Use details and key quotes from the essay to support your analysis.

DESCRIPTION

Deep Cold

Verlyn Klinkenborg

Verlyn Klinkenborg writes a column called "The Rural Life" for the New York Times. *His regular descriptions of nature's beauty and harshness rely on exact details and sensory details. As you read "Deep Cold," note how the author's language draws the reader into the world of an icy day.*

Words You May Need to Know (Corresponding paragraph numbers are in parentheses.)

gnashing (1): grinding or grating
muted (1): softened, made less ringing or resonant
rime (2): white frost
reservoirs (3): a place where water is stored for future use
brood (3): think deeply and with gloom

current (3): stream of water
paradox (3): a situation or statement seemingly impossible but also true
trepidation (3): agitation or fear

I f deep cold made a sound, it would be the scissoring and gnashing of a skater's blades against hard gray ice or the screeching the snow sets up when you walk across it in the blue light of afternoon. The sound may be the stamping of feet at bus stops and train stations, or the way the almost perfect clarity of the audible world on an icy day is muted by scarves and mufflers pulled up over the face and around the ears.

But the true sound of deep cold is the sound of the wind. Monday morning, on the streets of Cambridge, Massachusetts, the wind chill approached fifty below zero. A stiff northwest wind rocked in the trees and snatched at cars as they idled at the curb. A rough rime had settled over that old-brick city the day before, and now the wind was sanding it smooth. It was cold of Siberian or Arctic intensity, and I could feel a kind of claustrophobia settling in all over Boston. People went about their errands, only to cut them short instantly, turning backs to the gust and fleeing for cover.

It has been just slightly milder in New York. Furnace repairmen and oil-truck drivers are working on the memory of two hours' sleep. Swans in the smaller reservoirs brood on the ice, and in the swamps that line the railroad tracks in Dutchess County, you can see how the current was moving when the cold snap brought it to a halt. The soil in windblown fields looks—and is—iron hard. It's all a paradox, a cold that feels absolutely rigid but which nonetheless seeps through ill-fitting windows, between clapboards, and along uninsulated pipe chases. People listen superstitiously to the sounds in their heating ducts, to the banging of their radiators, afraid of silence. They turn the keys in their cars with trepidation. It's an old world this week.

MyWritingLab™ Reading Comprehension

1. Klinkenborg's description of deep cold makes frequent use of one of the five senses to provide its vivid sensory detail. Name the sense, and list some examples from the essay.

2. In Paragraph 2, Klinkenborg writes, "I could feel a kind of claustrophobia settling in all over Boston." What specific example does Klinkenborg use to convey this claustrophobic feeling?

MyWritingLab™ Discussion Prompts/Writing Options

When you write on any of the following topics, be sure to work through the stages of the writing process in preparing your paragraph.

1. Write about heat. You can call the heat "extreme heat," "deep heat," or another term to convey the heat you will describe. Concentrate on using sense words to explain the power and impact of this heat.

2. Klinkenborg describes the negative effects of deep cold. Write a description of the positive effects and the beauty of deep cold.

3. If your earliest years were spent in a warm climate, write about your first recollection or reaction to extreme cold weather.

4. Describe your experience of some type of extreme weather: a flood, a tornado, a hurricane, a forest fire, a sandstorm, and so forth.

5. Describe some element of nature (such as snow or surf) to someone who has never experienced it.

MyWritingLab™ Topics for Critical Thinking and Writing

1. Certain descriptions become so overused that they are called "clichés." Clichés include phrases like a "state-of-the-art" entertainment center or a party dress "to die for." Working with a group, compile a list of some popular clichés. Then, working alone, write about one cliché. Explain how it is used today. Include what the words of the cliché are used to describe, and give several examples of this usage. (For instance, a dress may be something "to die for," but some people refer to "a vacation to die for," and others talk of "a pizza to die for.") Then suggest better, more specific words to describe some of the items now linked to the cliché.

2. Choose a product you like. It can be a specific food, a brand of sneakers, a model of car, and so forth. Write a paragraph to describe this product, and be sure to use sensory details.

ILLUSTRATION

A Different Mirror (Excerpt)

Ronald Takaki

Ronald Takaki, born in Honolulu, is a historian known for his books on history, race, and multiculturalism. The following excerpt is from his book A Different Mirror. *In the book, Takaki argues that in studying America's history, we must study all the groups who have created America so that we "see ourselves in a different mirror." This excerpt focuses on specific details that illustrate the scope of America's diversity.*

Words You May Need to Know

ethnic diversity: variety of people, races, and cultures
discerned: recognized, perceived
Ellis Island: an island off the shore of New York City where many immigrants first landed in America
Angel Island: an island off San Francisco

Chinatown, Harlem, South Boston, the Lower East Side (of New York City): places associated with a variety of ethnic groups and races
derived: originated from
Forty-Niners: people who joined the Gold Rush of 1849, when gold was discovered in California
vaqueros: cowboys

The signs of America's ethnic diversity can be discerned across the continent: Ellis Island, Angel Island, Chinatown, Harlem, South Boston, the Lower East Side, places with Spanish names like Los Angeles and San Antonio or Indian names like Massachusetts and Iowa. Much of what is familiar in America's cultural landscape actually has ethnic origins. The Bing cherry was developed by an early Chinese immigrant named Ah Bing. American Indians were cultivating corn, tomatoes, and tobacco long before the arrival of Columbus. The term *okay* was derived from the Choctaw word *oke*, meaning "it is so." There is evidence indicating that the name *Yankee* came from Indian terms for the English—from *eankke* in Cherokee and *Yankwis* in Delaware. Jazz and blues as well as rock and roll have African-American origins. The "Forty-Niners" of the Gold Rush learned mining techniques from the Mexicans; American cowboys acquired herding skills from Mexican *vaqueros* and adopted their range terms—such as *lariat* from *la reata*, *lasso* from *lazo*, and *stampede* from *estampida*. Songs like "God Bless America," "Easter Parade," and "White Christmas" were written by a Russian-Jewish immigrant named Israel Baline, more popularly known as Irving Berlin.

Reading Comprehension

MyWritingLab™

1. Why do you think American cowboys adopted several terms, such as *stampede* from *estampida*, from the Spanish-speaking Mexican *vaqueros*?

2. Takaki writes, "Much of what is familiar in America's cultural landscape actually has ethnic origins." List two terms Americans borrowed from other cultures; list one skill; list one type of music.

MyWritingLab™ **Discussion Prompts/Writing Options**

When you write on any of the following topics, be sure to work through the stages of the writing process in preparing your paragraph.

1. Interview three people in your class. Ask each to tell you about his or her family background. Before you begin, prepare a list of at least six questions such as "Were you born in this country?" and "Do you know how long your family has been in America?" Use the answers as the basis for a paragraph on diversity in your classroom. You may discover a wide range of backgrounds or a similarity of backgrounds. In either case, you should have sufficient details for a paragraph or short essay about your classmates and their origins.

2. Discuss or write about three foods or dishes that are considered American but which originated in another country or culture. For each choice, provide specific details about its origin and current popularity.

3. Write about some cities or regions in America whose names are derived from another language. You might, for example, write about only Spanish place names and group them according to the states where these places are located. On the other hand, you could write about names from several languages and group them into Spanish names, Native American names, French names, and so forth.

4. Discuss or write about one ethnic group's contributions to American life and culture. You can use specific examples of contributions to language, music, dance, food, clothing, and customs.

MyWritingLab™ **Topics for Critical Thinking and Writing**

1. Takaki gives examples of words Americans use, like *Yankee*, that originated in another language. Write about words or expressions that Americans use that originated in another language. You can visit *http://en.wikipedia.org* and in the search box, type "list of English loan words." You will find lists of words from such origins as African, Chinese, Hawaiian, Indian, Native American, Italian, and Korean languages. In your own words, give examples of at least three American words that have interesting origins. Be sure to click on each word in the list for interesting information about the word's original meaning, history, and present-day meaning.

2. Write about your name. It might be Patrick Andrew DeLucca. Look carefully at each part of it. Is any part of your name, such as *Andrew*, a common name in your family? Do you know if you were named after a particular relative or ancestor? Is "DeLucca" part of an Italian or Spanish heritage? What nationality tends to choose the name "Patrick"? Once you have done a little research about the meaning of your name and have asked family members about their reasons for the name choice, write about your findings.

ILLUSTRATION

Meet the Neighbors

Peter Lovenheim

In this article published in Parade *magazine, Peter Lovenheim talks about the power of a community in which neighbors know each other and concludes that "If ever there was ever a time to break down the barriers that separate us and take advantage of the potential for companionship, it is now."*

Words You May Need to Know (Corresponding paragraph numbers are in parentheses.)

accelerated (3): increased in speed
potlucks (7): meals in which participants bring food to be shared

decentralized (7): separated
radius (7): limited area
stockade fences (10): an enclosure of upright fences

When Jodi Lee, a librarian, bought a home in 2004 near downtown Columbus, Ohio, neighbors told her about "Wednesdays on the Porch." From the first week after Memorial Day through early fall, residents take turns hosting a weekly porch party for their neighbors. It is a way to get to know one another, exchange information, and keep in touch. Jodi was encouraged to host one. She followed the advice and, a few weeks later, on her own front porch, met her neighbor Bill Sieloff. Four years later, he became her husband. "The wedding was almost like another Wednesday on the Porch," Jodi recalls, "so many neighbors were there." 1

Doug Motz, one of the founders, estimates that since these Wednesdays began eight years ago, about 75 different families have held more than 130 porch parties in the neighborhood. "It's a time for sharing—opinions on new restaurants, how to find good painters and home repair people—but it's primarily social," Motz says. "And the nice thing is, the hosts don't have to worry about cleaning up inside." 2

New traditions like these are a welcome exception to the trend favoring privacy over community, which goes back to the post–World War II flight to the suburbs. According to social scientists, neighborhood ties today are less than half as strong as they were in the 1950s. Recently, the trend has accelerated with suburban "McMansions," huge houses set back from wide streets with big backyards that further isolate neighbors from one another. 3

It was a tragedy ten years ago on my own street, in a suburb of Rochester, New York, that got me thinking about how we Americans live. One evening, a neighbor shot and killed his wife and then himself. Their two middle-school-age children ran screaming into the night. Soon, the kids moved in with their grandparents, and the house was put up for sale. 4

5   But life on our street seemed little affected. Asking around, I learned that hardly anyone had known the family well. In fact, few people on the street knew anyone more than casually. In an age of discount air travel, cheap long distance, and the Internet, when we can create community anywhere, why is it that we often don't know the people who live next door?

6   By not knowing our neighbors, we lose a crucial safety net. We also lose social and economic benefits: the ability, in a pinch, to borrow a cup of sugar or a dash of vanilla instead of making another trip to the supermarket, and the simple pleasure of daily, unplanned contact with people with whom we have become friends. Bucking the decades-long trend toward isolation, people around the country are finding new ways to break down the barriers that separate neighbor from neighbor.

7   In Reno, Nevada, during the last week of June, residents will celebrate their annual "Get to Know Your Neighbor Week." It's a celebration that has generated more than sixty-five simultaneous potlucks with thousands of participants. "We've created a decentralized model where neighbors invite neighbors from a three-block radius," Richard Flyer explains. "It's self-organizing; we provide a downloadable form for people to put the names and addresses on, and then everyone is invited to bring food."

8   Through these gatherings, Flyer says, neighbors have noted seniors among them who needed companionship and young people who lacked enough supervision. "These individuals were kind of invisible before," he says. "I know of two women who were recently widowed, and through the neighborhood gatherings, they connected with families for support. Another senior was alone, and neighbors helped him with shopping and landscaping."

9   When new people move into Hollywood/Grant park, a district of modest, single-family homes about two miles from downtown Portland, Oregon, the first thing Dennis Maxwell does is give them a homemade map of the neighborhood. It shows locations of families, names, children, pets, telephone numbers, and work numbers for emergencies. The effect has been to draw neighbors closer together. "Now we exchange child care, take care of mail and newspapers, and water plants during vacations," Maxwell says.

10   In Albany, New York's Center Square/Hudson Park, owners of six adjoining brick row houses have traded a bit of privacy for a lot of beautiful gardening. "Our tiny backyards were really shaded from the stockade fences between each unit," recalls one of the owners, Kathryn Sikule. "You really couldn't grow too much." Over time, neighbors agreed to take down their fences and merge gardens. Stone footpaths set among the joint garden now allow each resident access to the fully landscaped space and an uninterrupted view of a sunny garden scene. The result, Sikule says, has "brought us all together as a community."

11   In the U.S. today, more than 30 million people live alone. Add to that an economic recession that often puts travel and entertainment out of reach.

If there was ever a time to break down the barriers that separate us and take advantage of the potential for companionship, it is now. As a woman from Jackson, Mississippi, who identified herself only as Pamela, wrote to me, "If we all cared about our neighbors, we could change the world one street at a time."

Reading Comprehension

MyWritingLab™

1. Peter Lovenheim ends his illustration essay with a quote about the importance of knowing our neighbors from a woman identified as Pamela. Reread the quote. Then list illustrative examples from the reading that support this point.

2. In Paragraph 3, Lovenheim mentions the "trend favoring privacy over community." What examples does he give in Paragraphs 3 through 5 of this privacy trend? Explain how these examples illustrate the author's observation in Paragraph 6: "By not knowing our neighbors, we lose a crucial safety net."

Discussion Prompts/Writing Options

When you write on any of the following topics, be sure to work through the stages of the writing process in preparing your work.

1. Write about two or more of your neighbors who have been part of your life. They can be good neighbors, bad neighbors, or both.

MyWritingLab™

2. Have you ever been a good or bad neighbor? Write about your interaction with one neighbor. Illustrate this connection by providing specific details about your relationship with this neighbor.

MyWritingLab™

3. Would you prefer to remain detached from your neighbors? If so, use specific reasons to justify your answer.

MyWritingLab™

4. Begin this assignment by brainstorming with a group. Think about the many reasons why people in the suburbs do not spend much time getting to know their neighbors. For example, long working hours may have cut residents' time at home. Also consider what changes in daily life have made it easier to connect with people and establish friendships outside one's neighborhood.

Collaborate

Topics for Critical Thinking and Writing

MyWritingLab™

1. Think about one television series that depicted a happy family living in a suburb. Do a little research on the setting, characters, and plots typical of this series. Then write about the appeal of this series and how realistically (or unrealistically) it reflected life in the suburbs.

2. Peter Lovenheim writes that in our country today, "more than 30 million people live alone." What do you value more: your privacy or your connection to others? Also consider why privacy has become an issue in recent years.

PROCESS

Coming Over

Russell Freedman

In this selection from Russell Freedman's book, Immigrant Kids, *the author describes the difficult and often frightening process European immigrants of the 1880s to the 1920s endured when they looked for a better life in America. From the dark conditions of the Atlantic crossing to the terror of the examinations at Ellis Island, the immigrants found strength in their dreams and in their first glimpse of the Statue of Liberty.*

Words You May Need to Know (Corresponding paragraph numbers are in parentheses.)

impoverished (1): poor
fervent (1): passionate
penniless (2): without any money
foul-smelling (3): having an offensive odor
lounges (3): public sitting rooms
New World (5): the Western Hemisphere
the Narrows (5): a narrow channel of water between Brooklyn and Staten Island in New York City
foredeck (6): the forward part of the deck of a ship
jabbered conversation (6): rapid talk that can't be understood

din (6): loud noise
veered (7): swerved
scowling (7): frowning
maze (10): a confusing network of interconnecting pathways
nationality (12): the country a person belongs to
flustered (12): nervous and upset
rigorous (13): harsh, severe
momentarily (13): for a minute
indomitable (13): not able to be overcome
teeming (14): crowded, filled to overflowing

1 In the years around the turn of the twentieth century, immigration to America reached an all-time high. Between 1880 and 1920, twenty-three million immigrants arrived in the United States. They came mainly from countries of Europe, especially from impoverished towns and villages in southern and eastern Europe. The one thing they had in common was a fervent belief that in America, life would be better.

2 Most of these immigrants were poor. Somehow they managed to scrape together enough money to pay for their passage to America. Many immigrant families arrived penniless. Others had to make the journey in stages. Often the father came first, found work, and sent for his family later. Immigrants usually crossed the Atlantic as steerage passengers. Reached by steep, slippery stairways, the steerage lay deep down in the hold of the ship. It was occupied by passengers paying the lowest fare.

3 Men, women, and children were packed into dark, foul-smelling compartments. They slept in narrow bunks stacked three high. They had no showers, no lounges, and no dining rooms. Food served from huge kettles was dished into dinner pails provided by the steamship company. Because

steerage conditions were crowded and uncomfortable, passengers spent as much time as possible up on deck.

The voyage was an ordeal, but it was worth it. They were on their way 4 to America. The great majority of immigrants landed in New York City at America's biggest port. They never forgot their first glimpse of the Statue of Liberty. Edward Corsi, who later became United States Commissioner of Immigration, was a ten-year-old Italian immigrant when he sailed into New York Harbor in 1907. Here is how he later described the experience:

My first impression of the New World will always remain etched 5 in my memory, particularly that hazy October morning when I first saw Ellis Island. The steamer *Florida*, fourteen days out of Naples, filled to capacity with 1600 natives of Italy, had weathered one of the worst storms in our captain's memory, and glad we were, both children and grown-ups, to leave the open sea and come at last through the Narrows into the bay.

My mother, my stepfather, my brother Giuseppe, and my two sis- 6 ters, Liberta and Helvetia, all of us together, happy that we had come through the storm safely, clustered on the foredeck for fear of separation and looked with wonder on this miraculous land of our dreams. Giuseppe and I held tight to Stepfather's hands while Liberta and Helvetia clung to Mother. Passengers all about us were crowding against the rail. Jabbered conversation, sharp cries, laughs, and cheers—a steadily rising din filled the air. Mothers and fathers lifted up babies so that they too could see, off to the left, the Statue of Liberty.

Finally, the *Florida* veered to the left, turning northward into the 7 Hudson River, and now the incredible buildings of lower Manhattan came very close to us. The officers of the ship went striding up and down the decks shouting orders and directions and driving the immigrants before them. Scowling and gesturing, they pushed and pulled the passengers, herding us into separate groups as though we were animals. A few moments later, we came to our dock, and the long journey was over.

But the journey was not yet over. Before they could be admitted to the 8 United States, immigrants had to pass through Ellis Island, which became the nation's chief immigrant processing center. There they would be questioned and examined. Those who could not pass all the exams would be detained; some would be sent back to Europe. And so their arrival in America was filled with great anxiety. Among the immigrants, Ellis Island was known as "Heartbreak Island."

When their ship docked at a Hudson River pier, the immigrants had 9 numbered identity tags pinned to their clothing. Then they were herded onto special ferryboats that carried them to Ellis Island. Officials hurried them along, shouting "Quick! Run! Hurry!" in half a dozen languages.

10   Filing into an enormous inspection hall, the immigrants formed long lines separated by iron railings that made the hall look like a great maze. Now the examinations began. First the immigrants were examined by two doctors of the United States Health Service. One doctor looked for physical and mental abnormalities. When a case aroused suspicion, the immigrant received a chalk mark on the right shoulder for further inspection: L for lameness, H for heart, X for mental defects, and so on.

11   The second doctor watched for contagious and infectious diseases. He looked especially for infections of the scalp and at the eyelids for symptoms of trachoma, a blinding disease. Since trachoma caused more than half of all medical detentions, this doctor was greatly feared. He stood directly in the immigrant's path. With a swift movement, he would grab the immigrant's eyelid, pull it up, and peer beneath it. If all was well, the immigrant was passed on.

12   Those who failed to get past both doctors had to undergo a more thorough medical exam. The others moved on to the registration clerk who questioned them with the aid of an interpreter: What is your name? Your nationality? Your occupation? Can you read and write? Have you ever been in prison? How much money do you have with you? Where are you going? Some immigrants were so flustered that they could not answer. They were allowed to sit and rest and try again. About one immigrant out of every five or six was detained for additional examinations or questioning. The writer Angelo Pellegrini recalled his own family's detention at Ellis Island:

13   We lived there for three days—Mother and we five children, the youngest of whom was three years old. Because of the rigorous physical examination that we had to submit to, particularly of the eyes, there was this terrible anxiety that one of us might be rejected. And if one of us was, what would the rest of the family do? My sister was indeed momentarily rejected; she had been so ill and had cried so much that her eyes were absolutely bloodshot, and mother was told, "Well, we can't let her in." But fortunately, Mother was an indomitable spirit and finally made them understand that if her child had a few hours' rest and a little bite to eat, she would be all right. In the end, we did get through.

14   Most immigrants passed through Ellis Island in about one day. Carrying all their worldly possessions, they left the examination hall and waited on the dock for the ferry that would take them to Manhattan, a mile away. Some of them still faced journeys overland before they reached their final destination. Others would head directiy for the teeming immigrant neighborhoods of New York City.

Reading Comprehension

1. Russell Freedman notes that between 1880 and 1920, Ellis Island was known as "Heartbreak Island." Why? List four specific reasons from the essay.

2. In Paragraph 13, Freedman quotes another writer, Angelo Pellegrini, whose family had terrible anxiety about being detained. His sister, who was ill and crying for hours, was almost denied entry because of her bloodshot eyes. Assume the role of either Pellegrini's mother or sister, and describe the tense situation through one of their perspectives.

Discussion Prompts/Writing Options

When you write on any of the following topics, be sure to follow the stages of the writing process in preparing your paragraph or short essay.

1. Travel involves a number of processes. One of the most common today is the process of the security check at the airport. Using clear steps and specific details, describe this process for someone who has never experienced it.

2. Discuss or write about the steps involved in another process that involves some local, state, or national agency. For example, you can write about the steps involved in obtaining a driver's license, paying for a traffic ticket, getting a marriage license, applying for a green card, or obtaining a passport.

3. Write about a process that was new for you. You might write about the first time you registered for college classes, went through Customs in a foreign country, prepared for surgery, or took a medical test that required local or general anesthesia.

4. As it was in the late nineteenth and early twentieth centuries, America today is filled with immigrants. If you began your life in another country, trace the steps of your first entry into (and first glimpse of) America, and share the details of this journey with your classmates.

Topics for Critical Thinking and Writing

1. Using Russell Freedman's steps as a guideline, write your own version of the journey of the immigrants from Southern and Eastern Europe to New York City. Make this version your own by adding details about Ellis Island you find in research. For such details, try these sources:

    http://www.nps.gov/elis/ (This address uses "elis" instead of "ellis.")
    http://www.history.com/minisites/ellisisland/

    Your details can include two or more photographs of different stages of the journey. For selected images of Ellis Island and of immigration, see this source:

    http://www.loc.gov/rr/print/list/070_immi.html

2. Freedman's essay cites the experience of Edward Corsi who came to America at age eleven. Corsi describes the joy of the immigrants as they held their children up to see the first glimpse of the Statue of Liberty. To them, the statue seemed the first glimpse of the "miraculous land of our dreams."

Think about what a specific practice, process, or ceremony symbolizes about America. Then write about the power that this symbol holds for you.

PROCESS

Beauty and the Beef

Joey Green

Joey Green is a humorist, prolific author, and frequent guest on regional television and radio shows. His best-selling series, Polish Your Furniture with Panty Hose, *details hundreds of alternative uses for brand-name household products. Green previously worked in advertising and wrote commercials for Burger King and Walt Disney World. In "Beauty and the Beef," the author provides many colorful details as he shows, step-by-step, how a fast-food hamburger is made into a television star.*

Words You May Need to Know (Corresponding paragraph numbers are in parentheses.)

singed (4): burned on the surface, scorched

crevices (4): narrow openings

prissy (5): extremely proper

picturesque (6): visually attractive

preternaturally (8): beyond what is natural

When was the last time you opened a carton in a fast-food restaurant to find a hamburger as appetizing as the ones in the TV commercials? Did you ever look past the counter help to catch a glimpse of a juicy hamburger patty, handsomely branded by the grill, sizzling and crackling as it glides over roaring flames, with tender juices sputtering into the fire? On television, the burger is a magnificent slab of flame-broiled beef—majestically topped with crisp iceberg lettuce, succulent red tomatoes, tangy onions, and plump pickles, all between two halves of a towering sesame-seed bun. But, of course, the real-life Whoppers don't quite measure up. 1

The ingredients of a TV Whopper are, unbelievably, the same as those used in real Whoppers sold to average customers. But like other screen personalities, the Whopper needs a little help from makeup. 2

When making a Burger King commercial, J. Walter Thompson, the company's advertising agency, usually devotes at least one full day to filming "beauty shots" of the food. Burger King supplies the agency with several large boxes of frozen beef patties. But before a patty is sent over the flame broiler, a professionally trained food stylist earning between $500 and $700 a day prepares it for the camera. 3

The crew typically arrives at 7:00 a.m. and spends two hours setting up lights that will flatter the burger. Then the stylist, aided by two assistants, begins by burning "flame-broiling stripes" into the thawed hamburger patties with a special Madison Avenue branding iron. Because the tool doesn't always leave a rich, charcoal-black impression on the patty, the stylist uses a fine paintbrush to darken the singed crevices with a sauce the color of used motor oil. The stylist also sprinkles salt on the patty so when it passes over the flames, natural juices will be encouraged to rise to the meat's surface. 4

5   Thus branded, retouched, and juiced, the patties are run back and forth over a conveyor-belt broiler while the director films the little spectacle from a variety of angles. Two dozen people watch from the wings: lighting assistants, prop people, camera assistants, gas specialists, the client, and agency people—producers, writers, art directors. Of course, as the meat is broiled, blood rises to the surface in small pools. Since, for the purpose of advertising, bubbling blood is not a desirable effect, the stylist, like a prissy microsurgical nurse, continually dabs at the burger with a Q-Tip.

6   Before the patty passes over the flame a second time, the food stylist maneuvers a small electric heater an inch or so above the burger to heat up the natural fatty juices until they begin to steam and sizzle. Otherwise, puddles of grease will cover the meat. Sometimes patties are dried out on a bed of paper towels. Before they're sent over the flame broiler again, the stylist re-lubricates them with a drop of corn oil to guarantee picturesque crackling and sizzling.

7   If you examine any real Whopper at any Burger King closely, you'll discover flame-broiling stripes only on the top side of the beef patty. Hamburgers are sent through the flame broilers once; they're never flipped over. The commercials imply otherwise. On television, a beef patty, fetchingly covered with flame-broiling stripes, travels over the broiler, indicating that the burger has been flipped to sear stripes into the other side.

8   In any case, the camera crew has just five or ten seconds in the life cycle of a TV Whopper to capture good, sizzling, brown beef on film. After that the hamburger starts to shrink rapidly as the water and grease are cooked from it. Filming lasts anywhere from three to eight hours, depending upon the occurrence of a variety of technical problems—heavy smoke, grease accumulating on the camera equipment, the gas specialist's failure to achieve a perfect, preternaturally orange glowing flame. Out of one day's work, and anywhere between fifty and seventy-five hamburgers, the agency hopes to get five seconds of usable footage. Most of the time the patties are either too raw, bloody, greasy, or small.

9   Of course, the cooked hamburger patty depicted sitting on a sesame-seed bun in the commercial is a different hamburger from those towel-dried, steak-sauce-dabbed, corn-oiled specimens that were filmed sliding over the flames. This presentation patty hasn't been flame-broiled at all. It's been branded with the phony flame-broiling marks, retouched with the steak sauce—and then microwaved.

10   Truth in advertising, however, is maintained, sort of: When you're shown the final product—a completely built hamburger topped with sliced vegetables and condiments—you are seeing the actual quantities of ingredients found on the average real Whopper. On television, though, you're only seeing half of the hamburger—the front half. The lettuce, tomatoes, onions, and pickles have all been shoved to the front of the burger. The stylist has

carefully nudged and manicured the ingredients so that they sit just right. The red, ripe tomatoes are flown in fresh from California the morning of the shoot. You might find such tomatoes on your hamburger—if you ordered several hundred Whoppers early in the morning, in Fresno. The lettuce and tomatoes are cut, trimmed, and then piled on top of a cold cooked hamburger patty, and the whole construction is sprayed with a fine mist of glycerine to glisten and shimmer seductively. Finally, the hamburger is capped with a painstakingly handcrafted sesame-seed bun. For at least an hour, the stylist has been kneeling over the bun like a lens grinder, positioning each sesame seed. He dips a toothpick in Elmer's glue and, using a pair of tweezers, places as many as 300 seeds, one by one, onto a formerly bald bun.

When it's all over, the crew packs up the equipment, and seventy-five gorgeous-looking hamburgers are dumped in the garbage.   11

Reading Comprehension

MyWritingLab™

1. List the steps in the process of transforming an ordinary hamburger into a desirable object that Green describes here. Indicate which step in the process you think is the most unusual, clever, amusing, unnecessary, or wasteful.

2. Tell why you believe the advertising agency goes through the elaborate process described by Green when preparing burgers to be filmed for TV advertisements. Do you think the process is worth the trouble? For whom? Why or why not?

Discussion Prompts/Writing Options

MyWritingLab™

If you write on any of the following topics, work through the stages of the writing process in preparing your assignment.

1. Describe a situation in which you went through an elaborate process in order to appear more attractive, or to present yourself to the public in some other way that was different from the way you usually seem to others. Was the process difficult or expensive? What was the result? Was it worth it? Describe each step in the process, and study Green's use of vivid details to see how he paints a picture for the reader.

2. The process Green describes of preparing the burgers to be filmed does not represent truth in advertising because the normal appearance of the burgers is altered. Can you think of another television or online ad that does not reflect truth in advertising? Write a paragraph or short essay describing the deceptive tactics. As you brainstorm ideas for this assignment, make a list of ads that contain false or misleading information. Select one, and then list as many false statements and exaggerated/unrealistic images you can remember from the ad. Rank the items on this list according to emphatic order (least to most outrageous) before you start planning your work.

3. What does Green's essay reveal about the American obsession with food and fast food in particular? Use specific examples and quotes from the essay to support your premise.

MyWritingLab™ ## Topics for Critical Thinking and Writing

If you write on any of the following topics, work through the stages of the writing process in preparing your assignment.

1. Is the "food styling" Green describes dishonest? Should it be allowed? If you argue that it should be prohibited, predict how banning it might positively or negatively affect other types of advertising and public relations campaigns.

2. Evaluate Green as an author by examining his tone, word choice, and organization. Is the essay entertaining? Is it informative? Does he make a serious point? Give three reasons why his essay is—or is not—a good model for writing a process essay of your own. Incorporate specific examples from the essay that support your answer.

Text Credits

Page 6: Poe, Edgar Allan. "The Tell-Tale Heart." *The Pioneer.* January, 1843.

Page 75: John F. Kennedy. Inaugural Address. January 20, 1961.

Page 101: Mora, Pat. "Remembering Lobo." *Latina: Women's Voices from the Borderlands.* Ed. Lillian Castillo-Speed. Simon & Schuster, 1995.

Page 142: Buchanan, Edna. *The Corpse Had a Familiar Face.* Simon & Schuster, 2009.

Page 189: Will Rodgers. Speech at Columbia University.

Page 268: Churchill, Winston. "We Shall Fight on the Beaches." House of Commons of the Parliament of the United Kingdom. June 4, 1940.

Page 398: Klott, Gary. "Part-Time Jobs May Do Teenagers More Harm Than Good," from *South Florida Sun Sentinel,* September 1, 1996. © 1996. Used by permission.

Page 416: Excerpt(s) from WOULDN'T TAKE NOTHING FOR MY JOURNEY NOW by Maya Angelou, copyright © 1993 by Maya Angelou. Used by permission of Random House, an imprint and division of Random House LLC. All rights reserved.

Page 421: "Sheroes: Bold, Brash, and Absolutely Unabrashed Superwomen from Susan B. Anthony to Xena" by Varla Ventura, May 1998. With permission from Red Wheel/Weiser LLC.

Page 425: "Hunger" by Nilsa Mariano. From the book *Chicken Soup for the Latino Soul* by Jack Canfield, Mark Victor Hansen, and Susan Sánchez-Casal. Copyright 2012 by Chicken Soup for the Soul Publishing, LLC. Published by Backlist, LLC, a unit of Chicken Soup for the Soul Publishing, LLC. Chicken Soup for the Soul is a registered trademark of Chicken Soup for the Soul Publishing, LLC. Reprinted by permission. All rights reserved.

Page 429: De Jesus, Yesenia. "Bullet to Blue Sky." Pearson Writing Rewards student essay winner, 2010.

Page 433: Adapted version of "El Hoyo" from *Chicano Sketches: Short Stories* by Mario Suárez by Mario Suárez. © 2004. The Arizona Board of Regents. Reprinted by permission of the University of Arizona Press.

Page 437: From The Rural Life by Verlyn Klinkenborg, Copyright © 2003 by Verlyn Klinkenborg. By permission of Little, Brown, and Company.

Page 439: From A DIFFERENT MIRROR by Ronald Takaki. Copyright © 1993 by Ronald Takaki. By permission of Little, Brown and Company.

Page 441: Lovenheim, Peter: "Meet the Neighbors," from *Parade Magazine,* May 2, 2012. © 2012. Used with permission.

Page 444: "Coming Over," from Immigrant Kids by Russell Friedman, copyright © 1980 by Russell Freedman. Used by permission of Dutton Children's Books, a division of Penguin Group (USA) LLC.

Page 449: Green, Joey. "Beauty and the Beef," first appearance in *Spy Magazine,* 1987. By permission of the author.

Photo Credits

Page 1: Lucky Business/Shutterstock; **Page 20:** Arek Malang/Shutterstock; **Page 40:** René Mansi/Getty Images; **Page 44:** Chris Schmidt/Getty Images; **Page 52:** G-stockstudio/Shutterstock; **Page 60:** Robert Kneschke/Shutterstock; **Page 70:** Thinkstock/Getty Images; **Page 78:** Robert Kneschke/Shutterstock; **Page 88:** Pius Lee/Shutterstock; **Page 98:** Tyler Olson/Shutterstock; **Page 111:** Rido/Shutterstock; **Page 125:** Craig Wactor/Shutterstock; **Page 133:** wavebreakmedia/Shutterstock; **Page 164:** Sergey Nivens/Shutterstock; **Page 174:** Andrew Scherbackov/Shutterstock; Minerva Studio/Shutterstock; **Page 203:** Radu Bercan/Shutterstock; **Page 215:** Lipskiy/Shutterstock; **Page 229:** Chagin/Fotolia; Jupiterimages/Getty Images; **Page 241:** Robert Kneschke/Shutterstock; **Page 259:** Jarous/Shutterstock; **Page 268:** Stokkete/Shutterstock; **Page 274:** Tomas Del Amo/Shutterstock; **Page 282:** Graham Monro/Getty Images; **Page 283:** Ejwhite/Shutterstock; **Page 308:** Masson/Shutterstock; **Page 309:** Ammit Jack/Shutterstock; **Page 326:** Pete Saloutos/Shutterstock; **Page 327:** Mila Supinskaya/Shutterstock; **Page 342:** Peredniankina/Shutterstock; Rock/Wasp/Shutterstock; **Page 343:** Maridav/Shutterstock; **Page 358:** Diego Cervo/Shutterstock; **Page 359:** Christian Delbert/Shutterstock; **Page 391:** Brezzell/Shutterstock; **Page 392:** Blend Images/Shutterstock; XiXin Xing/Shutterstock; Bikeriderlondon/Shutterstock; **Page 396:** Pressmaster/Shutterstock.

INDEX